CW00385723

Rabbiting in the Highlands of Scotland Autobiography

– DOUGLAS COX –

FASTPRINT PUBLISHING
PETERBOROUGH, ENGLAND

First published 2009 by
FASTPRINT PUBLISHING
Peterborough, England.

Printed by
www.printondemand-worldwide.com

INTRODUCTION

My name is Douglas Cox, better known as Country Boy.

This is my true-to-life story of what happened to me when I was in my early twenties which was way back in time in the decade of the 1970s. I tell of how I would travel with my friend Barry, the long-distance lorry driver, up into the Bonny Highlands of Scotland and while Barry would stay up there haulaging all week long, I would be dropped off. I would sleep rough in my self-made bivouac in the vast fir tree plantations on a Laird's vast estate which stretched thirty miles long and twenty miles wide. The Laird's estate was absolutely out of control with rabbits and I would poach these rabbits all week long with my ferrets and then Barry would pick me up again on his back track home.

You readers must now have to ask yourselves, "DID I GET CAUGHT?" or "DIDN'T I GET CAUGHT?" poaching the Laird's rabbits. You will have to read my exciting and knowledgeable true-to-the-fact story to find out.

Now you readers sit back comfortably and read my true McCoy of a book which is the story of all lifetime's of stories on big time rabbit catching, plus many of my graphic, in great detail illustrations.

One evening I went into my local working men's club for a couple of pots of ale and I sat down with Barry who was a long-distance lorry driver. As we chatted, Barry told me he goes right up to the top of Scotland with his wagon and stops up there all week haulaging and comes back home at the end of the week. Now what Barry was telling me got me thinking about when I was up there out in the wilds of the Glens of Scotland on a rabbiting holiday, which is quite a while ago now. And on my way home from my holiday, dropping down through the Highlands, I went past a place that was overrun with rabbits, and a glint came into my eye. I asked Barry if he went past this place as he went up Scotland, and he said that he did, and the place was still abounding with rabbits.

When I went past this place it was one continuous length of fir tree plantations that ran a long distance along the side of the Highland road. In between the fir tree plantations and the Highland road, there was a wide grass belting, and the rabbits I saw that day as they were feeding along the woodland side, were in their multitudes. Now I scratched my head and got to thinking again, if I could get a lift up there with Barry in his wagon, I could go up there and ferret the rabbits all week. I could sleep rough in the woodland and Barry would be able to pick me up at the end of the week as he was on his way back home again.

I suggested this to Barry and he agreed that he would take me and he picked me up very early the following Monday morning. It was going to be a long distance trek to get there and I estimated it would be early afternoon when we would arrive at my destination.

I had looked on the road map and pinpointed where I wanted dropping off. There was a country road branching off of the main Highland road, and this quiet road was wide enough for Barry to travel along in his large wagon. The country road wound and meandered its way through this fir tree woodland and it was an ideal place to secretly drop me off. The woodland would conceal my intentions, and once Barry had dropped me off he could carry on along the country road which led him back on to the main Highland road.

Now I am a person who always likes to travel light, money in one pocket and a toothbrush in my back pocket, or that sort of thing anyway, just the bare essentials.

I had with me two ferrets which were tied up inside a small bag with breather holes stitched into it. When I arrived at my destination in the forestry fir tree plantation I would erect a small cage for the two ferrets to sleep in. I had made this cage portable and easy to carry. It was six sections of strong wire grille, all cut two feet square, and all six partitions could be laid flat and tied together. They could then be easily transported.

I also had with me a hundred rabbit purse nets which were all stuffed into my large poacher's pockets which were stitched inside of my large overcoat. I had a small dish with me for the ferret's to drink out of. I was going to spend four nights up there in the isolation of that fir tree forestry plantation so I took with me enough easy food to eat, that should be enough to keep me going. As an extra precaution I took with me half a dozen Mars bars. What's that saying, "a Mars a day helps you work, rest and play!" I will see if the manufacturers are right with that saying. I also took with me a big piece of mouth-watering, juicy pork crackling which I took from my old mother Edith's Sunday roast.

I stuffed all this food on top of my purse nets in my poacher's pockets and that was all the bare essentials I took with me. My sleeping arrangement, which I had thought out beforehand, was going to be a self-made bivouac which I was going to construct inside the forestry fir tree plantation once I had arrived.

That early Monday morning when Barry picked me up in his wagon, he looked at me gobsmacked. He said, "Where's all your luggage?" me replying saying, "It's all in my pockets." Barry looked at me, he scratched his head in bewilderment and said nothing.

I jumped into Barry's wagon and off we set for Scotland, and after quite a few hours of travelling we passed through Edinburgh and continued on and across the Firth of Forth Bridge. This is what I call the gateway to the Scottish Highlands. We then carried on travelling for several more hours before Barry turned off the main Highland road and headed across country on a secondary 'B' road. Barry had a drop to do with his wagon and we were now worming our way through the Grampian Mountains. The scenery was breathtaking, they call it Bonny Scotland and the beauty certainly catches your eye.

I am sure the solitude of the mountains was calling me to come. I could see herds of red deer on the snow-covered mountaintops and there were rabbits galore in the foothills and meadows.

The mountain road we were travelling on was becoming hilly, and Barry had so much weight on his wagon he had to keep dropping into crawler gear to get up some of the hills. There was a roadside café coming up and Barry said he was stopping off for a morning break.

I got myself a hearty English breakfast of bacon and eggs, and asked the waitress to put two extra sausages on my plate. The waitress commented that I must like my sausages. I knew that this was going to be my last square meal that I would get the chance to have until at least late Friday evening.

After I had eaten breakfast, or was it dinner, I got the spare milk that was on the table and went outside to Barry's wagon and got my two ferrets. I took them out of the bag that they were tied in and let them have a run around on the lawn outside of the café so that they could get a little fresh air and do their business. I then gave them the milk to drink and the two extra sausages that I had got. I broke them into small pieces and the ferrets ate them readily. Barry came out of the café and we were off on the road again, worming and meandering our way along the mountain Highland roads. After a few more hours of travelling we were nearing my destination, my drop off point.

I could tell Barry was becoming agitated, he was becoming hesitant about dropping me off and just leaving me there out in the wilderness all alone. He looked at me in a concerned sort of manner and said, "What happens if you freeze to death in the cold bitter nights?"

I told Barry not to worry about me, I was young enough and fit enough to throw off any bitter, rugged weather that mother nature could throw at me.

We neared the turn off point where the country road branched off and led away from the main Highland road, and I directed Barry down the narrow back road.

The pine forest came right up to the roadside but there was a bit of a park-up space that Barry could pull his wagon on to. No doubt it was a courting couple's parking place which was concealed under the woodland canopy.

Barry pulled in his wagon and we came to a standstill. As I was getting out of the wagon, Barry was getting himself all worked up and frustrated. Barry was rabbiting on and nattering like an old mother hen, saying, "You're sure you have enough clothes to keep you warm, are you sure you have enough food to eat, and what happens if there's a snow blizzard and you get snowed in and you haven't even got a raincoat?"

I said, "Barry, stop worrying."

I arranged with Barry that he would pick me up here at this point at ten o'clock Friday morning and on that note bade Barry farewell and disappeared into the surrounding forest.

As I weaved my way through the pine tree woodland, I could still hear Barry's wagon engine ticking over. I was sure Barry was waiting and thinking that I might have a change of mind and go back to him. There was no fear of that happening, my mind was intent on catching some rabbits.

As I made my way deeper into the woodland I heard Barry's wagon pulling away. As the wagon's engine got fainter and fainter until the sound disappeared into the distance, I pondered and thought to myself, there, I'm here now, and all alone in the seclusion of this pine forest. I had two hours and it would be nearly dark so I had to work fast and get me and the ferrets bedded down for the night.

I chose a warm little spot in the woodland under the shelter of a large bushy fir tree. The woodland around it was sheltered by thick, dense-growing pine trees. They would shelter me and the ferrets from any cold bitter winds that may blow through the night.

I untied the six sections of strong wire meshing I had brought with me to make the wire cage I was going to keep the ferrets in. I lashed them together with baling band and it was now erected into a small square cage.

At the woodside along the bottom of the fence line was some tall dried grass growing. I pulled handfuls of this and stuffed it inside the ferrets' cage that was now a warm cosy nest for them to sleep in. I took the two ferrets out of their bag and put them in the cage, tying the front of the cage so that they couldn't escape.

The ferret bag was wet with the ferrets peeing in it, so I hung it up in a fir tree to dry out. The ferrets were now snug and dry in their cage underneath the pine trees.

The vegetation was very sparse, hardly anything grows under pine trees, everything was bare, but there was a thick layer of old dry pine needles. I gathered big handfuls and threw them over the top of the ferret cage, just leaving a small hole at the front for the ferrets to breath. The heaped-up pine needles over the cage would now keep out any rain that may fall through the night, and also insulate the cage from the bitter cold weather.

The cage was now camouflaged against any roving eye that may come along. With the ferrets now bedded down for night, it was now my turn to get ready for bed.

I had thought it out well over the last few days how I was going to sleep, I was going to make myself a bivouac. I went into the woodland and got myself four long, strong branches. There were many old branches lying on the woodland floor which were just ideal for me to make my bivouac from. I stuck two branches into the ground and crossed them at the top and tied them in position with some baling band. I wanted to make the bivouac longer than myself so that I could fit into it easily. I stuck another two sticks into the ground just the same as the other two sticks and at a distance of two feet longer than I stood tall, leaving me with ample room to get myself inside. I now had to insulate the floor so that I would not be lying on the cold ground, so I gathered more branches and laid them on the floor of the bivouac.

I now wanted a roof putting onto my bivouac so I got myself a long branch and laid it within the crossed branches which I had stuck in the ground earlier. I now went and gathered a lot more shorter branches, these were going to put sides on my bivouac.

I laid them on the slant from the ground and leaning onto the long roof pole, all the way along either side of the bivouac. My bivouac was now complete and erected in a matter of no time. I now needed some warm dry bedding putting inside for me to snuggle myself into. So I went and got great armfuls of this dry grass from the woodland fence line and stuffed it inside of the bivouac.

I had made the bivouac extra large inside so that I could get plenty of dry grass inside. The thicker I could stuff the grass in the warmer it would be, keeping me dry and snug through the bitter cold winter nights that they have up here in the mountains.

That job now done, I went and gathered great big handfuls of dried dead pine needles and threw them over the top of the bivouac. I threw them on until they were heaped up high and covered the open end of the bivouac where my feet would be. The job was now complete and hopefully waterproof, if the heavens opened. As I stood back and looked at it, I could neither see my bivouac nor the ferret cage as they were camouflaged underneath the thick bushy-growing pine tree. Me and the ferrets would now be like the elusive pimpernel.

By now it was coming in dark so I got myself laid down at the open end of my bivouac and pushed my feet into the packed dry grass. Slowly but surely I made a hole in the middle of the dry grass, gradually worming myself deeper and deeper into my bivouac until I was in. I stuffed myself around a little to make myself comfortable. I had made a big ball of this dried grass which I pulled in at the back of my head. I was now sealed and enclosed within my bivouac, and as I lay there in silence, it appeared all snug and warm here inside.

I could hear some pheasants outside in the woodland, they were calling as they were going up into the trees to roost. I was now tired after a hard day's travelling behind me, and I started to drift off into a deep sleep. The next thing I knew I was awakened again by the pheasants calling as they were dropping out of their roosts in the trees. I was as warm as toast as I lay in the dry grass in the bivouac. I pushed out the ball of grass that was behind my head. It was just breaking daylight and I could feel the coldness of the morning air outside, I was eager to be up for a day's rabbiting ahead. The ferrets woke up and out of their grass nest, and looked as eager as me as to what lay ahead of us. Let's get at them rabbits.

The first thing that I had to do was to find some water for me and the ferrets to have a drink and I set off through the fir tree plantation. It was a bitter cold morning with a coating of white frost on the trees and I could see my breath as I breathed out. As I neared the edge of the woodland I went along light-footed so as not to break any branches under my feet. There was a grass pasture at the woodland edge and I wanted to see how many rabbits there were sat out feeding. I very slowly and quietly went to the woodside and peered down the grass meadow. I couldn't believe my eyes, there were rabbits galore sat out feeding.

I turned my head slowly and looked down the grass meadow at the other side of me and there were even more rabbits sat out on this side. My heart was pounding with excitement, thinking to myself, all these rabbits for me to ferret out later. As I looked further along the woodland edge the grass meadows continued on way out into the distance and there were many rabbits sat out all the way along. As I looked out in front of me there stood a big mountainside, it looked awe-inspiring to me. There was a hedgerow running from the foot of the mountain that ran down into the woodland again where I stood.

As I went out into the open and towards the hedgerow the rabbits saw me and scattered and disappeared into the fir tree plantation. As I got to the hedgerow my luck was in, there was a stream coming down from the mountainside.

I squat myself down by the side of the stream and put my numb cold hands into the freezing cold water. I drank a little out of my cupped frozen hands and I touched a little of the water around my face, giving myself a bit of a 'cat lick'.

I filled the ferrets' dish with water and headed back to my encampment. I took both ferrets out of their cage and gave them the water to drink. I was ready for a good hearty breakfast myself so I sat on a tree stump to eat one of my pork pies.

I was frozen stiff as I sat there, but I dare not light a fire for fear of being noticed by any roving eye that may be around. As I sat there on my stump munching away on my pork pie my ears cocked up, I could hear a horse clip-clopping down the road. Now I got to thinking, that quiet country lane is more than half a mile from where I am, I wouldn't be able to hear a horse clip-clopping that distance.

The clip-clopping continued, then I heard a familiar sound of a loud 'pop' followed by a 'wheeze', it was a capercaillie I could hear. He is our largest and most arboreal member of the grouse family. The male is a very ferocious, territorial, turkey-sized bird and will tackle man to defend his territory. The capercaillie has an unusual diet of eating pine shoots which makes its flesh have a resinous tang to it when eaten. The clip-clopping was getting forever closer, was he moving in to tackle me for his territory? I best move on and get out of his way. I got the ferret bag which had been freshening in the pine tree overnight and it was now nice and dry. I popped both ferrets into the bag and popped them into one of my big poacher's pockets inside of my coat.

Both my poacher's pockets were bulging out with the hundred purse nets I had brought with me. As I set off hurriedly to get away from the capercaillie I grabbed a big piece of pork crackling which had a thick piece of meat on it and ate it as I went. This would grease my insides and help fend off the bitter freezing cold weather.

I was now in search of these rabbits and their warrens. The rabbits usually make their warrens near to the woodside which are then near to their feeding grounds.

I saw the first rabbits' holes as I neared the woodside and I saw rabbits running ahead of me and bolting to safety as they went down their holes. The rabbit holes got more and more frequent as I headed closer to the woodside, it was one large rabbit warren. I headed up the woodside to survey the situation and it was just one big honeycomb of rabbit holes. Just one massive continuous rabbit warren. I stopped to scratch my head and to think of the best way to tackle the situation. I decided to start at the beginning of the rabbit warren, just setting my hundred purse nets on the best and most well-used holes of the warren.

I knew that if I missed any bolting rabbits they would just bolt away from that part of the warren and bolt down holes further along the warren. Them rabbits would not escape forever, I would get them later.

So I set all my hundred purse nets on all the best-used holes and everything was now set and ready. I pulled out my ferrets which were in their bag inside of one of my large poacher's pockets. They were both small bitches. My own preference is to use small dinky type ferrets, that way if the ferret anchors itself on to a rabbit, the rabbit is big enough and strong enough to drag the small ferret along and hopefully and often the rabbit will drag the ferret to the surface where I have a chance of grabbing the rabbit. I put my first ferret into one of the holes and reset the purse net tidily all ready for a rabbit to bolt into the net. The ferret looked back at me and I gently tapped her nose and off she went.

I went a few paces away and put the other ferret into the mouth of another well-used hole. The ferret had a smell around at the entrance of the hole, she arched her back and her hair stood up on end on her back as she scented the rabbits down in the warren. She gave a quick look back at me and then disappeared down into the warren. Everything fell silent.

I got myself into a squat-down position, as I waited and watched, observing where all my purse nets were set. The nets covered a large area of the warren. My heart was pounding, my adrenaline was flowing through my body, I knew there were many, many rabbits down here inside of this warren.

I had seen many rabbits running off the grass meadow only this morning and all the rabbits headed and made their way towards the safety of this warren.

I saw something flash past the corner of my eye and as I looked across I saw a rabbit bolting hell for leather across the warren. The rabbit had bolted from a hole with no net on it and it bobbed down another hole and disappeared. I knew I had a purse net set over that hole and as the rabbit went down the hole I saw the cord on the purse net tighten.

I sped across the warren silently, I must not disturb the other rabbits which are underground in the warren, any sudden noise now would deter any would-be rabbit from bolting out of the warren to safety.

I put my hand down the hole I had just seen the rabbit bolt into, I had to lie down to get my hand further down the hole. My finger tips touched something warm and furry and I grabbed hold of it with a firm hand and pulled it out. It was the rabbit all balled-up in the purse net. The rabbit had what we call 'back-netted itself'. I quickly shoved the rabbit's head back and broke its neck and took the dead rabbit out of the net, quickly straightening and resetting the purse net back over the rabbit hole.

As I looked back to where the rabbit had come from in the first place, the ferret was there, she had followed the scent of the bolting rabbit out of the hole. She had pulled the purse net off the hole entrance as she came out. I went over and reset the net again.

I picked up the ferret and popped her down another hole a few paces away and everything went quiet again. I went and put the rabbit I had just killed safely away from the rabbit warren.

The times I have just left the dead rabbit lying there on top of the warren, the ferret will come out of the warren behind my back, grab hold of the dead rabbit and drag it back down the hole. I will then have a lay-up with the ferret, waiting while she gets a bellyful of rabbit. It can be one hell of a time-consuming job waiting for the ferret to come out again. I have learned by my mistakes and learned to put the rabbits safely away from the warren.

All silence is broken as a rabbit comes hurtling out of a hole at the side of me. It hits the purse net with such speed and impact the purse net tether peg comes flying out of the ground. The balled-up rabbit in the purse net goes whizzing across the warren, coming to an abrupt standstill leaving it kicking and fighting in the purse net.

I move across silently and quickly and kill the balled-up rabbit. The ferret is there in the entrance of the hole so I gently tap her nose and off she disappears back down the hole again. I take the dead rabbit out of the net and put it safely into my poacher's pocket. When I get the time I will place it with the other rabbit safely away at the side of the warren.

The ferrets now are nowhere to be seen. They will be hunting and chasing the rabbits about below ground. As I look across the warren I see another rabbit bolting. It races across the warren, bobs down another hole and I see the purse net cord tighten, the rabbit has back-netted itself. As I race over I see another rabbit bolt, it bobs down the same rabbit hole as the one that's just back-netted itself. I put my hand down the hole and pull out a rabbit which hasn't got a net on it and I quickly kill it and pop it straightaway into my poacher's pocket. It is still fighting and kicking itself to death as it lays inside of my coat. I put my hand further down the hole and pull out another rabbit all balled-up in the purse net. It was this rabbit that had blocked up the hole so that the second rabbit couldn't get by to make its escape to safety back inside of the warren.

The ferrets haven't shown, they are nowhere to be seen, and all goes deadly silent again. I take these rabbits and put them with the other rabbits at the side of the warren. I hear a scuffle, I turn, I see two, three rabbits bolting across the warren, they have made their escape from unnetted holes. They disappear out of sight into the warren further up the woodland. This is where the 'long net' would have been worth its weight in gold. Just simply run the net out along the rabbits' escape route and the long net wouldn't have missed a rabbit.

I hear another scuffling noise behind me and as I look around sharpishly I have three rabbits all in individual nets. They are kicking and fighting in the purse nets trying to make their escape.

I quickly neck them and replace the nets over the holes. The ferrets are working well, they are bolting rabbits here, there and everywhere, but just nice and steady, just the way I like it.

It eventually all falls silent again then after a while one of the ferrets shows at a hole entrance. I go across and pick her up and put her safely back into her bag and back into my pocket. All the pandemonium we have caused in the rabbits' warren, striking the rabbits with fear, they are maybe becoming reluctant to bolt. If I am not careful I will have a lay-up on my hands, the ferrets may kill a rabbit and I may then have to wait an eternity for the ferrets to emerge.

The best policy is not to be greedy, get a few rabbits and when I think the rabbits are starting to get a bit stubborn and reluctant to bolt, it's wise to pick up ferrets and purse nets and move on. There's plenty of rabbits around here to have a go at anyway. I see the other ferret show, so I go and pick her up also and pop her into the bag with the other ferret.

They start chattering away like hell at each other now they are back together again, they are excited, they love their outings rabbiting, just as much as myself.

I pop the bag back safely into my pocket and I now pick up all the one hundred purse nets that I have set and scattered across the warren. I always count the purse nets down when I am setting them, and always count them back when I am picking them back up again. I don't like losing purse nets, it's totally slapdash and irresponsible to overlook any nets. A lost purse net leaves a telltale sign to the gamekeeper that I have been there in the first place. I count ninety-nine purse nets, I have one missing. I take them all out of my pockets again and count them all again, I still count ninety-nine, I have overlooked one somewhere. I go back across the warren looking for it but the purse net is nowhere to be seen. I know it's here somewhere, I must search until I find it. I hunt up and down the warren again and then I notice the purse net cord, it's pulling tight and leading down into a rabbit hole. I put my hand down the hole but I can't touch anything. So I lay myself down and put my full arm's length down the hole and I can just touch something with my finger tips. I grab the purse net cord and pull it to me, it's snagged up inside on something. I pull the cord tight and then hold it still. There's something tugging back on the cord so I keep jerking at the cord until it frees itself.

When I pulled it out it was a live rabbit all balled-up in the purse net. It had back-netted itself while I must have had my back turned on it. So it paid off this time, counting the nets down and counting them back up again.

I said earlier that when I put the ferrets into their bag I then put the bag back safely into my coat pocket. My past mistakes have taught me to do this. I remember well when I had been ferreting a rabbit warren one day, I put the bag with the ferrets inside on the surface of the rabbit warren while I went to gather up all the purse nets. When I went back to pick up the ferrets in their bag, the bag was gone. I had my dog with me that day and she was frantically digging into an entrance of a rabbit hole not far away. She kept looking at me and whining and then having another dig in the rabbit hole. She was trying to tell me that the ferrets were there. I tried in vain to get down to the ferrets but there was no chance, the ferrets, still tied inside of their bag, were too far down the rabbit tunnel.

What had happened while I wasn't looking was the ferrets had rolled about in their bag and into an entrance of a rabbit hole and rolled along until they were unreachable. So that day I used an old gypsy trick. I went to a bramble bush and cut myself a long thick briar, then I pushed the briar along the rabbit's tunnel and started twisting and turning the long briar. It got itself snagged on something with its sharp barbs and slowly and gently I began pulling the briar back out, and to my delight and relief it was the ferrets still tied up in their bag.

I have pulled many a dead rabbit out of holes with these long sharp bramble briars when the ferrets have killed a rabbit not far in from the entrance of the hole, and often the ferret follows the rabbit out with bleary eyes.

So learning by my past mistakes I will never let that happen again, I always put the ferrets safely into my poacher's pocket. So now I have all my purse nets safely gathered up and the net peg holes are covered over so as not to leave any telltale signs for the gamekeeper's roving eye.

Now to go onto another part of the rabbit warren a bit further along the woodland. It amazed me the length and size of this warren, it ran all the way along the woodside and by what I have seen, there was no end to it.

I started dropping my purse nets on the next section of the warren, it was adjacent to the warren where I had just ferreted. All those rabbits I have just missed are now laid up in here. There's many, many more rabbits in here besides them. This new section of rabbit warren is now all netted up and ready for a bit of action.

I slipped one ferret into a hole and off she went out of sight. I then slipped the other ferret into a hole a little further away and everything was silent. My adrenaline now starting to flow through my body again and my heart was pounding in excitement of what to expect. All silence was broken as two rabbits bolted together at the far side of the warren. They had both bolted from the same hole and the purse net balled-up the first rabbit, but the second rabbit was off like hell across the warren, running as if there was no tomorrow, and bobbed down another hole. I ran noiselessly across the warren, pushed my hand down the hole and pulled out the rabbit which had back-netted itself, quickly breaking its neck while it was still in the grasp of the net, and popping it into my poacher's pocket.

I then ran across to the other rabbit which was kicking and fighting trying to free itself from the tightly-pursed net. I quickly pushed the rabbit's head back breaking its neck, hurrying myself to take the rabbit out of the net, being careful and watching out for its flailing, kicking back legs as it kicked itself to death. I then had to quickly get them two nets back over them two holes before any more rabbits bolted.

The two nets were now set and back in position and all went quiet again. As I am squat down quietly waiting for more action, my ears prick up as I can hear my old mate the capercaillie again, its abbreviated slang name is the 'capper'. I got to thinking to myself, was he searching me out to protect his territory? It sounded as though he was singing somewhere as he was perched in a tree.

He was sending out a series of well-spaced-out 'clicks' which accelerated out into a 'drum roll', which was followed by the 'cork pop' sound, which sounds like a tight cork being pulled out of a bottle, and his continued song of 'gurgling' and 'wheezing' notes. He wasn't far away from me as he was perched in a tree but that elusive capper was nowhere to be seen. Was he casting his beady eye over me?

A bolting rabbit distracted my attention and as I sped over to grab the rabbit it disturbed the capper, but surprisingly he was silent as he flew directly over my head. He appeared to be a massive giant of a bird as he flew past me, out into the grass meadow and settled only a short distance away from me. This was a sight for me and never to be forgotten, I was gobsmacked and impressed as I watched him.

As I looked across the meadow, I saw another male capper join him, both cappers were keeping their distance between each other. I was becoming spoiled for choice between catching rabbits as they bolted and watching these cappers displaying to each other. My darting across the rabbit warren to bolting rabbits didn't seem to disturb or upset the cappers. To my surprise and delight a third male capper joined them on the grass meadow.

I was over the moon with the fascination, my eyes were transfixed on them as they strutted up to each other in a challenging form of display. I couldn't believe my luck as to what I was watching, all this was happening just a short distance in front of me and the rabbits kept bolting like hell at the back of me. I was that busy trying to kill one rabbit and watching the cappers displaying all at the same time, that the rabbit bit me sending its front teeth right the way through my thumb. That will teach me to pay attention to my business of catching rabbits.

The main purpose of this male capercaillie display I was witnessing was primarily to attract females. The grass meadow that they were on was the cappers' traditional 'DISPLAY GROUND'. The male capercaillie is polygamous and will have several females in his 'harem'.

Both sexes are big fine handsome birds, especially the male. His back is a chocolate brown, his large chest is a glossy green and his belly and tail are marked with white. He has a bright red patch of bare skin above his eyes and what appears to be a great big bushy beard on his chin, in my eyes an astounding magnificent bird. I kept racing backwards and forwards catching rabbits and resetting the purse nets and then watching the cappers displaying on the meadow in front of me and sucking my bleeding thumb all at the same time.

The cappers started moving in towards each other, they strutted aggressively to each other with their bodies swollen, their throats distended, their big bushy beards puffed out, their heads held in the air. One of the cappers leapt three feet into the air noisily flapping his wings, which is known as the 'flutter jump', and giving out his 'cork pop' sound of song. One of the other males crouched and then ran forward with his neck outstretched. He struck up into the air with noisily flapping wings, glided briefly and, fluttering back to the ground making even more noise with his whirring flapping wings, he plummeted back with a heavy crash-landing, nearly knocking the living daylight out of himself in the process. The other two joined in and did the same. What a fine spectacle this was to my eyes. All three cappers had by now got dangerously close to each other. They were bowing to each other, they were raising and lowering their wings as the they strutted threateningly and menacingly towards each other.

They were using their special 'belching' sound to ward each other off. Their backs were arched, their tails were arched over their backs, they ruffled their feathers on their necks, making themselves look thick, robust and powerful, and life-threateningly dangerous to each other. They all stood their ground, none of the three would bow and back off, and a battle took place. They were stabbing and pecking each other with their strong powerful beaks.

They were thrashing whirring, flapping wings at one another. These stand-up fights are not usually to the death, it's more often just threatening displays towards each other, but they have convinced me that they are life-threatening to each other. As I stood there watching and sucking my bleeding thumb I was completely mesmerized and gobsmacked at what I was witnessing.

A rabbit started screaming its head off somewhere on the rabbit warren and as I raced across the warren to see where the screaming rabbit was, I looked back across the meadow. The cappers were dispersing from their rivalry, a sad end to a magnificent sight in my opinion, a sighting which will never leave my memory. It must have been the screaming rabbit that had scared away the cappers, it certainly wasn't my presence.

My attention now fully back on my rabbiting, I followed the sound of the screaming rabbit. I located it in a hole but, out of my vision, the ferret would have hold of it. I kept myself silent and out of sight, I knew if that screaming rabbit saw me it would drag the ferret deeper down into the warren. I kept quiet and patiently waited, and as I bided my time I could hear the screaming rabbit getting close to the end of the rabbit hole. I saw the rabbit's backside appear just inside of the hole entrance, it was dragging my small bitch ferret to the entrance. I slowly put my hand down and make a quick grab at the rabbit, grabbing it by the scruff of its neck. When I pulled it out of the hole, the ferret was anchored onto the end of the rabbit's nose. I gently coaxed and persuaded her to let go of the rabbit and quickly broke the rabbit's neck.

I have now had my fair share of rabbits out of this particular part of the warren. This screaming rabbit may deter the other rabbits from bolting from the warren, so it's best that I pack up and call it a day. It's by now early afternoon and after this time of the day rabbits tend to lay up tight. They seem to have some sort of a siesta (snooze) in their warrens and are reluctant to bolt. And that was the end of my first day's ferreting in this secluded pine forest out in the wilds of the Grampian Mountains high up in the Highlands of Scotland.

A super day's ferreting, I remember it well, especially them cappers. I counted up my rabbits, thirty-eight I counted, that was an excellent bag of rabbits in my mind.

I now take the rabbits away to paunch them. There's a lot of weight in thirty-eight rabbits I can tell you, as with all the rabbits hung over both my shoulders I hump them well away from the warren. A pile of rabbits' guts may disturb the other rabbits that are still in the warren, and I don't want that do I. There's plenty more rabbits to be had there yet. I put the rabbits' guts in a pile well inside of the fir tree plantation and cover them over with dead pine needles, they are now out of sight of any roving eye. I legged all the rabbits and pushed them onto two good strong branches I picked from the woodland floor. The rabbits are now more easy to carry as I head back to my bivouac. The weight of the rabbits was still dragging me down so I had to stop and have a minute and as I stood there in the woodland cooling off, something whizzed by me. As it went flashing over the top of my head, I looked up and just managed to catch a glimpse at the tail end of a GOSHAWK as it weaved its way through the trees at great speed. The goshawk surprise-attacks its prey like a phantom bordering on the supernatural, its target prey is dead before they even know he's coming. A supreme and a top predator in my opinion.

I now set off again and on to my bivouac and hang my day's bag of rabbits up in the branches of the fir tree, they hang there concealed and out of sight. Now to feed my ferrets. I push my hand deep into a rabbit's chest and pull out its heart, it's all bloody, just the way ferrets like to eat them. I take another dozen or so hearts, that should be enough to fill their bellies. I leave the livers intact in the rabbits, that's used by the lady of the house when she's preparing the rabbit for dinner.

I note that these rabbits are in top prime condition, their kidneys are surrounded by thick snowy-white fat, that's the rabbit's emergency energy source if the winter weather becomes harsh and severe.

Now that my ferrets are bedded down for the night, bellies full of bloody hearts and snuggled up in their grass bed inside my manmade cage and all concealed and covered over with pine needles, any roving eye that may come along wouldn't even know the ferrets were there at all. I now grab myself a pork pie for my dinner. As I have an hour to kill before nightfall, I head back out through the woodland as I want to suss out the extent of the rabbit warrens where I intend ferreting over the next two days. I headed towards the warren where I had just been ferreting earlier and along and past that warren and the rabbit warrens just kept going on and on, there appeared to be no end to them. Rabbits were scampering here, there and everywhere as I walked through the pine forest making sure not to make a sound. I kept going to the woodside to see how many rabbits were sat out feeding and there was hundreds of them. On seeing me they all bolted down their warrens in the pine forest, all present and just waiting for me to ferret them out.

By now it was coming into deep dusk so I had to get back to my bivouac before it was too dark to find it. Once there I got

THE "GOSHAWK"
DARTS WEAVING AND
WHIZZING THROUGH
THE WOODLAND SURPRISE
ATTACKING HIS PREY
JUST LIKE A PHANTOM
BORDERING ON TO THE
SUPERNATURAL.

myself all snuggled up in my bivouac. It was early to bed and late to rise while I was up here in these hills, with the days being short and nights being long through the wintertime. Once it had come in dark I had nothing else to do but just lay there comfortable and warm in my bivouac. It gave me plenty of time to lay there and think, I could hear all the sounds of weird noises going off in the surrounding pine forest around me.

I could hear a long-eared owl hooting as it was perched in the trees above me. I could hear a dog fox barking which was not far away from me by the sounds of him. I could hear the vixen 'female' fox yapping back to him, she sounded as though she was up in the distant hills. There were many other strange sounds and noises which I could hear which I couldn't distinguish as I lay there in the silence of my bivouac.

I remember one of my old rabbiting mates called Ridgey who I mention in this book, he did exactly what I am doing now. He did the same as me, he got a lift with a wagon driver and slept rough in the woodlands just like I am doing now. But Ridgey made the mistake of going down into the village pub in the bottom of the glen, just simply to pass away the time of the dark winter evening. But the local people noted that he was a stranger in camp.

It must have been obvious to them that he was sleeping rough somewhere, and they kept an eagle eye on him. When Ridgey's wagon driver came to pick him up, the keepers and police pounced on him, together with a bag of rabbits that he had caught with the ferrets. I might add that was a different place in the Scottish Highlands to where I was, so I didn't fall for that trick, I spent my dark winter evenings laid tucked up in my warm bivouac.

I lay there just reminiscing about the day's bag I had just caught only that morning. I can never resist the temptation to do a bit of rabbit poaching, it's naturally in the body's GENES and bloodstream, that bit of devilment to do a bit of worldly poaching. As you will read in this book, I had more rabbiting permission than a person could ever wish for, but it lacks that anticipation and excitement.

Having to look over my shoulder all the time, having to slip through the undergrowth so that I go unobserved. Forever watching the birds fly by to see if they are telling me by their characteristic body language that there's someone about. The blackbird will be well ahead of me, he will be chattering away like hell in his own characteristic way, he will be telling me, "Watch out there's a stranger coming", "Watch out he's nearly upon you." Then there's my prided people who will take a rabbit from me for their dinner, they will make me a kind gesture and slip a coin in my hand. I will hear someone say to them in a low voice, "Where did you get the rabbit from?" and I will hear them whisper, "Doug got it only last evening, in that dark windy night that we had."

That's the big difference between having permission and doing a bit of worldly poaching. Anyway that's enough reminiscing from me, it's now time for me to get some beauty sleep in my bivouac, I have another hard day's ferreting ahead of me tomorrow.

With the warmth, comfort and contentment of my bivouac the night seemed to pass by within the blink of an eye. I am awakened early next morning by the pheasants again that have been roosting in trees nearby. I pushed my ball of grass away which lay at the back of my head. This ball of grass certainly did its job well, sealing all the cold out from entering my bivouac. I could now feel the freezing cold morning air outside and as I climbed out everything was white-over with the keen hard frost we had had through the night. The temperatures must have been well below freezing point but me and my ferrets had laid snug all night unaware of the freezing night. The ferrets were peering out of their dry grass nest all bleary-eyed. I got myself all prepared for the day's rabbiting ahead, and then sat down on my tree stump to eat one of my pork pies. As I was sat there munching I suddenly froze, I heard that horse clip-clopping down the road again, it was right at the back of me. I turned my head around very slowly and there it was, my old mate the capper, he was only a few feet away from me, and he was looking me dead in the eye. He had a harem of females strutting around behind him and he looked at me threateningly so I grabbed the ferret bag and grabbed the ferrets out of their cage and was off through the woodland.

As I turned to look back he was coming after me with flapping wings and as I turned to make my escape I got such a terrible thump in the middle of my back. It was the capper, he was attacking me, so I kept on running and left him to it.

I began netting up the warren where I had left the day before. I had noticed quite a number of rabbits running into this warren as I approached, all safely in the warren and ready for the taking hopefully.

My ferrets, now in the warren and among the rabbits again, they seemed as eager as ever to get at them rabbits. If these large warrens had have been nearer home, I would have completely surrounded a section of these large warrens with the long nets and then worked the warren with about eight ferrets. That way it would have panicked the rabbits into bolting and the surrounding long nets wouldn't have missed a single bolting rabbit. By doing it that way I would have caught many, many more rabbits than doing it the way I was now.

With these two ferrets that I am working now, all them rabbits in this large warren, and I know that there's plenty of rabbits in there, were just playing around with the ferrets. The rabbits will be just running along one tunnel and then down along another tunnel with the ferrets chasing on behind them here, there and everywhere. But I mustn't grumble, the two bitch ferrets are working very well, and they are bolting their fair share of rabbits.

By now the rabbits were bolting to the presence of the ferrets in their warren, and they were bolting every which way in between quiet lulls. I did the same as the day before, when I thought I had taken enough rabbits from that part of the warren. It's best not to get greedy. Once the rabbits had got tired of being chased around by the ferrets they are liable to get caught by them and then I would have a kill on my hands, and I know how long them kills can last sometimes.

I have seen me in the past having to wait hours upon end just waiting and waiting for the ferret to show itself. And then when the ferret does eventually show itself it looks at me all bleary-eyed wondering what all the fuss is about. I would sometimes have waited that long I would have a pile of snow on top of my head. So when the ferrets showed themselves I picked them up and gathered up all the purse nets, I then moved on to the next section of the rabbit warren.

Earlier on when I had been watching the rabbits come in off the fields I had seen half a dozen or so black rabbits running into this part of the warren. With fingers crossed for luck, hoping to catch a few of them, I sent in the monkeys (this is a slang words we use for ferrets, that's so if we are speaking in among the public they don't know what we are talking about, everything must be muffled in the poaching world).

I look up, I see a couple of rabbits bolting at the far side of the warren, I have both of them well balled-up in the purse nets. I run over silently and light-footed and grab one of the balled-up netted rabbits, I look up and I see another rabbit bolting not far from me.

Not having time to kill the rabbit in my hand and take it out of the net, I quickly wrap the purse net cord around the rabbit's body. This makes sure that the rabbit can't roll out of the net, and I put the rabbit into my big poacher's pocket alive. All in one mad rush, I grab the other rabbit which is kicking and fighting in the net by my side, quickly wrap the net cord around his body and pop it quickly into my big poacher's pocket alive.

I race across the warren silently to the last rabbit that has just bolted. I see it's half in and half out of the net and I make a quick grab at it. It's now freed itself from the net, but it's too late for the rabbit to make its escape, I have it firmly held in my hand. It's panicking and it's lashing out at me with its big powerful back legs. One of its big claws finds it mark and it's ripped my trousers and clawed a great gash in my leg. As I am trying my best to deal with this kicking, fighting, mad, crazy rabbit, another two rabbits bolt by the side of me and the rabbit in my hands starts screaming its head off. I quickly muffle it by putting my hand over its head and mouth, a screaming rabbit will put off other rabbits from bolting. The screaming has brought the ferret to the hole end so I tap her nose to go back into the warren. The rabbit in my hands has freed its head and it starts screaming its head off again. It's disturbed the rabbits that are laid in my pockets and there's one got its head stuck out of my pocket. As I am pushing its head back in, the screaming rabbit in my hand takes one almighty bite. Its big four front teeth have gone right through my finger, there's blood everywhere, my leg's drenched in blood also. This rabbit in my hands has done enough damage for one day, but as I am trying to grab its screaming head, I see the ferret running across the warren. It has a rabbit racing in front of it that came out of a hole with no net on. I see the rabbit bob down another hole but I know I have a net over that hole.

I see the monkey follow into that hole after the rabbit. I now have the screaming rabbit in my hand by the head, a quick push back of its head and the rabbit goes silent. It's a big old dominant buck I see as I push him into my poacher's pocket on top of another rabbit. I silently and quickly grab the other two netted rabbits and pop them, still in the purse nets and alive, into my poacher's pockets.

I now hurry over to where I saw the monkey follow the rabbit into the hole, as I am sucking my bitten bleeding finger. I peer down the hole end, I see nothing, but I do see the net cord pulling taut down the hole. I give the cord a pull and a tug, I am in no hurry now, everything appears to have gone still and silent. I feel a gentle tugging back at me on the net cord and as I pull the cord slowly out of the hole I see the tail end of my cream ferret. She has something brown down there with her, it's a rabbit and I keep pulling and dragging at the cord. I make a grab at the rabbit, my ferret is startled and she turns to bite my hand, but a quick smell and scent on my hand and she leaves me be. She turns back to the rabbit and bites hard into the back of its neck. The rabbit starts grunting and groaning, it starts kicking out with its back legs, but it's only its nerves, the rabbit is dead when I pull it out.

I send my ferret back down into the warren, I have to act fast while all appears quiet. I quickly go over to the edge of the warren and empty my poacher's pockets of their rabbits. I can now go back across the warren replacing these purse nets back over the holes. All my nets are now in position again, all poised and ready for the kill. I am now stood in silence over the top of the hole where I have just sent my ferrets in a moment or two ago. As I stand there I can hear rabbits rumbling and racing around in the warren's tunnel system below my feet.

There are many, many rabbits just here. My body is by now full of adrenaline, I can feel my heart pounding, I am eagle-eyed, I am watching every hole around me, any minute now all hell is going to break loose. I stand there still sucking my bleeding finger and oh so slowly gently rubbing my badly gashed bleeding leg.

I can hear a rabbit, he's right underneath my feet, it can't be more than a foot away. Below me, there's a hole right in front of me, any second now I am sure he will bolt out of that hole. My eyes are transfixed on watching and I see a rabbit's nose appear at the entrance of the hole. He's that close to me I can nearly grab him, but I leave him be, I see him pick up his nose, he's scenting the wind for danger. He doesn't know that I am stood just above him.

I hear rabbits rumbling and racing around at the back of him, he edges himself forward. I can now see his full head from the back. He pricks his ears up, he turns his head, our eyes meet, he looks panicky, he hesitates as he watches my motionless body, he half looks behind himself back down the hole. He senses something he doesn't like. He makes a mad dash for the safety of the outside of the warren. The purse net clasps around him as he bolts, the cord holds taut and the net purses-up. He's struggling and kicking in the net to try to free himself, but it's too late, I have him firmly now in my hands. I no sooner grab him when another rabbit bolts from another hole by my side, I now have two rabbits together in my hands. I quickly wrap the net cord around each of them and pop them into my big poacher's pockets alive. I have another two rabbits out at the back of me, they are both black rabbits, they quickly go into my poachers pockets.

These rabbits I now have here laid all balled-up within my big poacher's pockets, with it being dark inside there, will lay still and usually don't try to escape. I had no sooner got these rabbits into my big pockets when I see two, three, four rabbits bolting all together at the far side of the warren. This will be my other ferret working who's bolting these rabbits. I quickly and silently race over and grab them and put them safely away and still alive into my big poacher's pockets.

I hear a scuffle by the side of me, I turn, I see four rabbits racing across the warren all together. I watch one rabbit, it's another black rabbit, I see it bobbing back down into a netted hole. The other three rabbits bob into the same hole behind it. I smile to myself, thinking, I will have all them four rabbits.

I now have rabbits bolting everywhere around me. I push another four rabbits into my big poacher's pockets, my pockets are now fair bulging and bursting full. I grab more netted rabbits, I have nowhere to put them, I push them all balled-up in purse nets tightly under my arms. I can now hold no more and most of the rabbit holes are now unnetted. I see rabbits bolting here, there and everywhere. I am missing them as I watch them make their escape, but there's nothing much I can do now but go to the edge of the warren and relieve myself of all these rabbits. I quickly deal with the rabbits I have under my arms then I look across the warren and I see a ferret out. As I head across to pick her up, I see another two black rabbits all balled-up in purse nets. I quickly grab them and put them firmly under my arm. I pick up my ferret before she goes back down into the warren.

I head on back to the edge of the warren, I deal with the rabbits under my arm first, and then pop my ferret back safely into her bag. I can now empty my bulging, heavily-laden poacher's pockets of their rabbits. I leave the rabbits there safely at the edge of the warren. I pop my ferret into the safety of my pocket. I don't want her rolling down a rabbit hole while she is still in the bag.

I head off across the warren again to where I saw all of them four rabbits go into the same hole, and as I am going I am on the lookout for my other ferret, but she's nowhere to be seen. I peer down into the darkness of this rabbit hole, I see nothing, but I do see the purse net cord pulling tight down the hole. I get myself squat down and reach my arm down the hole, a bit of groping and I pull out a rabbit without a net on it. I quickly bend its head back and pop it into my big pocket. I pull out another rabbit and another rabbit after that, both without a net on. I can by now reach no further into the hole with my arm, so I start pulling at the net cord until I pulled out my final prize which was a balled-up, netted black rabbit. It was him that had stopped the other three rabbits escaping.

It's by now time to pick everything up, I don't want to get greedy. I have got a brilliant bag of rabbits here today, all I have to do now is find and pick up my other ferret. As I look across the warren, I see a white blur run out of a hole, it's a white 'ermine' stoat. I can't believe my bad luck, that stoat will have killed a rabbit down in the warren. My ferret will have come upon the stoat, the stoat has made its escape by leaving the warren, leaving my ferret down there with the stoat's dead rabbit. My luck was now out, I knew I could have a long wait now for the ferret to show herself, she would be gorging herself on the stoat's dead rabbit. I went across to the hole where the stoat had made its escape, I got myself down on my hands and knees and put my head down the rabbit's hole and listened. It was all silent, I could hear movement of neither rabbits nor the ferret. I had a rabbit scream down the hole to attract the ferret's attention and hopefully cause it to come out, but all stayed silent. I got myself a stick and pushed it as far down the hole as I could and rattled it around in the tunnel, but all remained silent, so I stood back and patiently waited. Time drifted on by and still no sign of my ferret. She will have got her bellyful of rabbit and then got herself snuggled up in the belly fur of the rabbit and gone to sleep.

The stoat that had caused all this to happen, I say was white. The stoat's natural summer coat is a nice chestnut or reddish brown with white body marking, but in winter especially up here in the Highlands of Scotland where the winter weather is cold and harsh, the stoat's natural body colour turns white for camouflage and the stoat is then called an ermine.

I went around several of the other rabbit holes and gave out a rabbit scream and rattled the stick around in the rabbit holes then

BIG DOG STOAT IN HIS WHITE WINTER ERMINE COAT.

SMALL BITCH STOAT IN HER SUMMER COAT.

OLD SAYING. "THE STOAT IS STOUTER THAN THE WEANY WEASEL."

WEASEL

WILD POLECAT

stood back again and patiently waited. But yet again all remained silent.

I got myself to thinking about my old Uncle Jake. He told me he was once out ferreting and he had got a lay-up with his ferret, he told me that he put his head down the rabbit hole and was listening and watching for any signs of movement underground. Uncle Jake heard the rabbit around in the tunnels, he says, and as he put his ear deeper into the rabbit hole, the rabbit bolted and hit uncle Jake smack bang in the ear hole. That thought made me smile a little.

By now the time was coming very late in the afternoon and normally if I am back home and this happens, I will block up all the rabbit holes and come back next day to pick up the ferret. But there was that many rabbit holes here on this massive warren it would be futile even to think of blocking them up, I had no spade with me anyway. All I could do now was leave my ferret to her fate and try to get her back first thing next morning.

It was coming into dusk by now and I had to get back to my bivouac before it got dark. I went around the outsides of the rabbit warren and began gathering up all my day's bag of rabbits. I had caught quite a lot of black rabbits.

These black rabbits are usually big, fine-quality rabbits and these were no exception. These black rabbits which are now to be found all over the British Isles, originate from when rabbits first colonized Great Britain many hundreds of years ago. In those distant bygone days, the men who were in charge of the wild rabbits were called 'WARRENERS'. They would purposely introduce tame black rabbits into their colonies of wild rabbits, and thereafter when the warrener noted the black rabbits missing, they would know their rabbits were being hit by rabbit poachers. An extra vigilance could then be taken to guard their valuable rabbits, which were big business in those days.

The tame, domesticated black rabbits interbred with the wild rabbits, and even nowadays the gene of the black rabbit still lives on. And occasionally the wild rabbit nowadays will throw a few black rabbits in her litter of young. Hence these black rabbits I have got in my bag of rabbits now.

Once my day's bag of rabbits were safely gathered up I had a quick glance around the warren, but my ferret was still nowhere to be seen.

I headed off and away from the warren and I now set to and

paunched them. I must get rid of some of the weight, if I keep carrying heavy burdens like this I will have arms down to my knees.

I open up a black rabbit and its kidneys are laden with pure white fat, as white as freshly-driven snow. This is the rabbit's energy reserves which will keep it going through the severest of cold bitter weather that's had up here on the mountains and in the glens of Bonny Scotland.

My rabbits are now paunched and all the rabbits' guts safely hidden away under the dead pine needles again. I must keep them guts out of sight of any roving eye that may be passing by.

I now leg all my rabbits and slot them onto two long branches. I give them a count, forty-two, that's another good bag of rabbits I have got, considering all the trouble I have had losing my monkey. Then off I went through the forestry tree plantation with my heavily-laden bag of rabbits and on towards my bivouac. Once there I hung them on the branches up in the fir trees all together with yesterday's bag of rabbits. They looked a fine bag of rabbits to my eyes as they hung camouflaged up in the trees.

I pull half a dozen hearts out of the rabbits and go feed my solitary ferret which is now back in her camouflaged cage. Afterwards, I get myself a quick pork pie for dinner, then I myself crawl into my camouflaged bivouac and get myself snuggled into my nest of grass. Once I have pulled my grass ball in at the back of my head, I am sure me and my ferrets and my bag of rabbits are now nowhere to be seen if any stranger passed us by. then I drifted off into a deep slumber sleep as I listened to the late pheasants calling as they went to roost up in the trees not far away.

I didn't seem to have been asleep an hour before the calling pheasants awakened me back up again. I pushed out my ball of grass from behind my head, it was cracking dawn already, I must have slept sound that night. When I crawled out of my bivouac I could feel the freezing cold mountain air hitting me, it was biting at my nose end, and it was white-over as though it had been snowing. I got myself a bit of breakfast, no sign again of Capper. I put a big piece of pork crackling in my mouth to stave off the winter chill, I put my ferret back into her bag and off we went through the woodland. When I arrived back at the warren where my lost ferret was, there were rabbits scurrying about everywhere. They stood out like sore thumbs in the snow-covered, or was it frost-covered, ground. I went to the rabbit hole where I had seen the ermine stoat come out, I got myself down on my hands and knees on the snow-covered ground and gave out a long drawn out rabbit scream.

I rattled a stick down the rabbit hole, and stood back and waited and, as I half expected, a small cream nose appeared at the entrance of the rabbit hole. The ferrets sometimes are a little bit hesitant about coming out straightaway, just like she was now. I had brought with me a dead rabbit from yesterday's bag of rabbits and I unhurriedly dangled the rabbit's head in front of her. She grabbed the rabbit's nose and hung on to it as though she was possessed. I slowly pulled her out of the rabbit hole as she hung on for dear life to the rabbit's nose, gently got hold of her and lifted her out, and popped her into the bag with the other ferret. I could hear them chattering together, they appeared glad to be reunited.

Through past experiences, I have noted that when a ferret lays-up with a kill like this one, the ferret will stay with that dead rabbit for quite a long time.

I remember clearly me and my old Uncle Ron were out ferreting and the ferret killed a rabbit down in the warren, and that ferret refused to come out. We were well up the road, and quite a long distance from home, so we had to leave her there, and didn't block up the holes. The following week me and my old Uncle Ron, who wasn't that old at the time, were back at the same place ferreting again. As we passed the warren where we had lost the ferret the week before, for just a matter of interest I went and rattled a stick in the rabbit hole where we had lost the ferret, giving out long drawn out rabbit screams at the same time. And to my delight a bleary-eyed ferret came out with her belly all bloated out full of rabbit. That just shows you after a whole week had passed on by the ferret was still present with the dead rabbit.

So that morning I was as pleased as Punch at having found my ferret again. I now headed away from that part of the warren and on to a new section of warren to where there appeared to be a lot of rabbit activity. Their holes were polished with continuous pounding of feet going in and out of them. The ground around was pattered and shiny, there were many rabbit runs leading from the warren and heading out into the open fields, which were the rabbits' feeding grounds. The runs were ideal for snaring.

I started netting up the holes, it had been so cold through the night I had a hard job getting the purse net pegs into the frozen ground.

I always like to get the bottom of the purse net well into the rabbit hole, doing it that way the rabbit is halfway in the net before he bolts from the hole. As I was squat down busying myself putting a net over a hole, there was a disturbance up in the treetops. As I look up, I see a squirrel racing hell for leather through the branches in the treetops.

I see a flash of white speeding behind the squirrel, there was something in hot pursuit behind the squirrel. I see the squirrel leap from one tree to another treetop, what a leap it was, it must have been all of a twenty-foot leap.

I see the blur of flashing white leap after the squirrel, and as it was in mid-air between the two trees I see it was a pine marten.

I was gobsmacked as I watched, and as the fleeing squirrel landed in the other tree, the pine marten landed with it.

It was all happening right in front of my very own eyes.

The pine marten as quick as a flash made a quick grab at the squirrel. I see it give one swift bite at the back of the neck, and the squirrel was dead.

The pine marten hadn't seen me squat on the ground, but it had now, and it set off like hell back through the treetop branches with the dead squirrel firmly in its mouth. What a brilliant display, that was such a rare sighting if ever I saw one.

The pine marten is a true native to the British Isles, its stronghold being the vast conifer plantations here in the Highlands of Scotland. It's about the size of a large domestic cat and in my view it's a real bonny animal. With its dark, red-brown body, a creamy-yellow throat patch, and with a long bushy tail it's a member of the weasel family. The pine marten often goes down rabbit holes in search of its dinner and often comes back out of the rabbit hole with its dinner in its mouth.

My attention turned back to this warren I was now ferreting. My two ferrets were working well and there were rabbits bolting left, right and centre. Within next to no time, my coat was bulging with live rabbits all balled-up in purse nets, even more than yesterday. I crammed and stuffed them into my big poacher's pockets, I stuffed rabbits under my arms, and even between my legs. They were really good bolting rabbits were these, and that's just with a pair of monkeys working together. I will bet these rabbits have never seen a ferret before in their lives. In between the pandemonium of bolting rabbits, I was just imagining how well these rabbits would bolt if I had had eight or nine ferrets working

THE SQUIRREL RACES THROUGH
THE TREE CANOPY LIKE LIGHTNING
BUT THE PINE MARTEN IS LIKE
GREASE LIGHTNING AS HE
CHASES HIM FOR HIS DINNER,

PINE MARTEN

RED SQUIRREL

GREY SQUIRREL

this warren with my long nets surrounding the whole area. In my eyes that is the ultimate ferreting, much, much better and by far much, much more fun than ferreting to purse nets.

The weather by now was turning rather bitter, my hands were numb with the freezing temperature. There was an idle, nithering wind blowing, and it was blowing straight through me instead of around me. By now my hands were so cold and numb I opened up a rabbit and put my hands inside into its warm guts to get them warmed up a bit.

It was coming on to sleet, then snow started coming down heavy. The sleet and snow was hitting me in the face like bullets as it was being hard driven by the nithering blowing wind. I had to put my rain gear on, which was a DUSTBIN BAG. I tear a small hole in the bottom of the dustbin bag, just big enough to push my head through, and then pull the bag down over my body.

I never wear a hat, I like to feel the wind blow through my hair but I use a carrier bag as a waterproof hat. I roll up the sides of the carrier bag and then turn it inside out, it now fits perfectly over my head. I am now completely waterproof and windproof.

The carrier bag and the dustbin bag are always of a dull colour so that I don't stand out like a sore thumb. I carry these waterproofs with me all the time, they tuck up neatly into the corner of my pocket. I don't even know that I have got them until I need them, and to think my mate Barry the lorry driver thought I had no raincoat with me. My hands are by now warming up a little as I have them deep inside the rabbit's warm guts. My face is so cold I think it's frozen up. I wipe my nose with my bloody old coat sleeve.

There's a blob of snot on the end of my nose, it's frozen up into an icicle. When I blink my vision is marred with something, I touch my eyes, my eyelashes are all stuck up with ice. There was a real snow blizzard coming down by now so I go and stand at the back of a tree for shelter.

As I have my back to the warren, trying to avoid the sleeting driving snow, I look back and I see a rabbit all balled-up in a purse net. This hard cold bitter weather doesn't bother the rabbits. I go and grab the rabbit and take it back to the shelter of the tree. As I have my back to the warren and I am taking the rabbit out of the net, I look back. I have another rabbit kicking and fighting in the net. Rabbits have a canny way of peeping out of their holes, when they see I have my back to them, that's the time the rabbit will bolt and make his escape to freedom, but alas, the purse net will have him.

The ferreting was easy on this bare ground underneath the fir trees, all the rabbit holes were exposed, and in the open and easily to be seen.

As the morning's ferreting went on, I kept moving on to different parts of the warren, and finished my final day's ferreting with forty-one rabbits, not a bad three days rabbiting, I do think.

Barry's eyes are going to pop out of his head when he sees this lot. What's that now, one hundred and twenty one rabbits altogether.

I gather together all the day's bag of rabbits and pee them. This is important, if the pee is left inside in the rabbit's bladder it will taint the taste of the meat.

To pee them I hold the rabbit by the head and stoke my thumb gently down between the inside of the rabbit's back legs, and the pee will readily squirt out.

I now paunch and leg the rabbits and slot them on to a couple of straightish tree branches and off I head towards my bivouac. There's no signs of that mad capper of a bird the capercaillie. Once I arrive back at my bivouac, I hang my day's bag of rabbits with all my other rabbits up in the branches of the fir trees. The tree branches were nearly bending double with all the weight they were holding. What a fine bag of rabbits they looked to my eyes as they all hung suspended in the trees.

I now put my ferrets in the cage and feed them some blooded-up rabbit hearts. They are now comfortable and bedded down for the night.

I myself was ravenously hungry, but I had nothing left to eat. All my pork pies and Cornish pasties were now gone and I had eaten my last Mars bar earlier that day. I went back through the woodland to fill the ferrets' dish with water from the mountain stream and when I reached the woodside I stopped to admire the beauty of the mountain in front of me. To me that was a sight for sore eyes, as the mountain stood there in all its magnificence.

As I stood there quietly gazing out under the cover of the woodland, a cock pheasant came out and started feeding in the grass field only twenty yards away from me. It hadn't noticed me as I watched it. A slight movement caught my eye further up the field but whatever it was that I saw disappeared back in the hedgerow.

I was by now engrossed in watching. I saw a slight movement

in the long grass in the hedgerow and it appeared to me that whatever it was, was trying to stalk the feeding cock pheasant in front of me.

The pheasant was quite unaware of what was going off around it, and I kept myself well undercover as I was peeping from behind a fir tree.

Whatever it was I was watching I could now just make something out as it peered through the long grass which was by now only a few yards away from the unaware feeding cock pheasant.

As I am now peering from behind the tree trunk, only with half an eyeball and not daring to flinch a muscle for fear of being seen, I see the pheasant cock its head up. It was startled and panicked, it struck up into the air and as it whirred up the unidentified animal leapt out of the grass after it.

It was a wildcat and it leapt up high into the air after the pheasant. The wildcat half glanced the pheasant with its taloned paw and the pheasant, now off balance, came crashing back down to the ground. The wildcat recovered its balance and also came crashing back down to the ground. The wildcat went reeling over sideways and it hit the deck by the side of the pheasant. By the time the wildcat recovered its balance, the pheasant whirred back up into the air again.

The wildcat gave one almighty leap, and with another glancing blow from it sharp taloned paw, it struck the pheasant at the back of its head and they both crashed to the deck together. As they landed the wildcat quickly grabbed the pheasant by the neck. The wildcat sprawled itself across the pheasant with its razor sharp fangs sunk deep into its neck, and the pheasant kicked no more.

The wildcat laid sprawled across the pheasant until it knew it was dead, everything went silent and motionlessly still.

I couldn't believe what I had just witnessed, one of the most cunning of animals having its kill right in front of my very own eyes, a spectacle I will never forget for as long as I live.

The wildcat still hadn't seen me as I was still peeping from behind the fir tree trunk with just half an eyeball.

The wildcat never picked up my scent as the wind was blowing from it to me. This was the first wildcat I had ever seen and I got a bit of devilment into my eye. I have screamed all sorts of predators into me, but never a wildcat. I decided to have a go while the wildcat was still sprawled across the pheasant not far out in the

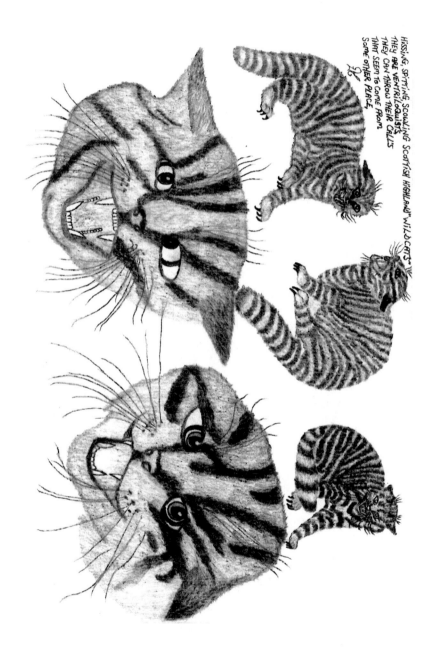

HISSING, SPITTING, SCOWLING SCOTTISH HIGHLAND "WILDCATS"
THEY ARE VENTRILOQUISTS
THEY CAN THROW THEIR CALLS
THAT SEEM TO COME FROM
SOME OTHER PLACE

field.

I kept myself flat to the tree trunk only daring to put less than half an eyeball around the tree. I knew that one false movement now and the wildcat would see me for sure and be off. I gave out a long, bloodthirsty, hair-raising rabbit scream. The wildcat acknowledged my scream instantly, it lay itself flat to the ground in the shortish grass. The grass must only be a couple of inches high at the most, but the wildcat seemed to virtually disappear out of sight. With its ears flat to its head all I could make out was just the tip of the top of its head. I could just make out its beady eyes as they peered eagle-eyed through the blades of grass, and they were looking directly at me behind the tree trunk.

I gave out another bloodthirsty, long, wailing rabbit scream and it again responded to my screams. It started crawling through the short grass dragging itself along on its belly as it came. Not wanting to give the wildcat too many screams, I withdrew myself very slowly to the back of the tree.

After a moment or two I slowly peered back around the tree again with one quarter of my eyeball, the wildcat was still there flat to the ground peering through the blades of grass. I gave out another long drawn out, pitiful, blood- curdling, wailing rabbit's scream.

The wildcat was advancing on me oh so very slowly, getting closer and closer as it crept and crawled along on its belly. It was by now only a few yards in front of me.

I could hear my belly rumbling with hunger, or was it the wildcat's belly I could hear, it was that close to me?

Something caught the corner of my eye and as I turned my head oh so very slowly to see what I had seen, there were two or three rabbits sat there out on the warren. They were acknowledging my rabbit screaming, 'rabbits and hares do also respond to DISTRESSED rabbit screams'.

I oh so slowly looked back at my wildcat, it had moved in even closer while I wasn't looking and I could by now make out the stripes on its head it was that close to me. I gave out another bloodthirsty scream.

I see it draw its back legs under its belly, it was getting ready to pounce. I see its nose twitching through the grass, I see it scenting the breeze that was blowing, it can't have liked what it was smelling. It half got up out of the grass, it seemed to ponder bewildered for a second, it looked directly at the trees I was behind, then it gave a nervous twitch with its body and, in the flash of an eye blinking, it was off like hell down the woodside. It leapt over the fence without touching it with its feet, it was racing along as though there was no tomorrow. It mad-panicked raced through the woodland, it raced as though the devil was up its backside as it sped across the rabbit warren, scattering the startled rabbits as it went.

I think the rabbits must have got the shock of their lives when they saw what was coming straight at them, and the wildcat appeared to disappear into thin air, just as though he had never been there at all.

The wildcat is another bonny animal in my eyes just like the pine marten. As he made his escape from me I could see the fine details of his body, his tawny, grey-striped fur with a bushy striped tail. The wildcat is known as the 'BRITISH TIGER', and his stronghold is also confined mainly to the Highlands of Scotland. The 'tom' wildcat can be up to 15lbs in weight, that's some almighty big cat, and they have a remarkable talent of being able to throw their calls like a VENTRILOQUIST.

Cats usually detest water, but not the wildcat, he has been known to swim out to islands to seek out fledglings of nesting birds.

The wildcat is not related to the domestic cat, it originates from Asia and Europe. The domestic cat originates from the 'WILD DESERT CAT' of Africa.

The prestige I got that day, not only seeing the wildcat but to actually scream it into me, was beyond all my dreams.

As I looked back across the field I could see the wildcat's dead pheasant. My stomach was rumbling with hunger and I got to thinking, I wonder what raw pheasant tastes like? I had to have something to eat, so I went and got the pheasant, all gratitude for an offering from the wildcat. I sat myself on a tree stump at the wood edge and I pulled the skin and feathers off the pheasant's breast. The flesh was a nice healthy pinky-red colour, and it looked ravenously enticing. I pulled my gutting knife out of my pocket, wiped the fur and blood off the blade, cut a small sliver of meat from the pheasant's breast and half-heartedly popped it into my mouth. To my surprise it tasted good, so I got stuck into it. As I sat there chomping away at my pheasant dinner and absorbing the scenery, looking at the bonny beauty of that mountainside in front of me,

I got to thinking again, there's a lot of predation, killing, territorial activities going on in this pine forest plantation here.

There's that goshawk who's whizzing through the woodlands looking for a quick dinner, and there's that 'ERMINE WHITE STOAT' who caught his rabbit dinner and lost it to my ferret. There's that pine marten I saw with that spectacular chase of that squirrel through the treetops which ended up as his dinner.

Then there's that once in a lifetime chance of seeing the elusive mountain wildcat stalking and catching this pheasant which he thankfully gave to me for my dinner. And never to be forgotten how I screamed him into me.

There's that hooting long-eared owl who no doubt will have his eagle eye out, or should that be owl eye, looking for his dinner as he perches in the treetops above my bivouac. And not to forget the yapping, barking foxes who no doubt at all will have their dinner lined up somewhere. And to top it all there's that mad capper of a bird the capercaillie who is fighting me for this territory, and last but not least all them rabbits my ferrets have caught for me.

I got to thinking as I took another mouthful of raw pheasant, is anything safe in this massive pine forest plantation here?

My belly now full, I got to thinking again, if I come back here ferreting again, I wont need to bring any food with me, I can eat like my ferrets, rough and ready, just eating raw pheasant and who knows I may try raw rabbit and share with my 'monkey' ferrets.

That's just me all over, I always like to travel light, just the bare essentials. Barry will be saying next time all in frustration, but you haven't even brought anything to eat with you.

I now head back to my bivouac with a bowl full of mountain-fresh spring water from the stream. My ferrets will enjoy this I am sure, it will help wash down the bloody hearts they had for their dinner.

I now crawl into my bivouac and get myself all snuggled up in the dry warm compact hay, now ready for a good sound sleep.

As I lay there thinking in the silence and warmth of my bivouac, I think it's up and off in the morning, it's Friday and Barry will be picking me up in his wagon. I hear my belly rumbling as it's digesting my bursting bellyfull of raw pheasant. My ears again suddenly prick up, I can hear Capper outside singing. He was sending out a series of 'clicks' and then sang out his 'drum roll' followed by his 'cork-popping'. Then singing his

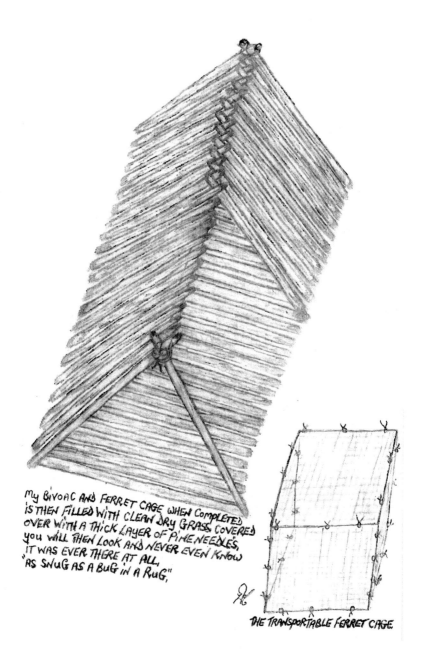

My Bivoac and Ferret Cage when completed is then filled with clean dry grass covered over with a thick layer of pine needles, you will then look and never even know it was ever there at all, "as snug as a bug in a rug"

THE TRANSPORTABLE FERRET CAGE.

my BIVOUAC CAMPSITE.

'gurgling, wheezing' notes, then singing out his series of 'clip-clopping' of a horse coming along a road, which left me there thinking, it sounds to me as though Capper is out gunning for me, and I drifted off to sleep listening as Capper lulled me to sleep.

The night passed quickly and I was awakened by the sound of a horse clip-clopping along the road. I pushed out the ball of grass from the back of my head which had been sealing me inside of my bivouac and when I looked out, who should I see but Capper. He's been waiting for me getting up, he was 'belching' at me, he was intimidating me. His tail was arched over in a 'big fan' over his back, his feathers were ruffled out on his neck, his beard under his chin was all puffed out, his head was held high with his beak stuck up in the air. He looked like a big fat turkey but looking thick and powerful, he looked awesome and ferocious, as he stood there sending out his threat calls to me with his series of 'cork pops' and then 'belching' at me. I think he was trying to frighten me. I think, if that mad capper of a bird doesn't watch out, one of these days I will be having him for my dinner, even if he does taste of resinous turpentine.

I crawled out of my bivouac and brushed him to one side. "Stupid bird" I say to him. I was busy, I had to get all my rabbits to the roadside, ready for Barry picking me up. As I went into the fir trees to get some of my rabbits, I got such a powerful thump at the back of my head. It was Capper, the mad crazy bird was attacking me. I turned around to him and he strutted up to me, he was taking me on to protect his territory. He got into a crouch then ran towards me, with his neck stretched out. He flew up at me with noisily flapping, whirring wings, and crash-landed back on the ground, making even more noise with his whirring, flapping wings.

I could easily have grabbed him and wrung his neck, but I wouldn't, I respected Capper. I was proud to be in his territory, he was only a dumb bird, I had to tolerate him, but I had to stand my ground to him.

As I wiped the back of my head where Capper had just hit me, I looked at my hand, there was blood on it, leaving me thinking, that damned bird has to be watched carefully, he will have my eye out if I don't watch him with care.

I pulled two poles of rabbits out of the fir trees, all was well with them, nothing had been trying to eat them while they had been hung up in the trees.

The fox is liable to come and take some of them, but to make sure the fox didn't take any, I had hung a smelly old jumper up there with my rabbits. The fox now will venture nowhere near for the fear of human scent.

I took one of the rabbits and had a look at it, it was as stiff as a board, all frozen up with the bitter cold freezing nights we had been having. I opened up the rabbit's belly flap, I saw ice inside there, my rabbits were as fresh as a daisy, as fresh as the day that I killed them.

I headed to the roadside with these two poles of rabbits. The road was quite some distance away and Capper was at me all the way, flying up over my shoulder and having a peck at my ear as he passed me by. The two poles of rabbits were now safely at the back of the hedge at the roadside and as I peered down the quiet country lane, there was not a person or vehicle to be seen anywhere. I went back for another two poles of rabbits, and Capper was still following me all the way, pecking and flapping his wings at my legs. I got to thinking, if I took the ferrets out of their cage, I could put Capper in there until I had finished hauling my rabbits, but I struggled on regardless, and kept pushing Capper out of my way.

I eventually got all six poles of rabbits to the roadside and out of sight at the back of the hedge. I had completely covered over my bivouac with dead pine needles, now I popped my two ferrets into their bag and popped them into my large poacher's pocket.

I covered over their cage with dead pine needles, I then stood back and looked at my campsite, and there was not a trace of me ever having been there at all.

My bivouac and ferret cage are now well insulated against the winter's snow and rain and the bedding will now be kept dry. I have enjoyed such a good three days ferreting here, my intentions are to come back here again.

I now get myself squat down at the back of the hedge with my bag of rabbits and wait for Barry to come along in his wagon to pick me up. As I was squatting there waiting, Capper had brought his harem of hens. I hear the sound of a big engine coming along the road and as I peered through the hedge to see if it was Barry, Capper's persistently pecking at my backside. I got laid low, it wasn't Barry, it was a farm tractor. It went by and carried on into the distance and disappeared out of sight.

I got squat back and waited quietly. Capper came over to me

and was persistently niggling and pecking at me. He was a fine looking bird was Capper, he would have been a fine looking bird plucked out ready for the oven. He would have weighed more than eight pounds. It's a pity his meat tasted of resinous turpentine, otherwise it might have been a different story. I got to thinking, I wonder if he tasted like that raw, he was big enough to last me all week here in food as I was living rough in this pine forest.

I hear another big engine coming along the road but as I peered through the hedge to see if it was Barry, I couldn't see properly because one of Capper's hens was stood on a broken-down stone wall and was blocking my view. As I peered anxiously, Capper pecking and biting at my hand, I saw it was a Land Rover coming so I got squat back down at the back of the hedge. The Land Rover passed on by and disappeared into the distance and when I looked at my hand, the old devil had drawn blood. I gave him a clout around the ear hole and shooed him away.

I now had a bleeding hand and the back of my head was still bleeding, all inflicted by that dumb capper of a bird, if he doesn't watch out he's going to end up as ferret meat. All Capper's harem of hens were stood perched on the broken-down stone wall. I heard another vehicle approaching and as I peered through the hedge and through the gaps in between Capper's hens, I saw it was Barry's wagon approaching. I jumped out from behind the hedge and Capper jumped out with me. I flagged Barry down, he pulled his wagon onto the grass verge right by the side of me, jumped out of his wagon and came around to me.

The mad capper of a bird was attacking me again, he was coming at me with ferocity, with his pecking, slashing beak and his whirring, flapping wings. And all Capper's harem of hens were kicking up a right old fuss, it was just like a hell hole of Bedlam.

I think it must have incited them all when they saw Barry and his wagon. With all the noise and commotion that was going off around me, I looked at Barry and Barry looked at me. I could see fear on Barry's face and he raced off and jumped back into his wagon.

I signalled to Barry to get onto the back of his wagon to take the rabbits from me. Barry opened his wagon door only slightly, he then sidled his way from the cab and edged his way along and onto the back of his wagon.

As I passed him a pole full of rabbits the capper was going mad crazy at me. Barry says to me in a panicky voice, "Are they some sort of pheasant Doug?" Capper flew up at me again and Barry shouted out, "Watch out Doug, they're going to kill you!" I passed Barry another pole full of rabbits and Barry says, "By, these are grand rabbits, is that them all?" I went to the back of the hedge and Capper raced after me, he was getting worse. Capper was going off his rocker, he was whirring high up into the air, hovering over me and then crash-landing his heavy powerful body at my feet.

He was giving out his 'DRUM ROLLS' and then his 'CORK POPS' and then started 'GURGLING' and 'WHEEZING', and then his characteristic 'clip-clopping' noise. He then whirred up into the air again and crash-landed down the side of my head, biting my ear as he crashed passed. I give my ear a rub, it's all wet and tacky, he's drawn blood again. His harem of hens on the broken-down stone wall were playing holy hell, it was like a pandemonium going off around me.

I passed Barry another pole full of rabbits but Barry wasn't there, I see him hidden behind the load on his wagon. Barry uneasily comes over and takes the rabbits from me and he says, "Is that it, have we got all the rabbits now Doug?" I shake my head. I put my hand up to my ear, it feels wet and tacky, I put my hand to the back of my head, it too feels wet and tacky. I bring my hand down and look at it, my fingers are covered in blood, my legs and hands are bleeding.

The mad capper of a bird was cutting and slashing me all over my body. I passed another pole full of rabbits up to Barry and he says, "That must be all the rabbits by now, surely." I shake my head, and go back behind the hedge, I hand another pole full of rabbits up to Barry.

I say to Barry, "One more pole of rabbits and that's the lot." Barry says, "Thank Christ for that, let's get the hell out of here and fast or somebody is going to get killed here."

I pass up the last pole of rabbits, Barry quickly throws them on to the back of the wagon.

Barry, I had to smile at him, hurriedly sidles himself back down the side of the wagon and slips quickly into the cab and slams the door shut behind him. I jump into the passenger side of the cab.

While the cab door was still open the mad capper of a bird was trying to get into the cab. I looked at Barry, he was freaking out with horror. I shut the cab door, shutting Capper out, and Barry set off with his wagon, his tyres screeching as we went. As I looked back through the window, Capper flew up into the air and circled around in front of us and he hit the windscreen of the wagon. I thought Barry was going to jump out of the cab window with fright. Capper dropped off the wagon and dropped onto the grass verge. I opened the cab window and looked back. Capper was unhurt, I could see him, he was up on his feet flapping and whirring his wings at us as we went.

Once we had got on our way homeward bound, and Barry had settled himself down, I must have looked like the Wildman of Borneo to him. With me sleeping rough, I must have looked rough, my longish hair must have been all over the place, it hadn't had a comb through it for nearly a week. I had nearly a week's stubble on my chin, I never had a shave while I was there. I must have been dirty too, I hadn't had a wash either only a 'cat lick' in that mountain stream. And to top it all my hands and face were covered in blood with that mad capper of a bird the capercaillie.

I tell Barry what the birds were, and that the capercaillie was a true BRITISH NATIVE BIRD, especially up here in the Highlands of Scotland.

Barry looks at me and says, "Let the capercaillie stay up here, let us get home."

As time went by, after that first ever encounter at ferreting these rabbits up there in those Bonny Glens, I came back quite a few times. Barry would always drop me off with his wagon in the early part of the week, leaving me to ferret the rabbits out for a few days. He would then pick me up again later in the week. With the number of times I came back here, I ended up doing all that full stretch of pine forestry plantation ferreting out the massive rabbit warrens, and catching many, many rabbits, and in all that time I always used that same bivouac, it became just like home from home to me.

My bivouac stood up to all the rigorous hard Scottish weather, the piled up dead pine needles over the top of my bivouac always keeping it dry inside, and my ferrets' cage also. But I did learn one thing the hard way, all the warm dry grass inside my bivouac was so inviting I would get many mice sleeping in there. So when I arrived on my first day, I would have to pull out my dry snug bedding and give it all a good old shake.

But alas, my way of thinking is "A CREATURE OF HABIT ALWAYS GETS CAUGHT". I went there once too often in this massive fir tree plantation, up here in the isolation of the

Grampian Mountains, high up in the Scottish Highlands.

But was it for the bad or was it for the good… READ ON.

I remember this particular day very clearly in my mind, it's as though it only happened yesterday, but it happened many, many years ago now, in those bygone days of yesteryear. Barry had dropped me off as per usual with his wagon and I was out on my third day's ferreting. As I was squat down low on top of a rabbit warren, all was quiet as I waited for the rabbits to start bolting.

Then suddenly I heard some woodpigeon come clattering through the treetops and my hair instantly stood up on the back of my neck. That told me to beware, there's someone in this part of the forestry tree plantation. I kept myself perfectly still and squat low with my ears pricked and cocked listening for the slightest of sounds.

I hear a couple of magpies, they come hopping from tree to tree as they pass me by. The magpies haven't seen me squat low, they are cackling away to each other in their own bird fashion way. They are telling me, "Watch out, there's a stranger coming." The magpies disappear further along into the woodland, I am now on red alert and, without making a whisper of a sound, I get myself up at the back of a fir tree trunk.

I peep around the tree trunk with just an eyeball and I listen and watch. I see a blackbird come TEAR-ARSING through the darkness of the pine trees, he's cackling his head off, telling me, "There's a stranger upon you." He perches himself on a tree branch above me, he hasn't seen me he's that busy eyeballing from where he's just come. He starts jinking his tail and chirping out madly to himself, he doesn't like what he sees by the looks of him.

He's off like the clappers as he goes TEAR-ARSING through the woodland. He's telling me, "He's upon you, be warned, take heed and be off with you."

The blackbird disappears out of sight through the woodland.

I am now left all alone again in silence. As I peer around the tree trunk and look into the gloom of the fir trees where the blackbird has just tear-arsed from, I see something moving about inside the gloomy woodland. I don't like what I see, it's a black Labrador dog. I get myself tight and flat up the side of the tree trunk and keep myself motionless.

I instinctively knew then that my number was up, I knew that the dog would pick up my scent and disclose my whereabouts.

As I am watching the dog with just half an eyeball from behind

"WOODPIGEON" CLATTERING
THROUGH THE TREE'S TELL'S
OF A STRANGER APPROACHING,

THE SQUAWKING CALL'S
OF THE "MAGPIE"
TELL'S OF A STRANGER
IN THE WOODLAND.

THE EYE BALLING "BLACKBIRD" is SHREIKING OUT
"GO BACK" "GO BACK" "THERE'S A STRANGER, COMING,"
AS HE GOE'S TEARARSING THROUGH THE WOODLAND
HE'S CALLING BACK "I HAVE WARNED YOU, THE STRANGER
is upon' you,"

the tree trunk, my ears prick up. I hear someone shouting to the dog, he's telling the dog to, "Seek him out lassie, he's in here somewhere, seek him girl." I peer around the other side of the tree trunk only with a quarter of an eyeball. I see a man, he's stood on the woodland side, he's peering into the woodland where I am, he's still urging his dog on to seek me out.

I can now hear the dog pitter-pattering through the dead pine needles on the woodland floor. I peep around the other side of the tree trunk, I see the dog, it's only a few paces away from me, it has it nose tight to the ground, it's following my scent where I have just come from.

The dog comes right up to the tree which I am hiding behind, the dog looks up at me and starts wagging its tail, I try to shoo it away, but it starts barking at me. I knew then that was it, my game was up.

I hear someone shout out in a Scottish tongue, "Ye best be coming out and show yourself."

I came out from behind the tree and looked at this fellow, he looked important. He had a deerstalker hat on and he had a great big bushy black beard that came down to his chest. He was a thickset fellow with big thick arms on him, leaving me thinking to myself, I had better not tackle this fellow, if he gets hold of me, he will shake me like a rat. It was no good trying to do a runner to get away from him, I was here in a massive pine forest in the middle of nowhere, so I sheepishly gave myself up and walked across to him. He says, "Na then laddie, what may you be up to?"

I say, in a croaked up tone of a voice, "I am trying to catch a rabbit or two with my ferrets."

He says, "Well, I am the keeper around this neck of the woods and ye should have sought permission from me first." I nodded and at that moment a rabbit bolted into a purse net. The fellow says eagerly, "Go on, go and catch it."

I ran over and killed the rabbit, which left me thinking, this fellow appears to be all right with me, he doesn't appear to be nasty-minded, he's not giving me a grilling for poaching his rabbits.

I went back over to him with the dead rabbit in my hand and said, "Aren't they good fat rabbits."

He says, "That's not a local tongue ye speak laddie." I shook my head and he says, "Where's your neck of the woods then?" I thought, he appears to be coming clean with me, and not appearing to be a threat. So I came clean and told him where I came from.

He says, "But that's hundreds of miles away." I nodded and he asks how I had got here, so I came clean with him again and told him. I looked at him and he had a big smile on his face, and he says, "Ye must like ya rabbiting." I nodded, he asked, "Where ye getting ya head down then?" As I told him, I pointed through the woodland towards where my bivouac was. He says, "Come on, let's go have a look."

By now the ferrets had come on to the surface of the warren, so I went and picked them up and popped them back into their bag. Me and this fellow then went through deep into the pine forest, I then pointed and showed him where my bivouac was.

When I looked around at him he had a big smile on his face that must have stretched from EAR TO LUG, and he says, "I will be damned. I have searched this woodland looking for you for quite a long time now, and I have kept walking past your camp and never seen it." As he looked up he saw four poles of rabbits hung and squat between two fir trees and he responded by saying, "You've got a good bag of rabbits by the looks of it." I nodded and he said, "Ye best be coming with me back to my cottage, I want to have a serious word with you." I nodded, feeling a bit guilty.

He says, "Gather ya rabbits together and take them to the woodside, I will come and pick ye up in the Land Rover." He helped carry some of the rabbits through the woodland and while he was gone for the Land Rover, I picked up all my purse nets that were set on the rabbit warren. I was still in suspense as to whether or not he was going to do me for poaching his rabbits.

It was by now early afternoon so I had just about finished rabbiting for the day anyway and had just about got my quota of rabbits when this fellow had caught me.

In the morning it was pick-up day with Barry, so I had a real good bag of rabbits to hand into this fellow's Land Rover.

He had game rails in his Land Rover so I hung all my rabbits on his game rails. A real good sight to my eyes were my rabbits as they hung there inside his Land Rover. It will be my luck now, for him to take me straight on down to the local nick.

I jumped into the front of the Land Rover with him and off we went. As we were driving along I said to the fellow, "Whereabouts do you live then?" He says, "Over that LALL HILL there." As he pointed, he was pointing at what I was calling a mountain, he was calling it a lall hill. "Lall" meaning little.

I looked down into the glen, it was just like picture postcard country. There were steep mountainsides running down into the glen, with densely planted pine forests on its bank sides. There was a BURN (STREAM) running along the glen bottom and I could see a wisp of smoke coming up in the distance. The fellow pointed to it and said, "That's my little cottage where you see that smoke coming from."

As we drove along making our way down into the glen, we went along a driveway, an avenue with mature trees at either side as it meandered down into the glen. All this was sheer beauty to my eyes. It was a gorgeous sunny winter's day and I saw snow-clad mountains and glens, a veritable winter wonderland, a winter wonderland which abounds with wonderful wildlife.

So this fellow didn't take me to the local nick after all. We pulled up outside his cottage and there were rabbits scampering around everywhere. I saw a herd of red deer running off into a woodland in the distance and the burn ran right in front of his quaint little stone cottage, leaving me thinking, this is my kind of country.

The fellow invited me into his cottage, leaving me thinking again, there he might call the police now, now that he's got me here. But he didn't, he put a giant-sized frying pan on to the large log-burning fire, he put some big thick rashers of ham into the pan, cracking half a dozen eggs by the side of it, leaving me thinking, he's making his own dinner, but he wasn't. He put the ham and eggs on to the table and said, "Here, get stuck into that." I ate it ravenously and after he had dined me, he pulled off his boots and pulled an armchair up in the front of the log-burning fire.

The black Labrador dog that had caught me came and laid down by the side of his feet. Then he introduced himself as, "BOB BLACK, but everybody around these parts call me BLACK BOB."

I introduced myself as, "DOUG," and to my delight he shook hands with me. As we were both sat down in front of the log-burning fire, Bob got chatting away and came upon the subject of how he knew I was in his woodland. He says, "Your cig smoke, I could smell it a mile away," and continued on to say, "you also left the odd footprint in the soft soil around the rabbit holes. Also, where you had paunched your rabbits, the fox had pulled them out of the cover you had hid them in, then the guts attracted the crows and I saw them feeding on them."

I patted Bob on the shoulder, complimenting him on his good

keepering.

The conversation then turned to my rabbiting and I told Bob all the different ways I catch rabbits. He appeared impressed and said, "There's plenty of rabbits around here for you to have a go at." My eyes lit up.

It was by now coming into late afternoon and I said to Bob, "I best be getting back to my encampment, before it gets too dark." Bob shook his head and said, "You can sleep here in the spare bed." Bob had told me earlier that he lived alone, he also told me there was a hutch outside that I could put my ferrets in.

I told Bob that my mate Barry was picking me up in the morning with his wagon. Bob says, "I will get you down there on time."

So that was the start of a good relationship I had with Bob. He tells me the next time I come I have to bring plenty of rabbit snares with me. He had a place where it was overrun with rabbits and that they were making good runs. That left me thinking of my old saying, "a creature of habit gets caught", but me being caught this time had really paid off.

Bob kept his promise, he had me down by the roadside with my rabbits waiting for Barry to pick me up. We parked at the roadside at the end of Bob's drive with his Land Rover. Barry had to pass this drive to get to my pick-up point which was just along the road a little.

As I saw Barry coming in the wagon, I jumped out of Bob's Land Rover and flagged Barry down. I could see a grim expression on Barry's face as he jumped out of his wagon. He starts playing hell, saying, "I told you Doug that you would get caught," and me calming him down saying, "Barry, Barry calm down." I introduced Barry saying, "This is Bob and he is letting me do a bit of rabbiting for him," and Barry and Bob shook hands.

I had well over a hundred rabbits to transfer over on to Barry's wagon. Barry was telling Bob, "You've dropped on a good rabbit catcher there with Doug, he will sort your rabbit problem for you." And on that, with all the rabbits loaded on to the back of the wagon, me and Barry drove away bidding Bob farewell as we went.

I heard Bob shouting in the distance, "Make sure you bring plenty of snares the next time you come, and don't forget to give me a ring." And homeward bound me and Barry went with me as pleased as Punch and thinking, all's well that ends well.

As time passed on by my friendship with Bob Black grew even

stronger… READ ON.

It was by now late February, the breeding season was upon me. I had already seen a few young rabbits about, so I left things be while the end of the breeding season and while I was waiting I got myself prepared and made plenty of snares. The summertime passed on by quickly, and I was eager to get back up into the Highlands of Scotland, back among all them rabbits in those Bonny Glens.

This time I was going to travel up there in my Land Rover and as I was expecting a decent bag of rabbits to bring back with me I towed a trailer at the back of the Land Rover. It was going to be a long drive up there.

It was by now early September, the end of the rabbit breeding season. I telephoned Bob Black, 'Black Bob', and arranged with him that I would be up at his cottage by early evening, and off I set. I left very early morning, all loaded up with my snaring gear. I had more than three hundred snares with me, that should be ample enough to get myself a good bag of rabbits.

I intended having my snares down for two nights, and then lift them, and then straight back home while the rabbits were still fresh.

It was a long, long drive to get up there, but eventually I arrived, I turned off the main Highland road and on to that country lane where I had guided Barry with his wagon, I was wondering to myself if Capper was still around.

As I drove along the very quiet country back road, there were masses of rabbits out feeding on the grass fields that ran alongside that massive fir tree plantation, the place where I had done all that ferreting so many times over the past. There appeared to be more rabbits there now than there ever was, it had been a good breeding season for the rabbits by the looks of it.

I turned off the quiet back road and on to Bob's driveway.

I wormed my way up that mountainside, the one that Bob called a 'LALL HILL', and on reaching the top I looked down into what was one of the bonniest glens I had ever set eye on. I drove down the hillside and along Bob's driveway, the avenues of trees at either side of the driveway made it look really picturesque.

As I drove along I see a large herd of red deer grazing on the hillside in the distance. I see rabbits scampering about everywhere, all big fat ones now by the looks of them, I was eager to have a go at them. As I drove into the courtyard in front of Bob's stone cottage, there were geese, chickens and ducks, and they scattered as I drove in.

Bob was there ready and waiting to welcome me. There, I thought, I have finally arrived all safe and well but tired.

Bob was all prepared for my arrival, he was going to put me up in his spare bed in his cottage. After a good night's rest, I was up at the crack of dawn the following morning. Bob was up before me, he was outside feeding his geese, chickens and ducks. After a good ham and eggs breakfast, which was far better than my usual pork pie, and defending myself against that mad capper of a bird the capercaillie, down in the forestry plantation.

Me and Bob set off towards the snaring grounds he had promised me. Bob led the way in his Land Rover, I followed on behind him in my Land Rover. We wormed our way through the hills and over mountaintops, and down through glens, the scenery was a real picture for sore eyes. Bob pulled up at the side of a pond and came to me saying this was his duck pond where he did a bit of wildfowling. He told me that when I paunch my rabbits to throw the rabbits' guts into the pond, and saying that the guts were good feed for the ducks and would attract many mallards in. Bob then pointed down into a large glen, saying that's where the rabbits were, and that the rabbits were in plague proportions down there. He says there were no sheep turned out so I would be okay to snare down there, and on that, Bob jumped back into his Land Rover and off he drove leaving me to it.

I looked at the place from where I was standing at the side of Bob's duck 'flight pond'. It was a very long glen stretching for nearly as far as I could see. Stretching way out into the distance, down the hillsides of the glen was a forestry fir tree plantation with a high deer fence around it. Below the trees were grass meadows on either side of the glen and I was thinking, that will be where the rabbits are feeding. In the bottom of the glen was a fast-flowing stream (burn).

I was eager to be at them rabbits, so I jumped into the Land Rover and got as close as possible to the scene as I could. I grabbed two bundles of snares and off I went.

I got myself onto the woodside and walked along. With it being a quiet secluded desolate area, the rabbits were sat out in their multitudes.

I could see the rabbits were travelling out of the fir tree plantation and underneath the high wire mesh deer fence and feeding in these grass meadows. The grass was rough and thickly growing but short, no doubt kept short by the onslaught of the feeding rabbits. This type of ground is ideal for snaring rabbits.

The rabbits' runs were leading from the forestry and leading way out into the meadows, which again is ideal for snaring rabbits.

Down in the bottom of the glen was a lot of densely growing 'sivs' which are a type of reed. The sivs ran all the way along the banks of the fast-flowing stream and the rabbits were making their runs through them so that they could drink from the stream, which again is ideal for snaring.

I was eager to be on and at them so I carried on along the woodside. There were rabbits galore, scampering about inside of the woodland. It was one great long rabbit warren inside that woodland, just like that fir tree plantation that I had been ferreting at the other side of the estate.

Now to start dropping my snares. There was an old tree stump which I took as a marker where my first snare started. The first run was a long main run leading way out down into the bottom of the meadow. If possible, it's best not to snare the main run itself, there will be many rabbits travelling along that run and any snared rabbits on it will be off-putting to other rabbits following on behind. So what I do is snare the good runs leading off or on to the main run, that way it will ensure snaring more rabbits. I got ten snares set on the runs which led onto the main run and I was confident they would all be 'struck' during the night. I got out my little sketchbook and drew a rough quick sketch of that run and its location, putting a circle on the sketch everywhere I had a snare set. The sketch is quick and simple and it does ensure I do not overlook any snares when I come back later. When I am setting hundreds of snares some can easily be forgotten, but not with my rough sketch in my pocket.

As I am down in the sivs setting a snare something catches my eye. I see a bird of prey flying low, it's quartering the sivs and hunting. As it flew in closer just skimming over the top of the sivs, I see it's a hen harrier. These birds fly low along the ground silently surprise-attacking their prey.

The hen harriers have a notorious name with the fraternity of shooting people. On shooting days, the gun will have a wounded game bird down, and as if from nowhere the hen harrier will swoop in and take the bird right from in front of the retriever dog's nose. When the hen harrier spotted me, it did a quick disappearing

FEMALE

MALE

"THE HEN HARRIER"
WILL SWOOP IN AND STEAL SHOT
GAME RIGHT IN FRONT OF THE
SHOOTING MAN'S VERY OWN EYES.

FEMALE
"HEN HARRIER"
WITH HER SHOT GAME
STOLEN DINNER.

trick.

I carried on further along the wood edge and I came across four main runs that ran way down into the bottom of the meadow. I could tell by the well-beaten runs there were many rabbits running here. The runs were zigzagging here, there and everywhere as they traversed and meandered around these main runs, over a large area. I set fifty snares in one big cluster, wherever a rabbit run I had a snare set there for the rabbit to hit. A quick pull out of my pocket, I had my sketch book in hand, a quick scribble and all my snares positioned and located with a rough drawing.

They are a big breed of rabbit up here and I always set my snares according to the size of the rabbits I am snaring. For a good clean catch or kill I must always catch the rabbit with the snare around its neck. I set my snares at five inches high, that's from the ground to the bottom wire of the noose. I do that measurement with my hand and I must make sure I do not touch the bottom of the run with my hand as I am measuring, any hint of human scent on the run bottom will stop the rabbit dead in his track. And also as I walk along I never put a foot on their runs.

I now head on further along the wood edge and I see rabbit runs coming underneath the deer fence all the way along the fence line. I don't like to snare rabbits where they are going underneath a fence or through it. Some snarers do, and they will tie and tether their snares to the fence. But to me, when a rabbit is tethered to the fence the vibrating, shaking fence from the fighting rabbit in the snare does and will put off many rabbits as they ago along their runs. I like to put my snares where the old snarers of yesteryear would set their snares and that is way out in the middle of the field, that way the rabbit is running freely and will run headlong into the snare.

I also like to study a run before I set my snare. I scan the run bottom closely, looking for the 'little beat', that is where the rabbit is putting his front feet, and then setting my six strand snare directly over the top of the little beat.

As the rabbit comes along his run at a fair old hop, he will put his front feet on the little beat. The rabbit's got his head in the noose now, but he doesn't know that and he will go out on to his next quick hop, and the snare noose tightens around his neck. I have my snare double half-hitched onto a wire tealer, and I have tension in the set wire noose. That way, if a rabbit brushes past it, the tension in the noose flips the snare back into its original position over the run, leaving the set snare all ready and waiting for the next rabbit that happens to come along that run.

I stand back and look at the snare, I see it gently quivering and blowing in the breeze with the grass, it looks alive as it is poised there waiting set and ready. It's virtually invisible as I see the grass blowing around it.

The tether peg I heel in level with the ground and there's nothing there visible for the rabbit to see. If the ground is hard or stony I have with me a screwdriver which I carry in my back pocket, that will locate an entry for my tether peg.

As I am setting snares on the runs that are leading through the sivs and on to the banks of the stream, I notice mink 'scats', which are droppings, and as I look around I see small scats, and that tells me there is a mink with cubs about.

There's no doubt about it, they will take their fair share of my snared rabbits. The cubs will stay with their mother until late autumn. The mink was once upon a time all caged animals for their valuable fur. The mink originate from North America, but they are experts at escaping and are now breeding successfully in our British countryside.

As I move further along the stream, I come across an old wooden five-barred gate and I see three main rabbit runs leading through it, but somehow they look different. As I look closer I see bigger beats on the run bottoms and they are set apart further than rabbit beats usually are.

These are hare runs. Bob said he would have some hares if I caught any. I calculate that there will be at least half a dozen hares using these runs. I set two snares on each run about fifty yards apart, that way any screaming snared hare will not deter any other hares from using their run. I purposely put down strong snares with strong tethers. The hare is a big strong animal, he can snap a snare like a carrot with his big strong back legs. I have with me some wooden tealers which I have brought with me purposely for this job. I stick them into the ground alongside of the snare and out of sight of the hare. The wooden tealer is stuck up and out of the ground about four inches.

So now when the hare is snared, he will run around and wrap himself around the wooden tealer with the tether, he is now limited in movement holding him firmly and well and truly caught.

I now carried on back up the bank of the stream and there were

WILD MINK
WITH HIS KILL

rabbit runs leading down through the sivs and to the water's edge. The rabbits were jumping across the stream to feed on the other side. What's that old saying, "the grass is greener at the other side of the hedge". In this case it was a stream.

So I set a snare where the rabbit was landing with his front feet, with my snare bang over the little beat. So now when the rabbit jumps the stream, as soon as his feet touch the ground, his head will be in the snare noose and on his next hop the noose will tighten around his neck. There were quite a lot of rabbits jumping here along the stream so I went along the bank and snared on all the runs where the rabbits were jumping the stream. I noticed fresh mink scats as I went along. There's no doubt about it, these mink will take their fair share of these rabbits tonight if I catch any. I now head back up to the top of the meadow and back along the wood edge.

I came across about twenty good runs which were all running straight out into the middle of the meadow. The way I snare such runs as these is to set my snares in long straight lines. This is done so that I can easily locate my snare. I then go to the next run to it and set another snare level with the last snare. I go along all the runs and set my snares in the same way.

By the time I have a snare on every run, they are all in a long straight line. I now go about twenty yards down the run and further away from the wood edge, and set another row of snares.

I set several rows of snares along all of these runs and I can now easily locate them when I return by just walking along the rows of snares. On this particular setting I have twenty snares in one row, and I have five rows altogether, so in total I have a hundred snares set on these twenty runs. I can tell there are many rabbits running here so every snare I have set here will be struck during the night.

I now carried on along the wood edge. By now I had many snares set and I stopped to have a five minute break. As I sat on a tree trunk a buzzard came flying past and settled in the top of a fir tree not far away from me. I like the buzzard, he's one of my favourite birds of prey. I might add he's a damned good rabbit catcher, the rabbits are petrified of him. As I sat there a PEREGRINE FALCON came flashing past me, he is another of my favourite birds of prey. The peregrine saw the buzzard perched in the treetops and circled around and came in at the back of the buzzard. As the peregrine swooped past it knocked the buzzard off its perch.

PEREGRINE

BUZZARD

BUZZARD AND PEREGRINE
MOB FIGHTING IN MID-AIR COMBAT.

The buzzard soared high into the sky with the peregrine hot in pursuit of it. It looked as though the peregrine was challenging the buzzard to a real combat.

The peregrine flew high overhead of the buzzard and then it fell in to a 'stoop', speeding and twisting as it plummeted down on the buzzard. The buzzard saw the peregrine attacking from above.

At the moment just before contact, the buzzard turned on to its back and bared its razor-sharp talons and hooked beak and as the peregrine struck at the buzzard, the buzzard struck back with its outstretched talons.

As the peregrine went CAREERING past at a breathtaking speed, the buzzard struck at it with its powerful hooked beak.

It was only a 'mock fight'.

They were challenging each other for the supremacy of the skies. As I sat there on my tree stump watching this territorial battle taking place, right in front of my very own eyes, the mock fighting carried on for quite a while. Then they both disappeared over the treetops and out of sight, still fighting as they went.

I remember I was once sitting quiet in a quarry watching a pair of peregrine falcons training their young to kill when a flock of feral pigeons flew high overhead. Both peregrines set off after them with one of their young following in hot pursuit behind them. The wise old pair of peregrines were working together as a team. They split up as they neared the feral pigeons. The female peregrine, which is the larger of the two sexes, singled a pigeon out of the flock, she was using herself as a decoy as she flew below the pigeon, distracting the pigeon's attention.

The tiercel, which is the name of the male falcon, is much smaller than the female and he was flying high overhead of the distracted pigeon.

I was sat there gobsmacked and watching with my eyes transfixed and not daring to blink for the fear of missing something.

The tiercel, high above the pigeon, went into a stoop with electrifying speed. He must have been breaking the sound barrier as he hit the pigeon at the back of its head with his hooked pointed talon.

The pigeon never stood a chance, it never even saw the tiercel coming. As the pigeon fell fluttering to the ground, the female peregrine swooped in catching hold of the fluttering pigeon while still in mid-air. By now the pursuing young peregrine had caught up with where all the action had taken place.

I looked to see where the tiercel has gone and I saw him sat high up on a rocky edge. He was watching the female hand over the flapping, flailing pigeon to her youngster, all still in mid-air.

The immature youngster let the pigeon go. By now the pigeon had recovered its senses and in a bedraggled state made a last ditch attempt to reach the safety of the quarry.

The younger peregrine made a poor attempt at re-catching the pigeon. The wily old tiercel was watching all this taking place from his rocky position, his beady eyes missing nothing.

I saw him jump into the air, he gave out one of my favourite bird calls, fell into a stoop and again hit the pigeon with a massive great strike to the top of its head.

This time the pigeon fell lifeless, heading towards the ground. The now learned young peregrine swooped in and grabbed the pigeon while all still in mid-air. This time the youngster didn't let go, and off he went with his prize of a dinner, which left me all gobsmacked with what I had just witnessed and all in front of my very own eyes, phew! They are one hell of a bird and one of my favourite birds of prey the peregrine falcon.

Anyway I am getting myself a little distracted, let me get back to the real job of rabbit snaring.

I have by now well on to three hundred snares set. It is hard work setting that many snares and it can cause me to get a sweat on, and that's bad practice when snaring. I must never set my snare with sweaty hands, any hint of human scent and the rabbits will back off their runs and I won't get a rabbit. So it's always best to have a break and cool off.

I now leave this heavily-snared area and set off further up the wood edge, rubbing my hands in grass as I go to get rid of any human scent on my hands. I am now about finished dropping my snares, but I come across some runs where there are a lot of dead branches laying about on the ground. The branches are laid across the rabbit runs and as I look closely, I see the rabbit's 'BEATS' as he is jumping over the branches. I set my snare bang over where his front feet are landing, and that should take him by the neck as he is going out on to his next hop, or is it jump? I set another dozen snares here, and that's it for the day.

As I look along the side of the fir tree plantation, it stretches way out into the distance, which will be rabbit-infested just like where I am snaring here. As I look to the other side of the glen, it's just the same there, the fir tree plantation stretching way out into the distance further than the eye can see. And there will be no doubt about it I am sure, that will be rabbit-infested also. It is all untrodden territory for me but I will be at them rabbits in the near future.

By now it's coming onto mid-afternoon so I head back along the wood edge the way I came and I am now passing by my snares which I set earlier. As I am nearing that cluster of a hundred snares I set, I see a patch of white there that wasn't there earlier. I look further across and I see a rabbit jumping and kicking, there's something brown laid not far from it.

As I come upon the white I see it's the white belly of a dead rabbit in a snare. I take the snare from around its neck, straighten out the snare and re-shape it back to 'pear shape' and re-set it again over the run in exactly the same place. I go across and kill the rabbit that is kicking and jumping in the snare. As I look further across the cluster of snares, I see another four rabbits caught up in snares so I empty them all and re-set them. These are early rabbits, they have come out into the late autumn sunshine to feed early and have a run around. I have my rabbit carriers with me which I carry in my pocket. Each is just a heavy-duty two-inch ring, with three lengths of short strong twine on either side of the ring. Each length of twine has a slip knot at the end which I slip over the rabbit's back legs. Each holder or carrier holds six rabbits and can then be slung over my shoulder, making it easier to carry the rabbits.

I carry on along the wood edge, I am taking caught rabbits out of the snares all the way along.

I eventually get back to where I dropped my first snares and I have by now got four rabbit carriers, full and strung over my shoulders. That's a good start to my rabbit snaring up here in these here hills. I have a bag of rabbits even before it's got dark.

I now head back to Bob's small cottage, worming my way back across the hilltops in my Land Rover. I stop off at Bob's flight pond and as I get out of the Land Rover, I see a party of mallard strike up off the pond. I paunch the rabbits and throw the guts into the pond, the mallard are going to have a birthday party when they see this lot.

I noticed the pond was a bit sparse of vegetation, it looked bleak and hostile out here in the middle of nowhere. I will have to have a word with Bob later. As I dropped down into the glen where Bob's cottage was, the late evening sun was just sinking down over the hilltops in the distant Grampian Mountains.

Bob was there in the courtyard on my return and he commented that I had caught some rabbits already. He had a game larder there where he hung all his game that was shot in the shooting season and he let me hang my rabbits in there. When I opened the game larder door, there was hardly any room for my rabbits. There was more than two hundred brace of grouse and at the back of them were the carcasses of three red deer hung up. Bob said he was awaiting the gamedealer picking them up. It was cold inside the game larder. It was fitted with a fine GAUZE on the window and air vents, which allowed a breeze to pass through and to keep the flies out, which is ideal for hung game, and my rabbits.

We then went inside the cottage where Bob had got the dinner cooking on the log-burning fire. He had a stew pot simmering as it sat on top of the burning logs and in it was venison, one of my favourite meats. There was big dumplings, carrots, onions and potatoes simmering with it, which left me thinking, this is home from home here. I looked around to see if Bob had got my slippers out, but I couldn't see them.

Over dinner I told Bob I had more than three hundred snares set and he commented that they should be good snaring rabbits as they have never been snared before.

A bit later on that evening we got ourselves washed and changed and he took me down into the village where we had a few pots of ale in the local pub.

When I looked up at the name of the pub they called it the 'POACHERS ARMS'. I looked at Bob and Bob looked at me, then he smiled and said, "There Doug, you should feel at home here."

We wasn't late home that night, early to bed and early to rise. When I am in bed I lay there thinking, I have all them snares set. It makes me restless, leaving me tossing and turning. I am sure I feel every rabbit that hits the snares.

It was a perfect night for rabbit snaring, there was a steady wind blowing, which takes away the silence. It was overcast with low clouds leaving the night black and there was a steady drizzle of rain coming down, which keeps the rabbits on their runs, rabbits hate to get their feet wet. A most perfect rabbit snaring night, and I drifted off to sleep. It was Bob's rooster of a cockerel that woke me up early next morning. Bob was nowhere to be seen, he'd beaten me up out of bed again.

I had a quick breakfast and off I went, eager to be back to my snares. The rabbits had better have watched out where they were putting their feet last night, otherwise they will be in my bag this morning.

By now it was just cracking daylight as I approached my first set of snares. I always go back the following morning on the same route as I dropped the snares, doing it that way I know where all my snares are.

Adrenaline now coursing through my body and full of optimism, there were rabbits scampering about everywhere as I strained my eyes to see them in the dim light of morning.

As I approached my first snare I could see nothing, and as I got closer I saw the snare laid on the ground. It had been pulled out straight had the snare wire, that's what I call a 'knock'. The rabbit had been in the wrong position when it had hit the snare. My intentions were to snare tonight also, so I reset the snare again a foot further along the run. If I hadn't already caught this rabbit in another snare, there was a good chance this snare would take him tonight.

I had another snare not far away, at the back of some sivs, and as I peered around the sivs, I saw I had a rabbit in it. It was dead and had the snare firmly around its neck. I emptied the snare and re-set the snare in exactly the same position, this dead rabbit told me I had the snare in the right place.

The re-set snare will now catch his mate tonight, if I haven't already caught it in another snare. I move on.

I had three snares set all in a line a little bit further along and as I looked I saw two rabbits in the snares, both dead. My little sketch I drew told me I had ten snares set around here, I went around and located them all. They had caught six rabbits so I re-set them all and moved on. I looked again at my sketch, I had fifty snares set in a cluster further along, most of the snares were exposed out on the open ground. As I looked across the area, I could see I had a decent catch, there were rabbits snared up here there and everywhere. I could see white bellies of rabbits as they lay 'jam side down'. I emptied and reset all the snares, making sure that I had located all fifty snares.

I mention the saying 'jam side down', that's when a rabbit is laid on its back exposing its white belly which is easily to be seen. When the rabbit is laid jam side up, that's when a rabbit is laid on its belly exposing nothing but its camouflaged back which is hard to be seen.

I now moved on.

My next place was them hare runs that ran under that old wooden five-barred gate. As I leant on the gate I could see something, it had its head nuzzled in the sivs with its backside stuck out, it was a big mountain hare. I grabbed it and quickly killed it, what a beauty it was, as I held its back legs up to my chest it ears were trailing the ground.

I had six snares set here, I went around them I had another two hares, big fat hares they were. Bob wanted these and I was sure he would be proud of them. I estimated there were at least half a dozen hares using these runs, so I re-set the snares again.

I now moved on again.

As I look across the sivs I see some carrion crows, they are flapping and flying about where I know I have some snares set. That's a sure sign I have rabbits in the snares there, but before I get there, I have some snares set where the rabbits are jumping the stream.

I come to where my first snare is set but there's nothing there. Then as I look closer I see the snare tether leading down into the stream. I pull up the tether and there's a rabbit's head in the snare, but that's about all. The rabbit has been eaten, it's that mink and her cubs that have taken it.

I tidy up the snare and re-set it, it might be a waste of time, but I carry on up the stream.

I have six rabbits caught that went to me, there were a further five rabbits in the snares that went to the mink. I re-set all the snares again. I never know, the mink may have moved on.

I now move on again to where I saw the crows flapping around, I have a lot of snares set here. The first snare I come to, the crows have eaten the rabbit. They have the canny ability to skin the rabbit and slither the meat from the bone, which leaves me with nothing but skin and bone and the rabbit's head minus its eyeballs left in the snare.

They have a big powerful beak do the carrion crows. They are known as a 'murder of crows', and I know for sure they keep to their name.

I moved on. My little sketch I keep handy in my pocket tells me I have a hundred snares set here. I have them all in rows, and twenty snares in each row. As I move along the rows, the marauding pack of carrion crows have decimated a lot of the rabbits. I ended up with about forty of the rabbits and the rest went to the crows.

I moved on. I have several snares in and around some sivs. I come across a rabbit that has a snare around its body. The rabbits have the ability to be able to jump through the hoop of the snare without even touching it. This is not done intentionally by the rabbit, he is unaware that the snare is there in the first place, but often it catches the rabbit by the body just like this rabbit I have here now. Often the rabbit will pass through the noose and then hook it around one of his back legs or even catch himself with a toe.

I came across another rabbit in a snare and when I looked closely at it, it was in a real old mess as it was tangled up in two snares together. The rabbit was dead, and what it had done was, it had caught itself in a snare and as it fought and kicked in the snare it pulled out the tether peg from the ground. The rabbit had then set off along the run again still with the snare around its neck and still dragging the tether peg behind itself as it ran. It then ran headlong into another snare and got itself caught again.

The rabbit now fought two snares together, leaving itself in a tangled up mess like it was now, with snare wires trapped and wrapped all the way around its body and its legs and between its toes.

There's no wonder I can't sleep at night when I have my snares set. I have sometimes had rabbits like this one I have in my hands now and I can't untangle them. The wire has been that deeply knotted in its fur and the wire has got that twisted and contorted around its backs legs and toes, I have given it up as a bad job, and put the rabbit in my poacher's pocket out of the way.

I now moved on again.

As I was walking along towards another snare, I saw it is untouched, but at that same moment a rabbit jumped up out of the sivs and got straight on to its run and headlong into the snare I was just looking at.

It fascinates me seeing little incidents like this happening as I watch on. That rabbit was making its escape going hell for leather along its run to safety only to be snatched up by the snare. And often in cases such as this the rabbit hits the snare with such speed and force it breaks its neck on impact.

I move on again and I see another rabbit, this one is all tangled up in a snare. The rabbit is dead but the snare wire is all kinked up. These kinks must be straightened out to allow the eye of the snare to slide up and down freely. I pull the snare taut on the tether peg and then using a second spare tether peg I rub it up and down the snare wire. That removes all the kinks and the eye of the snare can now run freely. I put the snare back into shape by putting the noose around my bent knee and pulling it tight. A quick adjustment with my fingers and the snare is back into pear shape again, and now all ready for resetting over the run again. If a snare is so kinked up and unusable, I carry spare snares with me. These snares are pre-set in a pear shape, so a quick adjustment and they are ready for setting on the run.

I now carry on for a distance emptying and resetting snares and resetting knocked-over snares. I have had quite a few predators at my rabbits, my best mate the buzzard has taken one or two, but I am not against him taking the odd ones for his dinner. The mysterious and elusive mountain wildcat has eaten one or two, I can always tell the characteristic ways of the cat when he has been at my rabbits.

They always eat them in the snare. He always starts eating the rabbit from the back of its neck and then makes his way down the shoulders, that's the telltale signs of the cat.

Then there's the badger which I call Billy, he too has been around and eaten a few of my rabbits. I can always tell by his characteristic ways of eating also. Like the cat, Billy leaves the rabbit in the snare while he's eating it also, but he always goes into the belly and under the ribcage first. He is after the heart and liver, he them moves down and takes the kidneys and then eats the soft tender meat that the kidneys sit on underneath the back.

I now move on again and it takes me upwards to some snares I have set on a rocky bankside. The first three snares that I come to all just have rabbits' heads in them.

There was a strong smell of the fox, which I call 'SNAGGLEPUS, my elations for catching rabbits here were dampened. I know the extents that the fox will go to when he's about taking my rabbits.

That's the foxes characteristic telltale signs that he was here, he just leaves me with the heads in the snare. If he can't pull the rabbit's body off by the head, he will chew through the snare wire with his razor-sharp teeth.

Some gamekeepers like rabbit catchers to go rabbit snaring on their estate, that way the rabbit catcher can inform the keeper where the foxes are working. Bob will be very interested when I

"BILLY" THE BADGER

SCOTTISH HIGHLAND CATTLE

WILD RUGGED HIGHLAND MOUNTAIN GOATS

tell him about his fox. As I move around my snares the fox has taken many of my rabbits just as I had feared.

I now move back up to the woodside, I am heading to the place where the rabbits were jumping over the branches. I see three, four, five rabbits in snares, there are some dead and some alive. I see another a bit further away that's laid jam side down.

As I move in I see something unusual, and as I move in close I see I have caught a stoat in the snare. Now that's a rare catch. The stoat is one of Bob's arch enemies. They prey on game birds and have to be controlled, so I grabbed a big stick and hit it over the head. That snare is now useless as that stoat's scent will linger on that snare nearly forever. Any rabbit approaching that snare on its run will back off and go nowhere near it. So I picked up the snare and I pushed it down a rabbit hole.

The way this stoat got itself caught in the first place, which was unlucky on the stoat's behalf, is that it will have been following the scent of a rabbit along its run. The rabbit, on coming to the snare, has knocked the snare to one side and left it hanging low over the run, the stoat has then come along and has gone through the snare noose, and the stoat has been unlucky enough for the snare to tighten around its belly.

These stoats up here in the Highlands of Scotland turn white in winter which camouflages them in the snow. When they are snow white they are called 'ERMINE'. Their fur was at one time valuable to the fur trade and was in big demand. There are only three British animals that turn white in the winter, the other two being the PTARMIGAN and the MOUNTAIN HARE. They must camouflage themselves well in the winter's snows, if they don't the eagle-eyed GOLDEN EAGLE will have them for his dinner, for sure.

And that's it now for my first night's, or is it day's, snaring.

I have now been around all my snares and I now have about sixty to seventy rabbits to carry back to the Land Rover. Not a bad bag or rabbits I thought, now for the hard part of the job, and I carried the rabbits back to the Land Rover in two trips. The weight of the rabbits was fair cutting into my shoulders by the time I got them there I can tell you. I had to keep stopping as I went to take more early rabbits out of the snares, but I eventually got them all loaded in the Land Rover and off I went, as pleased as Punch that I had had a successful night's snaring.

On the way I stopped off at Bob's duck pond, paunched the

rabbits and threw the guts into the water. The guts which I had thrown in the day before had all gone, the mallards must have eaten them.

I thought again as I looked across the bleak, uncomely pond, I will still have to have a word with Bob about that.

Bob was in the courtyard when I arrived back. He had a big smile on his face when he saw all the rabbits, and said, "You've had a good day's snaring there by the looks of it Doug." And Bob's eyes lit up when he saw the big hares I had got for him.

I hung the rabbits in the game larder. There was a bit more room now the grouse and deer had gone. The deer are shot with high-powered rifles high up in the hills on Bob's vast estate that he keepers. The stalkers pay a lot of money to go there stalking the red deer.

And that was the end of the day for me. I went inside of Bob's cottage and had a well-earned drink of 'Rosy Lee', a pot of tea.

It was early to bed that night and early to rise next morning. Bob was nowhere to be seen again, he also appears to be an early riser.

I was back at the scene of the snaring fields at the crack of dawn. Just before dawn is a time when the snares start catching and killing, it's what I call the 'morning run'.

Often when the rabbits come out in the early evening, the grass is dry and the rabbits will go out on to feeding grounds without using their runs. But in the early hours of the morning, dew has usually settled on the grass as the rabbits make their way from the feeding grounds. They will get on to their runs to keep their feet dry. As I said earlier, rabbits hate to get their feet wet.

I am picking my snares up this morning, the snaring is over for the time being. As I am heading across to my first run of snares, the heavy morning cloud is just beginning to allow the morning light through. First light is the finest time of day to be up in my opinion, not a soul about, just me and my animals and birds. I can fair feel that fresh morning air going deep into my lungs. As I am upon my snares, I am startled by a herd of red deer. They come stampeding from below the hillside, I am sure they hadn't heard me, I was only walking quietly, they must have picked up my scent on the wind.

There must have been thirty to forty deer in the herd and they stampeded right across my first lot of snares. One of the hinds was snatched up sharp and was pulling and tugging her back leg from the ground. She must have had her back leg caught in one of the snares. She gave a big snatch with her back leg and she was free, and she rejoined the rest of the herd which had by now headed down into the bottom of the glen. And luckily for me they headed away from the snaring fields where all my snares were set.

It appeared to me that deer and sheep must have the same characteristic manner. They will walk along a rabbit run and purposely put their foot into the snare. The sheep have seen the snare, unlike the rabbit, but they have this funny hare-brained idea to put their foot in the snare. So I never snare where there is livestock in the field, especially sheep.

As I move in close and have a look at my snares I see the deer have trampled them in badly, and some of the snares are missing. The deer must have snagged their legs on them and pulled the tether pegs out of the ground.

As I am busying myself picking up the broken snares, I see a rabbit as I look over the tops of the sivs. It's caught in a snare and it's alive. I go over to kill it but before I get there I see another two rabbits caught in snares. My luck's still in, all is not lost. I pick up this run of snares and put all the broken ones into my pocket, I will sort them out later.

As I set off again to my next run of snares, I look down into the bottom of the glen. The herd of deer have disappeared out of sight. The red deer are purposely kept out of the forestry plantation by a high, wire-meshed, deer-proof fence, but the fence gets broken down in places and the deer do get into the forestry plantation.

Once the deer are in they lose their escape route where they have entered through the broken fence. The fir tree woodland is bare of vegetation so the deer eat the bark and damage and ring bark the trees. This kills the trees and the deer end up dying of hunger in their scores.

The deer have to be culled by 'FORESTRY KEEPERS' who shoot them twelve months of the year.

I head across my snares, emptying and picking them up as I go. I am catching as many rabbits as I was the day before. Sometimes I can have the snares down for too long a period and the rabbits do sometimes become aware of the snares. The rabbits do actually stop and look for the snares on their runs, I have been rumbled, they will then purposely stop using their runs. He's not as dumb as he may appear is the humble rabbit. When this happens it's best that I pick up my snares and snare elsewhere.

On the odd occasions I have had two rabbits caught in one snare. How this happens is that when the doe rabbit is going along her run, the buck rabbit is following her and trying to mount her. She will be in season ready for breeding. As the doe rabbit hits the snare which catches her by the neck, the buck rabbit is on her back and he gets his front legs in the snare as the noose is tightening and the snare holds them firmly caught together.

I now head across country to where I have my half a dozen snares on them HARE RUNS that go under that old wooden five-barred gate. I see something big and brown as it is struggling in the snare, it's a whopping big mountain hare. These hares are down in the lowlands for some reason, they are usually high up on the hilltops. They are still in their brown camouflaged coats but when the winter snows fall they will for sure turn to a bluish white. When I get to this hare I have caught, I see he is tightly wrapped around a second peg I have stuck in the ground. The hare has gone around and around this peg which shortens the tether which then restricts the hare's movements, this then stops the hare lashing out with his big powerful back legs and maybe breaking the snare.

I look across at the other hare run, I see another hare laid jam side down, his big white belly stands out like a sore thumb.

That's five hares I have had off these three hare runs, Bob will be pleased when he sees what I've got for him. I now head along the bank of the stream.

My first snare I had set where the rabbits were jumping the stream. All there is in the snare is a rabbit's head, the rest was the remains of a mink-eaten carcass.

As I went along the bank of the stream I see the mink have had more than their fair share of my rabbits, the mink and her cubs have fed well. They will be laid up somewhere around here sleeping it off with big fat bloated bellies full with my rabbits. I have to accept nature's ways and shake my head at my losses.

I move along and head back up the glen side, I have many snares set here. As I arrive amongst my snares I see a 'MURDER' of crows flapping and flying around, a sure sign I have had a good kill. I see I have many rabbits caught in my snares, and I see many rabbits that are just skin and bone. Again, nature's ways have struck, and now the marauding carrion crows have taken their toll on my rabbits. I shake my head at my losses and empty and pick up all my snares. I head on further up the side of the glen and I pick up the strong smell of Snagglepus the fox.

I see my first snare has just a rabbit's head in it, that's a sure sign it's the work of Snagglepus. My next snare and the one after that all have just heads in them.

As I look higher up the bank of the glen, I see some large rocks and I go on up to investigate. The smell of the fox is growing stronger the closer I get to the rocks and when I get there I see the carcass of a dead rabbit laid by the side of the rocks, it has no head on it. That will be one of my rabbits no doubt.

I see a narrow opening leading into the rocks and as I get closer I see the ground faintly padded down. I put my head into the opening, it stinks of Snagglepus the fox, this is where he is laying up for the day.

I take off my sweaty jumper and put it as far inside the opening in the rocks as I can. That will now contain the fox in the rocks, that fox will not venture out while that sweaty jumper is there.

I see another entrance leading into the rocks, I take off my sweaty gypsy scarf from around my neck and bung that into the rocky entrance. I will inform Bob about this fox when I return to the cottage.

I still have a few more snares to lift higher up the glen. I come to where I have a snare set but I cant' see it. I search around but fail to find it. I know it should be exactly where I am looking, it's down on my rough sketch as plain as day, and then I see a short length of tether leading into the sivs. I grab hold of it and give it a pull, and lo and behold I pull a rabbit out of the sivs. My sketch has done its job well.

I can set snares and when I return to them the following morning often they are missing. I can search high and low for them, there is no signs that anything has been struggling in them, they just vanish into thin air, never to be seen again.

I head on up to the wood edge. I have another four rabbits where I had caught and killed the stoat earlier. All my snares are now safely gathered in, a fine bag of rabbits I have too. I carry them back to the Land Rover in three carries.

I head down out of the glen in the Land Rover and on to Bob's flight pond. All the rabbit guts I threw into the pond the day before have gone.

Them mallards are going to be that fat on these rabbits' guts they won't be able to fly.

I paunch these rabbits and throw the guts into the pond, just like Bob had told me to. I now head off across the hilltops and back down to Bob's cottage in that picturesque glen.

Bob was in the courtyard when I arrived, he looked over my rabbits as they lay in the Land Rover, and his eyes nearly popped out when he saw the big fat mountain hares. He held them both up in front of him and he had a big smile on his face that must have stretched from 'ear to lug'. He said, "By, these are crackerjacks Doug."

As me and Bob were hanging the day's bag of rabbits in the game larder, I knew Bob would be on red alert when I told him about the fox holed up in the rocks.

The fox is the top predator to the gamekeeper and must be caught at all costs, so I half-heartedly said to Bob in a muffled, unconcerned low voice, "There's a fox holed up in them rocks." A moment of silence went by, Bob was thinking he hadn't heard me properly, and then he said, "Did you say there's a fox holed up?" I nodded.

He was all ears when I told him of its whereabouts. Bob knew the place well saying he'd had numerous foxes out of them rocks. I told Bob that I was holding the fox in the rocks with my sweaty jumper and gypsy scarf and on hearing all this, Bob dropped everything, which was my rabbits, and off he went rushing into his cottage.

I think I must have triggered something off in his brain, he was now on red alert. He rushed out of the cottage as fast as he rushed in, he had two double-barrelled twelve bores in his hands and he whistled up his dog which was running around in the courtyard.

Bob rushed across into an outbuilding and drove out an 'argocat'. He shouted to me in his hurried state saying, "Come on Doug, hurry up, jump in. Let's be going and getting that fox." His dog jumped in at the back of us and off we went towards these rocks where the fox was still hopefully holed up. Bob knew the route well as he manoeuvred the argocat across the rugged terrain. These argocats can go virtually anywhere, it is an eight wheel drive, all-terrain vehicle.

Bob came to that stream where I had been snaring. He never even hesitated when we reached the stream, he just drove the argocat straight down the bankside of the stream. The front end hit the streambed hard as it thudded in and we were nearly in an upright position. As I lurched forward on the impact, the dog in the back came flying over our shoulders. There was fast-flowing water in the stream, it was fair gushing around us was the torrent of water. Bob shouted over the top of all the noise, "Hang on now, it's getting a bit rough here." I clung hold of the dog under one arm, with both shotguns in the same hand, and somehow I hung on grimly with the other hand. Bob revved the argocat's engine and all eight wheels started driving and skidding. The water in the stream went a funny colour as the argocat wheels skidded and churned the mud up on the streambed. The argocat shot forward we started floating. With the argocat being an all-terrain vehicle it floats like a boat as well.

We ploughed on up the stream with the spinning wheels in the water driving us along. Bob looked up the other bankside and nosed the argocat into the bank. I looked up the bankside, it was sheer and rugged, and I shouted out in an uncertain voice, "You're never going up there."

Bob shouted back, "Hang on now, while I take her over the bank."

The argocat started climbing the bank and as it left the gushing water all eight wheels I saw were slithering, sliding and skidding. The argocat was now pointing straight up into the sky. The dog panicked itself free from under my arm and tumbled back into the back of the argocat. I hung on grimly and with the argocat's engine fair screaming and all eight wheels biting and gripping into the ground, we shot forward and up and over the bank. Now safely at the other side of the stream, I said to Bob, "Don't ever put me through that again." Bob said, "That's nothing Doug, that's just a simple task for the argocat."

I looked behind me and the dog was still there, all crouched up in a corner, shaking like a junior aspirin, its teeth chattering as though something had frightened it.

Off we go again. We now head on further up the glen side, bumping and bouncing along as we go. It's certainly a big short cut the way Bob has come, it would have taken forever to get here if we had taken the way I came in the Land Rover.

We are now nearly upon the rocks where the fox is still hopefully holed up. Bob stops short of the rocks with the argocat, turns off the engine and parks up. Bob says in a whispered voice, "I don't want to frighten the fox with the noise of the argocat's engine."

Bob ushering me to be silent by putting his finger up to his mouth, we loaded both twelve bore shotguns with 'BB cartridges'. Double-barrelled guns they were and BB is the size of the shot in a cartridge. It is a heavy shot purposely for shooting big predators like Snagglepus the fox.

Bob quietly passed me a handful of spare cartridges which I pushed into my pocket. We both approached the rocks silently and light-footedly. I went ever so quietly and down wind to the entrances to the rocks and removed my sweaty jumper and sweaty gypsy scarf, and ever so quietly moved away again. I stood in a good position about twenty yards away from the rocks with the wind blowing from the rocks and to me. Snagglepus couldn't pick up my scent now.

Bob silently signalled his dog to him, it was a small, heavy-muscled Jack Russell bitch. She was all battle-scarred around her head, face and body from past encounters she had had with foxes. She was Bob's special foxing dog, most gamekeepers usually have one.

Bob sent her to the rocks, he then went and stood in a good position about twenty yards away from the rocks and with the wind blowing from the rocks to him. Snagglepus couldn't pick up Bob's scent either. Between us both we had the rocks well covered. I watched the Jack Russell as she hunted up and down, she was getting herself all excited as she was picking up the scent of the fox.

She goes to the entrance of the rocks, she sticks her nose into the rocks, I see her body arch up, I see the hair on her back stand up on end. She's now scented the fox and she disappears down into the rocks, all I hear now is silence except for the wind blowing around my ears. I stand there with my eyes transfixed on the entrance of the rocks, I hold my gun ready, I see Bob is poised for action also. Any fleeing fox now trying to make its escape has to pass me and Bob first. As I stand there waiting I hear muffled dog barks coming from within the rocks, it sounds like the Jack Russell is on to the fox.

I see something moving at the entrance to the rocks, I push the safety catch of the twelve bore shotgun forward, my gun is now ready for firing.

I see a white muzzle appear at the entrance to the rocks, I see it lift its nose into the air. It's scenting the wind trying to pick up any danger scent in the wind.

I see a beady eye look straight into my eye, my adrenaline is really flowing now, my heart is pounding like a big bass drum, my eyes are transfixed on the snout I see in the entrance of the rocks. I see Bob, his eyes are transfixed on me, he knows by my body language that I have seen something, I dare not flinch a muscle to make him aware of what I am seeing. But Bob takes the hint, I see him push forward the safety catch on his twelve bore shotgun. And with the flash of an eye, the fox is out and up over the rocks and out of sight before I even have time to take snap shot at it.

I see Bob lift his gun to his shoulder, I hear one big almighty bang, the blast of the gun ricochets all around the glen. The almighty bang disturbs all peace. I hear a jay go off squawking through the woodland in sheer panic, I see a flock of woodpigeon in the woodland at the far side of the glen, they are tear-arsing out of treetops panic-stricken to death with the deafening bang. I see Bob, he never moves from the position from where he is stood. I look over beyond the rocks, I see no fleeing fox make its escape. I see Bob drop open the barrels of his gun, I see an empty spent cartridge shell eject from the barrel. Bob quickly and silently reloads the empty barrel with another BB cartridge. Then his gun is silently closed and all ready for action again.

Bob stays put where he stands, he looks at me in silence, I stay put where I stand. I still hear muffled barking coming from within the rocks and that tells me there must be another fox in them there rocks.

Normally the Jack Russell would have come out chasing the fox as it bolted, but not this time, she's staying down in them rocks for a good reason.

I can still hear muffled barking coming from deep within the rocks, the barking is getting louder and clearer by the minute, there's something on the move within them rocks.

Again without any notice, I see a flash of red and another fox is out, it flashes over the rocks just where the other fox went, and again I never had the chance to take a snap shot at it. The Jack Russell is out with it and races after it over the rocks.

Again I see Bob lift his gun to his shoulder, and again there's one almighty bang. The great bang shatters all silence, and then there is silence.

Bob makes a move this time, he drops the barrels of his gun to make it safe, I do likewise. Bob says, "That's it Doug."

We climb up over the rocks and there they are, I see two dead foxes laying there not far apart. The Jack Russell is on top of one of them, she's fair trying her best to rip out the fox's throat and her face is all red with blood. I don't know whether it's her blood or the fox's blood that's on her face.

Bob looked at me and said, "There, I am well rid of them Doug."

It was a big 'dog' fox and his vixen; they are such bonny animals in my opinion. If the fox only knew just to kill and eat vermin and leave game birds alone I am sure they would be welcomed in the countryside.

These two foxes we had just got were easy to bolt, but that's not always the case. You will get some foxes which are stubborn and reluctant and will not bolt. If the terrier dog doesn't kill the fox, the fox can and will kill the terrier dog, so it's not all a one-sided affair.

There are other perils for the terrier dog also, if the fox is laid up or holed up in such rocks like we had just encountered, the fox has the ability while down there within the bowels of the rocks to leap from one rocky ledge to another. The terrier dog may try to follow the fox and may not have the ability to leap like the fox and may fall short of the rocky ledge and fall to its fate below. The terrier dog may then become trapped, never to be released. In the end, in circumstances like that, it will die of starvation. Also, if a fox does get on to a rock ledge which may be above the terrier dog, the fox now has an advantage point and can now bite back at the terrier dog below. Constant biting and snapping at a terrier dog below with his razor-sharp teeth can rip and tear a dog to ribbons and shreds. So you can see a fox sometimes will not just give in easily.

So back to these two foxes we have just shot here on these rocks. Bob's as pleased as Punch with the outcome and picks both foxes up with his terrier bitch still hanging on to one of them for dear life. She won't let go, so Bob throws all three of them together into the back of the argocat, and off we set back again. We had to go back across that dreaded fast-flowing, high-banked stream again, which we did eventually manage to negotiate, and off we went across the rugged hilltops and eventually arrived back at Bob's cottage.

Bob stood there in the courtyard priding himself on what he had just shot. He asked me to go fetch some baling band from an outbuilding as he wanted to string up the foxes in the courtyard for his boss, the Laird of the estate, to see. Putting them on show like this gives the Laird encouragement when he sees such predators as foxes hanging there. The Laird then knows his gamekeeper is doing a good job of pest control which is saving his game birds.

As I was rummaging about in the outbuilding looking for some baling band, I saw great big bundles of old-fashioned 'gin traps' hung on the wall. I mentioned all the gin traps I have just seen to Bob and he told me they were used by the old rabbit catcher of the estate, which was many years ago now, said Bob.

He went on to tell me the rabbit catcher would catch hundreds of rabbits with the old gins in a week of trapping. The old gin trap is now illegal and was deemed as barbaric and doing injustice on the rabbits.

The trap would be set on the rabbit runs, or in the entrances of the rabbit holes, and then covered over so the rabbit couldn't see the trap. The rabbit would then come along and tread on the trap plate which triggered the jaws of the trap, the teeth of the jaws would hold the rabbit firmly by the upper part of its legs.

The rabbit and the trap were held there securely by a tethered chain. Nowadays there is a new modern version rabbit trap. The trap, known as the 'Fenn Rabbit Trap', has larger jaws than the old gin trap, which catches the rabbit by the chest, killing the rabbit instantly by crushing its heart. The new modern Fenn trap is much more respectable and lenient on the rabbit. And that was the first lesson that Bob had learnt me, how the old rabbit catchers of yesteryear worked.

And that was my first ever encounter at snaring rabbits up in them there Grampian Hills in the Highlands of Scotland on my mate Bob Black's, or is it Black Bob's, estate.

Snaring rabbits is an 'art', on its own. Successful rabbit snaring can only be acquired by actually putting it into practise. The more you snare the more accustomed you become, learning where and how to set your snare, and gradually the hands become dexterous and the 'fine art' of rabbit snaring will appear.

I asked Bob if I could long-net the rabbits at night the next time I came up here and Bob nodded his approval. I suggested long-netting them rabbits where he had caught me poaching the rabbits with my ferrets.

Bob again nodded his approval, and told me there were more rabbits down there than there ever was, the place was overrun with them. In many cases, the more the rabbits are persecuted or hit badly by such as myxomatosis, the more prolific the rabbits breed the following year.

I was all ready and destined for home. The following morning I was up with the larks and I loaded all my rabbits into the Land

Rover. I have made two decks in the back of my Land Rover so that I can lay my rabbits in without squashing them. I also have rails up in the roof of the Land Rover so that I can hang the rabbits up there also.

I had a real fine bag of rabbits which I was really proud of. Just short of two hundred rabbits I think I caught on that snaring expedition. I didn't need the trailer, I could get all the rabbits in the Land Rover. So I pushed the trailer up the side of Bob's cottage and left it there while later. Bob gave me the hindquarters of a red deer to take back with me, he knew I had a love for venison.

I wanted a good north wind blowing for when I came back again, which was the ideal wind for them rabbits which I intended long-netting. And on that note I bid Bob farewell, and said that I would give him a ring when the wind was blowing right, then off I set on that long, long drive back homeward bound.

Read on. There's more to come, all this because a creature of habit gets caught, and Bob caught me, and it was for the better not the worse.

After a few weeks had passed on by, the weather forecast was looking good, there was strong northerly winds moving in, which is what I had been waiting for. I was eager to get back up there and get at them rabbits.

I rang and informed Bob that I was on my way back up again, and that I would be arriving by late afternoon the following day. I had prepared two long nets for the occasion, both my long nets were each one hundred yards long. That's one hell of a distance when they are end to end with each other, and I know there's one hell of a lot of rabbits there where I intend long-netting.

I took with me plenty of freshly-cut privet pegs, they will withstand the weight and impact of the rabbits when they hit the long nets. It appeared to me as though my twelve bore shotgun had a job to do there so I dismantled it into three pieces and put it into the locked-up compartment in the Land Rover. It is safe in there, and out of sight until wanted.

I also took with me my .22 rifle. There is forever rabbits up there for me to pick off and that will help me build up a good bag of rabbits.

I also took two bags of rabbit snares, they are there then if needed. This time I am taking my dog with me. My dog is part of my life, wherever I go she goes, she's my buddy and is well trained for the fieldwork which you will find out later.

The following morning me and my bitch were on our way very early, it was well before the crack of dawn. We had a long journey ahead of us, up into them there hills up in the Grampian Mountains high up in Scotland.

After a long journey we arrived at Bob's on schedule, and it was off to bed early that evening after that long journey.

I was up bright and early the next morning, I had plenty of time to kill that day. Bob said to me, "You're not doing anything for few hours are you Doug?" I wasn't long-netting the rabbits while that night, so I shook my head saying, "No." Bob said, "I have a fox laying out on the hills somewhere," and added that he had had the lamp on him but he had been too far away to take a shot at him.

If Bob has a fox roaming about on the estate he will go out in the middle of the night trying to pick up the fox with the high-powered lamp, which is plugged into the argocat. He will have with him a high-powered rifle, which will pick off the fox at long distance.

So when Bob says the fox was too far way, it's important not to have a lucky pot-shot at him. If Bob misses, that fox will forever be lamp shy, and the fox will never give Bob another chance of a shot at him again. So it's important that the fox is within killing range of the high-powered rifle. The fox must be eliminated at all cost, they cause so much damage killing the game birds.

Bob carries on to say, "We can have a rough shoot all at the same time if you want Doug, while we are trying to walk up the fox."

So Bob handed me a handful of 'BB' cartridges to slot into my twelve bore, if we did come across the fox.

We set off in the argocat across the rough terrain ground. Bob was heading high up into the hills to where he had seen the fox. When we arrived at our location, I slotted a couple of five-shot cartridges into my gun, all ready for any game that may present me with a shot, making sure the 'BB' cartridges were at hand and ready if wanted.

We set off walking up the rough ground, with Bob about fifty yards apart from me. Bob had his old faithful Labrador with him for hunting and retrieving any game that we shot. That's that Labrador which caught me when I was ferreting that fir tree plantation.

Bob also had with him his small Jack Russell terrier, she was a good hunter, but her main job of the day was to bolt any fox that may go to ground. 'Jesse' they called her and 'Candy' was Bob's Labrador. I had my dog with me, she is a sheep cur, she also had a good nose on her for hunting, 'Pup' is her name.

As me and Bob walked along the rough grass, with our dogs out hunting and searching the ground in front of us for any game that may be laid out, I looked across and I could see that Candy was getting excited. She had her nose close to the ground and her tail was wagging, she had picked up the scent of something. A cock pheasant struck up out of the grass in front of her, Bob pulled his twelve bore to his shoulder, there was an almighty bang and the pheasant crumpled and fell to the ground.

The bang of the gun startled another pheasant out of the rough grass. It circled and flew right across in front of me and I let fire and missed. Keeping my gun to my shoulder I gave it another barrel, it folded and fell to the ground, and Pup went to retrieve it. As I looked across Bob was taking his bird from Candy's mouth, and off we set again, with the dogs out in front hunting again. As I watched my dog she was starting to look interested in something. She hunted the grass in front of her, with her nose scraping the ground, then stopped and looked directly into a clump of grass. She arched her back and I could tell by her body language that there was something laying tight in the grass just in front of her. She moved in slowly, her tail wagging oh so slowly from side to side, her head cocked to one side with her eyes transfixed. She went in to a lurch position then she pounced and stuck her nose into the grass. When she pulled her head up she had a rabbit in her mouth and she retrieved it back to hand still alive.

I have specially trained Pup to do this job, catching me many, many rabbits. As they are laid on their seats in the grass, also catching many pheasants like this.

I put up my thumb to Bob, and off we go again, with the dogs out in front hunting again. I have trained Pup never to go too far out when she is hunting, that's so that anything she may get up is then in range of the gun.

We came to some boggy ground. I had my boots on but there were some sivs growing there, which are a type of reed that grows in clumps that rise above the water level, and I used these as stepping stones to get me across the boggy ground, keeping my feet dry.

I hear the characteristic sound of a 'Jack Snipe' and as I look across, I see the Jack Snipe as it is zigzagging at great speed away from Bob. He misses it with his first shot. The Jack Snipe is flying so fast it's soon way out in the distance by the time Bob gives it a second barrel. The Jack Snipe crumples to the bang of Bob's gun, Candy is eagerly watching and races off to retrieve it. A pair of mallard duck strike up out of the reeds in front of Candy. They veer and fly my way and I let fire at the drake and it folds up. His mate rises high and fast as it veers up into the sky but it folds up to my second barrel and Pup runs out to retrieve

I see Candy retrieving the Jack Snipe back to Bob. The zigzagging flight of the Jack Snipe and the common snipe are a real difficult presentable target to the shooting man. As the snipe zigs to the right, by the time the shooting man has pulled the trigger, the snipe has zagged to the left and off the snipe goes, zigzagging its way to safety.

I see Pup coming back through the reeds, she has the drake mallard in her mouth and she quickly retrieves it to hand. Then off she races again, she can count can Pup, she saw two ducks drop to my gun, and Pup's soon back with the second mallard duck.

Me and Bob now head across country, we head towards a clump of trees which are out in the boggy land. By now my feet are saturated so I stop using the sivs as stepping stones and I now splash through the water regardless.

We come to a sheep netting fence and I see Bob break his gun and take out the cartridges before climbing over the fence. A wise move I thought, better to be safe than sorry, so I did the same.

As we approach the clump of trees Jesse flushes up a woodcock making such a clattering noise. I see Bob reload quickly and pull his gun to his shoulder. The woodcock heads into the trees, dodging and swerving as it flies between branches. The woodcock folds and falls from a single shot from Bob's gun. A woodpigeon comes clattering out from the back of the trees and as it clatters between two trees I take a snap shot at it. There's a cloud of blue feathers that follows it to the ground, Pup races off after it.

I look across at Bob, he's having difficulty finding the woodcock. Woodcock leave no scent that's why Candy was having difficulty finding it. It was a futile job for her she had no chance of finding the woodcock with her nose.

We searched up and down but failed to find it, my dog and Candy hunting here, there and everywhere. I turned and looked behind me and who should be sat there but Jesse, she looked as pleased as Punch with the woodcock in her mouth.

The woodcock has a quaint, interesting lifestyle. The mother woodcock, when she is moving her young chicks, has the ability to carry them between her thighs as she is flying, one chick at a time of course. When the woodcock is crouched on the ground, the camouflaged feathers make it invisible. They also have very large eyes which have a greater field of view behind the head than in front of the head, giving them the ability to see danger approaching when they are feeding.

There's an old saying about the woodcock which goes like this, "for fools are known by looking wise, as men find woodcock by their eyes". But alas the woodcock wasn't wise enough, he will be in the cooking pot tonight, a real delicacy is the woodcock to the eating connoisseurs.

Me and Bob now head across country and start climbing the side of a mountain. As Bob said to me, "We'll have a walk up that lall hillside."

Once we eventually reach the top we are now walking across the moorland heather, with all three dogs out hunting in front of us. We hadn't gone very far when the dogs started getting interested in something, they had winded and scented something in the heather. I could tell with how my bitch was working, she was on to something close on by. As my Pup lurched herself forward, all at the same time a whirr of wings come bursting out of the heather, it was a covey of grouse. Bob quickly dropped a right and a left, even before I had time to get my gun to my shoulder. As I let fire I missed, but keeping my gun to my shoulder I dropped one with the second barrel. I see the dogs running across to retrieve them. I see little Jesse, she's having difficulty getting herself over the long heather, but Jesse wasn't going to be denied, she has already proved she is a retriever by bringing that woodcock back to hand. She dives low and travels along underneath the long heather, and all three dogs return with a grouse each. They looked proud of themselves as they handed over the grouse with wagging tails, except for Jesse she only had a stump for a tail, docked off when she was a lall baby.

Bob's boss, the Laird of the estate, let's him shoot a grouse or two for his own table, a perk of the job you could say. We now head on along the hillside, more of a mountainside to me, and we come to a bare peat hag. These hags are everywhere along the hillsides. They are like a long natural trench which has been made by constant water running off the mountaintops. In places the peat is very soft in them there hags and you have to cross the hag with care as the soft peat can work like quicksand and will suck you under if you tread in the wrong place.

As me and Bob was down in the bottom of this hag gingerly trying to cross over, I see Bob pull his gun to his shoulder and there was a quick double bang. As he fired, I looked up and I see a couple of carrion crows, they are plummeting to the ground, both dead in the air together. That was crack shooting from Bob, I never even saw the carrions coming.

These birds are well rid of off the estate, they cause havoc with the game birds by killing the young poults and stealing eggs from the nest. I expected Bob to leave the carrion crows where they lay dead but he didn't, he gathered them up for some reason. I asked no questions, Bob knows what he is doing.

As I look across the hillside I see a flash of red as it disappeared down into a hag. I tap Bob on the shoulder and point and as we stood there and watched, a fox came out of the hag. Bob's double bangs from his shotgun must have frightened the fox as it was laying-up in the heather.

It was a long distance away and, as we watched him, the fox ran up the mountainside and disappeared out of sight.

Bob looked at me with a sparkle in his eyes, then winked at me saying, "I think I know where that old rascal's heading," and off we went in the direction where the fox disappeared.

Bob was still clutching hold of them two carrion crows for some reason. As we went along the mountainside, or along the lall hillside as Bob was calling it, I looked across at my bitch. She was showing body language that she'd picked up the scent of something. As me and Bob watched, she had her nose tight to the ground. As she hunted about in the heather a big mountain hare jumped up right at the end of Pup's nose, and it raced off down the hillside to make its escape.

Bob lifted his gun to his shoulder to shoot it but I stopped him saying, "Leave it, my Pup will give the hare a run for its money."

My bitch sets off after the hare as it races hell for leather down the hillside. The hare has a lot of white on its body, it's turning white into its winter coat. With there being snow on the ground most of the time in winter up here in the mountains, the hare's coat turns naturally white for camouflage.

As me and Bob watch on from our good vantage point which is

halfway up the hillside, we can now see a hare course taking place, right in front of our very own eyes.

By now my bitch has caught up to the hare, she's right up its backside and if the hare has a shit now, Pup will get a mouthful. I see Pup strike at the hare to grab it but as she strikes the hare turns at an acute angle and my bitch misses and ends up with a mouthful of fur. My bitch has now overrun the hare and the hare is now running the other way. Pup stops dead in her tracks. She quickly spins around and off after the hare again.

The hare is heading for that clump of trees where we had just shot the woodcock and woodpigeon. My bitch by now is back up the hare's backside and they both disappear into the trees as me and Bob eagerly watch on. The scene in front of us all goes quiet and Bob says, "She's lost it." But I know my bitch, she won't give in easily, she has a good nose on her, if she's lost the hare by sight she'll find it again by scent.

Bob says, "She's fast isn't she."

I tell him, "Pup is in her prime, she's only four years old." I carry on to tell Bob, "Some of the best lurchers are bred from my breed of dog, the sheep cur, it's their intelligence and rough coat that is sought after. Put my Pup with a good, fast-running dog and you finish up with a supreme lurcher."

Bob gets his stuttering head on, he's pointing, he says, "Look, the hare, it's coming out of the far side of the trees."

We see Pup, she's out of the trees. From our good viewing point halfway up the hillside we are looking down on them. Pup can't see the hare for the long patch grass but I have trained Pup to work to hand signals. I wave my hand to gain her attention, she sees me. I wave over to her to go over to her right, Pup acknowledges with her nose tight to the ground and her eye cocked watching my hand signals. Pup keeps moving on over, she crosses the patch where the hare has just passed, she picks up the hare scent, and off she goes running like hell with her nose tight to the ground.

We see the hare prick up its big lugs, it's heard Pup coming through the long, stumpy grass. As the hare speeds away, Pup breaks cover from the grass, she sees the hare and the course is back on again.

They are both running fresh again now they both had a bit of a breather and they both race across the flatland. They are both travelling like the wind. Pup has more speed than the hare on a straight run and Pup is soon back up the hare's backside again. She's striking, striking, striking at the hare and Pup keeps missing, missing, missing the hare as it keeps tear-arsing across the flatland. It's racing as if there's no tomorrow. Bob is clutching tight hold on my arm as we watch an unbelievable hare course. Then it gets even more exciting, another hare has sprung up out of the grass, it's jumped up right at the other hare's feet.

My heart leaps into my mouth. I think, what's Pup going to do now? The times I have told Pup in the past, always stick to the first hare, that's tired just like her, the other hare is fresh and full of running. I watch Pup with pride, all my training has finally sunk into her head, she keeps herself on the first hare.

By now I can see both Pup and the hare are getting tired, and by now the hare has got on to its run. It's heading straight for the sheep netting fence which me and Bob had climbed over earlier. The hare follows its run straight through the fence but the hole in the fence is too small for Pup to get through. She hesitates, I can see her thinking, then she remembers where she crossed through earlier with us and she's now through the fence. By now the hare's lolloping along at the far side of some long grass, it's come right alongside of Pup, and it doesn't know it, it hasn't seen Pup and Pup hasn't see it.

The hare has now stopped, it's sat up on its back legs, it's looking around to see where Pup is. It's lost Pup, or so it thinks. We can see Pup as we stand halfway up the hillside, they are only yards apart and neither of them knows it, the long grass is covering each other. I don't know if it was luck on Pup's behalf, but she set off in the right direction and as she pushes her head through the tussocks of grass, Pup sees the hare at the same time as the hare sees Pup. The hare darts around some stumpy long grass, Pup uses her brains, she bobs the other way around the stumpy grass and wallop the hare's in Pup's mouth, a quick shake and the hare is no more.

As Pup was retrieving the dead hare to hand, I looked at Bob. He was scratching his head, he had a big smile on his face that must have stretched from EAR to LUG, and was saying, "By, what a good hare course that was Doug." My bitch now back, I take the hare from her mouth.

Bob said, "Come on Doug, we have a fox to catch."

We head off across the side of the lall hillside to where we had seen the fox disappear. Bob seemed to know where he was heading and took us to a place where the ground levelled out.

Bob looked at me and shushed me with a finger over his mouth and he ushered me to keep the dogs at heel.

Bob lent down and started looking closely at the ground, he pointed in silence, there were fresh claw marks in the soft peat, they were the claw marks of a fox.

I saw they were leading into the entrance of a hole. Bob ushered me away in silence and we stood about twenty yards away from the entrance. We stood where the wind was blowing from the hole and blowing towards us, any would-be fox in there now would not be able to scent us. We loaded our guns with 'BB' cartridges, then keeping Pup and Candy at heel, Bob sent Jesse the Jack Russell in to hunt. She went up and down scenting the ground and to the entrance of the hole. She poked her nose in scenting the wind warily, then I see her arch her back and her hackles stood up on the back of her neck. She pushed her head inside the hole and hesitated for a moment as she scented the air, then disappeared into the hole.

Me and Bob stood in silence and at the ready with our guns. After five minutes of silence and no signs of Jesse, Bob looked at me with a concerned eye. Bob and me waited another five minutes but everything stayed silent, I could see Bob was worrying about the safety of Jesse.

Bob whispered to me that it was a 'FALSE FOX EARTH'.

A lot of gamekeepers make these fox earths and they are positioned in a place where foxes are known to frequent. The keeper will dig a long trench with a dry warm nest chamber at the end and then line the sides and floor with stones. The nest chamber has two entrances so that when the terrier goes in to one entrance, the fox can escape out of the other entrance.

The nest chamber is filled with clean hay to encourage the fox to lay up there. The walled-out trench and nest chamber is then covered over with flat stone slabs and then covered over completely with soil or peat.

It now looks all natural and homely to the unwary fox. Every now and again the keeper will put dead carrion at the end of the entrance and any would-be passing fox will then scent the dead carcasses and will be lured across. He will find the false earth and hopefully lay up there. The two dead carrion crows which Bob had shot earlier were for the purpose of baiting and luring the fox to this false earth.

Quite a while had passed by now at this false fox earth and I could see Bob was becoming more concerned. Everything remained silent. No signs of Jesse or the fox.

I see Bob making his way across to the entrance of the fox hole and I see him push his ear deep within the entrance. He hears the muffled barking and growling of Jesse, and he hears bloodthirsty, muffled snarls and growls coming from the fox. They are having a real battle down there by the sounds of it. There was nothing me and Bob could do but wait so Bob comes over to me and there we patiently wait. Jesse had been down in the fox earth a long time by now.

As I stand there gazing across the mountaintops admiring the beauty of the distant scenery, I stand with my back looking away from the fox earth. You could say I was lacking attention. I catch a sudden movement out of the corner of my eye then I get one almighty bang in my ear hole from Bob's shotgun. I look back sharpishly and I see the fox down and kicking itself to death.

If Bob hadn't been stood there I might have missed that fox with daydreaming. I see Jesse come flying out of the hole and pounce straight on top of the now dead fox.

Jesse went into the hole sporting clean white hair. I look at her now and her white hair is now blood-red. Bob anxiously looks over Jesse, the fox had bitten her badly around the head. The end of her nose was badly ripped and half hanging off, there was bad gashes around her neck and shoulders.

The fox had had a real old go at Jesse by the looks of her. As Bob is inspecting over her body, he says, "She will live to fight another day. It's just a few more battle scars on her body."

I look at the fox as it lays there dead, it's a big dog fox. He's badly battered around his face where Jesse had had a go at him. And that was the end of our rough shooting for the day, and Bob got his fox at the end of the day.

A diagram sketch of the "False Fox Earth" can be found in my other book – "The Life and Times of a Country Boy, autobiography of a Yorkshire lad", "Doug".

Bob throws the fox over his shoulder and off we head back to Bob's cottage. Once there I laid out the produce of our rough shoot in Bob's courtyard and I see Bob stringing up the fox, that's for his boss, the Laird of the estate, to see. I count our day's bag of game. There are two pheasants, one rabbit, that's simply because there isn't many rabbits high up in the mountaintops, we have a

Jack Snipe, one woodpigeon, a pair of mallard ducks, one woodcock and three red grouse. Not a bad bag of mixed game, I thought, not forgetting the two carrion crows and the red fox, and the hare which Pup caught.

Bob came across and looked at our shooting efforts of the day and said, "We will have them three grouse and the woodpigeon for our dinner tonight. Woodpigeon tastes like best steak to me. You pluck and I will cook." And on that I did as I was bid, I started plucking. The grouse and woodpigeon are easy to pluck out, they only need a good quick shake, or so to speak, and the feathers fall off.

Bob made a fine meal of them that night, and we were spitting the pellets out as we ate. It was feet up then after that connoisseur of a dinner, a good lay up for me, in front of Bob's log-burning fire. I needed plenty of rest, I am out long-netting rabbits tonight.

It was well after dark when I set off netting that night, the rabbits need plenty of time to get well out on to their feeding grounds. A quick check to see if I had got all my gear then I chucked it all into my Land Rover together with my .22 rifle. I was going to use that later, I had everything worked out to plan.

I drove down Bob's drive to the quiet country lane at the bottom and when I got to the place where Barry used to drop me off with his wagon there was a ride there that went into the fir tree plantation. A ride is a track through the woodland and I drove the Land Rover onto it and parked up. I was now as close as I could get to the rabbits.

I had my two long nets in a large hessian sack which I threw over my shoulder and tied securely onto my back. My hands were now free to do other jobs. My two hundred yard length of rope was in the sack with the nets, this was to bring the rabbits in off the feeding grounds and into my nets. I had a quiver full of long-net pegs which I strapped onto my belt.

I am now ready. I leave Pup in the Land Rover and off I set through the fir tree plantation towards my first rabbit setting where by now the rabbits should be way out on their feeding grounds.

As I am going along through the tree plantation I pass by my old bivouac but it's too dark in this woodland to be able to see it. I carry on through the woodland and to where them massive warrens are which I have ferreted so many times. I have been here so many times in the past that it almost feels like home sweet home.

I am sure my old mate the mad capper of a bird the capercaillie will be roosting somewhere over my head in the treetops with his harem of females. As I go stealthily along I don't hear any rabbits scampering around in the woodland. That's a sure sign to me that all the rabbits are out on the feeding grounds. I now come to the edge of the woodland and the strong wind is hitting me hard in the face. I had my compass over this place a long time earlier when I knew I was going to long-net the place which has now given me the right wind tonight.

As I stood there silently at the woodland edge, I looked out across the grass meadow in front of me. Out there was the rabbits' feeding ground. It was pitch black out there, the sky was overcast with thick dark cloud. I was eager and itching to get at them rabbits. I looked at the time, I could just make out the hands of the watch face in the dim light of the night, it was just coming on to midnight. I could just make out the lines on the palms of my hands.

An old poacher's saying is that, "if you can just make out the lines on the palms of your hands, the night is right and perfect."

I very carefully climbed over the fence not daring to make a sound for fearing the rabbits would hear me. The wind was howling off the mountaintops and across the rabbits on their feeding ground and hitting me hard in the face. The trees were fair clattering in the strong wind and that makes the rabbits feed further away from the woodland so that they can hear predators approaching. The rabbits will not hear or see me, I am light-footed, in dark clothing, and the wind is blowing my scent away from them. By the time they do know of my presence it will be too late, the trap will be set. I am going to long-net the setting where I used to get a drink of water from the stream. There are many, many rabbits feeding out on this meadow.

I take my first one hundred yard long net out of the hessian sack. This sack makes no rubbing or shuffling noises for the rabbits to hear with their big acute, sensitive lugs, it's all done in silence.

I now strap my hessian sack that holds my other long net on my back and my hands are now free to do other jobs.

The long net has two iron spikes on it called 'end irons', there is one at either end of the long net. These end irons hold the net taut once the net is run out along the woodside.

The long net is threaded on to one of the end irons and I

unwrap the loose end iron from the neck of the net and stick it firmly into the ground. I now head off down the woodland side dropping my net off in links as I go.

My net is now fully stretched out along the woodland edge and I now pull the net taut as it lays on the ground.

I now take my other long net which was on my back in the hessian sack. I stick its end iron into the ground at the end of my other run-out net then I drop the second net in the same manner as my first net.

So now I have my quiver strapped to my belt and I draw out a peg which is about three foot long. The long net has a top and a bottom line running all the full length of the net. It's these lines that are held taut by the end irons.

I lift the bottom line right at the end of the net, wrap it once around the bottom of the long net peg and stick it firmly into the ground. I now wrap the top line at the top of the same peg and my net is now being held upright. I now take ten paces straightening my net as I go and stick in another peg. I do this all the way along both of my nets, and that's it, both my nets are now stood up erect and blowing in the wind, which bellows the net out like one big long sack. The nets are now all ready for the onslaught of rabbits that's going to hit them.

The setting of these two long nets takes about fifteen minutes, which is all done in the silence and the black of the night. The rabbits out there feeding have not got a clue what's happening, their escape into the woodland is now cut off by nets.

I am now right at the end of my nets and I now get my two hundred yard length off three-eighths thick, strong nylon rope. I tie the end of my rope to the fence. I have done this sort of long-netting so many times, yet at this particular moment, when my nets are up and ready for the kill, my heart always starts pounding like a big bass drum. It's a wonder the rabbits cannot hear my heart pounding and scarper for the nearest cover.

So with my rope in my hand I set off along the woodside away from my nets. I carry on until my rope is at full stretch, now I start moving out into the meadow where the rabbits are out feeding. My rope is now taut in my hands, it's strung out way across the meadow and I am by now at the other side of the rabbits with the woodland and my nets way out across yonder.

With the strong wind now blowing hard at my back, my human scent is now wafting across the rabbits. The rabbits now panic, my scent puts terrifying fear up their arses and they run hell for leather across the meadow to make their escape into the safety of the woodland. I hear the pattering of feet running close on by me, it's the rabbits that I hear as they are fleeing from my presence, but I don't see them in the darkness of the night.

I start lashing and whipping my rope across the meadow and I hear rabbits screaming way out yonder in the distance. They are hitting and balling themselves up in the long nets. Now with adrenaline surging through my body, I now know the nets are doing their job so I keep on whipping and lashing my rope. I must keep on panicking the rabbits to flee for cover, there will be rabbits out there still on the meadow. They will be laid tight squat in the grass, they will be panic-stricken with fear, but one tap up the rabbit's arse with my rope as I drag it over the meadow and panic-stricken rabbits will be up out of the grass and off like bats out of hell for their distant woodland. By now, I can hear rabbits screaming blue murder, they are not far in front of me now, I am now at the far end of my nets at the opposite end to where my rope is tied to the fence.

I am now upon my net and I see dull faint white bellies of rabbits jumping all tangled up in my nets. They are screaming as if there's no tomorrow. I must leave them rabbits be for a moment, my rope runs about ten yards away from the full length of my nets and there will be rabbits down there which have stopped. They can see their mates caught in my nets and they are sat in between the nets and the rope. I whip and lash my rope and pull it tight up the full length of my nets and the rope gives them sitting rabbits a final tap up their arses. As the rabbits leap forward with shock and leap straight into my nets, my rope has now done its work. I now run to the end of my net and I dimly see two, three or is it four rabbits all tangled together in the net. They are screaming like hell and I put my hand gingerly in among the rabbits.

I must watch my finger ends. I go to grab one of the rabbits and I hear snap, snap, snapping of teeth clashing together. I whip my hand out sharpishly, the damned rabbits will not let me kill them, they are all balled-up together. I grab the top line of the net, I give it a quick shake and the bundle of rabbits separate a little, I now put my hand in again and I grab one of the rabbits by the back of its neck, keeping my fingers well away from his big front teeth. With my fingers now under his chin, supported now by my thumb at the back of his neck, I give a quick flick back of his head and I

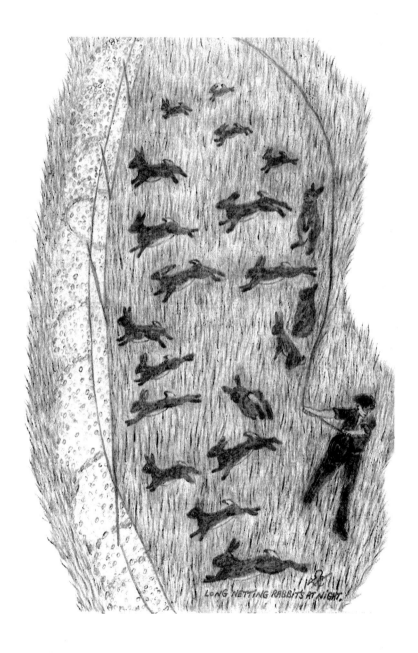

LONG NETTING RABBITS AT NIGHT.

hear and feel a slight click as his neck breaks. The rabbit falls away limp in body as it kicks itself to death. Another three quick flicks and clicks and all four rabbits lay dead still tangled in the net. I now leave them where they lay. I go another two paces down the net and there's more rabbits to be killed. As I am flicking and I feel and hear a lot of clicking sounds, I see more and more rabbits down the nets. I head down the length of my nets killing and leaving as I go and by the time I am at the end of both my nets I have had a good kill, I have rabbits dead all the way down my nets. There is no time to have a rest.

I now go back down my nets taking the dead rabbits out, usually a quick shake of the top line and the dead rabbit falls out of the net.

I have a real good bag of fat rabbits by the time I gather them all up and get them all together. That job now done,

I now go back along both my nets taking the pegs out as I go and pushing them back into my quiver which is strapped to my belt.

That job now done, I now pick up my nets and I pull out my end iron from the ground. This job should be done with care, they must not be tangled up anywhere, I am going to drop them again tonight for even more rabbits.

I take a yard of net in my hand keeping the top and bottom line together. I form it into a link and slide it on to the end iron, one link at a time until the full length of the net is on the end iron. I now wrap the second end iron and its top and bottom lines around the neck of the bundle of net. Then strapping the two end irons together that net is now all tidy and all ready to drop again. I do the same with my other net and then pop them both back into my hessian sack. And my last job is to gather in the full length of rope.

I am now all ready to go along the side of the fir tree plantation and on to the next rabbit setting.

Now that I am not rabbit poaching, I now have full permission from Bob the gamekeeper, I remember I carried on that night. The wind kept blowing hard and I long-netted another two rabbit settings, getting some good bags of fine big fat rabbits.

I finished netting that night quite a while before daybreak so I decide to lamp a rabbit or two with my Land Rover.

I headed on back through the fir tree plantation. It was really dark inside that woodland and I was nearly bumping into trees it was that dark. I heard a tawny owl hooting in the treetops above my head, I heard rabbits scurrying about in the woodland, I heard a fox barking in the distant hills, or is that mountains, I heard croaking coming from the treetops not far away. I thought to myself, I wonder if that's my old mate that mad capper of a bird the capercaillie.

I carry on and grope my way through the woodland and on to where my Land Rover is parked up. Pup is there waiting to greet me when I arrive. I grab my .22 rifle and load it up with bullets and Pup is giving me a hard smell over with her nose, she knows I have been catching rabbits she can smell them on my clothes.

I drive the Land Rover along the ride which goes through the fir tree plantation. The ride brings us to a wooden five-barred gate and I stop to open the gate which takes us on to the grass meadow where I had long-netted earlier. As I pull the Land Rover through the gateway I see rabbits across the meadow in the Land Rover headlights. Pup has seen them too and she's watching them with her beady eyes through the windscreen. She's whining and getting herself all excited. Pup has done this lamping rabbits many, many times, she knows her job.

I go and close the five-barred gate behind me and as I get back to the Land Rover I see a rabbit run across and sit in the headlights. I make a grab for the rifle but by the time I have slotted a bullet from the magazine into the chamber the rabbit has moved on. I put the Land Rover into first gear and crawl away from the gate and onto the meadow, with my headlights now scanning the ground in front of me. I catch a glimpse again of the rabbit, I lift my rifle and as I take aim the rabbit hops on, it's now sat in full view in the headlights. It's got its back to me as it crouches down grazing and I have my sights on him but I can't see his head. I give a little rabbit squeal with my mouth, he lifts his head and I pull the trigger. The bullet hits him at the back of the neck and he slumps to the ground without even giving out a death kick.

As quick as a flash Pup is out of the Land Rover and in the blink of an eye she has the rabbit in her mouth and is back into the Land Rover.

I throw the rabbit into the back of the Land Rover and on we go again. We carry on along the woodside picking rabbits off with the rifle as we go. These are rabbit settings that I have gone across once this evening with the long nets, there are a lot of rabbits which I have missed.

I pick up a pile of rabbits which I caught earlier with the long nets, by now they have cooled off with the cold early morning temperatures, and off me and Pup go again. As per usual Pup is in her prime position on the passenger seat watching for rabbits through the windscreen. We head across the grass meadow to where I saw rabbits in the distant headlights.

I am now at the point where I saw them rabbits and I slowly swing the headlights around the meadow.

I pick up a rabbit's eye as it is at one side of the headlights, it's laid flat to the ground squat in the short grass.

I quickly grab my rifle, Pup is up on to the dashboard with her front paws, she is eyeballing everything I am doing. I get the rabbit into the scope of my rifle, I put the cross on to the brain part of his head and slowly squeeze the trigger. The bullet is bang on target and the rabbit jumps three feet into the air. Pup stays put where she is, she knows she has seen more than one rabbit, she marks the dead rabbit's location with her dog brain.

I slowly move the Land Rover on a little with the headlights scanning the ground as I go, I have my rifle resting on my knee and ready. I see another rabbit and I have to shoot fast or he will be up and off. He drops quickly with a dumdum bullet in the head, there is no crack from my rifle, it has a silencer fitted on the end of the barrel.

I see another rabbit, I have him on the dim edge side of the headlights. I get my scope on to him, in the dim of the lights I can just make out the cross on his head and I pull the trigger. He jumps high into the air, that's another head shot down. There's no more rabbits just here but I see more across the meadow in the distant headlights. I pick up these dead rabbits first, or Pup does. I turn the headlights off and let Pup out of the Land Rover, she's under my legs like a shot and off she disappears into the darkness of the gloom. I sit there in the darkness of the cab, Pup will find them dead rabbits with her powerful hunting nose.

I have the Land Rover door half open, I see Pup poke her nose through it, she has the dead rabbit in her mouth, I take it from her, and off she races again. I feel at the rabbit's head, its skull has been shattered by the power of the bullet. I throw it in the back of the Land Rover with the other rabbits. Again I hear Pup at the door, she has another dead rabbit in her mouth, I take it from her and off she disappears again, she's no nincompooch, she knows how many rabbits I dropped.

I hear her again panting at the door, I open it and in she jumps with the last rabbit in her mouth. She takes the rabbit into the back of the Land Rover herself and I hear her having a good sniff round in the back. She's just checking to see if all the rabbits are there.

I turn the headlights back on as I set off again. Pup, like a flash, is back on her front seat watching for the next rabbits to appear in the headlights.

We carry on around the grass meadows picking rabbits off as we go. These meadows would have been overrun with rabbits but they have all fallen foul of the long nets earlier.

It's by now daylight so I pick up the rabbits I netted earlier, they are by now cold and stiff, and head off and on to Bob's duck flight pond.

As I get there I see many wild duck get up off the pond and I see a party of greylag geese get up with them. They make their escape by flying low across the moor, honking their heads off as they go.

No doubt they have all been brought in by all these rabbits' guts I keep throwing into the pond. They will be back I am sure. There's another load of rabbits' guts here for them if and when they return.

As I am paunching these rabbits, I hear blackcock calling in the distance. I was eager to see these blackcock so I quickly paunched all these rabbits and did as I had been told by Bob and threw all the guts into the pond.

I quickly load up my Land Rover with the now paunched out rabbits and head out across the moorland to where I had heard the blackcock calling.

I got as close as I dare to the blackcock with the Land Rover and then parked up and headed across the moorland on foot.

I could hear the blackcock calling out ahead of me, by the sounds of them they were just over a stone wall.

As I peered over the wall, there they were, four blackcock in their, what is called, 'ARENA ON A LEKKING GROUND'. They were only a hundred yards away from me in the heather.

They were stood out in their own territories. They were 'hissing', 'bubbling' and 'crowing' at each other, which was loud enough to be heard right the way across the moor.

I see another blackcock come and he lands in a fir tree not far away in the forestry plantation.

He starts crowing back at those on the lekking ground. I could see this was going to build up into a right old 'ritual contest' of

"BLACK GROUSE" OR "BLACKCOCK" ON THEIR "LEKKING GROUND". THESE BIRDS ARE OUR ONLY TRUE NATIVE BIRD. UNIQUE ONLY TO BRITAIN AND CAN BE FOUND NOWHERE ELSE IN THE WORLD.

matchmaking, and it was all happening in front of my very own eyes.

I look across and see more gathering on a stone wall not far away. Another one flies in as he passes over the top of my head, he circles around over the top of the blackcock which are crowing and sticking their chest out at him.

He settles on the lekking ground and takes up his position in his own territory.

The female 'greyhens', which the blackcock are fighting for supremacy for, are nowhere to be seen. They will only appear here on the lekking ground in the mating season.

By then the dominant males which rule the roost will have the preferences over the greyhens. As I am still peering over the stone wall I see blackcock appearing from all directions. They are flying in and circling the lekking ground and dropping in on their own territory.

There are two sat perched in an old tree not far away, they are having a stand-up battle with each other. It's a wonder the old tree branches can take their weight as they are bouncing up and down throwing their weight at each other. The blackcock are a big strong heavy game bird. Only that mad capper of a bird the capercaillie is larger.

I am distracted from my attention to the blackcock when I hear the chorus of a flock of white-fronted geese. As I look up to see a V-shaped skein of geese, they are 'yodelling' to each other as they pass overhead.

The chorus of a skein of geese is an ear-catching, stirring sound to me, and as I watch they set their wings and drop in lower.

They circle over the duck flight pond which I have just fed with rabbits' guts and settle on the pond.

My attention is caught yet again as I see a skein of greylag geese. They are doing their aerobatics in the sky as they are coming in to land on the flight pond.

They are 'whiffling' and plunging downwards in a 'side-slipping dive', 'rolling' and 'tilting' as they plunge downwards.

They circle the flight pond and land on the water.

I see parties of mallard and widgeon, and a whole host of other breeds of wild ducks.

I think they are going to have a birthday party when they see all the guts I have just thrown in for them.

As I look back at the blackcock on their lekking ground, I see a party of teal as they come sweeping low over the ground. They are swooping and wheeling that low to the ground the blackcock duck their heads low as they pass over.

As the teal skim low over the stone wall they pass me by like whistling bullets, and to my amazement there's a huge blackcock stood perched on the wall only twenty yards away. He ducks his head low as the speeding teal pass over him. I could see his feathers lift up from the backdraught of the teal. I had been so absorbed in everything going off around me, I hadn't noticed this massive blackcock appear at the side of me.

What a fine big bird he was too, the largest blackcock I had ever seen. He totally ignored me as I stood there crouched up at the back of the stone wall.

He started throwing out his threat calls to the other blackcock on the lekking ground. There must have been nearly twenty blackcock out there by now all in their own territorial patch.

This big powerful game bird by my side started throwing out his challenges, with his head held high, tail 'cocked' and 'fanned' with his red wattles puffed out above his eyes and his red comb expanded. The 'lyre tips' of his tail were fanned out, what a magnificent spectacle he was.

He sent out a threatening 'sneeze' and a 'tsueesh' and followed with a 'roo-oo, roo-oo' call. Then he got himself down in a crouched position on the wall top and started giving out other threat calls with a 'rookooing', 'crowing' and 'hissing' and a whole host of other queer noises. With an almighty beating and thrashing of his wings, he took to the air, he circled overhead of the battling blackcock below, then he dropped into the 'main arena on the lekking ground'. He towered above the rest. All-comers came at him but he drove them out of his territory.

The beaten blackcock were 'bowing' and surrendering in a submission posture, with their wings trailing the ground, and the giant of blackcock was chasing them off. What a scene I was witnessing, I couldn't believe my good luck. When I look across I see a blackcock crouch low and run for cover. The other blackcock instantly acknowledge his body language and they too make a mad scarper into the safety of the cover, leaving me a little bewildered. I am sure it wasn't me that had frightened them, then I heard my old mate the buzzard.

He was soaring and circling and calling out, it was him that had panicked the blackcock. In my experiences the buzzard puts the 'fear of God' into most animals that he preys on.

Even these massive, heavily-built game birds the blackcock, and all within the blink of an eye, there wasn't a blackcock to be seen anywhere. All that fascinating display was now over.

He's an intriguing bird is the blackcock and he's also known as the black grouse. The capercaillie is the only game bird which is bigger and stronger than him. The blackcock is our only true native bird, he is unique to this country and can be found nowhere else in the world.

I now head on and back to Bob's cottage.

I have had a long night long-netting rabbits and I am now getting tired. All I want now is a good breakfast and a few hours sleep. When I arrive back at Bob's he's nowhere to be seen as usual.

I hung up the night's bag of rabbits in Bob's game larder and then off I went into Bob's cottage for a good breakfast.

Bob had everything laid out waiting for me. He had left some thick rashers of ham and a big goose egg and all I had to do was cook it.

The big goose egg filled my entire dinner plate, and the taste of the homebred ham was mouthwateringly delicious.

Bob was making me feel really at home here, just like home sweet home, but he still hasn't got me any carpet slippers.

I wasn't late up out of bed that day, my main job was to run out the long nets and straighten and tidy them up. They would then be all ready for the final night tonight long-netting more rabbits.

I take the nets on to the meadow at the back of Bob's cottage and I run my nets out just like I do when I am netting at night, but now that it's daylight I can see what I am doing.

I pick up the top line of the net and hold it waist high then I go along the net sliding the surplus net mesh back along the lines.

During the night while I was out rabbiting, the strong wind has a tendency to blow the netting along the lines. So what I am doing now is putting everything back into its proper position.

As I go along my nets, at the same time I am checking the lines of the net to see if they have been half chewed through by the netted rabbits. If they have, I have to repair them straightaway. If I don't the lines will snap on me during the night.

I now have my nets all ready and checked and all ready for tonight. As I am busying myself I see someone coming. It's a young woman and as she comes across the meadow, it looks as though she has just dropped out of the mountaintops.

She has a sheep crook in her hand and two sheepdogs with her. As she comes close to me I see she is a pretty woman with long flowing blonde hair. She looks at me and gives me a great big smile, it was just like a breath of fresh mountain air.

I thought to myself, is she an angel or is she for real? She's now introducing herself as Helen. She has big deep-blue eyes just like the colour of a swimming pool, she nearly knocked me off my feet with her beauty.

I introduced myself as Doug, but Helen replied by saying, "Yes I know all about you Doug, Black Bob has told me all about you."

I got to telling Helen about all the rabbits I was catching for Bob, and saying to her about the vast amount of rabbits there was on the estate. Helen gave me that great big smile of fresh mountain air again and replied by saying, "There's not that many rabbits around these necks of the woods, not compared with my place."

This left me thinking, I know seeing is believing, and I know the rabbits here on Bob's place are out of control.

So with Helen saying that, it left me thinking again, well how many rabbits has she got on her place? Helen says, "I will show you around my place", and to my delight Helen invited me round for dinner that afternoon. Now I can see how a man can be tempted at an offer like that, so I accepted Helen's offer.

Helen pointed towards a great big mountain way out across the moorland and said, "My place is just over yonder at the back in that lall hill." I can see where Bob gets his phrase from now by saying that lall hill. They mean little when they say "lall", some little I think.

That's a mountain Helen is pointing at, anybody can see that. Helen bid me farewell and said she will see me a bit later. I closed my eyes expecting a kiss, but when I opened my eyes again she was walking away.

Helen had truly captured my attention, I felt as happy as a pup with two tails. Now that Helen had gone I had to finish off my nets, they were wet through, they always get saturated by the early morning dew that's set on the grass. They have to be dried out to work to their best ability if they are going to catch rabbits tonight.

Bob has two clothes posts in the courtyard. I take a long net off its end iron and carefully thread the net on to a length of baling band. I now tie the baling band tight between the two clothes posts. I can now spread the long net along the baling band which will open it up. I do my other long net in the same way.

The strong wind is still blowing hard and it will dry my nets out in no time. A little later that afternoon, I set off to go to Helen's. I decided to walk there, Helen said her place wasn't far away, just at the other side of that lall hill. I left a note on the kitchen table letting Bob know I had gone for dinner to Helen's. I went along what I call the foothills, following a track that someone had made with a quad bike. They are an all-terrain vehicle and will go practically anywhere. They are four-wheel drive with big balloon type tyres for the rugged terrain. The track led me high up into the hills which then levelled off. As I looked across I could see a large flat heather moorland and I could see grouse shooting butts, leaving me thinking this must be one of Bob's grouse moors. I continued on along the moor edge.

I have brought my dog Pup along with me and I see her pick her nose up and stick it into the air. She was winding the scent of something laid in the heather. I stopped and watched her as she slowly hunted about in the heather. She concentrated her attention on a small area of heather and I was starting to get myself a little excited. I have watched Pup many times in a hunting stance like this and more often than not she will put something into the game bag.

I could tell with her body language she was upon something laid there in the heather. She stopped and poked her nose out and I stood there watching full of anticipation of what it was she was on to. She had something pinpointed in the heather right in front of her. I saw Pup's back arch up, her tail wagging slowly from side to side, her eyes were watching for the slightest of movements. Then she slowly lurched herself down just like a cat going in for the kill, made one quick fast pounce into the heather and right in front of her nose a red grouse bursts up in the air. Pup made a quick grab at it and missed. Another grouse burst out of the heather right by the side of it and Pup made a pounce at it. She hit the grouse with her paw, it tippled itself off balance and crashed back into the heather.

I see a whole covey of grouse burst up out of the heather just as if from nowhere and I jump back startled. I see the grouse on the ground, it's by now recovering its senses and it strikes back up into the air. I see Pup leap into the air after it, she misses again and is left with just a mouthful of feathers, and yet again the grouse crash-landed back into the heather. As Pup crashes back down just by the side of the flailing grouse I see her make another grab and she has the grouse firmly in her mouth. Pup retrieves it back to me still alive. I think Bob will be none too pleased if he knew I had just taken one of his grouse. I quickly neck the grouse and pop it into my large rabbiting pocket, it might be a nice treat for Helen, maybe she never gets the chance of a grouse for her dinner.

I now carried on along my walk to Helen's place. When I reached the moorland edge I could see Helen's small stone cottage in the distance. It was nestled in at the bottom of the hills and I could see she had a bit of a farmyard to her place.

I made my way down off the moorland and down into the grass meadows below and I see many rabbits as I head on to Helen's. I make Pup walk at heel, I could see Helen had sheep out grazing.

As we head along, I see rabbits running about everywhere. Pup kept looking at me and I kept looking at Pup. She was eager to be after the rabbits, but I held her at heel, we mustn't upset the sheep.

As I reached Helen's place she was there waiting to greet me. She had a pen full of sheep in the fold yard which was just in front of her quaint little cottage. Helen looked as pretty as ever as she invited me into her cottage. As we are going through the doorway I see a couple of dozen rabbits hung there, they are good fat rabbits and all paunched. As I look them over I see they all have a bullet hole in their heads. I comment about them to Helen and to my delight she says they're for me, she says she has only just shot them with the .22 rifle.

This left me thinking, this woman is made for me, she can even put the bullet smack in the rabbit's head. Helen sits me down at the table for dinner, she is busying herself in the oven which is at the side of a large log-burning fire. I see an old-fashioned meat turner hung there, it's what they call a 'bottle Jack'. You wind up its mechanism and then hang a joint of meat on the hook at the bottom. The bottle Jack is then hung over the fire and the wound-up mechanism turns the joint of meat slowly allowing it to cook evenly. A simple contraption but very efficient in its cooking.

Helen put a plate in front of me and I couldn't believe what I saw on my plate. It was grouse again, but not the grouse I was going to give her, that was still in my coat pocket.

It looked to me as though the Laird supplied everybody with his grouse. As me and Helen chatted over dinner, me with a whole grouse on my plate and Helen with a whole grouse on her plate, we were spitting out the pellets as we chatted away. Helen told me she was the shepherdess for the Laird and that she looked after two hundred ewes. "That's female breeding sheep." she says. The land she shepherds on and Bob's land he gamekeeps on is all on the Laird's massive estate.

After we had feasted on our grouse dinners, all courtesy of the Laird, Helen gets out a bottle of Scotch whisky saying, "This is good for the digestive system you know Doug", as she swigs off a glass. And on that Helen says, "I just have to finish off these ewes in the fold yard and then I will take you and show you what a plague of rabbits looks like. You may think Bob's land is overrun with rabbits but just you see what I have to show you." And on that we go out of her cottage and Helen is now climbing into a pen full of sheep. Helen is trimming the sheep's feet and she says she is looking for any foot rot that may be in their feet.

As I watched on, I was looking at and admiring the 'tup', that's a male ram sheep. He was a big fellow with big strong curled-around horns. He had a red-dye-marked collar strapped around his neck which was held on firmly with a leather harness around his chest.

This indicates to the shepherd how well the tup is working. Every time the tup mates with a ewe he leaves a red dye mark on the ewe's backside that let's the shepherd know that ewe should now be pregnant with a lamb or two. I saw Helen having a bit of difficulty holding down one of the ewes while she was trying to work on its feet, so I climbed over into the pen and held the ewe for her. As I was leaning over holding the fighting, struggling ewe I felt one hell of a wallop up my backside and ended up on the floor among the rest of the flock of sheep. When I came to my senses I looked up and I saw the mad crazy tup looking me dead in the eyes with his devilment-looking eye. He's now running at me with his head held low and he's now head-butting me while I am still down and out on the floor. I grab him by the horns to try to hold him off, he's a big powerful animal. I see Helen rush in and grab him and I pick myself up from the floor and make a run for it straight through the middle of his flock of ewes.

The mad crazy tup must be thinking I am a threat to his ewes. I went to climb over the pen fence but by now the tup has gone off his rocker and he breaks free from Helen's grip. I see him come charging at me knocking his ewes to one side as he comes. I am on top of the pen fence, just about to jump to safety, when I get another almighty head-butting thump up my backside. I go flying up into the air and as I come down I land headfirst into the muckheap.

As I pick myself up I see Helen stood there, she has a big, breathtaking, heart-leaping smile on her face that must have stretched from ear to lug. Helen's now wiping my face with a lily-white handkerchief and, with her deep blue eyes now upon me, she is looking me deep in the eyes. I close my eyes expecting a kiss, but when I open my eyes she is walking away again.

It must have been all the shit on my face that was putting her off. What do they call shit these days, is it manure?

Helen's flock of sheep and that big ram-head of a tup now done, we set off to take the sheep into the low-lying grass meadows. Helen's two sheepdogs were shepherding the flock of sheep while we were following on behind on the quad bike.

I sat at the back of Helen on the bike while my Pup laid on the rack at the back. The rabbits that Helen had shot and given me were tied and hung up on the back of the quad bike. They were big rabbits which were dangling down over the wheel arch with their big ears near on trailing the ground.

As we drove along, the old tup kept stopping and looking at me, giving me the dead eye, but Helen's sheepdogs kept driving him on.

I could see by now that the rabbits we were seeing were starting to build up into big numbers. Helen turned her head as we drove along and said, "You haven't seen nothing yet Doug."

Helen dropped off the sheep into a meadow, we then carried on along her grass pastures. Helen's two sheepdogs then jumped on to the front of the quad bike which was by now laden down with all us lot on it. And the rabbits we were seeing were getting thicker and thicker as we drove along.

It is by now coming on to late afternoon which is the ideal time for the rabbits to come out feeding. Helen is now driving along the side of a fir tree plantation, it's the same woodland that runs on to Bob's land. It's one great long forest that stretches way out into the distance as far as the eye can see.

As we turn a bend around the fir tree plantation, Helen taps me on the leg and says, "Watch out." And as we go around the bend in the woodland, I can't believe my eyes at what I see. There are rabbits running off the grass meadows and into the woodland in their hundreds, and as she drives further along the rabbits are in their multitudes and running off the meadows in droves.

I said to Helen, "Stop, turn the bike engine off, let me get my breath back." I got off the bike and stood there flabbergasted with all the rabbits I am witnessing with my very own eyes.

Helen said, "What do you reckon to all that lot then Doug?" I shook my head in disbelief. I walked across to the forest side and looked in, it was just one mass of rabbit warren, in there, just like everywhere else I had been to in these forestry plantations.

Helen said to me, "You catch all these rabbits if you want Doug." I replied by saying, "I can see that a rabbit catcher like myself might be tempted at an offer like that."

Helen says, "There's more rabbits yet to be seen," then she looks at me and smiles, saying, "you haven't seen nothing yet." So on the bike we jump, dogs and all, and off we go. We wind and turn through the grass meadows as we travel along on the quad bike, and we see rabbits upon rabbits and believe me the rabbits were in big numbers. Everywhere we travel across.

As I look over Helen's shoulder as she is driving the bike I can see we are heading down towards a river, what the Scottish people call a 'burn'. I see a lot of rabbits running in off the grass meadows and to the riverbank.

Helen's now driving us along by the side of the river, I see hoards and hoards of rabbits running in front of us. Helen half turns her head towards me, smiles and says, "You still haven't seen nothing yet Doug."

This leaves me thinking, well how many rabbits is she going to show me? Helen's now turning a bend around the river and she turns and says, "Watch out Doug, now you're going to see what a lot of rabbits looks like."

We are now around the bend of the river, and what I see I don't believe. The grassland in front of us turns from green to brown, but the brown is moving. I don't believe it, the ground is nearly brown with rabbits, there must be more than a thousand rabbits running in front of us as we travel along. They are all bolting for the cover of the riverbank.

I tell Helen to stop the bike, let me take in what I am seeing. Helen pulls up, turns the bike's engine off and says, "What do you reckon to all that lot then Doug? I want you to catch all that lot if you can." I was flabbergasted, what could I say, I was speechless.

As we sit there silent on the quad bike, the mild winter sunshine shining on our backs, all that could be heard was the strong wind that was still blowing and the babbling river by our side.

As we sit there in silence I keep hearing a plop splash, plop splash. I look towards the river and I see a big trout plop out of the water and splash back in again then I see another trout jumping. I tell Helen, and as we watch on we see trout leaping in and out of the water everywhere.

Helen says, "This is the Laird's private stretch of river where he does a lot of fishing, fly casting with his rod." Helen looks at me with a bit of devilment on her face and says, "Would you like a couple for your dinner?" What could I say but yes. I have no sooner said yes, and off Helen goes towards the riverside. I say something to Helen but she shushes me to be silent. What Helen is doing now is she's laying herself down right by the side of the water, she has her jumper sleeve rolled right up to her armpit and she's now groping her arm in the water with her hand underneath the river bank. As she gropes her hand up and down, I see Helen's arm go still, she's now doing something with her hand.

As I stand there just watching I think to myself, whatever is Helen doing down there? I see Helen's hand grab sharpish at something, and to my surprise she whips out a great trout from the water. She throws it on to the riverbank and it's flipping and flopping around. It's now flipped itself down a rabbit hole and I run to grab it, but it disappears out of sight. I thrust my arm far down the rabbit hole and I can just touch something wet and slimy. I grab at it firmly and pull out the trout and as I hold it up to show Helen, another trout comes whizzing past me. It's Helen throwing another trout out of the river. So now I have two great trout in my hands.

Helen gives me a radiant smile and says, "That's what they call tickling trout, is that Doug."

So now we all pile back on the quad bike, with me sat at the back of Helen as she drives and with Pup at the back of me laid on the rack. Helen's two sheepdogs are laid on the rack at the front of the bike together with the big bundle of rabbits Helen shot for me which were hanging over the back wheel arch of the bike. And now we have these two whopping great trout which I have tied together by the gills with baling band and that are now hung down from the handlebars. It's a wonder the quad bike can carry us all.

Helen's now driving us along the side of the riverbank and she's showing me the extent of all them rabbits we have just seen. The riverbank as far as the eye can see is just one big long continuous length of rabbit warrens. So now I have seen what Helen wanted to show me which was all the rabbits on her place,

TROUT
TICKLING

and wow has Helen got a rabbit problem, and all mine to catch says Helen. And on that Helen says, "I will now take you back to Bob's place, hang on tight, it gets a little rough along here."

As we went along there was yet more multitudes of rabbits running across the front of us, Helen had to weave around them on the quad bike. We went along the bottom of the foothills and there were meadows that stretched way out into yonder where there were rabbits running everywhere, as many as ever we have seen. The rabbits were running into one massive long rabbit warren that stretched all the way along the foothills.

Helen stopped the quad bike and said this was the place where she got a lot of rabbits to feed her dogs on. I saw out in the meadows there were a lot of sivs.

We walked out into the meadow and Helen stopped and pointed into a clump of sivs saying, "There do you see it?"

I peered into the sivs and I saw a rabbit laid tight squat on its seat in the sivs. I was that close I could nearly have reached out and touched it. The rabbit jumped up and bolted for safety to the distant warren. As we walked on there were many rabbits laid up in the sivs, and when they were disturbed they all bolted in the same direction of the large warrens. Helen said, "When I want some rabbits for dog food, I just come along here quietly and when I see a rabbit laid on its seat in the sivs, I just hit it over the head with a long nobbler stick. And it's not long before I have all the rabbits that I need." Then she said, "I can also catch all these rabbits if I want to."

We now set off again on the quad bike, dogs and all, and on towards Bob's place. We come to the top of a steep ravine and Helen says, "Hang on tight now." I put my arms around Helen and hold on grimly and tightly as she goes down the steep ravine side. I look behind me and I see Pup is hanging on for dear life on the rack at the back of the quad. I see Helen's two sheepdogs sat on the rack at the front, they appear none too concerned.

The quad bike bounces its way down the rugged ravine side and Helen looks back to see if we are still there. At the bottom of the ravine I see a wide, fast-flowing stream and a narrow wooden footbridge across it.

Helen turned again and said, "Hang on tight now." I shut my eyes in fear, the wooden bridge was only just a bit wider than the quad bike and it had no side rails. I could feel the bridge swaying as we were crossing it. Halfway across I opened my eyes and looked down and I could see the rapid-running stream cascading over the rocks below us. I closed my eyes again and awaited my fate, then I sighed with relief as we reached the other side. Without even hesitating Helen set off up the other side of the ravine, it was sheer and the quad bike was struggling to get up with all the weight on it. We bounced and bumped as the quad went up the rocky terrain.

We finally reach the top and as I look from the top of the ravine I can see Bob's place in the distance. Thank Christ for that, I thought.

Helen delivered me safely into Bob's courtyard and said, "Right, you can let go of me now Doug." And on that I thanked Helen for a lovely dinner and said that some time in the near future I would be back to have a go at her rabbits. She nearly knocked me off my feet as she gave a kiss when I wasn't expecting it. That made my day, and off I went like a pup with two tails.

I now go to take my long nets off Bob's clothes line, they will be dry by now, and I thread them back onto their end irons and pop them back into the large hessian sack. They are all dry and tidy now, all ready for long-netting more rabbits later on tonight.

Tonight is going to be my last night long-netting the rabbits along that fir tree plantation on Bob's place, for this particular visit anyway.

It is by now becoming dark and I will give the rabbits a few hours to get well out on to their feeding grounds. I look up into the sky, it is thick with cloud, really overcast, and the north wind is still blowing as hard as ever, a most perfect night for long-netting rabbits. I now go into Bob's cottage to watch a bit of television with him. As I lay back there in my armchair, I see a portable battery on charge on the sideboard and I ask Bob what he uses that for. Bob smiles to himself and says, "That's for when I am out at night on poacher watch, when I am after someone such as the likes of you." Bob is having a little rib at me for when he caught me ferret poaching his rabbits. I get myself to thinking, Bob has a lurcher outside in the dog kennels. I say to Bob, "Is the lurcher outside any good at lamping rabbits?" Bob chortles saying, "She's one of the best." I have nothing to do for a few hours, until I go netting them rabbits later on tonight, I remember, and I get a rare old sparkle into my eyes. So I say to Bob, "Let's try her out on a few of the rabbits around the cottage." Bob looks at the timepiece on the stone shelf above the fireplace and says, "Aye, we can do, you have a little bit of time to kill haven't you."

So on that, we throw our field togs on and get ourselves prepared for a bit of rabbit lamping with his lurcher running bitch. Bob unplugs the rechargeable battery from the mains electricity supply. He threads his belt through the carrying clips and straps the battery to his back. Bob then goes into the cupboard and takes out a big lamp.

He plugs the wire on the lamp into the socket on the battery and we are all ready to be off. We now go to let Bob's lurcher out of the kennel. She has a quick five minutes run to empty herself and Bob shouts her back. I could see she was getting herself all excited, she knew where she was going, and I could tell by just looking at her that she had done it all before.

Blue, Bob calls her. I can see where she gets that name from, she has a rough shaggy hair of blue. Bob slips a length of baling band under her collar I get my Pup from out of my Land Rover. Pup has to come with us, after all she is on her rabbiting holidays just as much as I am.

Bob says in a quiet voice, "Keep Pup at heel." We come to a wooden five-barred gate which is at the side of Bob's cottage, it leads us through into some rough grass pastures. The weather is perfect for lamping some rabbits with Blue. The sky is cloudy and overcast, it is a pitch black night and the wind is blowing strong through the old trees that are around. Just an ideal night, the perfect weather also for me long-netting the rabbits later on tonight.

I hear a muffled click as Bob turns on his flashlight. He shines the light around the rough grass pasture and I see rabbits' sparkling eyes everywhere. Blue is snatching and pulling at the baling band slipper lead, she is eager to be at them there rabbits. Bob snatches Blue back to his side. My Pup is eager to be at them rabbits and I silently beckon her back to my heel. Bob says in a low whisper, "There's too many rabbits together just here, we want them in ones if we can."

We walk on a little further, out into the middle of the rough pastures, and as we walked through the rabbits they looked oh so unconcerned. They kept having a nibble at the grass, then sitting up on their back legs having a good look at the light shining on them, then hopping a little further along the pasture then stopping and having a good look back at us behind the lamp. That's fatal for the rabbits when I am out with the rifle, the rabbits are so curious that when they think they have reached the safety of the cover side, they stop and look back. I am usually waiting for them to stop, and I will be following them in my powerful scope. The moment they stop they get a dumdum bullet in their head. What's that old saying, "curiosity killed the cat"? In the rabbit's case it's, "curiosity killed the rabbit".

I could tell by all these rabbits we were passing our way through now, that they had never had a lamp across them, they were to damned tame.

When a rabbit has been lamped with a gun or with a dog, or whatever, they become accustomed to danger, they run when the lamp shines on them, or they keep hopping along and will not stop. That's what we call then, the rabbits are 'lamp shy'. Bob now whispers to me again and says, "There's too many rabbits here, we'll move further on up the hillside."

We trogged on a little further with both dogs at heel, and we walked in the darkness of the night with the lamp switched off.

We come to a broken down stone wall, we clamber over it in silence, we are by now well away from them lowland rabbits.

Bob switches the light back on, it picks up a rabbit about hundred yard away further up the hillside, it's on its own grazing by the looks of it. The lurcher sees it, she's looking straight down the light's beam. I thought this bitch knew her job, now I know she does. She's pulling like hell at the slipper lead, Bob releases her and she's off just like a phantom through the night. The rabbit just sits there looking at the light, it's dazzled, it doesn't see Blue coming. Blue's running at full pelt, she lurches down and strikes at the rabbit, all at the same time. The rabbit hears something coming upon it, it sticks its lugs up and, as Blue's teeth are just about to clamp shut, the rabbit jumps up into the air at the same time. Blue misses it and her speed takes her careering on. The rabbit hits the ground and stands up high on all four legs. It's now on red alert with its lugs pricked high, it must be wondering what the hell has just flown underneath it. Blue has tippled head over heels in all her excitement and the rabbit's eyes are now focusing on the tippled-over lurcher. The rabbit's lugs prick forward, it shakes its head, maybe trying to recover its senses, and like a bat out of hell it makes a quick run for it.

Bob follows the rabbit with the lamp, the rabbit disappears down a small burrow, that was one hell of a lucky rabbit.

I see Blue is back up on her feet and she's up and down hunting for the rabbit but she soon stops. She knows she's lost the rabbit, and she straightaway returns back to Bob. That's a well-trained dog that will do that. Bob quickly puts Blue back on the slipper lead which is the old length of baling band. Bob says quietly that he has trained her to come back to hand when she loses the rabbit, that way she doesn't disturb any other rabbits that are around. I realized that, I thought.

We now move on a little further with the lamp switched off and my Pup still at my heel.

I keep mentioning my dog called Pup, as I tell my stories which have happened over many bygone years. I always have a bitch, they are always house dogs, come field dogs. When my old bitch which is called Pup dies, I straightaway after a lot of grief get in another Pup to replace my old one. My sister Ann, who I live with, always gives her a proper name, but I always call them Pup. Everywhere I go Pup goes and everywhere Pup goes I go, and everything I eat Pup eats which may be some old cock pheasant Pup's caught. Well, I might not help eat that with Pup. So this Pup I have with me now is a recent Pup, she's about four years old and in her prime. I have already taught Pup a lot of my old rabbiting tricks, and Pup has a good hunting nose on her and has the speed and agility to catch any rabbit or hare breathing. So now you know when I mention my bitch's name 'Pup' it doesn't mean to say she's a young pup. She might be my old Pup, and may be a different Pup which you read about earlier, but they all end up being my old faithful Pup.

It is the first time the Pup I have with me now has ever been out lamping rabbits. I mean for the dog to catch in the lamp, she's done plenty of lamping with me shooting the rabbits with the rifle. Pup appears to be a little green at the job, she hasn't learnt to look down the light beam to see the rabbits, but I am sure she will soon learn, she is intelligent enough.

By now me and Bob and our two dogs have moved further along the hillside. Bob switches the light back on and the beam picks up a rabbit only twenty yards away. Blue the lurcher has it in her glimpse straightaway and without any hesitation Bob slips Blue. The rabbit instantly sees the lurcher tear-arsing towards it and it sets off as if there's no tomorrow. Blue is straight on to the rabbit's backside, she strikes at the rabbit and picks it up with ease. Bob clicks Blue back to him.

There's no whistling or shouting that will disturb other rabbits that may be around, just a simple click and Blue's back to Bob handing him the live rabbit. As Bob takes the rabbit he hasn't got hold of it properly, the rabbit falls to the ground and off it goes across the field. Blue goes bounding after it. All in a few dithering seconds Bob has the light flashing across the field again, but his lamp is not needed, Blue has the rabbit firmly in her mouth.

Bob hands me the rabbit and I quickly break its neck. I let Pup have a quick smell at it then pop the rabbit into one of my big poacher's pockets inside of my big coat. We move on a little, Bob flashes the light back on, we get two rabbits in the light. Bob slips Blue and the rabbits split as Blue is upon them. Bob keeps the light on the rabbit which Blue is chasing, the other rabbit races half-blinded towards us. I see Pup has seen it, she's eager to be off after it, so I set Pup at it and off she races into the dark of the night.

I look across the field, Bob has the light on the rabbit and Blue together, she catches the rabbit on the second strike. As I am watching Bob taking the rabbit from Blue's mouth, I see a movement out of the corner of my eye. It's Pup and she has the other rabbit in her mouth. I kill both rabbits and pop them into my poacher's pockets.

Bob's light beam is so powerful, it's a small 'spot' beam, and when it hits the rabbits' eyes it dazzles them. Like Pup's rabbit she just caught, that rabbit ran off into the darkness, but its eyes will have still been dazzled. I am sure Pup will have caught it easily, she is now learning the art of lamping.

We move a little further and we soon have more rabbits in the light. Bob slips Blue on to one and before I know it Pup is off after another one.

Blue has her rabbit in the flash of an eye but she's no sooner caught it when another rabbit comes running across the light beam. Blue sees it, she gives the rabbit in her mouth a quick shake and drops it. She's now off again after the other rabbit and she's straight up that rabbit's backside. Bob keeps the light on the rabbit's eyes with Blue in view in the light. Blue strikes at the rabbit, it slips and slides to one side of the snarled-up, biting teeth. Blue turns and strikes again, she misses. The rabbit twists and turns from every strike from Blue, but another strike and Blue has the rabbit firmly in her mouth.

Bob clicks Blue in and takes the rabbit from her mouth. We go across to pick up the other rabbit, it's there laid dead on the ground, that quick shake of the rabbit from Blue killed it. I see Pup come into the light, she has a big fat rabbit in her mouth. I quickly pop the rabbits on top of the other rabbits in my big poacher's pockets. We now move on again.

Bob flashed the light again and I remember what happened next caused absolute chaos.

I see a whole host of rabbits up on the hillside. Blue sees them all and she's pulling that hard she's nearly pulling Bob's arm out of its socket. I see a rabbit flash by past us, Pup sees it and she's off like a bullet out of a gun after it. Blue's that excited she snatches once too hard, the slipper lead snaps and Blue's off up that hillside like a shot as she follows Pup chasing the rabbit. It's heading straight for a whole host of rabbits on the hillside. Bob's cursing like hell at his bad luck that the dogs have got away, but he still keeps the light trained on the rabbit and both dogs.

I don't believe it. I see some horses come galloping across the front of us lit up by Bob's flashlight. I see Pup and Blue, and the rabbit they are chasing runs smack into the middle of all the rabbits. Now I see mayhem. Pup and Blue and all the mad crazy horses go stampeding among all the rabbits. I can see the rabbits eyes popping out when they see what's suddenly come upon them. I see rabbits scattering and leaping everywhere, I see the horses lashing and kicking out with their back legs at the dogs, I fear the worst. Horses can and will kill dogs, especially when they are in an agitated frenzy, like they are now. I have trained Pup to keep away from horses, training her to give the horses a wide berth as she runs around them.

Let's see if my training has paid off. I see the shell-shocked rabbits, they are panicking, they don't know where to run to find safety. I see one rabbit run straight into the jaws of Blue, I see her give it a quick shake and drop it and the rabbit lays kicking itself to death on the ground. I see horses come charging in to get Blue and I see Pup come racing into view in the lamplight. She's racing between the horses and Blue and if I hadn't have known better I would have said Pup was trying to distract the horses from Blue. Both dogs disappear into the darkness and Bob can't shine the light on the dogs because the horses are in his way. I tell Bob to turn the light off, it will give the dogs a better chance if the horses can't see them. With the light now off, we stand there in the darkness of the pitch black night.

The wind is fair blowing hard across the hillside and we hear rabbits screaming in the near vicinity. That's the dogs killing rabbits. One of the horses comes up to us nuzzling us with his

"Run Like The Wind"

nose. I take hold of his head collar and pat and stroke him, he's now settled down. More horses come across to me and Bob and we take hold of them by their head collars. Bob says that they are the Laird's horses, and he has turned them out into this meadow without telling him.

The horses are all around us by now and they have all settled down by the looks of them. By the sounds of it the dogs are okay also. I keep hearing rabbits screaming as me and Bob are holding three of the horses with the other horses around us. Bob says, "There's a paddock across yonder, let's see if we can get the horses into there." So we set off leading these three horses by their heads and to our luck the rest of the horses follow on behind.

As we are heading across to the paddock we keep on hearing rabbits screaming, the dogs are catching well by the sounds of them.

We get to the paddock, Bob opens the wooden five-barred gate and into the paddock the horses do go and Bob secures the gate behind them. We now head on back up the hillside, back towards the dogs. Bob picks up a dead rabbit, he feels at it and says, "It's still warm, the dogs have just killed it and left it." Bob hands me the rabbit to carry.

As we head on up the hillside, I am trying to get the rabbit into my big poacher's pockets in my coat, but it wont fit in, the pockets are already bulging full with rabbits. Bob stops and waits for me to catch him up, he's now handing me another three rabbits he's picked up. I now have that many rabbits upon me and my hands full I cannot keep up with Bob. To my relief I see Pup come into the light of Bob's lamp and I beckon her to me and keep her at heel.

Bob sees I am laden down with rabbits and he says, "You stay there, I will go find Blue," and on that he disappears over a small hill. Me and Pup must have been sat there for ages in the darkness on the hillside when my ears prick up, it's Bob shouting at Blue. I look behind me and I see Bob's light flashing about everywhere, he's having difficulty holding the lamp straight by the looks of it. I hear Blue racing down by my side in the darkness, I hear her panting like hell as she passes me by. I can hear Bob shouting like hell, "Blue, Blue, come here Blue." He flashes his light zigzagging it across me and manages to flash his light on Blue. She has a live rabbit in her mouth, I click her to me and she hands me the rabbit. I look back and Bob's flashlight is still flashing around everywhere,

I think to myself, what's up with the man?

Bob finally gets to me, both his arms are full of rabbits that the dogs have killed and which he's picked up, and he has the lamp balancing in his fingertips. I help Bob sort out his rabbits and laden him down. Now we are both laden down with rabbits as we head down off the hillside.

Once we reach the low lying pastures we head on towards Bob's cottage not far away. I have Pup close by my side and Bob has Blue back on the now tied back together baling band slipper lead. We don't want anymore rabbits, we have as many as we can carry.

I remember what happened next was my first ever experience with a dog. Bob was shining a light to see where we were going in the blackness of the night.

He keeps flashing the light around the grass pastures as we go and the light picks up a pair of eyes in the sivs. Bob says, "It's an old ewe." That's a female sheep and ewe in slang is pronounced as 'yow'. It's eyes are sparkling and shining as it peered out of the sivs and into the light's beam.

"It's a fox," I whisper to Bob. The sparkling, shining eyes disappear into the sivs and I see Bob getting himself all agitated. I say in a whisper, "Have I to go get the gun?" Bob's cottage is only a couple of hundred yards away by now. Bob Looks at me, I see his face in the glimmering shade of the light, he shakes his head to me and says, in a low whisper, "No, the lurcher will take him." We move off slowly towards the sivs. I see Blue start pulling hard on the slipper lead, I see her pick her nose up into the air, she's scenting the wind, which is blowing straight into our faces. That's to our benefit, the fox will not be able to pick up our scent. Blue is now pulling so hard she's nearly pulling Bob's arm out of its socket as she's picking up the scent of the fox. I thought to myself, this dog's done this all before. I could tell that by her body actions.

As we reach the sivs they drop down into a gulley and I keep Pup close by my side, I don't want her messing things up. Bob shines the spot beam light down into the gulley, I sense an eerie silence down there, we see nothing. Bob flashes the light beam around but there's still nothing to be seen. Me and Bob know there's a fox down there somewhere, it can't be anywhere else but down in the gulley.

I smell the strong, pungent scent of fox in the wind and, as Bob is flashing the light around, we see a rabbit come scurrying out of some sivs. The rabbit looks panic-stricken and that tells me and Bob there's something about down there. Bob says, in a low whisper, "Go down there with Pup and try to flush the fox out." As I get myself into the bottom of the gulley, Bob is shining the light so that I can see where I am going, it's rough ground down there and I could easily fall and do myself an injury. Bob keeps leaving me in the dark as he shines the light around watching for the fox to do a runner.

Pup's hunting around in the sivs. If there's a fox in there Pup will find it, she has a good nose on her but she's no foxing dog.

Pup's now hunting in the sivs where the rabbit just scurried from and she's getting herself all excited. Her tail's wagging away like hell and she has her nose hard to the ground. In the shadow of the lamp's light I see something flash out at the far side of the sivs. Bob flashes the light on it, it's the fox.

It heads along the bottom of the gulley, just like a phantom in the night as it's making its escape. I hear Bob shout to the lurcher, "At it lass!"

I'm now all in the darkness, Bob's forgot all about me. I oh so carefully grope my way back up the side of the gulley. I keep Pup by my side, I don't want her to mess up the fox chase. I am eager to watch, I have never seen a fox coursed by a lurcher before.

As I reach the top of the gulley, Bob is there flashing the light around. I see he's slipped Blue, but I don't see her. Bob says, "She's gone over the bank chasing the fox." He no sooner said that than he picks up the lurcher in the lamp's beam, she's racing hell for leather across the grass field. Bob flashes the light in front of her, there it is, the fox. Blue is catching up the fox fast.

These grass fields where we are, they are flat with no fences around, this is ideal for coursing.

Blue is now upon the fox, it stops and turns, bares it teeth and scowls at the lurcher. That doesn't seem to bother Blue, she goes straight in and makes a grab at the fox. As she grabs, the fox jumps into the air and Blue goes tippling head over tail. The fox is up and away, and Blue is up and back on her feet in the flash of an eye.

Bob follows both of them with the light, he purposely keeps the light out of Blue's eyes, he doesn't want to dazzle her, and yet again Blue is back on the fox's tail. Me and Bob are racing across the field trying to keep up with the chase. Blue grabs at the fox and the fox grabs at Blue.

By the time me and Bob get on over there, Blue and the fox are tightly locked together, they both have each other by the throat. As they both lay there the fox is scowling and chomping hard with its razor-sharp teeth, Blue is gripping hard and growling. There's blood and snot coming from them as neither will let go. As they both lay there, I can hear their throats gurgling as they try to draw breath.

Me and Bob look at each other. Pup is scowling and shaking behind me and I say to Bob, "What do we do now?" Bob says, "There's only one thing we can do. You grab hold of the fox by the back end and I will grab hold of the lurcher and we'll drag them back to the cottage."

Bob's cottage is by now only just across the grass field we are in. I say to Bob, "But, what are you going to do then, when we get there?" Bob says, "I am going to shoot the fox then when I get my rifle, that will make the fox let go of the lurcher."

So I grab the fox by the tail. He didn't like that, he's fair hissing blood at me, but he wouldn't let go of Blue's throat. Too right he wouldn't, that would have been certain death to him.

Bob now grabs the lurcher by the tail and off we go manhandling them both across the field. We both struggled as we dragged both of them along, both the lurcher and the fox objected and dug in their feet, both were scowling and growling at each other. The harder we dragged them the harder each bit into the other's throats, neither was going to release their death-defying grip.

As me and Bob fumbled along in the darkness of the night, Bob had his lamp turned on, but what good it was I don't know. He had it tucked under his arm while he used both hands to hold the lurcher and the lamp was shining up in the air most of the time.

Now I got to thinking as we struggled along toward the cottage, the fox didn't deserve to be shot with a bullet in the head. It was brave enough to fight and tackle a big dog like the lurcher, Blue was three times the size of the fox. In my mind the fox deserved a decent escape but I knew it wouldn't do any good trying to convince Bob of that. So as me and Bob struggled along, with the lurcher and the fox objecting all the way as we went, I am silently scheming and plotting to myself how I can release the fox without Bob realizing it.

As we started across rough rocky ground, I stumbled upon a boulder, I reckoned to slip and fall, and as I fell I gave the fox one almighty yank on its tails. With the fox gripping hard on the lurcher's throat, this caused the lurcher to stumble forwards, and this in turn caused Bob to stumble forward. Bob tripped himself and over he fell, dropping with his full bodyweight on top of the lurcher. As the lurcher gives out an almighty yelp it opened its mouth, which released its death-defying grip on the fox's throat. At the same time as I was falling on purpose I sunk my teeth deep into the stump of the fox's tail. The fox screamed blue murder with what I've just done to it and this made the fox open its mouth and release the blood-curdling grip on the lurcher's throat.

So with this all happening at once and all at the same time, both the lurcher and the fox released their throat grip at the same time. I now snatched hard at the fox's tail again and this caused the fox to jump towards me. It couldn't get past me so it darted between my thighs, and as it went through it panicked and sank its razor-sharp teeth deep into my ankle. I looked back behind me and I saw the fox in the dim light of the night. He was off like a bat out of hell as he made his escape.

The lurcher sets off after the fox. By now Bob's picked himself up off the ground, he's got the lamp in his hand and he has the light's beam on the escaping fox. But it's too late, the fox comes to a five foot stone wall and without even hesitating, the fox runs and climbs the wall. All at the same time, as it reaches the top, Blue jumps up at it snapping her jaws at the fox, but it's too late, the fox disappears over the wall.

I see Bob shining the lamp over the stone wall but, alas, we never found that fox. And that was my first ever encounter with a lurcher dog coursing the fox at night.

We now head back to Bob's cottage. The rabbits that we have just caught I hang them up in Bob's game larder together with the rabbits I long-netted the night before, and not forgetting Helen's rabbits that she gave me.

The evening has passed on by well and it's by now a few hours after dark. Those rabbits down at the forestry tree plantation will by now have had plenty of time to get well out on to their feeding grounds.

This is going to be my final night long-netting and then it's homeward bound for me and Pup. I look up into the sky and it's thick with cloud, really overcast, and the north wind is still blowing as hard as ever. A most perfect night for long-netting rabbits.

My long nets and all my gear I now put into my Land Rover and off me and Pup do go. I go up Bob's private driveway to the top of the hill and then drop down the hill at the other side which takes me to the quiet country road. This then takes me past the place where my friend Barry the wagon driver used to pick me up, the part of the forest where my bivouac is.

It was all along the other side of this forestry plantation that I long-netted the rabbits the night before, so I carry on for a good distance along the quiet country lane. I want to bypass where I long-netted last night and get myself on to a new breed of rabbits, new territory so to speak.

I now come to another ride which runs through another part of the forestry plantation and I drive along this ride which takes me deep into the forest and on to the other side of the woodland. This is where the rabbits are that I am going to long-net tonight. They will be well out on the grass meadow feeding by now, so I park my Land Rover in the woodland for the night. I leave Pup in the Land Rover as per usual when I am long-netting.

I remember I carried on that night and had two good successful drops, getting myself two good bags of rabbits.

On the third drop, my last drop of the night, I had been around the feeding grounds with my rope and when I got back to my net I hadn't many rabbits caught in my first net. I ran along the net killing the few rabbits I had caught and set off along my second net. I saw something caught, it was far too big for a rabbit, and its kicking and fighting was really making the net bounce and shake. In the gloom of the night it was hard to tell what it was but as I got myself upon it my nose told what it was, there was a really strong smell of fox. I had caught old Snagglepus in the net and he was kicking up a right old fight as he fought the net. I left him be for a while to quieten down a little and I carried on down the net killing the few rabbits I had caught. I don't always get it all my own way when I am long-netting rabbits, anything can go across them rabbits and spook them before I get there, such as this fox, he had spooked these rabbits in tonight. Billy the badger may go across them and spook them in or maybe a big owl, so I do expect poor kills sometimes.

Over the years of long-netting rabbits I have had several foxes in the nets, and badgers, and I have had cats and pheasants. One night I remember I got a whole covey of partridges tangled up in my nets, that was a bonus for me was that. I have even had sheep all tangled up in the nets, they usually smash the nets to smithereens.

The hedgehog is the worst thing to catch in the long net. He will get all tangled up and then ball up, trapping the net inside his balled-up belly. What a job it is trying to get him out of the net.

I now made my way back along the net to the netted, captured fox, hoping he may have escaped by now, but alas, there he was all tangled up in the net. I stood there watching him fight the net.

I grabbed him by the tail pulling hard at him, hoping it would pull him free and I could then let him be on his way. There was no chance, the net was all tangled around his legs and in his toes. It was also all tangled in his mouth and around his head, he was well and truly netted.

As I pulled and tugged at his tail he somehow turned and grabbed hold of my foot and his four needle-sharp fangs sank deep into my foot. I only had light footwear on and he kept a firm hold on my foot and wouldn't let go. The pain was bringing tears to my eyes and I had to get his fangs out of my foot somehow, otherwise I would be there while Bob came looking for me. I had a thick, felt-type jumper on, so I took my jumper off and threw it over the fox's head. I then grabbed hold of his muzzle with my hands safely on the outside of my jumper and I forced my fingers in between his teeth and tried to force this jaws apart. But the harder I forced his jaws apart the harder he sank his teeth into my foot. He was wreathing and writhing and fighting and kicking the net all at the same time. The old fellow was panic-stricken.

I forced my fingers deeper into his mouth and I could feel his razor-sharp teeth penetrating through my thick jumper. He crunched his grip even harder and I felt terrible pain as his teeth sank deep into my fingers. I gave one almighty pull and parted his locked jaws and my foot was now free of his fangs. I quickly pulled my foot out of his mouth and all at the same time I pulled my fingers out of his mouth and jumped away double quick before he had time to grab again. I jumped away that fast I ended up on my bruised backside. I could hear blood and snot coming out of the fox's nose, he'd gone into a frenzy.

He'd gone berserk as he struggled and bounced about in the net. Now I was free I made sure not to go near him again. With the long-netting of these rabbits now over, I hobbled away and went to pick up my Land Rover, nursing my bitten fingers as I went.

I drove to the scene of the netted fox and I shone my headlights on him. He was still a balled-up mess as he lay tangled in the net, his eyes staring and sparkling like diamonds in the Land Rover headlights.

There was nothing else I could do, so I fetched the .22 rifle out of the Land Rover, put the end of the barrel to the back of his ear and pulled the trigger. All fell motionless and silent and after quite a struggle I managed to untangle him from the net. I put the fox in the back of the Land Rover for Bob to hang up in his courtyard for his boss, the Laird of the estate, to see.

This hung-up fox now tells the Laird Bob is doing his fox control properly.

I now carry on and empty the nets of the few rabbits they have caught then I pick up my nets and put them in the Land Rover, the night's long-netting rabbits now over.

How I have explained all this long-netting, 'pegging' is the slang term for it, it may all sound easy but I can assure you it is not. It's a fine art is the setting of a long net.

In my early years of learning to set the long net I have had it in terrible tangles, so badly tangled I have had to go home without even catching a single rabbit. But as time went by, by learning to run the long nets out in the daytime, that's so that I can see what I am doing, and teaching myself how to put angles in the net, this allows the long net to go around corners and around contours of the woodlands, after many, many hours practice and the keen willpower and interest to learn I eventually learnt the skills and the fine art of setting long nets.

Using the long rope is the best way to bring rabbits in off their feeding grounds and into the long nets. Some people may have used a dog to hunt out the rabbits, but any rabbits laying tight squat in the grass the dog may easily pass by, oblivious of them being in the grass. The long rope misses none.

I now go around and pick up the rabbits I caught earlier, and as I am driving along I am picking off rabbits with the rifle as they sit in the beam of the headlights.

By the time it breaks daylight I have a fine bag of rabbits to show for my night's hard work.

I now head off to Bob's flight pond to paunch the rabbits and throw the rabbits' guts into the pond for the wild duck to feed on. As I approach the flight pond, I remember the geese I saw the morning before and I decided to see if I could pick one off with my rifle. It will be a treat for me and Bob to have a goose for dinner tonight.

I pull the Land Rover up short of the pond. There's a lall hill just before the flight pond and I stalk along to the pond keeping myself low at the back of the lall hill. I creep to the top of the hill and peep over, and there they are, a whole flock of greylag sat on the pond, they are about seventy-five yards away from me. I slowly slide the rile up and rest it on top of the bank and pick out a big fat goose in the rifle's scope. But he's sat at the wrong angle, he's facing straight at me as he's sat on the water. If I shoot now the powerful bullet will pass through deep into his body and damage his flesh.

I lay patiently and wait for him to turn side on, I am going to place the bullet into the base of his neck, just where the neck joins the body. That's a deadly point on his body as the bullet will cut his windpipe in two. I see the goose slowly turn his body broadside on and I quickly get him into my scope and put the cross hairs on to his neck. He's now bang in the right position and I gently squeeze the trigger. The silencer on the rifle works well, all I hear is a muffled shot, and the goose is down and flapping its wings like crazy on the water. The rest of the geese fly up in alarm. Off they go into the sky honking their heads off as they go.

I look back and I see my goose now lays still on the water. As I stand up on the bank and look down to the flight pond I see what looks like a shooting butt. I go down to take a closer look and I see it's a well built 'sunken butt', it's been stoned out to ground level. It's so well camouflaged into its background I only noticed it because I was looking down on it from the banking top. I walk around the edge of the flight pond, I see more butts all sunken into the ground.

There's five butts in all, all surrounding the flight pond. I notice mink scats as I go around, that's droppings, and as I look up a gulley that runs up into the peat hags, I see two bins concealed in the banking side. I see they are full of wheat and down by the side of the bins I see a mink cage trap set. It has a piece of jointed rabbit inside it for bait.

So it looks as though Bob is feeding this flight pond with corn to attract in wild ducks and geese. I cast my eyes across the pond, I keep meaning to have a word with Bob about this pond.

I now bring my Land Rover to the pond side to where I can paunch my rabbits. I send Pup out to retrieve the goose off the water, Pup is a good all-round dog for the field work, I have taught her to do most jobs.

I watch Pup head out and grab the big fat greylag goose. It's that big she's having a struggle to swim with it in her mouth.

It may interest you readers to know the greylag goose is the ancestor of all domesticated geese, all except the Chinese Goose, which is a different breed of goose altogether. It may also be of interest to you that I was once told that the temperature of a wild duck's feet is 'absolute zero', and to me that appears to be true. The wild duck can stand roosting on ice on a lake, and can stand in that same place without moving and its feet do not melt the ice and fall through. And also the wild duck can stand there in the same position without moving and its feet do not stick to the ice. So to me, what I was told appears to be true, and also it seems to me, if a wild duck can do that, a wild goose must be the same.

Pup's now back with the greylag goose and I now have all my rabbits paunched and all the guts thrown into the pond for the wild ducks and geese to feast themselves on. I now head off across country back to Bob's place. When I get back Bob gives my bag of rabbits the once over. He sees the brush (tail) of the fox sticking out from underneath the pile of rabbits and he pulls it out and holds it up high. I look at Bob's face and he has a smile that stretches from 'ear to lug'. He goes eagerly to hang it up in the courtyard.

Bob now sees the goose and his eyes light up and sparkle. He says, "You pluck, I will cook."

I take my bag of rabbits to hang up in the game larder and I see the larder's nearly full again. Bob's had a party of guns out grouse shooting. I see three red deer hung up also. Bob had also been out with a deerstalker shooting a deer or two. So Bob had also been keeping himself busy.

My job now is to pluck that goose ready for dinner this evening. It is a fine big fat goose and it weighs out at just over six pounds. There's enough here for three of us so I should really invite Helen to dinner, she may well give me a farewell kiss before I leave for home in the morning.

With me being out long-netting rabbits all night long I was feeling a little tired so off I go to get a few hours sleep. I didn't seem to have my eyes shut for very long when I was awakened by screaming pigs, and that was enough to get me up out of bed. I look at the clock on the mantelpiece, it's twelve o'clock midday, I have had just two hours sleep. I go out into the courtyard and I see

Bob is feeding the pigs, that's what the pigs are squealing for. Bob sees me up bright and fresh again and he asks me if I will give him a helping hand, me replying saying, "What, with feeding the pigs?" Bob replies, "No, I want you to hold them while I cut them." This word 'cut' is a slang term for castration. I agree to help Bob.

Bob now has a saucepan full of boiling water in one hand and a bottle of antiseptic lotion in his other hand, and off we both go into the pig hole (sty). It's a litter of ten-week-old piglets Bob is going to castrate.

I ask Bob why he castrates them and he says, "As the young male pigs grow older they begin to come sexually active and they try to mount the young 'gilts', which is female pigs. This continuation of repeated mounting helps reduce the weight of the young male piglets. So I remove their knackers which then takes away the piglets' sexual urges, which then allows the piglets to grow fast and put on weight."

I hear a quad bike come into the courtyard and I peer over the pig hole door. It's Helen, she's arrived for her goose dinner.

Bob grabs hold of one of the male piglets and tells me to let the pig stand in between my legs. I now grab hold of the pig's legs, one leg in each hand, and I now have to hold the pig firmly by nipping my knees tight into the pig. The piglet's knackers are now exposed.

I hear a titter, it's Helen watching us over the pig hole door. Bob's now reaching into the saucepan of boiling water and he pulls out a razor blade. The boiling water has now killed all the germs on the razor blade and Bob's now smearing antiseptic lotion on the piglet's exposed knackers, due to me holding the piglet's legs apart.

Bob's now squeezing one of the knacker pouches taut so the skin is now tightly stretched and, with the hands of a surgeon, Bob makes a small incision into the knacker pouch. A little extra squeeze from Bob's hand and out pops a knacker. Bob throws the knacker over the pig hole door and Helen ducks to one side so that she doesn't get the knacker in her face.

The knacker no sooner disappears over the pig hole door, when I hear a chomp, just like a set of teeth snapping together. Helen can see what I can't see at the other side of the pig hole door, but she keeps looking at me and tittering.

This piglet in my hands has now been castrated. There is hardly any blood coming from where Bob made his surgical incision.

Bob now smears everything over with antiseptic lotion, to

prevent infection, and I release the piglet. Off it goes shaking its tail and puts its nose straight into the pig trough full of pig meal.

It appeared to be no problem at all for the piglet.

Me and Bob now pressed on and castrated the other piglets, and each and every one of the knackers went over the top of the pig hole door, and each and every time I heard a chomp just like teeth snapping shut. I look to see what Helen keeps tittering at.

I look over the pig hole door and then I see what Helen sees, it's her sheepdog. It's been catching the knackers and swallowing them whole. Bob says to Helen, "If you've come for your goose dinner you are a bit too early." Helen says, "I've come to invite you and Doug down to my place on a woodpigeon shoot." Helen carries on to tell me and Bob there's vast raiding parties of woodpigeon feeding on a game crop of kale.

Me and Bob jump at the idea of a bit of woodpigeon shooting and we take up Helen's offer.

Helen says, "We have to act fast while the woodpigeon are feeding ravenously." Helen carries on to say she knows where the woodpigeon are roosting overnight so we can do a bit of roost shooting also.

The time now was just turned one o'clock in the afternoon. It doesn't get dark while five o'clock time so that gives us a couple of hours of shooting the woodpigeon on the kale and finishing off the evening shooting them as they come into the woodland to roost.

We arrange to meet Helen shortly down by the kale field, and off Helen goes on her quad bike. I watch Helen go way out into the distance across the low-lying glen and I see her climb that mountainside, what Helen and Bob call a lall hill, and watch Helen disappear over the top.

I turn around and I see Bob has got his twelve bore shotgun strung over his shoulder. He has a bag of something in one hand and an even bigger bag of something else in his other hand. He throws everything into his Land Rover and I head off to get my twelve bore from out of my Land Rover and a spade?

By now Bob's pulled his Land Rover right up in front of his cottage and he's carrying four boxes of cartridges out of the cottage and putting them into his Land Rover. Each box contains twenty-five cartridges. Bob's now coming out with another eight boxes of cartridges.

I say to Bob, "It looks as though you intend to do a lot of shooting." Bob nods. Now Bob's heading back into the cottage, he says he's putting the goose dinner into the oven to let it cook slowly. "That will now be ready by teatime," says Bob.

Me and Bob now head off in his Land Rover and on towards that kale field down on Helen's place. It's not a long drive, just around a few narrow country lanes which takes us around that mountainside, or that lall hill. When we arrive at the field edge, where the kale is, Helen is already there waiting for us. There's not a woodpigeon to be seen anywhere. Helen has her shotgun under her arm and all three of us walk into the field. The kale is about two foot high, it is a type of cabbage plant and it has been grown as a supplement feed for Bob's pheasants and also a winter feed for Helen's flock of sheep. The harsh winter winds and snow have laid it flat in places. Helen is dumbfounded as to where all the woodpigeon have gone to.

I shout to Helen, "Watch out!" as a couple of woodpigeon come flying low over the tops of the hedgerow. Helen quickly pulls her twelve bore to her shoulder, a quick right and left and both woodpigeon are dead in the air together.

The bangs from her gun were unbelievable. Now literally hundreds of woodpigeon clatter up into the air and the sky has turned from sky blue to woodpigeon blue. There must be more than two thousand pigeon circling over the field, they were all out of sight when we arrived feeding at the bottom of the kale.

Now to get ourselves established for a good woodpigeon shoot. By now all the woodpigeon have disappeared out of sight. Helen has two big bags with her and I stand and watch. Bob's now coming into the field with his two bigger bags. Helen and Bob separate themselves by about sixty yards apart, and I stand there watching them both. I have my keen eyes watching distant woodpigeon as they fly backwards and forwards at the far side of the kale field. I am trying to locate the woodpigeons' flight path.

I look at Helen and then Bob, they have by now put up their own camouflage nets in the hedgerow.

I look across the kale field, by now I have seen a lot of woodpigeon keeping on the same line as they drop into the kale to feed at the far side of the field. I notice a lot of woodpigeon settling into a large solitary old oak tree, there they can scan the area for danger approaching.

I look back at Helen and Bob, I see them putting out their woodpigeon decoys. They are using two different types of decoy.

Helen's decoys are of a flat type made purposely so that they can all be stacked together taking up very little space. Helen is positioning on a laid patch of the kale. Her decoys are fitted onto a stem which is stuck into the ground holding the decoy raised up. The wind can now lift the decoy which allows it to move slightly, making the decoy look lifelike to the unaware woodpigeon.

I look at Bob who's further on up the field. The decoys he is setting are of a full-bodied bird, these are bulky decoys which takes a large sack to put them all in. Bob lays his decoys on another laid patch of kale, they are just positioned on the ground making it look as though they are feeding. All Helen's decoys and all Bob's decoys are all positioned facing into the wind, that's the natural way woodpigeon feed.

As I now look across both sets of decoys everything looks so convincing. I look for Helen and Bob, but they are nowhere to be seen, they have just vanished into thin air. Then I hear Bob shout, "Doug, Doug!" and now I see him and Helen further along the hedgerow. All I can see is their peeping eyes from within their camouflage nets. Bob says, "Go make yourself a hide somewhere."

So I go and grab my twelve bore and as many of Bob's cartridges as I can stuff into all my pockets. I also grab my spade and take that along with me, and off I go to the other side of the kale field.

I have no decoys like Helen and Bob, neither do I have a camouflage net, I have to make do with what I have got, that's nothing.

I head towards the old solitary oak tree which I have been observing, there's some sort of woodpigeon flight path there by the looks of it. I am by now about sixty yards away from the old oak tree, there's some laid kale there, this is where I will position my hide.

Just at the edge of the laid kale and where the kale grows two foot high, I make my hide. In between the standing kale I dig in with my spade, the soil is soft and easy digging. As my hole gets deeper and deeper, and by putting all the soil I dig around the edge of my hole, the hole I dig is now getting deeper twice as fast.

My hole is now dug in double quick time and my full body is now in my hole with just my arms, shoulders and head above the level of the ground. I now have the freedom to move my arms to shoot my gun, but I am now also concealed out of sight of the roving woodpigeons' eyes by the two foot growing kale all around me.

I now load my twelve bore shotgun and wait for the woodpigeon to arrive. As I peer through the kale into the skies above me I see a solitary woodpigeon fly in, it perches in the old oak tree not far away from me.

I keep myself motionless, I must not let the woodpigeon see me, he's scanning the field around him, he thinks everything looks at peace. He now takes off again and unknowingly flies low over my head. I leave him be, he carries on and circles the field of kale, and off he disappears into the distance. He will be back, he's gone to pass on the message to the other woodpigeons that all appears safe. That woodpigeon is what we call a 'scout'.

I stay still and wait, but I don't wait for very long before I hear a flock of woodpigeon clattering their wings as they settle in the old oak tree. I stay still and wait, and I get my thumb on to the hammer of my gun. I am eager for action to take place. The twelve bore which I am shooting is my old faithful gun. The time in my life when I was coming up here to this massive Laird's estate high up in the Grampian Mountains in Scotland I was only in my twenties.

I remember acquiring this gun, it was back in 1966 when I was only seventeen. At that time I used to go the livestock market every Saturday with my father. My father was always dealing, with pigs and horses mainly, but he would buy and deal with almost any livestock such as cattle, sheep, goats, donkeys. You offer them for sale and after a lot of bartering and hand-slapping my father would buy them. Every time we would go to this livestock market I would always find time to go up into the city centre to a well-established gun shop. There were always many, many guns there, all in gun racks in long rows along the walls. You could pick them up and test them to your shoulder to see if they fitted you well.

I remember that Saturday when I was there back in 1966 I saw a twelve bore on the gun rack and it instantly caught my eye. I picked it up and pulled it to my shoulder, it fitted me to perfection. It was what they call a game gun with twenty-eight inch barrels It had a well-grained walnut butt and the engraving it had on and around the hammers was out this world. I had to have this gun. I saw the gun shop owner and he wanted thirty-three pounds for it. That was a lot of money in those days. I had no money in my pockets, but I told the gun shop owner I knew where I could get some money, and as I rushed out of the shop I told the man, "Don't sell it, I will be back."

I raced back to the livestock market and I saw my father, he was just paying someone out for a gallower (a slang name for a horse) he'd just bought. My father had a great wad of notes in his hand. I told him about the gun and my father played holy hell with me for wanting such an expensive gun.

Now ever since I was a young lad and still at school my father always had more than two hundred pigs in the yard back home, and every morning I would muck out the pig hole (sties) before I went to school. My father was always a bad payer of wages, so instead of him paying me he would give me some small pigs. When eventually they would be big and fat and ready for market, I would then get paid for what the pigs made at the livestock market.

I had my pigs in at the market that day and they had made thirty pounds, so my father reluctantly paid me.

So, off I rush back to the gun shop and I offer the gun shop owner only the thirty pounds that I have. He refuses, he wants the full thirty-three pounds for the gun. At that time I only had a fold-up four-ten shotgun which I would poach with. I offered the four-ten 'to boot' together with my thirty pounds in exchange for the twelve bore.

The gun shop owner appears interested but wants to see the four-ten shotgun. That's hidden in my father's motor down at the livestock market together with a brace of pheasants and a hare I shot out of the motor window on our way to market this morning.

So off I rush out of the gun shop to fetch the four-ten, telling the gun shop owner as I go not to sell the gun.

I have the four-ten hidden behind the door panel of my father's motor. I break the four-ten into two halves which are held together by a hinge in the middle. I slot the barrel down my coat sleeve and rest the butt of the gun up the side of my body. I now close up my coat and now you can't even tell at all, that's why they call the fold-up four-ten a poacher's gun.

Off I rush back to the gun shop and when the owner sees me he says, "Where's your four-ten then?" I shiftily open up my coat and pull out the four-ten.

The gun shop owner raises his eyebrows as I do so. He's now inspecting my four-ten and he says he will only give me two pounds for it. So I am still a pound short of the thirty-three pounds he wants for the twelve bore I dearly want.

I now scratch my head and have a think. Then I tell the gun shop owner about the brace of pheasants and the hare and he now wants to see them to see if they are fat.

So off I go again and back to the motor at the livestock market. I have my big poacher's coat on and it has a big poacher's pocket stitched inside it. I conceal the two pheasants and hare and close up my coat, and off I rush back to the gun shop. The owner sees me and he says, "Where are they then?" I shiftily open up my coat and pull out a pheasant and as the owner feels to see if it's fat I now hand him the other and then the hare. I have brought a smile to his face, he likes what he sees. Our deal is now clinched and my twelve bore is finally bought.

Over the years I have shot just about everything with that gun. A gunsmith once had a look at my gun and he told me I must look after it well, it was worth a lot of money. He told me 'Roper & Son' made the gun, making only the most select of guns. He felt its lightness and he weighted it, it weighs only six and a quarter pound. He also told me it's one of a pair that had been especially made for a lady. So it appears my twelve bore has got a bit of history to it also. And that is how I acquired my old faithful twelve bore which I now have with me as I am shooting woodpigeon in this field of kale high up in the bonny glens of the Laird's massive estate in Scotland.

As I am there patiently waiting for the raiding woodpigeon to arrive on the kale field where I stand in my man-made dug-out hole, I peer through the kale and there's still about twenty woodpigeon sat perched in the old oak tree not far away. From where I hide, I could easily shoot one or two of them as they sit there, but that's not very proper is it.

I hear fluttering wings behind me, I look back, and it's a great flock of woodpigeons. They have caught me off guard and have landed in the kale right at the back of me. Then I see another great flock coming over the boundary of the kale field.

They appear to drift sharpishly over towards Helen and Bob who are concealed in the hedgerow behind their camouflage nets. Is it their decoys that are luring the woodpigeon in? I hear a double bang of a twelve bore go off and I see two woodpigeon fall from the sky. I see the flock scatter and spread out and I hear another double bang go off and yet another two woodpigeon fall from the sky. It looks as though Helen and Bob are on good shooting form. The bangs from their guns startle the woodpigeon again me, them in the old oak tree and those that had settled in behind me. They all scattered in panic. Now I have woodpigeon everywhere above my head.

I quickly pull both hammers back on my faithful old twelve bore and butt it into shoulder. A quick double shot and two woodpigeon come tumbling down to earth.

The other woodpigeon don't see me hidden in the kale and they continue to circle the field around me. I quickly reload and yet another two woodpigeon come tumbling from the sky. I hear shot after shot coming from Helen and Bob and I see dead woodpigeon raining out of the sky around them.

Now the woodpigeon are coming in on to the kale field in a constant stream. They are feeding hard, they are ravenously hungry. The bitter cold weather we are having on this day is why the woodpigeon are raiding the kale. It's a well known fact amongst shooting men that whenever the woodpigeon are feeding hard like they are here today, if the shooting men keep themselves out of sight of the woodpigeons' roving eyes they will keep on coming in, appearing oblivious to the banging guns. And me, Bob and Helen did do this and the woodpigeon kept on coming in one constant stream and we kept on shooting raining pigeon out of the sky. By now we had many woodpigeon laid dead on the kale field around us.

There came a lull in the woodpigeon feeding, there's not one to be seen around anywhere. I take this golden opportunity to go quickly out and set up a few decoys for myself. I gather up half a dozen dead woodpigeon and go to the hedgerow and break a few twigs from the bushes.

I am going to set my decoys where the kale is laid flat to the ground where the passing woodpigeon can see them. I get one of my dead woodpigeon and push a twig deep up its backside, I now face the woodpigeon into the wind, which is the natural way, and push the other half of my lengthy twig into the ground. Now the twig is helping to hold up the pigeon. I now get another lengthy twig and push it into the ground, the other half of the lengthy twig is pushed deep down the woodpigeons throat which now holds my pigeon upright, now my woodpigeon is stood there looking all natural and that. It only takes just a few minutes to set up my half a dozen decoys and back to my dig-in hole I go. I peer back through the kale at my decoys, they look lifelike.

I now keep myself still and wait for the woodpigeon to start coming back in. As I am scanning the sky with my beady eyes I see woodpigeon coming. They are high in the sky and I watch them circle the field of kale. They are now passing overhead and they look just in range to me. Up I jump and let fire at the leading bird. I miss, but keeping my twelve to my shoulder I drop my sights onto a bird at the back of the flock and I take a more careful aim.

This time I am more accurate, the bird comes spinning down out of the sky. It looks as though it's a lucky pellet that has hit it in the head.

I turn and I see a big flock coming in low over the hedgerow. They are passing close on down by my side. I lock my gun on to the leading bird and fire and to my surprise two birds fold up and hit the deck. I drop another bird with a snap shot as they head out across the field of kale, they are heading straight for Helen and Bob. I hear repeated bangs as the woodpigeon pass over their heads. I see woodpigeon dropping out of the flock here, there and everywhere.

That was a lucky shot of mine to drop two woodpigeon with one shot, you have to be accurate to get one with one shot. There's about three hundred pellets in a twelve bore cartridge shell, all depending on what size shot you are firing, and with all these pellets it may sound easy to hit a bird, but I can assure you it's not. I hear more banging coming from Bob and Helen and I peer through the kale.

Their woodpigeon are now heading directly to me and at the last moment I pick up and fire. The bird crumples and as I watch it I don't like what I see, it's heading straight for me! I duck low as the woodpigeon passes just over my head, the draught from it parting my hair, and it drops that close on to me I reach out and pick it up.

I turn and see another big party of raiding woodpigeon arriving, they are way out to one side of me. They turn, they have seen my decoys and they are down on the ground in an instance. I watch them and I don't think they like what they see. It's their dead mates now and they can tell they are dead. It spooks them and up they all rise and I get off a quick double shot at them. I hear bang, bang, banging coming from Helen and Bob and I keep replying bang, bang, back to them. There's woodpigeon in the sky all around us. It's now just one big frenzy of shooting. There's woodpigeon raining out of the sky as they are folding up to the banging guns.

I look across the kale field and I don't believe what I see. It's Helen and Bob, they have come out of hiding from behind their camouflage nets. That's spoiled the day, now the woodpigeon have seen them they are dispersing and the marauding, raiding woodpigeon have gone. That was a bad mistake on Bob and Helen's behalf coming out of hiding.

I turn and I see a lone woodpigeon fleeting by my side. I hastily go to pull the hammer back on my gun, it slips off my thumb as the hammer is half back. The gun goes off, I see kale stalk bend and tipple over from the shot from my gun.

That so easily happens with hammer guns, that's why nowadays shotguns are made hammerless. When the safety catch is pulled back, the shotgun is safe.

But when the safety catch is pushed forward both barrels are instantly activated for firing a much safer shotgun when they are hammerless.

My ears prick up, it's Bob whistling from the other side of the kale field. He's shouting to tell me we have packed in and to gather my birds, he's wanting to be off for the roosting woodpigeon shoot.

So up I climb out of my self-dug hole and I quickly fill it back in, we don't want accidents to happen do we. Now to pick up the dead woodpigeon that are scattered in close proximity around me. I know when I filled all my pockets with Bob's cartridges I put about fifty in my pockets and I now only have two left. That gives me an idea of how many bird I have to pick up.

This reminds me of a person I once knew. As you readers know, as I write this story, I am in my late fifties, but as I shoot these woodpigeon here now on the Laird's estate I am only in my early twenties so I can now look back in time. This person I knew they called him Alan and he was woodpigeon shooting crazy. He would have people all over the country looking out for woodpigeon feeding hard on certain areas. Once the woodpigeon had been located feeding hard Alan would be notified.

Alan one day received an urgent telephone call. It said woodpigeon seen feeding hard on laid barley, get yourself up here fast. Alan was up and off to that scene double quick.

Alan arrives on the scene at midday. He's shooting by himself and he sets his camouflage net up and lays out his decoys. The woodpigeon come thick and fast all afternoon, they are flying in from three different angles at him. Alan is flat out shooting as the marauding raiding parties of woodpigeon swoop in on to the laid barley. By five o'clock at teatime Alan had shot all his cartridges, so he had to pack in. He knew he had a lot of woodpigeon laying dead out there in the barley, too many for himself alone to pick up. It was summer time and the evening was early, plenty of daylight left yet, so Alan telephones up a local field sport shooting magazine. He tells them about his good afternoon of woodpigeon shooting and it may be a good story for them to put in their magazine. They say they will send out a journalist straightaway. Alan knows he wants several woodpigeon gatherers, one journalist wouldn't be enough. So he tells the editor of the magazine the field out here is a little boggy and if their vehicle gets stuck in the sludge it will want more men to push out their vehicle.

So now Alan waits for the journalists to arrive, and while he waits the woodpigeon keep on streaming in large flocks of raiding parties. Alan playing hell with himself for not bringing enough cartridges.

The journalists duly arrive on the scene and their four-wheel drive vehicle startles all the woodpigeon that are out of sight feeding in the barley bottom. There's just one massive swirling flock of woodpigeon now all in the air together. The sky now is not sky blue but woodpigeon blue.

There's three journalist arrive and Alan shows them where the woodpigeon lay dead out in the barley field. For quite a while the journalists search the barley and gather all the dead woodpigeon. They keep on throwing pile after pile of woodpigeon onto a farm track, and as they throw them down Alan lays them all out in neat tidy lines.

Now all the birds are safely gathered in they are counted, and it's a record bag. Alan now holds the record for woodpigeon shooting. I forget the exact number but it was just over 700. Maybe that record has been broken since, I don't know.

I have more to tell you about Alan later in my story. Now back to these woodpigeon I have shot here on the kale field up here in the Bonny Glens of Scotland.

I gather up about three dozen birds, I think that's what the number was anyway. I now go across the kale field to Bob and Helen where they are gathering up their birds. They have a big pile of birds between them. They have shot far more birds that me. Bob backs his Land Rover into the kale field and right up to the pile of birds. I count them as the birds are being thrown into the back of the Land Rover. If I remember rightly it was a hundred and twenty birds. Put my birds together with them and that takes the bag of woodpigeon to just over a hundred and fifty. Not a bad afternoon's shooting I do think.

Bob's itching to be off woodpigeon roost shooting, so me and Helen jump into the Land Rover alongside Bob. We have around about an hour and half before deep dusk sets in. Helen guides Bob along narrow country lanes as we head on towards where Helen says a lot of woodpigeon are roosting overnight. Helen's now guiding us through a gateway that leads into a grass meadow. "It's a bit boggy in this meadow," I tell Helen.

She says, "It's nothing the Land Rover can't get through." Helen no sooner says that than the Land Rover slides and slithers to a stop. Bob tells me and Helen to get out and push. Helen's sat beside the passenger door and she looks out through the window and sees all the sludge. Helen refuses to budge and I come out in sympathy with Helen, I refuse to budge. So Bob attempts to let the Land Rover get itself out of the sludgy, boggy field.

Bob pulls the red-knobbed lever back in the cab and the Land Rover is now in low gear box and four-wheel drive. It edges itself forward about three inches and then skids to a stop. The tyres want more traction. Bob does this repeatedly, keep putting full lock on the steering wheel edging the Land Rover backwards and forwards. The Land Rover is gradually manoeuvring itself around finding different ground. The rugged, deep-treaded tyres now find good traction ground. It's now gripping and out of the sludge the Land Rover does come, and off we go across the meadow.

I must add, Land Rovers themselves claim the Land Rover is the most versatile vehicle in the world, that was way back in time in 1970. Then along came the smart, posh Range Rover which was the gentleman farmer's Land Rover and since then, as all you readers know, there's now a flood of all different makes of four-wheel drive vehicles made in countries all over the world. Anyway, back to our woodpigeon roost shooting.

We are by now alongside a fir tee plantation and Helen says, "This is where the woodpigeon are roosting overnight." Bob drives the Land Rover into the plantation and parks it up out of sight, we don't want the Land Rover frightening the woodpigeon do we. Again I dip my hands into Bob's cartridge boxes and fill my pockets. We now head off along the woodland side with our twelve bores over our arms. Helen drops herself off first and disappears into the edge of the woodland, I drop myself off about a hundred yards away from Helen and Bob carries on a little further. I get myself into the edge of the woodland and hidden behind the trunk of an old oak tree. I see Bob go into the woodland about a hundred yards further along from me. As I stand there hidden out of sight behind the old oak tree, I look around me. Behind me is a dense, thick-growing fir tree plantation and along the woodland edge in front of me is a row of old oak trees. It is now winter time and the oak trees are bare of their leaves. Ideal for us to see the woodpigeon coming in to roost, ideal for us to shoot at woodpigeon passing overhead.

I see yellow flowering prickly gorse bushes growing along the woodland edge in between the old oak trees. There's an old saying about these yellow flowering gorse bushes, which goes like this, "WHEN THE YELLOW FLOWERS ARE OUT, KISSING IS OUT". 'Out' meaning there are no flowers growing on the bush, but that never happens. The yellow gorse bush flowers three hundred and sixty-five days of the year. And as you know kissing is never out, that also is done three hundred and sixty-five days of the year.

As I stand there in silence behind my old oak tree I hear rabbits scurrying behind me in the fir tree woodland. It's nice and warm inside there for the rabbits, and up in the fir treetops it will be warm for the woodpigeon also. I see a big rabbit sat looking at me but Bob's given me orders not to shoot the rabbits here, we are here to shoot woodpigeon. So I take my eyes from the rabbit and look into the sky for approaching woodpigeon.

By now we have less than an hour before darkness falls upon us. I scan the sky in front of me, I pierce my eyes over the distant meadows. I see a lot of small specks on the skyline, my eyes are affixed upon them, they are getting closer and closer and the small specks are getting bigger and bigger. I feel my heart pounding with expectation as I clutch right up to the old oak tree. As I peep around the trunk there is a massive flock of woodpigeon, they are heading straight for us as they head for this fir tree plantation. I grip on to my faithful old twelve bore's hammers, I click them both back. The woodpigeon are now upon us, I hear their wings beating as I jump out from behind the tree. I quickly take aim at one of the leading birds, there's a big bang as I pull the trigger, the woodpigeon folds. Without taking the gun butt from my shoulder I line the barrels on another as they fly overhead, it folds to my second shot.

I hear bang, bang, banging as this large, strung-out flock pass over Bob and Helen. I look to my left and I see two woodpigeon coming crashing down through the treetops, Bob has hit his targets. All at the same time I look to my right, I see another couple of woodpigeon coming spinning down in answer to Helen's shots. And still all at the same time I am hurriedly fumbling in my pockets for another couple of cartridges. All goes silent again except for the strong wind lashing through the branches of the treetops.

I say I am fumbling for cartridges I have loose in my pocket, it can be a dangerous practice can this, but it is a safe practice if you are careful. I remember a terrible accident happening and the story goes like this. This chap took his youngish son out shooting, his son was shooting a twenty bore shotgun. These guns are ideal for the youngish lads to learn to shoot, they are much smaller than the twelve bore shotgun. The chap was carrying his son's twenty bore cartridges loose in his pocket. The following day this chap was on a shooting peg and the driven pheasants were coming over him thick and fast. In his mad haste to reload his twelve bore he accidentally and unaware grabbed hold of one of his son's twenty bore cartridges. He was that engrossed in watching for more pheasant coming, he slotted the cartridges into the chamber of his twelve bore and then snapped shut the barrels. More pheasant came over the chap's shooting peg where he stood. He dropped a pheasant with his first shot, but when he fired his second shot, his gun did not go off. This happens on the odd occasion and the chap thought no more of it, thinking it was a dud cartridge. He was that engrossed watching for more pheasant coming, he just dropped the gun barrels which ejected the spent cartridges. But he was that engrossed he did not take note as he ejected the cartridge shells and he quickly reloaded his twelve bore with another two twelve bore cartridges. What the chap didn't know was that it was not a dud cartridge that misfired, in his haste he had loaded his twelve bore with a twenty bore cartridge. The twenty bore cartridge is much smaller than the twelve bore cartridge, too small to sit in the chamber of his twelve bore gun. The chap did not know that the twenty bore cartridge had slid down the barrel of his gun and got itself wedged, and he'd now just reloaded his gun. He'd now got a twelve bore cartridge aiming straight at the twenty bore cartridge that was wedged in the gun barrel. The chap saw another pheasant coming, he picked up his lethally loaded gun, let fire and 'BANG!' The twelve bore cartridge had blasted into the twenty bore cartridge and the barrels of his gun just simply exploded, the blast of the explosion hitting him full in the face. He was a lucky man, he survived the accident. So you shooters now beware, you have been told.

I am distracted from my reminiscing by flapping, fluttering wings. There's a flock of woodpigeon settled in the old oak tree right above my head and they haven't seen me as I stand close to the side of the tree trunk. I see three woodpigeon all perched on the same branch, they are all in a line together. I could easily let fire and get all three with one shot, but that wouldn't be playing the white man would it.

I hear Bob let off a couple of barrels and the woodpigeons above me panic and scatter, and they fly any way which they can. I get off a couple of shots at them and a second or two after I see another two drop out of the flock to Bob's gun. I hear another double bang coming from Helen, I look, I see yet another two woodpigeon crumple and fall from the flock. Helen and Bob are getting off far more shots than I am, all I have heard for the last ten minutes is bang, bang, bang, bang, banging, coming from them. The woodpigeon must be favouring their trees to roost in rather than my trees.

As I stand there hidden behind my old oak tree trunk scanning the low skyline in front of me, I spot a couple of carrion crows and they are heading straight for me. I tuck myself tight behind the tree and the carrion crows have now altered their course, they are now heading straight for Bob, I hope he has seen them coming. I now see a flock of woodpigeon coming, they too are heading straight for Bob. The woodpigeon fly faster than the carrion crows and they soon overtake them. The flock of woodpigeon are by now soaring overhead of the trees where Bob stands, but there's no shots fired, I bet Bob hasn't seen them coming. The carrion crows are by now upon him and I think to myself, well, where's Bob he's not seen them. And then I see it, I see a carrion crow crumple up and then I hear the delayed bang of Bob's gun. I see the second carrion crow duck and dive to make its escape, then I see it fold up and crumple as it falls to the ground and then I hear the delayed bang from Bob's gun. So Bob had seen them coming after all. He had purposely let the woodpigeon go by, he was waiting for the carrion crows. Well rid of from the estate, Bob will be thinking to himself.

I say I saw the carrion crows coming from far way, I knew they were carrion crows simply because there were only two of them, that's how they fly, in pairs. The rook is a very similar bird in appearance but they usually fly around in flocks.

Bob and Helen are shooting very well, I keep on seeing woodpigeon falling out of the sky where they are stood. Here comes a woodpigeon over me now so I pick up and have a crack shot at it as it flies over the treetops. It comes side toppling down as I hit it and drops on the woodland floor in a blue cloud of feather. It's only winged so I race over and grab it, I have my hand around its body holding its wings firmly tucked in. I give it a quick bang on the head up the side of a tree trunk, it's now dead. I have a feel at its breast meat. It's a big fat bird and its crop is bulging full. A lot of people when they have plucked out the bird, which is very easy, and gutted it leave the full crop intact on the bird. The crop is usually full of good healthy vegetable leaves and this enhances the flavour of the bird when cooked.

By now dusk is coming in fast. I see someone running towards me as they duck and dodge through the trees. It's Bob and he says he's run out of cartridges and he's off to the Land Rover for more. I see more woodpigeon coming at us, and while I am looking at the woodpigeon coming Bob's in my pocket and out with a couple of my cartridges. They are quickly loaded into his gun and bang, bang down comes another two woodpigeon. Bob now races off and disappears into the woodland. By now the dusk of the evening is bringing in many, many woodpigeon off the surrounding fields and it's not long before I am in the same position as Bob, I now have no cartridges left.

So now I head off through the woodland to Bob's Land Rover. I pass by where Helen is supposed to be stood, but she's not there. By the sounds of all the banging I can hear going off, I can guess where Helen is. As I head on through the woodland, I see dead woodpigeon laid everywhere on the woodland floor. These are all Helen's trophies that I see. I now reach the Land Rover which is nearly invisible as it's parked underneath the thick growing branches of the fir trees.

Bob and Helen are having a right old go at the woodpigeon. They are by now streaming in from the surrounding fields as they are coming here to roost. The woodpigeon are coming in from every direction. All three of us stand with our backs to each other, choose which way the woodpigeon come in now, we have them covered. There's a big flock just come in, the bang, bang, banging of the guns has put panic among the woodpigeon. They are swirling about over our heads everywhere I look, and everywhere I look I see dead woodpigeon raining out of the sky. I look at Helen and Bob, they have cartridges stuck in their mouths, that's why they are shooting faster than me.

I try it, I stick a couple of cartridges in my mouth, putting the steel or metal end within my lips. I see another big party of woodpigeon coming in low over the fields. They haven't heard our banging guns, they don't know what the hell they are heading themselves into. They swirl over our heads, I get a quick right and left at them. I quickly reload - much, much quicker this time, I put my two fingers across the cartridges in my mouth and they both slot into the chamber of my gun together.

I don't believe what I see, the sky is blue with woodpigeon, talk about putting the cat among these woodpigeon. As we all stand back-to-back to each other shooting, I keep on getting cracks and thumps at the back of my head. I turn and what do I see, as Bob and Helen are bang, bang, banging away, every time they reload they are ejecting their empty cartridge shells, and it's them that are flying across and hitting me at the back of my head.

I feel someone grappling in my pocket, I look and I see it's Helen, she's taking some of my cartridges. I feel someone grappling in my other pocket. I look, I see it's Bob, he's also taking some of my cartridges. They are not my cartridges really, they are Bob's cartridges, they are the ones which I took earlier. They aren't even Bob's cartridges really, they have all been supplied by Bob's boss the Laird of the estate. They have been purposely supplied to Bob for vermin and pest controlling these woodpigeon. They have to be kept under control. Woodpigeon feeding hard on a certain crop, usually in vast marauding raiding parties, can soon devastate a farmer's field full of crop.

That's it, we have no cartridges left. We have run out of ammunition, as all three of us just stand there looking up at all the woodpigeon swirling over our heads as they are coming in to land in the fir trees to roost. It's grown deep dusk by now and it's got a bit too dark by now to pick up the woodpigeons we have shot. Bob says he will be back at first light in the morning to pick up the birds with his retriever dogs.

I hear pheasants calling each other up into the trees to roost deep within the fir tree plantation. My ears prick up, I hear clip clopping coming from within the woodland. It's my old mate the mad capper of a bird the capercaillie, he's calling up his harem of

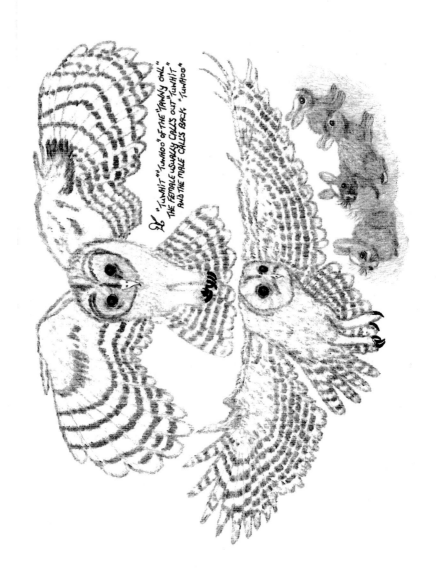

females into the trees to roost overnight. I see a tawny owl as it comes flitting past. It lands in the trees again where we stand, it's hooting out to us, saying, "It's time for you to go home now. Let me and the nightshift now take over." So we all clamber into Bob's Land Rover and off we go. Helen this time guides us around the muddy parts of the meadow. She knows the land here like the back of her hand, after all she is the shepherdess around these parts of the woods.

We now get on to the narrow winding lanes and as we drive along Helen says, "Do you want to see some rabbits Doug?"

I nod, yes I would. Bob has a lamp in the cab of his Land Rover, it's what he uses for lamping foxes at night, and Helen plugs the lamp into a socket on the dashboard. She shines it over the hedge into the grass meadow and I see eyes, hundreds of eyes shining in the lamp's light. As we drive along the narrow country lanes Helen's shining the light in different meadows as we drive along. Everywhere I look on the Laird's massive estate in the Grampian Mountains high up in Scotland the rabbits are out of control. They are in plague proportions.

"You can have all these," says Helen. Helen shines the light in another meadow, but I see no rabbits. Helen says, "That's unusual, there's usually hundreds of rabbits around here." Helen shines the light around the meadow, then we see the problem, we see a pair of eyes shining like diamonds as they sparkle in the lamp. It's now got laid tight squat in the short grass as it peers out at us. Helen says, "That's a Scottish wild cat, that's why there's no rabbits around. They have all scarpered."

A little further along the lane Bob pulls up and Helen gets out of the Land Rover. She has her quad bike parked in the kale field where we shot the woodpigeons earlier. Helen will now make her own way home, and just when I was least expecting it, Helen leans back into the Land Rover and gives me a whacking great kiss on my lips. Helen bids me farewell and have a safe journey home and that she will see me again the next time I come up. And off me and Bob go in the Land Rover and back to Hunter's Lodge which is Bob's cottage.

So as Helen says, I am homeward bound tomorrow, but first I need some sleep. I am knackered, but before I sleep I need something to eat, I am starving so me and Bob sit down to an evening meal.

I mention to Bob the pond high up on the moorland, the pond

which Bob always insists that I throw all the rabbits' guts into for the ducks and geese to feed on. Bob tells me that he feeds the flight pond to attract in the wild ducks and geese, and that the flight pond is shot regularly by him and a team of guns. Bob carries on to say he has a grouse shooting day coming up in three weeks time, and that he is a man short to help with the day's shooting. Bob asks if I would come up and help him out. How could I refuse an offer like that.

Bob carries on to say that after the grouse shooting he and the team of guns will be going up on to the other moor to have an evening wildfowl shooting on the pond I feed for him with all my rabbits' guts, and that he would invite me to shoot with the team of guns if I came and helped him out. With a big smile on my face I accept Bob's offer. Bob's still talking, he's now saying, "Then in gratitude for helping me, the following evening I will take you out lamping rabbits with the rifles."

My eyes lit up at that offer. Bob's still talking and I am all ears now. He says he will take me on to the estate where the rabbits are overrun, completely out of control. I shake Bob's hand, his offer I have now accepted.

I was early to bed that night, and up with the larks early next morning as I was setting off homeward bound.

Now to load my rabbits into my Land Rover, the rabbits which I caught long-netting. I can just about get them all in without having to use my trailer, that can stay up the side of Bob's cottage until needed. I am sure with all these rabbits on the Laird's estate, I will need the trailer in the near future, maybe next time when I lamp the rabbits with Bob.

These treble decks I have in my Land Rover to load my rabbits on to I have designed so that I can take them out. It's all just a simple set of boards that are laid together in the back. There is a sill at either side of the Land Rover and I lay a set of boards across these sills, which now makes a bottom compartment. I now lay wooden spacers at either sides of these boards, and lay another set of boards on top of these spacers. That gives me a middle compartment and a top compartment. These compartments together will hold way over a hundred big fat rabbits. Now the rabbits do not get crushed or squashed on top of one another. And to carry even more rabbits, I have three long hazel poles up in the roof of my Land Rover. I tie two rabbits together by their back legs and then hang them over the poles. These poles will hold well over a hundred big fat rabbits.

But now I have come to load all my long-netted rabbits, my Land Rover is full to bursting at the seams with big fat rabbits. I have a pile left which I can't get in but I don't want to use my trailer yet if I can help it. So I start loading the pile of rabbits into the foot compartment on the passenger side of my Land Rover. I fill the foot compartment level with the passenger seat, I still have more rabbits to get in. So I load them on to the passenger seat. The seat's now full and still I have a few more rabbits to get in. There's a space between the passenger seat and the driver's seat and I just manage to get all my rabbits into this space. Phew!

I look up and I see Bob has opened the back door on my Land Rover. I see him stuffing in woodpigeons in between all my loaded up rabbits. I stand and watch him, he's squeezing them into small gaps where I thought there were no gaps. These are all the woodpigeons that we shot on the kale field. I don't believe what I see, Bob gets every single woodpigeon into my Land Rover, now my Land Rover certainly is bursting at its seams.

I now look at the suspension on my Land Rover, the big springs look a little flattened out. The strong, heavy-duty tyres look a bit flattened at the bottom also, but apart from that everything looks okay.

Bob says, with a big smile on his face, "You will never make it home Doug, you have too many rabbits on board."

Pup my dog always sits on the passenger seat so I will have to make room for her somewhere. I will have to put her on top of the rabbits that's loaded on to her passenger seat. I push her and shove her and manage to get her on top. Now Pup's banging her head on the roof of the Land Rover.

I now bid Bob farewell and tell him I will see him in three weeks time for the grouse shooting day, and off me and Pup go in the Land Rover. As we travel along Bob's private road I look up and I see Pup looking down at me. I see her head banging on the roof as we go, Pup looks rather sheepish to me. I remember, as we climbed the lall hill that leads from Bob's cottage, I didn't think the Land Rover was going to make it to the top. I slipped it into four-wheel drive and into low gear box and we just managed to make it to the top.

I stopped at the top to make myself comfortable for the long journey home. I was badly wounded from my last few days. My backside was terribly bruised from where Helen's ram of a sheep had head-butted me, and then there's that mad crazy fox which I caught in the long net. My fingers were elastoplasted up, and where it had bitten clean through my boot I had elastoplasts on my toes also.

But my wounds all disappeared as I now gazed from the top of that lall hill because the scenery I saw was amazingly eye-catching. There were great big mountain ranges all around me and the tops of the mountains were all clad in snow. The mountains went way out into the distance as far as the eye could see. Below me was the low-lying Bonny Glens, where all the rabbits were, and I saw the vast forestry fir tree plantations which just simply disappeared into the distance. Wow, was this beauty to my eyes.

All this beauty I look at is all one massive estate which belongs to the Laird and everywhere is out of control with rabbits, all at my mercy if I play my cards right. When I think about it, wasn't I lucky when I got caught poaching Bob's rabbits that day.

I hope you are enjoying reading my story of what happened on the Laird's massive estate which all happened many years ago now way back in the 1970s. It gets even more exciting, read on.

The time at home soon passed on by and Bob's grouse shooting day was upon me. I arrived up at Bob's cottage late afternoon the day before the day's grouse shooting. Bob was in one of the outbuildings in the courtyard, he was feeding a couple of well-grown, ginger-red-coloured 'Tamworth' pigs. Bob says he is fattening up the pigs into bacon pigs, and that when they are big enough and fat enough he will slaughter them himself. He says, "I will then salt them down into bacon and ham."

These Tamworth pigs are good tasting, I can vouch for that myself with all the breakfasts I have had at Bob's.

As I walked out of the pig hole (pig sty) and into the courtyard, I looked over a high stone wall and I saw a couple of ponies turned out in a grass paddock. Bob tells me this is where the deerstalkers zero in their rifles before going off into the hills stalking the deer. Bob says he takes deerstalkers out regularly and that it is big business for his boss, the Laird of the estate. He says that's why they call my cottage 'Hunter's Lodge'.

Me and Bob go into his cottage, I am eager to ask Bob a question. I ask him, "How many woodpigeon did me, you and Helen shoot on that roost shooting we had just before I went home last time I was here?"

Bob smiles at me and says, "Just under two hundred

woodpigeon."

"Wow!" I say, "That was a good bag of woodpigeon."

Bob nods. So, put them woodpigeons together that me, Helen and Bob shot on the kale field in the late afternoon, which was just over one hundred and fifty, and I total that to be about 350 woodpigeons we shot altogether. Wow, that's one hell of a lot of woodpigeon. So, with all us three shooting we still only shot half the number my friend Alan shot when he broke the British 'record' for shooting the most woodpigeon which was just over 700 woodpigeon. And Alan shot them all by himself.

Bob's now telling me about the grouse shooting day ahead of us tomorrow. He tells me there will be nine paying guns shooting. These shooting men pay a lot of money to the Laird for a day's grouse shooting. The Laird himself will also be shooting.

"Tomorrow," says Bob, "there will be four grouse drives throughout the day. There will be two grouse drives in the morning and then it will be all stop for lunchtime. A ready lunch will be taken by us lads that are driving the grouse and will be eaten up on the moorland tops. After lunch we then have another two grouse drives." Bob then carries on to say, "I want you, Doug, to be a 'picker-up' with your dog on the first two drives of the day. I will show you what to do when we get up there on the hills." Bob carries on speaking and I am all ears, "The first drive after lunch is a big grouse drive, and there will be many grouse sent over the waiting guns in the shooting butts."

Bob keeps on speaking and I am all intent on listening to him. He says, "My boss, the Laird, has asked me to ask you if you will be a loader for him. The Laird shoots double guns. I have told the Laird you are pretty nifty with a gun yourself, and if you accept his offer to load for him you must look reasonably smartly dressed."

How could I refuse. I accepted the Laird's offer, leaving me thinking how lucky I was to be offered the chance of being the Laird's loader for the day.

Bob's now going into the clothes wardrobe. He pulls out a gamekeeper's suit and he's now handing it to me, saying, "Here, try that on, see if it fits you."

The suit was all neat and tidy on a coat hanger and it was made of a fine quality Scotch tweed. I tried it on and it fitted me up to the 'nines'.

Bob gave me the once over and said, "Now try the hat on."

It fitted me as if it was my very own, I felt a bit like a

millionaire as I stood there in it. And on that it was early to bed that night and early to rise next morning.

I was up bright and early that morning but Bob had beaten me up out of bed yet again. He was out in the courtyard preparing for the day's shooting ahead of us. I put on my fine keeper's suit, and I must add I looked a proper 'Bobby Dazzler' in it.

Just as I was going out of the cottage to meet up with Bob I bumped into the postman. He said, "There's some letters here for Black Bob."

I look at the letters and they are addressed to Bob Black. The postman says, "Everyone around here calls Bob 'Black Bob'."

I now go out and meet Black Bob in the courtyard. He was all smartly dressed in his fine gamekeeper's suit, just like I was, and the pattern of his Scots tweed was exactly the same as mine. Bob tells me our keeper's suits are the Laird's own personal tweed pattern which belongs to the Laird's family and estate which goes back generations.

Bob tells me the shooting men are all meeting up at the Laird's big house. So we set off there in Bob's Land Rover.

I see my Pup there, she's snarling and snapping at Bob's two retriever dogs. Pup's not used to being thrown in with other dogs.

We drive along a well made driveway which went along through the lowlands of the mountains. I see in the distance a castle and Bob says, "That's the Laird's big house," leaving me thinking, that's some hell of a house.

We were by now upon the castle grounds and we came to some wrought iron main gates. They were painted in gold leaf and were hinged on to two great stone pillars. On each pillar stood stone statues of royal red deer stags sporting massive twelve point antlers. There's me sat with my suave posh gamekeeper's suit on thinking, wow, what am I coming into here, I am only a humble rabbit poacher?

We carry on along the driveway. It's a strong, well-built castle I see, it has big towers to it with TURRETS around the top. The castle is set in the middle of about a hundred acres of grounds which are big, suave, posh lawns with flower beds. Wow, I think, the Queen will be coming out to greet us next. But no, I see a well-dressed chap coming out to greet us instead.

Bob says, "This is the Laird of the estate."

What a fine gentleman he looked too. I thought he was a tall chap in his fifties. He had a fine quality deerstalker tweed suit on with a deerstalker's hat on his head. The pattern of his suit was just the same as mine and Bob's.

The Laird's now coming over to us and I see at the bottom of this short trouser legs, which are called 'plus fours', and at the top of his long stockings he has 'BLUE FEATHERS' pinned on. That is the name given, but it's actually ribbon.

The Laird is now putting his hand out to greet me, he's now shaking my hand, he's now introducing himself to me. He's treating me as though I am royalty, when in fact I was not long since poaching the rabbits on his vast estate.

The Laird tells Bob the shooting men have not arrived yet, they were down at the local, the Poacher's Arms, having breakfast. The Laird's now having a quiet word with Bob. Now the Laird is speaking to me, he says, "Bob tells me you have agreed to be my loader."

I tell him with a big smile on my face, "Yes."

The Laird's now smiling back at me, he says, "That's good. There will be a lot of grouse coming over the shooting butts on the third drive of the day after dinner time, I will have to shoot two guns, it will be rapid shooting."

The Laird's now admiring my gamekeeper's suit I am wearing and he says I am looking smart. And on that the Laird walks away tipping his deerstalker hat as he goes.

Bob drives on and parks his Land Rover in front of the Laird's castle. So we are now waiting for the party of shooting men to arrive. I have a steady stroll in front of the castle, I feel all privileged here especially with my gamekeeper's suit on. As I am admiring the Laird's castle I see rabbit scats all over the smart suave lawns, the rabbits are making a terrible mess.

I saw a belting of fir tree woodlands which surrounded the entire perimeter of the castle grounds and I walked across the big lawn towards these fir trees. I saw rabbits running everywhere off the lawns and into the woodland. I went and peered into the woodland and I saw a large rabbit warren. I walked along through the woodland, and what I saw I didn't believe, there were rabbits, rabbits scurrying around everywhere I looked. I continued on through the belting of woodland trying my best not to stand on the poor little rabbits. My eyes were sparkling as I watched, they were big fat rabbits more like. The rabbit warrens I see in there were just one big continuation of warrens that continue on all the way around the castle grounds. I must leave these rabbits for now, I must not get my gamekeeper's suit dirty, but I will be back.

As I head on back towards the Laird's castle I see Bob doing something in the back of his Land Rover. He tells me he's making a 'BEATER'S FLAG', he says he's one short, and I watch him. Bob has some hazel sticks in the Land Rover which he had cut from the hedgerow. The hazel sticks are about three feet long and about one inch thick, and the small branches have been trimmed off to a smart finish with both ends of the stick rounded off. Bob now gets a light coloured polythene bag, the ones that farmers use around the farmyard, such as bags which have had sheep nuts in them or maybe fertilizer bags. Bob now cuts out one side of the polythene bag and he's now rolling it on to the hazel stick, ensuring he leaves a handle on the stick.

Bob has a lot of empty twelve bore cartridge shells in the Land Rover. He gets one and cuts off the steel end of the cartridge case and slits down the length of the plastic shell. He now pulls it apart to open it up and clasps it around the rolled-up bag that's wrapped around the hazel stick. The slit cartridge now grips tight around the stick and Bob now hammers in a couple of tin tacks which holds the cartridge shell in position. He now tin tacks a few more slit shells along the stick which firmly hold the polythene flag on the stick. And that's it, the 'BEATER'S FLAG' is now complete and ready for using.

Bob now holds it up and gives it a 'CRACK'. "A simple job," says Bob, "but a long-lasting job."

I look up and I see a convoy of vehicles coming along the driveway towards the Laird's estate. They are all smart four-wheel drive vehicles by the looks of them. What do I see behind them? It's a convoy of old banger cars following on behind. There must be a vintage car rally going on somewhere. What's that I see behind them? It's someone on a quad bike.

The smart four-wheel drive vehicles are now parking up in front of the Laird's castle, it's the team of shooting men arriving for their grouse shooting day out. Now the convoy of old banger cars are parking up. Oh, I see who they are now, it's all the beaters and flankers arriving. These are local people from the surrounding glens and it's their job to send the grouse over the shooting men who are stood in the shooting butts.

Now here comes the quad bike, now I recognise who it is, it's my beloved Helen. She has her faithful sheep cur with her who's sat in a big basket at the front of her quad bike. Helen comes over and gives me a peck on the cheek. She tells me she is going to be a beater today. Helen's sheep cur will get a lot of squat grouse up out of the heather. It's a good bitch is that, she has a good nose on her, I have seen her hunting.

I look across to the front of the castle and I see all the shooting men gathered together. The Laird's stood with them, they are having a toasting drink of whisky before setting off for the grouse moors. All the shooting men are looking very smart in their countrymen's suits, and there's some well-dressed women with them escorting the shooting men. They all have their retriever dogs with them for retrieving back dead grouse to hand. All these shooting people I see in front of me are all well-to-do gentry, multi-millionaire type of people. They will pay the Laird a lot of money for the day's grouse shooting today. I know in the 1970s, which is the decade I am speaking of, even in those distant days it cost about £150 to shoot a brace of grouse. That was a lot of money in those days, but not a lot of money to these gentry people.

I now see Bob go over to the gathering of shooting people. Bob pulls out a leather wallet from his pocket, in the wallet is a series of numbers. Each shooting man pulls out a random number, that allots the number of the butt the shooting man will shoot from. Bob's now telling the shooting men what they cannot shoot. Do not shoot any hares and do not shoot any blackcock, that's black grouse. The day's shooting is all well organized and properly conducted, and on that everybody is ready for the shooting day to commence.

The shooting men and their womenfolk and their retriever dogs all jump into their smart four-wheel drive vehicles. Me, Bob and Helen together with about twenty beaters, flankers and picker-uppers (I will tell you their job as the story progresses) all jump into a covered trailer which is pulled by the farm tractor. It's a bit of a squeeze once we are all loaded in and we are all seated on bales of straw which are positioned around the inside of the trailer. All our hunting dogs and retriever dogs, plus my dog Pup, are all piled in the trailer also. They are all sat in the middle at our feet, most of them anyway. There's some that are trying to run over the tops of our heads, they are giddy and excited at the shooting day's prospects. And the other dogs with them, all being cramped up together in the confines of the covered trailer, are snarling and snapping at each other. We are really one big happy family all snuggled in together.

Our tractor and covered trailer lead the way up onto the moorland. The shooting men's smart four-wheel drive vehicles all drop in line and follow on behind us in the tractor and trailer. It's a long way up on the top of the moorland and as the tractor goes along the rugged bumpy old moorland track, us inside the trailer are being bumped and bounced around, causing fur to fly with the dogs. Then as the tractor goes down a steep slope us inside the trailer all slide forward. We have to watch our fingers and our arses as the dogs are snapping and biting at each other.

The tractor's now passing over a burn, that's what we call a stream. Then the tractor now is climbing up a steep slope and everybody who was all piled up at the front of the trailer has now slid to the back of the trailer. And on the tractor goes, weaving and turning along and up the moorland track until we finally reach the top.

We are now in God's Country, I can see for miles as I look across the bonny Glens of Scotland. This is the finest of fresh mountain air that my lungs can breath.

There is a large wooden hut I see nestled nearly out of sight on the moorland edge. This is called a 'shooting box', and is where everyone gets their lunch at dinner time which is after the second grouse drive of the morning which will be about midday.

All the vehicles are parked up over the moor edge so that the grouse cannot see them. We don't want the grouse surprised or alarmed do we.

Everybody now drops off their bags, and everything else they don't want, at the shooting box. All the shooting men want is their twelve bore shotguns with them. By this time all the beaters and flankers have left for the distant moorlands a long time since. They will head out keeping themselves out of sight of the grouse, we do not want them disturbing yet, do we, not until the guns are in their butts and ready anyway.

By now the shooting men have taken their short walk and are now at the intended line of butts. Each shooting man goes off to his allotted butt number, the number which they drew out of Bob's special leather wallet. They take their twelve bores from out of their gun carrying holdalls. They have been kept in there for safety reasons. The shooting men and their guns are now all ready, all they have to do now is keep themselves low in the butts and wait for the grouse to be driven over them.

Bob has told me what to do and where to go so I go there and sit myself down on a small banking side. I get myself snuggled into the long heather and out of sight and Pup, my dog, lays down by my side. She is now my retriever dog.

I peer out across the moor in front of me, not a soul to be seen, everybody is keeping themselves low and out of sight.

Bob has given me a walkie-talkie to use. There's about half a dozen people out there on the moor who have walkie-talkies with them and these will keep us all in touch with what's going off out on the moor.

I hear someone talking on the walkie-talkie, it's Bob telling the beaters to set off. Now the grouse drive is in progress. The beaters are way out across the moor and they will be spread out across the moor in a line. They are advancing nearer to us all the time, waving and cracking their flags to disturb the grouse up out of the heather. Their dogs will be out hunting in the heather in front of them.

When a flurry of grouse jump up the beaters will wave their flags at them. The grouse will fly on a few hundred yards and then settle back down in the heather. The beaters as they go will put up even more grouse, forever sending the grouse nearer and nearer to the waiting guns.

Down either side of the grouse drive are the waiting flankers. It's their job to keep the grouse on course to the waiting guns and they are funnelling the grouse along. They will be sat squat in the heather keeping themselves out of sight. They will be watching with their beady eyes, scanning the moorland in front of them, and they will see a big covey of grouse heading across the moor. If they are heading bang on course to the waiting guns the flanker will sit tight and out of sight leaving the grouse heading across the moor. He peels his eyes as he watches them go.

If the big covey is veering off course and is drifting across the moor towards him, the flanker is now crouched that low in the heather he is poised there just like a mountain leopard watching its prey. When the big covey of grouse is upon him, he will spring up out of the heather waving his flag. The grouse are so startled they panic and veer sharply back and head back to where they have just come from. There's a line of beaters there waving their flags at them and the grouse now veer the other way and head on down along the moor. The big covey of grouse is now back on course heading on towards the waiting guns in their shooting butts.

With my eyes peeled I peer over the heather and I see the big covey of grouse as it gets closer to the butts. I see no shooting men, have they seen these grouse coming? I look back at the grouse and they are by now upon the butts then they veer sharply upwards and over the butts they go. They are spread across three, four butts, and at the last second I see the shooting men rise to greet the grouse and I hear bang, bang, bang. I see grouse crumpling from the sky, so the shooting men were not asleep at all. My dog Pup was and the banging guns woke her up. Pup's now vigilant.

It's mine and Pup's job now to mark the positions of the dead grouse that are falling, we have to find them and pick them up after the drive is over. Something catches the corner of my eye, I look and I see it's a flanker who has sprung up out of the heather. He's waving his flag like crazy, and then I see them, they are just like small dots on the horizon. It's another covey of grouse and I see the flanker has just managed to turn them in the nick of time. I hear more and more bangs coming from the shooting butts and I see grouse falling from the sky here, there and everywhere.

I am marking and memorizing where I see every bird drop, I look at Pup who's peering through the heather. She will be doing the same as me, remembering where she sees the grouse drop. Here comes that big covey which I saw as small specks on the horizon. They are now streaming over the butts, I hear the repeated bang, bang, banging of the guns and I see grouse falling everywhere. I look down by my side and I see Pup, she's observing everything that's going off out there on the moor.

I am that busy looking at Pup, I hear bang, bang, banging coming from the guns. I look up sharpishly and I see more birds falling from the skies. I never even saw them grouse coming, I will have to pay more attention.

I look back across the moor and I see way out in the distance white things moving about. As the white things get closer and closer, now I see what it is, it's the beaters, they are all in a long straight line across the moor. They are all waving and cracking their flags as they come. The beaters are still a long way out across the moor. There are still many grouse in front of them as they advance closer and closer to the shooting butts. I keep on hearing the bang, bang, banging of the guns as grouse keep on passing overhead of the butts. I keep on marking countless grouse that keep on falling from the skies.

There's one grouse I see and as it passes overhead of the butts I see it take the impact of the twelve bore shot, but it does not drop.

It continues on across the moor and it's jinking and swerving about as it goes. It's been wounded badly by the looks of it. I keep my eye trained on it, it's by now just a small speck in the sky. Now I see it just crumple and fall and I mark its position where I see it fall. Me and Pup will retrieve that later when this drive is over, and that's now by the looks of it.

I turn, I see the beaters, they are by now nearly upon the shooting butts. I hear a whistle being blown near to me. I hear a hunting horn being blown at the far side of the butts. That's a signal to the shooting men to stop shooting. The drive is over, and that's the end of the first grouse drive of the morning.

It's the beaters' job now to gather together in a group and head off on to the second grouse drive of the morning. The beaters yet again have to walk a long distance way out across the moorland, which eventually will take them to the far side of the next grouse drive. Once there they can have a good old rest. Meanwhile the shooting men come out of their butts, they want their own dogs to go out and retrieve the grouse they have shot themselves.

My job now is to take my dog Pup and retrieve the dead grouse which I marked earlier which have dropped well away from the shooting buts. So off me and Pup go.

There are several people like myself who have been marking the grouse when they to the guns they are spread out all the way along the shooting butts. They are professionals, they do this 'picking up' for a living. They will maybe be working three or four retriever dogs all at once.

I now send my Pup out into the heather hunting. Where I am stood I marked four grouse that had fallen just hereabouts. I see one half-hidden in the heather and I pick it up. Then I feel something nuzzling my leg, I turn, I see Pup there, she has a dead grouse in her mouth. I take if from her and fondle her ear, telling Pup she's a good dog. Off Pup goes again hunting in the heather. Pup's not gone long before I see her with another grouse in her mouth. I go over to meet her coming and Pup drops the dead grouse at my feet. She's excited, she's wagging her tail as she leaves me. She now has her nose stuck in the heather, she's pushing the heather aside with her head as she goes. She makes a grab at something and comes up with a grouse in her mouth. It's still alive, it's only been winged. Pup hands it to me, not letting go until she knows I have firm hold of it, and I kill the grouse by bumping its head on a boulder.

Me and Pup pick and gather many grouse as we go along. Pup has marked the birds very well as the shooting men shot them. Pup must have a good memory. As we head across the heather, I have been watching a shooting man working his own retriever dog. He has called over one of the picker-uppers and he says to him, "I have a grouse down just here and me and my dog can't find it."

Now the picker-up has his three dogs hunting and searching around in the heather, so now there's four retriever dogs looking for this elusive grouse.

The shooting man says, "It's only just here somewhere", as he points with his finger.

I send Pup in to help with the search, but Pup looks at me, she's not interested. So I carry on looking for the grouse myself with all the four dogs hunting and searching the heather. But alas the grouse is nowhere to be found. I look up, I see Pup, she's way out across the heather from us, I see her tail wagging, she has her nose tight to the ground and she disappears down into a hag. I know Pup is on to something, I can tell by her body language. I stand and watch the area where Pup has disappeared into and I see a grouse run out of the hag. It has a wing down, it's a runner. I see the grouse get squat in the heather and I see Pup race out of the hag, she's hot on the grouse's scent. A quick grab into the heather and out comes the grouse in Pup's mouth. So that's another fine retrieve from Pup.

Now to try to find that grouse I saw which was hit badly before continuing on way out across the moor before falling. I had marked the grouse falling against a hag, a hag is like a gutter where all the water drains down from the hilltops. When I reach this hag, I send Pup out hunting but she doesn't appear to be picking up the grouse's scent. She's hunting with her nose tight to the ground, but still we have no luck detecting this eluding grouse. As I am stood there on the top of the hag watching Pup hunt and scratching my head at the same time, I look down into the hag. I see ice on the water, it's been freezing in the night. I see a hole in the ice and I see fresh, unfrozen water on top of the ice. Now that tells me that hole in the ice has recently been made, could it be our elusive grouse in that hole? I go to investigate.

The ice on the water is very thin, but the water is only shallow. I only have my boots on so I use some sivs for stepping stones. I manage to reach the hole in the ice without getting my feet wet. I push up my sleeve, I don't want to get my smart gamekeeper's suit wet do I, and I put my hand into the freezing cold water. I feel nothing there, then I feel under the ice around the edges of the hole and I touch something. I reach in further, I grab what I am touching and pull it out. It's a soaked grouse, its body is still slightly warm. That's another grouse safely retrieved.

Me and Pup now head on back to the shooting men over at the shooting butts. I see many dead grouse lying on top of the butts and I see many, many empty cartridge shells lying on the butt floors. The shooting men have now all finished and are ready for moving on. They have got there twelve bores safely in their gun sleeves and slung over their shoulders.

The shooting men, beaters and flankers do exactly the same thing again on the second drive of the morning. And of course me, Pup and the picker-up men also follow on behind them, and another successful drive is accomplished.

After this second grouse drive is over it's now got to dinner time and it's everybody back to the shooting box, which is a large wooden hut where we can all get our lunch. When I arrive there I see Bob putting all the dead grouse into a temporary larder. This larder will prevent the grouse getting flyblown. The small mesh that covers the larder is too small for the flies to enter but does allow the breeze to blow through keeping the grouse cool. It's a fine bag of grouse we have got so far, about fifty brace and the days only half over. There's still two more grouse drives to be had yet after everyone has eaten.

These birds we are shooting, their full name is 'red grouse'. The shooting of these birds in big numbers is not detrimental to the survival of their species. I will just explain the red grouse's characteristic way of life.

To begin with red grouse are a totally wild moorland bird, they cannot be bred in captivity, their staple diet is the heather. They will also eat a few insects and berries. They breed out on the moorland in the spring of the year. By late summer they 'pack' together in large coveys or 'groups', and by late winter the large coveys begin to disperse. They separate into breeding stock and these red grouse now become territorial. Their territory has the best heather to feed on and the non-breeding red grouse now have nothing to feed on. Wherever they land on the moor they get ousted off by the territorial birds. The non-breeding grouse now become starving, they have no energy to fight off the freezing cold bitter temperatures that the moorland throws at them and they naturally starve to death. So the shooting we are doing now is only culling their numbers ensuring there's enough red grouse left for breeding stock.

So the morning's bag of grouse are now safely hung up in the temporary game larder and I see a lot of people now gathered at the shooting box. There's shooting men, beaters, flankers and picker-uppers, plus all their snapping, snarling, squabbling retriever, hunting dogs, now that they are all together. And there I see my beloved Helen among the crowd.

Bob's now introducing me to a chap. "This is Big Jim," says Bob, "he's the gamekeeper who looks after the other side of the estate for the Laird."

By, what a big fellow Big Jim was. He had a great long, bushy beard just like Bob and his gamekeeper's suit which, as you readers now know, was the Laird's family's tartan tweed.

Big Jim says to me, "I hear you're pretty nifty at rabbit catching. There's enough rabbits on this estate to keep you busy."

I ask Big Jim where his living abode is. Big Jim points across the distant mountain tops and says, "Twenty miles over the tops of them lall hills."

I think, that's another that calls these mountains LALL HILLS. I say to Big Jim, "That's a long way away where you live."

Big Jim says, "The Laird's estate is vast, it's twenty miles wide and thirty miles long." He carries on saying, "And everywhere you look in the glens it's just one big infestation of rabbits, they are in plague proportions." Big Jim looks at me with a glint in his eye and says, "Now it's your job to catch all the rabbits for the Laird."

I looked at Big Jim silent and gobsmacked.

By now it looks as though everybody is getting their dinner, or is it just a lunch? I poke my nose inside the shooting box, a long, well-made wooden hut, it's like royalty inside there. It's a big room with a wood partition in the middle. I see a long table in the middle of the room, the table has a long white tablecloth on it. I see all the shooting men sat around this table. The table is bedecked with delicacies. It's piled heavens high with food on it.

I see caterers, I see waiters with uniforms on, they are topping up glasses with sparkling, bubbling champagne for the shooting men. I see the Laird sat there, he's toasting his glass of champagne to the shooting men. The Laird spots me peeping around the door and he says to little me, "Don't forget Doug, you are loading for me on the next grouse drive after lunch."

I nod to the Laird and slip away.

I now go to the other end of the shooting box, I look inside, it's bare, it's glum, it's empty. This is the beaters' side of the hut.

I now see the beaters. It's by now a glorious sun-shining day and all the beaters and everyone else are sat on hillocks of heather outside in the sunshine. I go and sit down by the side of my beloved Helen. Everyone is eating their packed sandwiches. I pull out my lunch, a MARS BAR. I say to Helen, "The shooting men are all being treated like royalty in the shooting box."

Helen tells me, "It's all paid for by the courtesy of the Laird."

I see Bob going around everybody as they are sat on the hillocks of heather, he's giving everybody something. Bob's now coming over to me and Helen. He gives Helen an envelope, Bob's now giving me an envelope. I open it, it's money. Helen gives me a big radiant smile, which to me just looked like a breath of fresh spring mountain air. Helen says, "That's your wages for helping on the grouse shooting."

I see my dog Pup, she's pinched somebody's chicken leg, she must be hungry like me. Pup's now got her head down, she's having a drink, no doubt to wash her chicken leg down. She could have saved me some. I go over to where Pup's drinking, it's a spring, it's fair bubbling and gushing out of the ground. I have a drink to wash my Mars bar down, this is the purest of pure water a man could ever drink. Pure, unadulterated, unpolluted mineral spring water.

As I am writing this story it's now the year 2008 and in this time and age, man has tapped these mountain springs and bottled it and distributed it all over the world making a turnover of two billion pounds. Maybe me and Bob could tap and bottle this moorland spring here. Helen could sell it in her spare time in between her shepherding, she could label the bottles as the 'Laird's special mountain mineral spring water'. We could have made a massive fortune in those days of the 1970s.

As I sit there in the heather on the hillock, I see the shooting men coming out of the shooting box. They are getting themselves ready for the big grouse drive of the day. What happens next I will never forget for the rest of my life.

I am ravenously hungry, my Pup must be ravenously hungry too because she still keeps on trying to pinch people's sandwiches.

I get up and head over towards the shooting box and I beckon Pup to follow me. Helen's sheep cur dogs follow us on behind, by now both of them have got matey with my dog Pup. Just as I am about to go through the door on the beaters' side of the hut, the Laird sees me and he says, "This is the grouse drive that you are loading for me Doug, you can come with me in my motor." I acknowledge the Laird and off he goes to get his vehicle.

I now go through the beaters' room of the hut and there's another door that goes through the wooden partition into the shooting men's room of the hut. I peep around the door, I see the waitress, she's all dressed smart in her pinafore waitress's dress. She has her back turned to me, she hasn't seen me. I see on the table a whole host of food, most of it has hardly been touched. I see a big fat turkey on a silver tray, it's only been half sliced into. I see full cooked lobsters and crabs that haven't even been touched. I see piles of sandwiches on trays, I see thick slices of beef, chicken drumsticks and a whole host of other mouthwatering things to eat. I see bottles of champagne that haven't even had the cork taken out. I sneak in while the waitress's still not seen me. I wrench the big leg off the turkey carcass and I bite off a big mouthful making sure I don't take my fingers with it. I throw a big thick slice of beef to my Pup. She's that hungry she catches it and swallows it whole.

Helen's two dogs now have their front paws up on the table, they grab the chicken drumsticks and as they crunch into the bones the waitress hears it. She turns and what she sees she doesn't like. She rushes over and scats and waves Helen's dogs off the table.

Now the waitress is grabbing at my turkey leg. I pull away as she grabs and she's now snatching again. I set off around the table, she's chasing after me crying, "You can't have the turkey leg, dinner time is now over."

I know her game, the Laird has paid for all this food, and now what's left the waitress is wanting to take back with her to resell it again.

The waitress is still after me wanting her big turkey leg back. I race around the table, there's another door at the end of the hut, I head out through it, the waitress is in hot pursuit behind me. I am now outside, I do a quick left-hand turn, it takes me around the corner of the hut and down an alleyway. It leads to the game larder. Many feet have trodden this alleyway as people have gone backwards and forwards to the game larder and it's treacherous underfoot with wet, thick, slimy black peat. I slither and slide my way up this alley, and still the waitress chases after me for her turkey leg back.

I come to another side door which goes back inside the hut and as I race in, I see Helen stood there, she's come for her dogs back. By now her dogs and my Pup are up on the top of the table ransacking all the food. All three of them are snarling and snapping at each other over the food. All their growling has now been heard by the other dogs outside the hut. All them dogs now come piling in and straight on to the top of the table.

I now see a load of men coming barging in, it's the beaters, flankers and picker-uppers, come for their dogs back. What a pantomime that is now going off inside this hut. I take my advantage, I grab some more thick slices of beef and I stuff it into my pocket. I grab a whole lobster and a bottle of champagne to wash it all down later. I see Helen, the little tinker, she's stuffing her pockets with chicken drumsticks. As I head away leaving everybody to it, now everybody's grabbing and stuffing their pockets.

As I come out of the beaters' end of the hut, I see the Laird sat there in his smart four-wheel drive vehicle. I quickly hop in by the side of him, my Pup gets laid at my feet, and off we go. As the Laird drives away, I look back and I see the waitress, her face and smart waitress's dress is covered in black slimy peat. That calamity that day inside the shooting box will stay in my memory forever.

We now head downhill off the moorland tops towards the third grouse drive of the day. The 'big drive' as the Laird calls it, that's why he's wanting me to load double guns for him. 'Rapid shooting' the Laird calls it. Everybody else is following on behind us, there's all the shooting men in their smart four-wheel drive vehicles behind us just like a convoy. Behind them is the tractor, pulling the covered-in beaters' trailer which is full of beaters, flankers and picker-uppers, not forgetting their snarling, biting retriever-come-hunting dogs.

We head on down the moor road which is beauty in itself. Down either side of the moor road are avenues of mountain ash trees, these are about all the trees that will grow up here at this high altitude.

As we travel along I am chewing away at my thick slices of beef. The Laird sees me and he says, "You shouldn't have brought that Doug, there was plenty of that up in the shooting box, you should just have taken that."

I smile at the Laird.

We now reach the foothills of the high moorlands and we now drop on to a newly-laid moorland road. The Laird tells me it's only recently been constructed and says "It's to save us time and eliminates everyone from doing a lot of walking."

The new moor road was made of compounded rock and the Laird tells me all the rocks are from a natural source which can be found up here just below the surface of the ground. We are now turning off the new moorland road, all the shooting men follow us in their smart four-wheel drive vehicles, but the tractor and beaters' trailer carry straight on along the new-made road.

The Laird tells me, "The beaters and everyone else have a long, long way to go to get to the far side of the moorland." He says, "When they eventually reach their destination they will drop themselves off one at a time until they are all lined out across the moorland, and when everyone is in their positions the grouse drive will commence. By then," says the Laird, "all us shooting men will be in our positions in our shooting butts."

The Laird is now parking up his vehicle and all the other shooting men park alongside us. The Laird says, "This is now the hard bit." He points up a glen, which is what we call a valley or a ghyll, which stretches way, way up to the top of the moorland. "That's where we are going," says the Laird. All the shooting men are by now laden down with gear. They have their twelve bores in their carrying holdalls, which are strung over their shoulder, plus boxes of cartridges on top. I was no exception. The Laird loads boxes on top of boxes of cartridges on to me and I tell the Laird, "It looks as though you intend to do a lot of shooting!"

And off we all set up this high rising valley or glen. As we climb higher and higher the glen opens out into a wild valley. By, what beauty it was to my eyes. We see big moorland sides reaching high into the sky at either side of the valley. We reach a stone shooting butt and the Laird stops and says this is where he is shooting from. I see a line of stone shooting butts leading right up to the top of the valley head and the rest of the shooting men carry on up the valley and on to their own allotted shooting butts.

I turn around and I see the Laird taking out his guns, they are a matching pair of twelve bores. The Laird tells me they are made to measure to his special requirements. I pick one up, it's very light in weight. They are twenty-eight inch barrels, that's what they call a 'game gun'. There is the most intricate of engraving on the breech mechanism and trigger guard, and they have the finest of walnut stocks (butts). I see a gold disc embossed into the butt, only the finest of guns carry these gold discs.

We are now ready for the grouse to be driven over our heads. I felt as proud as punch as I stood there at the side of the Laird with my smart gamekeeper's suit on. The Laird's pair of twelve bores are now loaded and I have one at the ready waiting to pass it on to the Laird once he has emptied the gun in his hand. All we have to do now is wait for the grouse to appear.

As the Laird is peering and skinning his eyes over the top of the butt, I feel into my pocket and pull out my lobster. I crack its shell, the Laird hears the shell crack, looks at my lobster and says, "You shouldn't have brought that with you Doug, they are very expensive. There were some in the shooting box you could have had for free."

I look at the Laird and smile, and I give him a piece of lobster. I now feel into my other pocket and pull out the full bottle of champagne. As the cork pops out of the bottle the Laird hears it. He now sees the bottle of champagne, his eyes sparkle, and he says, "You shouldn't have brought that Doug, there was some in the shooting box you could have had for free."

I look at the Laird and smile, and pass the bottle to him for him to have a swig. The Laird looks at the label and says, "This is expensive champagne. It's just the same brand we had in the shooting box."

I look at the Laird and smile.

Now the Laird is taking a great big swig out of the bottle and he says, "This lobster is making me thirsty."

We hear calling out, "Go back! Go back!"

We look up into the sky and we see grouse passing by over our heads. The Laird instantly pulls his gun butt into his shoulder. He has only time to get off one quick shot and a single grouse falls out of the small covey to the bang of his gun. I quickly pass over the other fully-loaded gun. I compliment the Laird on his quick shot he got off then I pass him the champagne bottle. I tell him, "That deserves a drink." The Laird takes the bottle and has a good guzzling swig. I pass him more lobster.

We hear more banging guns coming from the other shooting men in the butts further up the valley. We see grouse dropping here, there and everywhere. We have the walkie-talkie in the butt with us and we can hear the beaters talking. We hear shouting and flag-cracking coming from the background on the walkie-talkies.

That's the beaters we hear driving the grouse forever closer to us in the shooting butts. I take a swig of champagne. The Laird takes the bottle from me, now he's swigging the champagne. I pass him more lobster.

We see a flanker high up on the moor top, he's waving his flag like a mad crazy man, then we see a covey of grouse coming our way. They are high in the sky, the Laird lets fire at a leading bird, it crumples to his shot. Momentarily he pulls the gun butt from his shoulder, he eyes up another bird and quickly lets bang, another grouse bites the dust. The flanker's still waving his flag like a mad crazy man. I snatch the empty gun from the Laird, I thrust the other full gun into his hands. There's more grouse over our head, the Laird picks up and lets fire, another bird crumples. And yet again the Laird momentarily takes the butt from his shoulder before eyeing up another bird which he takes with the other barrel.

If the Laird had kept the butt of his gun to his shoulder that would have been deemed by the shooting fraternity as a 'right and a left'. The Laird says he has difficulty keeping the gun butt to his shoulder. I pass the Laird another complimentary drink of champagne.

We hear constant bang, bang, banging of shots going off in the high up butts further up the valley. We see grouse raining out of the sky. We hear the beaters constantly talking to each other on the walkie-talkies, they are keeping each other well informed on what's taking place right across the moorland. I pass the Laird another swig of champagne.

The Laird tells me this is a massive drive the beaters are driving. He tells me they are coming across three vast moors altogether. He says they come across a moor called Dallow Glen Moor which then carries on across another moor called Scar Moor Ridge.

In all these three moors together there are thousands of grouse. The Laird tells me the reason these butts we are in now were purposely positioned in this valley bottom was to give the shooting men high birds to shoot at. The Laird points up to the top of the moorland in front of us, then he turns and points up to the top of the moorland behind us. So now when the grouse are driven over us shooting men in the butts in the valley bottom, the grouse are flying from one moorland top to the other moorland top making the birds high which presents us with difficult shots.

I look, I see the lobster has all been eaten; I look, I see the bottle of champagne is now empty. The Laird has 'drank' most of the champagne or should that be 'drunk'? The Laird to me looks a little bit tipsy and tiddly.

I see more grouse coming over the top of the valley head and I nudge the Laird, he hasn't seen them coming. The Laird ducks low and then springs high and he quickly takes a leading bird. And yet again the Laird momentarily takes the gun butt from his shoulder and then pulls the butt back into his shoulder before taking a tail end bird. I quickly pass him the other gun. I hear the beaters on the walkie-talkie, one of them is saying there's a massive covey of grouse passing low across the moorland. He says there must be more than three hundred grouse in the covey. I look at the Laird, the Laird looks at me, then the Laird says, "That's one hell of a big covey of grouse."

We hear one beater ask where they are on the moor, another beater replies they are just skimming over the top of Kiss Brig Bents.

The Laird says, "The grouse are quite a distance from us yet". By now the Laird has many dead grouse strewn around our butt laid in the heather. We see more birds coming in the distance and they head straight over the head of the flanker. The birds are veering away from me and the Laird in our butt and the flanker doesn't flag them back over to our way. We watch the birds as they drift down the valley and these birds we see in the distance somehow just don't look right to me. As we watch them, for some unknown reason they turn and veer our way and we duck low in our butt as the birds come closer and closer. They are now all but upon us and the Laird springs up to shoot but I spring up and put my hand on the gun's barrels and pull it away. I shake my head at the Laird and say, "They are blackcock, Black Bob has told us not to shoot them." The Laird pulls his gun down.

The shooting men in the butts above us further up the valley are doing plenty of shooting by the sound of all the banging guns going off. We keep seeing plenty of grouse falling from the sky, so they are shooting well.

We keep on hearing the beaters over the walkie-talkies shouting at each other as they are driving the moor. The massive covey of grouse has been spotted again by another beater. We hear them shouting their heads off, "Flag 'em! Flag 'em!" That's the flagging at the grouse to keep them on course and heading towards us in the shooting butts. The beaters are getting forever closer to

us as they drive the moor forward.

By now the grouse are coming at more regular intervals and by now the Laird is going into a frenzy of shooting. I am going into a frenzy of passing loaded guns to him and reloading.

I say again, what happens next will stay in my memory forever.

We again hear the beaters over the walkie-talkie, we hear "Flag 'em! Flag 'em!" They say the massive covey of grouse is now going over the ridge.

The Laird says, "The Ridge, that's just over the top of the valley in front of us".

We see another small covey of grouse, they are high in the sky. the Laird drops one and then a pause as per usual. The birds are plummeting to earth. I quickly pass the other loaded gun to the Laird as we see more grouse coming. I look up, the Laird looks up, and what the Laird sees he doesn't like. The last grouse he has just shot, it's coming side-tippling out of the sky, and all within the flash of an eye the dead grouse hits the Laird smack bang in his face. The Laird goes reeling backwards and he hit's the deck, plonking his arse bang in the middle of a pool of water on the butt floor.

I look up and what I see is a sight for tired eyes. The massive covey of grouse come speeding like bullets over the top of the valley head. I don't have to think what to do next, I pick up the Laird's gun put it to my shoulder and get a double shot off at the speeding grouse. Both barrels find their mark. I know the Laird's gun is loaded because I have just loaded it for him. I snatch the gun out of his hands as he is sat there in the puddle of water. I thrust the empty gun into his hands and say, "Quick, load that."

I look up, the sky is black with speeding grouse, a quick right and left and down come another two grouse. I look back down at the Laird, he's just closing up the loaded gun. I again snatch it from him, and again thrust the empty gun into his hands. I tell him, "Here, load that quick."

The Laird's moaning and saying, "I am the shooting man here, you are the bloody loader."

I ignore his moans. I look up, there's grouse streaming overhead, I drop two stone dead from the front, without loitering about. I grab the other now loaded gun from the Laird. The Laird's saying, "Pull me up out of this bloody puddle, give me back my guns here."

I ignore the Laird's pleas. I look up, I see the tail end of the massive covey of grouse just leaving. A quick double bang from the Laird's gun and I have another two grouse down.

I hear the Laird, he's still moaning, saying, "Give me my bloody guns here. I am the shooting man here, pull me out of this bloody water."

So I do as he asks. The Laird's now looking over the butt wall with a gun I have just loaded for him, but there's nothing there for him to shoot. I say, "They have all gone my friend." All we see is a line of beaters stood on the valley head. We hear a whistle being blown, we hear a hunting horn being blown, the grouse drive is over.

I am sure I will keep this in my memory forever.

The Laird's now complimenting me on the four right and lefts I have just had. I tell the Laird about Alan who broke the British record for shooting the woodpigeon in one day, just over 700 I tell the Laird. I carry on to tell him Alan is a keen enthusiast on shooting, and that Alan himself goes grouse shooting in the Yorkshire Dales. I tell the Laird Alan also holds a record there. He had three consecutive right and lefts at the grouse and a plaque was put on the shooting butt to commemorate his 'HAT TRICK'.

The Laird says with a big smile on his face, "Maybe we should have a plaque put on this shooting butt to commemorate your 'quadruple' of right and lefts."

I give the Laird a big smile.

We went on that day and had another successful grouse drive, and then the grouse shooting was over for the day. It was then everyone together and off we all went down off the moorland and into the glen bottom and back to Bob's cottage, the Hunter's Lodge.

All the grouse from the day's shooting were laid out in Bob's courtyard and counted. And if my memory serves me right we counted 298 brace, that's one hell of a big bag of grouse is that.

All the shooting men are now gathering together again in Bob's courtyard. There's still another good two hours of daylight left yet, and all the shooting men have been invited by the Laird to finish the evening off with a spot of wildfowling on Bob's flight pond. That's the pond where I throw all the rabbits' guts into when I have been out rabbiting. And Bob kept to his word that if I helped him out on the grouse shooting day he would invite me to the wildfowling evening. That's just what Bob did and he also invited my beloved Helen.

As you readers know, Bob's flight pond is high up on the moorland tops. Bob put me and Helen in one butt to shoot as a twosome. A little along the flight pond side Bob positioned himself in a shooting butt there. The next shooting butt along from Bob was positioned Big Jim who you now know is the keeper for the Laird at the other side of the vast estate some twenty miles away. The Laird positioned himself in the next butt on, that butt is underneath a main duck flight path, this is where most ducks that come are expected to fly over. The following two butts on from the Laird were two shooting men who had been grouse shooting today.

The whole of the flight pond is now surrounded by us shooting men, and Helen of course. So now, whichever way the ducks fly in we have them covered. Many wild geese are expected to fly in also.

Ducks and geese naturally feed at night and about an hour before nightfall is when the ducks and geese begin to fly out to their feeding grounds. The term used for this by wildfowlers is the 'evening flight'. After the ducks and geese have fed through the night on their feeding grounds, at daybreak the ducks and geese fly off and seek refuge on a large expanse of water where they can safely rest up for the day. So, when the ducks and geese leave their feeding grounds, the term used by wildfowlers is the 'morning flight'.

So, now all us shooting men are positioned in our shooting butts around Bob's flight pond at our evening flight. We now have one hour of daylight left, we are ready.

There are seven more shooting men who were shooting grouse today and they are positioned elsewhere, they have gone to a large loch. This is where the ducks and geese rest up for the day. Two of these shooting men have gone out into the middle of the large loch in a rowing boat and they have taken their guns with them. The other five shooting men are spread out in a long line along the shore of the large loch. They have their guns with them too, they are now ready.

I still have my walkie-talkie with me from the grouse shooting, it's stood at the front of me and Helen as we stand in our shooting butt. The shooting men on the loch still have their walkie-talkies with them too. Me and Helen can hear them talking to each other, and we can hear the two shooting men in the rowing boat. They are telling the shooting men on the shoreline of the loch that there's a large raft of ducks and geese roosting out in the middle of the loch. The shooting men in the rowing boat say, "We are all but upon them, they have spotted us, they are becoming agitated."

"They are up in the air!" shouts one of them.

Me and Helen are listening intently as they speak and we hear over the walkie-talkies two double bangs from their guns. We then hear the same double bangs with a delayed response noise coming from over the distant hills. Again over the walkie-talkies we hear repeated bang, bang, banging of guns from the shooting men on the shoreline. Again me and Helen here the same bang, bang, banging with a delayed response noise coming from the distant hills.

By now me and Helen are all tensed up as we stand in our shooting butt. We are scanning and peeling our eyes into the sky looking for ducks and geese coming into our vision. Surely something must be coming into our direction soon. Then I hear whistling wing beats of wildfowl. Now Helen nearly knocks me over, I turn and she has her gun to her shoulder. She takes a quick right and left. I look up into the sky where she's shooting and I see a big party of mallard, they are passing over our heads like speeding bullets. I see two of the mallard are crumpled up and falling to earth. "Good shooting," I say to Helen.

The speeding party of mallard pass over our heads that fast I don't have time to get a shot off. I see the mallard as they go whizzing over Bob's head, I see another two ducks crumple and fall to another double bang from Bob's gun. The mallard continue whizzing on over Big Jim and the Laird. The party of mallard are keeping to the edge of the flight pond. They are circling, they are now passing over the heads of the two shooting men.

I hear bang, bang, banging of guns, I see mallard plummeting to the ground. As the rest of the party of mallard continue whizzing on, I don't believe what I see, the mallard have circled all the way around the flight pond, they are now coming back over mine and Helen's heads. This time I am ready, I quickly stand and pull my gun to my shoulder, and yet again Helen beats me to shoot. I am distracted. This time I see three mallard crumple and fall from just two bangs from Helen's gun. That's a bit of fortunate shooting on Helen's behalf. There were two mallard flying close together and she's hit both of them with the spread of pellets. I am that intent on watching Helen's birds fall and complimenting her on her good shooting I never got a shot off. I see the big party of mallard whiz off and disappear across the moorland with at least a dozen ducks less than when they first whizzed in.

Everyone around the flight pond leaves the dead mallard where they have dropped, we will gather them later.

My Pup and Helen's dog at our feet are getting themselves all excited with all the banging guns going off. I bend down to cosset them and as I bend I hear Helen's gun snap shut. Before I have time to stand up from my stoop, Helen's petite bum collides with my bum and she knocks me skittling onto the butt floor. As I knock the dogs off me from licking my face, I hear honking geese over our heads, and from my laid down position on the butt floor, I look up and see two pink-footed geese come tumbling from the sky. Another good right and left from Helen.

I quickly rise to my feet, I peer over the top of the butt, I see yet more geese falling as they pass over the other shooting men. I now hear bang, bang, banging coming from over the walkie-talkies, and hear the same bang, bang, banging from over the distant hills. I hear another double bang come from my left, it's Bob shooting.

Helen again has her gun to her shoulder. She's beaten me yet again to the draw. I see a party of shoveler ducks passing overhead and I see three of them fall from the sky. Helen says, "I think I missed one of them." I think Helen is being modest, I am sure it was me who missed.

Helen taps me and says, "Duck down." So I quickly duck low and I peer over the butt, there's two geese flying straight towards us. With my gun at the ready as I watch them coming closer I think to myself, there's something amiss with these two geese coming. They are now upon us, I rise up to shoot, I hesitate, Helen doesn't. She lets bang with both barrels and they both crumple to the bangs of Helen's gun.

I tell Helen, "They are not geese you have just shot, they are a pair of shelduck. They look like geese at a distance."

By now it's coming into deep dusk, I hear bang, bang, banging coming from all directions. There's that much banging coming over the walkie-talkies it's making it vibrate around on the butt top.

I hear splash, splash, splash as dead ducks keep dropping in the flight pond. I hear honking, gaggling, yodelling of white-fronted geese passing overhead. It's by now got too dark to see them.

All that can be heard now is the wing beats of ducks as they pass us on by. I can hear that familiar quacking of mallard. I can hear goldeneye, they are making a loud whistling noise with their wings. I can hear cock wigeon calling out their far-carrying whistle, a sound that once heard is never to be forgotten.

Our evening flight of wildfowling is now over, it's by now a pitch black night. I can't see a foot in front of my face, but my eyes will soon grow accustomed to the darkness.

Me and Helen and our dogs go out of our shooting butt. I hear Bob and all the other shooting men, they are sending out their dogs to retrieve their shot ducks and geese. As the dim light casts over the flight pond, I see dogs splashing around everywhere. I hear shooting men who must be stood on the water's edge. They are whistling and shouting at their dogs giving them directions on where they think the ducks and geese lie dead.

I feel something touching my leg, it's Pup pawing me, she has a big drake mallard duck in her mouth. I take it from her and off she goes again and disappears into the darkness of the night. There's Helen out there somewhere at the back of me, I hear her making a fuss of her dog for retrieving something back to hand. We gather together many ducks and geese.

All the shooting men have now gathered together at the far side of the flight pond. Bob has now brought his Land Rover to load everything into. "It saves walking and carrying," says Bob.

The Land Rover is now laden with many dead ducks and geese. Me and Helen jump in the Land Rover by the side of Bob and off we go down off the moorland. I look behind us and there's a procession of headlights following on behind us with all the shooting men's vehicles.

When we arrive back at Black Bob's cottage, the Hunter's Lodge, the shooting men who have been shooting over on the large loch are already there waiting to meet us. Now with Bob's courtyard light on we unload our heavy burden of dead ducks and geese. We lay them in a neat tidy line, several lines I might add, what a good bag they look too. As I browse my eyes across them, I see mallard, teal, wigeon, shelduck, many different breeds of ducks.

I cast my browsing eyes across the geese. I see white-fronted geese, pink-footed geese, greylag geese, many different breeds of geese.

Bob allows each shooting man a pair of wildfowl of their choice, that's compliments of the Laird. The shooting men also get a complimentary brace of grouse from the day's grouse shooting.

The rest of all the ducks and geese are now hung in Bob's game larder together with all the grouse that were shot earlier this day. The game larder is by now jam-packed full. Bob says, "The gamedealer will pick them up in the morning. He will pay a good price for this lot." Which all helps the Laird run a well organized estate.

If my memory serves me right we shot 129 head of wildfowl on that evening flight. Not a bad bag I do think.

Everyone's now heading off home. Someone taps me on the shoulder, I turn, I get a great whacking kiss on my lips. It's Helen, she's bidding me good evening. And off she goes on her quad bike with two big fat mallard ducks in the basket at the back and her dog laid on the seat sandwiched between her legs. She's one belter of a lass, is that Helen, a lass of my dreams.

Me and Bob now head off and into his cottage we go. Bob's now looking in the oven at the side of the big log-burning fire. He's pulling out a big tray, it's got four whole cooked grouse on it and he says he prepared these earlier. Bob's now got two grouse on a plate for me and two grouse on a plate for him. Bob's now bent down in the oven again, he's now pulling out a tray full of cooked potatoes, carrots and turnip all in onion gravy.

Me and Bob eat like a couple of lords in this cottage all courtesy of the Laird. After our lord's banquet of a dinner I pull my big armchair up in front of the log-burning fire. I look around me, Bob's still not got me a pair of slippers.

Bob's now laid back comfortably in his old rocking chair by my side. I get to telling Bob about his flight pond, I tell him it's too cold, it needs some shelter. I tell Bob I have planted several flight ponds in the past with willow trees and that I would plant his flight pond if he wanted me to. Bob nods in agreement with me. I tell Bob there's some willow trees growing down by the riverside not far away.

As you readers know, Bob promised to take me out lamping rabbits the evening after for helping him out on the grouse shooting day today. Bob kept to his promise so I tell Bob that tomorrow daytime I have all to myself before the rabbit lamping in the late evening. So it was agreed that I would go willow tree planting for him tomorrow, and on that it was early to bed that evening.

I was up bright and early the next morning and still again Bob was up before me. When I went out into the courtyard, the argocat was stood there with the engine ticking over. As I'm getting myself ready to be off Bob says, "Have a look around the flight pond, see if Pup can pick up any dead ducks that we might have overlooked yesterday." Then as me and Pup are setting off in the argocat Bob shouts after us, "Check the mink trap while you're there too."

Off me and Pup go across the rugged terrain, bumping and bouncing as we go, and we finally arrive at the riverside. These willows I am about to take are 'crack willow' and in the past these willows have been what they call 'polled', meaning cut back. Once this happens it encourages the willow tree to sprout new branches very quickly and the new branches grow in clusters and as straight as an arrow. I look at the crack willow I am about to cut, I see they are in clusters and straight. There's some of them more than twelve foot long and a good inch thick.

I set to work cutting them. I have with me a junior hacksaw and I saw the straight branches off deep at the main base of the tree. As I cut them I keep on loading them on to the back of the argocat, the straight branches are green and in full leaf. You can grow them practically all year round, this also includes other willows such as 'pussy willow' and any other sort of willow I should imagine.

If you are not planting the willow straightaway when you have cut them, put them in a barrel with about eighteen inches of water in, and within a matter of a few short weeks the branches will root heavily right up to the top of the water level.

I now have the argocat laden to capacity and off me and Pup go to Bob's flight pond.

It's now all simple to plant the willow. I get one of the branches I have cut, it must be more than twelve foot long. I am stood at the edge of the flight pond in thick, wet, sludgy peat, which is ideal growing conditions, and I just push the willow branch about two feet into the ground. And that's all there is to it. That will now quickly root and grow.

I want to make this flight pond nice and warm and welcoming to the wildfowl, so I plant willows so that when they grow they will be shielding off the bitterly cold north-westerly winds that blow up here.

All my big pile of willows now planted I stand back and admire them, they look perfect as I look across them. It will not be long before they grow tall and bush out making it warm and welcoming for the ducks and geese when they arrive.

While I have been planting these willows I have been watching my dog Pup, she has been hunting the surroundings of the flight pond. I have seen her bringing back dead ducks she has found that were shot the day before.

I now go and investigate Bob's mink trap. It's nestled and concealed in some sivs at the side of the flight pond and it's been baited with a jointed rabbit. I gingerly move forward and what I see makes me anxiously jump back.

There it is, it's a mink in the cage trap and it's biting ferociously at the wire cage trying to escape. It has a rich, glossy, dark brown fur coat.

These mink that run wild in Britain are not native to this country. They were originally imported from around the world and kept on mink farms purposely for their valuable fur which was made into expensive fur coats. But the inevitable happened and they escaped and now run wild in the British countryside. They now create total havoc among other wildlife, killing in a frenzy. And that's not only to land animals and birds, they are the finest of swimmers, diving to deep depths and creating havoc among the fish also.

I will leave this mink alone, Bob will deal with it.

I now go to see what my Pup has found and retrieved. I see a pair of mallard, a duck and a drake (female and male). I also gather a teal and a wigeon, and on that, our mission now accomplished, me and my Pup hop into the argocat and off we set back to Bob's cottage, Hunter's Lodge.

When I arrive there I see Helen's quad bike parked there in the courtyard. I switch of the argocat's engine and now I can hear pigs screaming their heads off. I go round to the pig hole (sty) and I see Helen and Bob. They are trying to get a rope around the nose of one of the pigs. They say they are going to slaughter these two large Tamworth pigs and they say they want me to give them a helping hand.

The reason why they are trying to get the rope around the pig's nose is so they can lead the pig out of the pig hole and to where they want to slaughter it.

As I now look back through time, back in the olden days a lot of people would keep pigs down on their allotments (big gardens) purposely to slaughter for their own tables. While the pigs were still young they would pierce a large, heavy-duty ring through the end of their nostrils. So now, when the pigs were big and fat and ready for slaughter, they would put a rope through the ring at the end of the pig's nose. And with the nose being a vulnerable, delicate point they could lead the pig to anywhere they wanted it.

Helen and Bob are doing it all wrong, these two Tamworth pigs have no rings in their noses, so Helen and Bob are trying to get their rope around the full snout of the pig. This is now a strong point of the pig, he is now big and strong enough to pull Helen and Bob into the next county. So I go into the pig hole and show them how it should be done.

Now there is no ring I have to use the next best alternative. I have the noose rope in my hand as I push the pig up by the side of the pig hole. All this activity that's going off around the pig is all new to him. He is agitated and screaming, and he has his mouth open as he screams. So I quickly slide the noose deep into his mouth and pull the rope tight and his big teeth at the front now hold the rope firmly. The rope is now on a weak, vulnerable part of the pig and he can now be lead and pulled anywhere we want him.

We now pull him out of the pig hole and there's holy hell being played by both of the pigs screaming their heads off.

Me and Helen pull the rope around a strong wooden post slowly pulling the pig in. The pig's head is now held firmly against the strong wooden post and he can now move his head nowhere. In comes Bob with the loaded humane killer gun, he quickly puts the end of the gun on the centre of the pig's forehead and 'bang', the pig drops like a sack of potatoes to the floor. Now we hear only one screaming pig coming from the pig hole.

This humane killer gun I speak of shoots no bullets for safety of the people. It is loaded with a powerful 'cap' which when fired explodes a 'rod' which shoots down the short barrel of the gun and enters the brain to about six to eight inches. As fast as the 'rod' shoots out of the gun it shoots back in again. The humane killer gun is now all ready for its next victim (once it's reloaded with another 'cap') and that's over this pig hole door by the sounds of all the screaming that's going off inside.

There, so now our large Tamworth pig is laid kicking itself to death on the floor. It's only its body nerves kicking out the legs.

Bob moves in with a long-bladed, razor-sharp 'sticking knife'. He sticks the full length of the knife blade deep into the pig's throat and as the knife is drawn out blood gushes out with it. It's the beating pig's heart that is pumping the blood out. The sticking knife has severed the pig's jugular vein.

The cobble stones we stand on and where the now dead pig lays are spotlessly clean. We don't want the pig dirty once we start butchering him, do we.

We now have to get the dead pig from the floor and laid onto what slaughter men call a 'scratch'. This is like a heavy-duty stretcher which holds the pig up high while the butcher men go to work on the slaughtered pig.

Bob is now slitting behind the strong guider on the back legs of the pig and is now inserting a 'camel' into the slits. A camel is a specially shaped piece of heavy-duty wood which has serrated, notched, saw-like teeth at each end. This now holds the pig's back legs apart.

Bob now attaches a strong rope to the centre of the camel and the rope is then attached to a chain lifting gear and the big fat Tamworth pig is hauled up into the air. The chain lifting gear has a weight scale at the top and it weighs in pounds not stones. Our pig weighs a whopping 400lbs. A butcher would buy this pig on the 'HOOF' meaning live weight, which our pig is. It's still intact, we haven't gutted it yet. The butcher would say it weighs 20 'score', score meaning a group of 20. So 20lbs equal one score and twenties into 400 equals 20 score. So now you readers know how the butcher weighs his animals on the 'hoof' alive.

This weighing scale that Bob is using is what he weighs the red deer on when they have been stalked up on the hill. So now when the gamedealer comes to pick up a consignment of deer he will know how much each individual deer weighs.

So we now have our pig suspended up in the air and we now lower the pig on the 'scratch'. Me, Helen and Bob can now set to work on butchering the pig.

The whopping pig is absolutely covered in long ginger hairs and all these hairs have to be removed. As you readers know, when you buy a joint of pork from the butcher's shop the joint has no hairs on it.

These hairs have to be scalded off. We have with us in the courtyard an electric boiler and it's brimful of boiling water. We now have to ladle the boiling water over the pig and the boiling water soon makes the strong bristling hairs soft. We have with us a specially designed scraper each and me, Helen and Bob now set to work scraping all this hair off the pig, with a lot of pouring boiling water over the pig and a lot of scraping the hairs off.

We finally get the pig hairless, not 'hirsute' anymore. The still screaming pig in the pig hole wouldn't recognise his mate now if he saw him. We now have him looking all prim and proper.

So now that job is done we now have to give the pig a 'manicure', or is that 'pedicure', we have to pull off all the pigs toenails. This is a job for Bob with all his weight. At the back of the special hair scraper is a hook and this hook is stuck in at the back of the pig's nails and Bob gives a sharp yank and the nail comes off completely. Another few yanks and Bob has all the pig's nails off. So now that's both them jobs done.

We now haul the pig back up into the air with its back legs still held apart by the 'camel'. Bob pulls out another long-bladed slaughter man's knife and what they call a 'steel'. Bob slides the blade of the knife down one side of the steel and this steel puts a razor-sharp edge on the knife. An expert slaughter man can do this so fast you can hardly see the blade of the knife.

With the pig suspended up in the air Bob runs the blade of the knife right the way down the pig's belly. All its guts fall out, and with a little help from Bob, straight into a bin below. The guts now out, Bob's now gone in for the liver and it comes out blood red. Bob's now poking about in the pig's ribcage and he comes out with a big pig's heart in his hands.

Bob's now got a big razor-sharp meat cleaver in his hands. He's now lifting the cleaver high into the air and with one whacking great chop he hits the pig right between its open back legs. The meat cleaver slices down the centre of the backbone, and then another great whacking chop takes the cleaver to the ribcage. A few more lighter chops through the ribcage and on through the middle of the pig's head, and the pig falls into two halves. The pig has now been butchered and is hung in a cold store to let the meat set.

The other pig in the pig hole goes the same way.

Helen's now jumping on her quad bike and she asks me if I want to go down to her homestead tonight for a drink. I tell her that I can't, Bob is taking me out rabbit lamping. I see Helen's eyes light up and she gives out a plea to Bob, saying, "Let me come Bob."

Bob's a big softie with Helen and he nods his approval to her. She's now off to get her rifle from home and I shout to her as she's leaving, "Be back here tonight at 10 o'clock prompt." And me and Bob now go into his cottage.

It's by now only just become nightfall and we have to give the rabbits plenty of time to get well out on their feeding grounds. I am itching to be at these rabbits. Bob has told me this part of the Laird's estate is absolutely out of control with rabbits. This leaves me thinking, everywhere I have looked so far on the Laird's vast estate is absolutely out of control with rabbits, so just how many rabbits are there out where Bob's taking me? PHEW, I bet they must be in their thousands.

Me and Bob kill time waiting for zero hour to arrive by getting ourselves a good meal inside us. And by the time we have got all our gear together, and rifles and bullets all ready, it's by now coming up to 10 o'clock at night. There's someone coming through Bob's cottage door. It's Helen all bright-eyed and cheery and that's our signal to be off.

I remember that evening quite clearly in my mind. Just as all three of us were leaving the cottage, Bob's telephone rings and Bob answers it. Bob appears to be agitated on the phone, it's a chap called Jock and he's telling Bob he has seen poachers lamping the deer in the bottom of the glens. I can see Bob's really upset with himself. He puts the phone down and then picks it back up again. Bob's now talking to Big Jim who's at the other side of the of the Laird's vast estate. Bob quickly arranges to meet Big Jim on a lonely highland road.

Bob slams the phone down and says in a hurried voice to me and Helen, "Come on you two, you will have to help in catching these deer poachers. We will have to postpone the rabbit lamping for tonight."

This leaves me thinking, I am all right going out catching poachers? I am as much of a poacher as these poachers we are going out to catch.

All three of us quickly jump into Bob's Land Rover and race off out of the courtyard. We race along a rough old cart road that takes us through lonely secluded glens. The headlights are shining on many rabbits as we go along.

The cart road eventually leads us on to another small back road and Bob says, "This is the road the poachers are lamping the deer on," and adds that very few vehicles use this road. Bob says. "It's too early yet for the deer. They drop off the hills in the dead of the night to feed in the meadows of the low lying glens which shelters them from the bitter cold mountain winds."

Bob plugs a spotlight into the dashboard of the Land Rover and he's now passing the spotlight to me. He says, "Here, flash that along the meadows at the side of the road, see if you can see any deer."

I do as Bob says and flash the light around but all I see is hundreds of rabbits' eyes flashing back at me. Bob chunters to himself, "It's Big Jim's job to keep these rabbits under control but he's not doing a very good job is he?" Bob then looks at me and says, "This is your job now Doug, to keep these rabbits under control."

Those words from Bob sounded like music to my ears, all these rabbits at my mercy, wow!

As we drove along that mountain glen back road I flashed the spotlight around and we must have passed by thousands of rabbits as we went. I see a pine forest plantation in the distance, that will be where the rabbit warrens are, and I am thinking to myself, I will have to have a look around this place at a later date, now that I am the rabbit catcher.

Bob says, "The deer haven't dropped off the hills yet, the poachers will be laid up somewhere waiting."

I look out ahead of us and I see a Land Rover in our headlights. It's big Jim parked up and he is stood there waiting for us to arrive. He says he has seen no signs of the poachers.

Bob says, "We will lay up at the top of 'Hell Hole Rocks' and watch for the poachers coming from up there."

We drive on and Bob turns off this lonely deserted back road on to a track and Big Jim follows us in his Land Rover. We start climbing up this mountain side on a rough old bumpy track. The Land Rover is bouncing and bumping as it goes over large rugged stones on the track. Bob has to use the low gearbox four-wheel drive to get us up there. Halfway up the mountain side Bob turns the Land Rover around and parks up right at the edge of a rock face and turns off the headlights and engine. Big Jim parks up his Land Rover well at the back of us and out of sight.

Big Jim comes over and gets into our Land Rover. Now it's a big squeeze, they are two big hefty men are Bob and Big Jim. Helen sits on my knees as we are now sandwiched between the two big buggers.

All four of us sit there in total darkness with the Land Rover brinking over the edge of this rock face. Any vehicles that now come along that quiet lonely highland back road we will be able to see as we look down. I am sure we will not be spotted halfway up this mountain side where Bob calls 'Hell Hole Rocks'.

As we sit there peeling our eyes waiting and watching for any headlights approaching Big Jim and Bob are now discussing how they are going to catch the poachers when they appear. Me and Helen are listening to them intently.

Big Jim and Bob are now telling me and Helen how they once caught a notorious deer poacher on their estate. They say they were doing a spot of work up on a hill called 'Black Hill'. Bob says, "I was at one side of Black Hill and Big Jim was at the other side of the hill when we heard a big rifle being fired. We had the walkie-talkies with us."

Big Jim says, "I saw the poacher through my telescope and he was loading a dead red deer stag on to the petrol tank of his scramble motorbike. I informed Bob of what was happening as he couldn't see the poacher from his position on Black Hill. There's a track up on the low-lying mountains where the poacher is. It's the only way down off the mountains, so me and Bob planned to apprehend this poacher on that track. We had to be fast in getting there, the poacher was already making his escape."

Helen's fair gripping my hand in tension as she's sat on my knee sandwiched between Bob and Big Jim as they are telling us their poacher story as we all sit in the Land Rover. I look at Helen, I think she is loving the story.

Big Jim says, "I race across the side of Black Hill and I reach the track before the poacher gets there."

Bob says, "I have to cross a ravine to get to this track, and I have to cross it in a cradle which I pull along by ropes. I have Zak with me, my Alsatian dog, he's a good poacher catcher is Zak. As I am hurrying to pull this cradle along to get myself over the ravine Zak has his front paws up on top of the cradle, he knows what's going off. We see the poacher go whizzing by us on his scramble motorbike but there's nothing me or Zak can do. The poacher has beaten us to it, and I see he has a fine red deer stag strewn over his motorbike. He has his big rifle strapped over his back and he makes a rude gesture to me as he whizzes by."

I think Helen is full of tension listening to this story as she's now gripping her arms tight around my neck. I hope you readers are enjoying my story. Remember, all this happened way back in the 1970s. These are the words I recall Bob and Big Jim saying.

Bob says, "I got on my walkie-talkie, I knew big Jim couldn't see the poacher coming, and I tell him."

Jim says, "The poacher's coming straight at me so I stand in the middle of the track and put my hand up to stop him. I knew the poacher couldn't turn off the track, there was a steep slope down one side and the deep ravine down the other side of the track. But the poacher's not heeding my 'stop', he's coming straight at me. He's now upon me so I pull my arm back and clench my fist, and with one great punch I hit him smack bang in the nose. The poacher goes reeling backwards as he falls. The scrambler motorbike carries on and careers down into the deep ravine with the red deer stag still strapped to the bike.

"The poacher's now picking himself up from the ground. He's shaking his head and, by, what a big fellow he is. He's towering above me, and I am a big hefty man. And he has arms on him as thick as my thighs. The poacher, he's now rubbing his nose, he sees blood on his hand, and it's me who's put that blood there. He looks at me with his evil devilish eyes and I don't like what I see.

"He's now taking his big rifle from off his back, I stand there aghast and speechless. He pulls the rifle back and gives me a great whacking thump with the gun butt right underneath my ribcage.

"I am out for the count and as I lay winded on the ground I look up and I see Zak the Alsatian. He has leapt on to the poacher and he has him by the wrist of his shooting arm. The poacher, he pulls Zak up clean off the ground. He's a big heavy dog is Zak, but the poacher's shaking Zak around like a rag doll. Zak falls to the ground hurt and whimpering, he's never tackled a giant of a man like this before. While Zak is still down and out on the ground, the poacher grabs Zak by the front legs and he's pulling them wide apart. This is a vulnerable point on a dog, this can split a dog's heart clean in two. Then as if from nowhere in comes Bob."

Bob says, "I see the poacher, he's trying to kill my dog, so I rugby tackle him from behind. The poacher hits the deck hard and he now let's go of Zak. I now have the poacher by the arm."

Big Jim says, "By now I have recovered my senses and I quickly move in and grab the poacher by the other arm. I see Zak back up on his feet, he has the poacher by the bottom of his leg. We now have the poacher beaten. Oh no we haven't, the poacher's now climbing to his feet and he's now picking me and Bob up off the ground. The poacher he's as strong as a bull, he's just like a mad crazy grizzly bear. He's now spinning us around on his arms, Zak's down there spinning with us. He's now whirling us that fast I drop off, I see Bob drop off. I see the poacher bend down, he's now got his fingers in Zak's mouth and he prises his jaws open and throws Zak to one side.

"The poacher, he now grabs hold of the front of my coat as I still lay on the ground. His eyeballs look dead into my eyeballs and I see the biggest clenched fist I ever did see in my life. It's massive, it's right in front of my very own eyes.

"The poacher says in a blood-spitting voice, 'Do you want some more, this is what I do for a living is fighting'. I hear Bob say, 'Let him go'. I don't know if Bob was telling me to let the poacher go or if Bob was telling the poacher to let me go, but the poacher let go of me. Now the poacher is off down the track and heading away from us.

"The poacher still has his big rifle in his hands and Bob pulls Zak safely by his side and says, 'That mad crazy poacher is liable to shoot Zak'.

"By now the poacher has disappeared out of sight into the glen bottoms. Bob now heads off too, saying he's heading for the cottage in the bottom of the glen. He says he is going to inform the police of the poacher. Bob told me to try to recover the poached red deer stag from the deep ravine, we will show that as evidence when the poacher reaches court."

Bob says, "I did inform the police they had a dangerous man armed with a rifle on the Laird's estate. The police did respond in full force, and they did capture that mad crazy poacher of a man. And the poacher eventually reached court and was severely dealt with.

"It was also found out the poacher was at one time a professional wrestler and also in the underworld he was a champion bare knuckle fighter. This poacher was a persistent notorious deer poacher on the Laird's estate and not long after his court hearing me and Big Jim received terrible threatening letters. One morning I found a red deer stag's head stuck on the wrought iron gates at the end of my driveway.

"The Laird's estate is so vast, it covers 150,000 acres, and with just me and Big Jim keepering it, it's hard work keeping control of all the poaching that takes place. At times the deer poaching gets so intense the Laird has to call in a special team of SAS-type people who specialise in poacher patrolling. They call themselves 'Country Guards', they are ex Royal Marines, and it's all carried out in military discipline. They will stake out a notorious deer poaching black spot and they have with them high-powered infrared 'scopes so that they can see into the night.

"They catch their fair share of deer poachers, but word soon spreads around the surrounding area that there is a poacher patrol team working. Then the poachers will lay quiet for a while and when the 'Country Guards' leave, back come the deer poachers again. It's a non-stop surveillance all the time," says Bob.

Do you readers think that was an exciting story that Bob and Big Jim have just told us? Helen certainly does, as she's sat on my knee now I can hear her teeth chattering together.

So, as me and Helen now sit together sandwiched between Bob and Big Jim in the front of the Land Rover which is parked on the top of what they call 'Hell Hole Rocks', we are all peeling and skinning our eyes looking down below us watching and waiting for these deer poachers to arrive tonight.

I feel Helen jump and she says, "Look!"

We all look, and we see headlights down on the narrow highland back road. It's the poachers, they are back again but they have no chance of seeing us halfway up this mountain side. As they drive along the road they are shining a spotlight out of the window, they are trying to pick up the deer in the light as they feed in the low lying pastures.

Big Jim slides the window open on our Land Rover. We see the poachers' vehicle stop, they are shining their spotlight beam on something out in the pasture. We hear the crack of a big rifle being fired, and we now see the vehicle drive away and disappear around the mountain side.

Bob says, "They have shot a deer. The poacher who has shot it will now be out of the vehicle which has now driven off to safety and will lay out of sight for a while. The poacher who has just shot the deer will, in total darkness so as not to be seen by the roving eye, now go out to the dead deer. He will stick it in the throat with a knife and bleed it. Then he will carry it back to the side of the road and lay low to wait for the vehicle to return.

"We will wait," says Bob. "I want to catch the poachers in possession of the dead deer so that I can use it as evidence when the poachers appear in court."

Bob was right with his shrewd, wise calculating words. We see the headlights of a vehicle coming back along the road and we see it stop in exactly the same place as it stopped before. It no sooner stops and then sets off again.

"That's it," says Bob, "the poacher's now back in the vehicle with the deer."

The poachers are now speeding down the road to make their escape and Bob quickly starts up the Land Rover to intercept the poachers. Off we set down the rough rugged track which leads us off the mountain side, bumping and bouncing about as we go. We are going along in near on total darkness. Bob is driving without the headlights on and he says, "We must not let the poachers see us yet, I want to surprise-attack them."

We see the poachers' headlights speeding along the road below us, they are going to beat us to the road end. Bob says, "Hold on tight now." Bob's now got his foot flat to the board on the Land Rover's accelerator and we are now speeding down the mountain side. We are bouncing and bumping that high mine and Helen's heads are hitting the roof of the Land Rover.

Helen's crying out, "If this is the mad crazy poacher you was telling us about earlier, then I want to get out and go home." No one's paying any attention to Helen's pleas.

We are now off the mountain side and the speeding poachers are all but upon us but they haven't seen us yet in the darkness. Bob now flashes on our headlights as we screech out into the middle of the road and come to an abrupt stop.

The poachers are now bang at the side of us and their headlights are shining and glaring into the cab of our Land Rover. I don't know who's the most shocked, the poachers who have just seen us spring abruptly in front of them or us who can see their vehicle smashing into the side of us.

Helen jumps that high in fear and excitement she jumps off my knee and on to Bob's knee. The poachers screech around the back of us, how they did that I do not know. There's a trench that runs at either side of the narrow back road, but they managed to get their vehicle between the trench and our Land Rover.

Bob's now playing hell with Helen, he's saying, "Will you sit still girl, get off my knee."

We see the poachers tear-arsing off down the road, so Bob screeches the Land Rover around in the road and screeches off after them. We are catching them up fast, our headlights are now shining on the poachers' vehicle. It's a battered old van they are in, our Land Rover has more speed and we are now screeching up at the back of them. Bob's flashing his headlights like hell at them signalling them to stop. But the poachers are having none of that, they screech on and down the road.

Bob puts his foot down hard to the board, the Land Rover powers forward and rams the back of the poachers' van, but the poachers screech on regardless. Bob rams them repeatedly but to no avail will the poachers stop.

So Bob uses different tactics. He's now trying to overtake the poachers' van but the road is only wide enough for one vehicle. The trench still runs at either side of the road and we are going to finish up in it, there's nothing surer.

But somehow, I don't know how, Bob's now ranging up alongside of the poachers' van. We can now see the poachers, there's two of them and they both have balaclavas over their heads. Big Jim's half hung out of the Land Rovers window and he's shouting at the poachers, "Stop the bloody van!"

The poachers put their fingers up at Big Jim, then I feel our Land Rover swerve hard. I feel and hear a smash and crunching metal screeching together, Bob's now ramming the side of the poachers' van.

The poachers, I don't believe it, they are ramming us back, and on we go tear-arsing and screeching along the narrow highland back road.

I glance forward ahead of us and what I see in the headlights I don't like, it's a narrow wooden bridge. It's looming straight ahead of us and it's only wide enough for one vehicle. We are all but upon it, someone has to give way, but by the looks of the determination on Bob's face, he's not going to give way.

The two poachers look panic-stricken by looking at their body language. They are racing to get their van to the narrow wooden bridge first. The bridge, it's here, and both vehicles are still locked together side by side. I pull Helen tight into me, I close my eyes, I hear and feel an almighty smash, I hear crunching and screeching of metal, and then our Land Rover stops.

I open my eyes, we are on the bridge. I look down at Helen, she has her head underneath my coat. I turn and I see Big Jim, he's dashing out of the Land Rover. I turn the other way, I see Bob, he's dashing out of the other side of the Land Rover. Me and Helen are now dashing out of the Land Rover. We run along and down by the side of the bridge and I see the poachers van turned upside down. It's in a narrow, fast-flowing river. The water's not deep, the van is only half submerged.

I see Big Jim racing out into the river, he quickly opens the poachers' van door and pulls out a poacher. He drags him through the river and throws him on to the river bank. Bob grabs the poacher.

Big Jim's now back in the river again, he's pulling another poacher out of the van. Big Jim throws this poacher to the riverbank together with his mate. Big Jim says to me, "Here, hold him Doug." Big Jim's now back in the river again, he's getting the poached deer from out of the van.

The poacher I have been put in charge of is coughing and spluttering, and he's struggling to get away from me. I release my grip on him, if he wants to make his escape I won't stop him. Who am I to restrain the poacher, I am as big a poacher as these two poachers are, only I am only a rabbit poacher not a deer poacher. Big Jim now throws the poached deer onto the riverbank and Bob's now telling Big Jim to retrieve the poachers' rifle from the van.

By now Helen has reversed the Land Rover off the bridge and is now shining the headlights down on to the riverbank. We can now see the poachers clearly.

Big Jim's now back with the poachers' rifle and he throws it on to the riverbank. Bob turns his restrained poacher over on to his back and he pulls the poacher's balaclava off from over his head. It's a woman and she's pleading, "Let me go Bob."

Big Jim turns over the other poacher and he pulls the poacher's balaclava off from over his head. It's another woman and she too is pleading, "Let me go Jim."

It looks to me as though these two poachers know Bob and Jim.

"Aye, we know them all right," says Bob, "they have been felling trees on the estate for the Laird. They have got to know the lay of the land well and where the deer are roaming."

The two poacher women plead with Bob to let them go but Bob is having none of it. Bob and Jim are now throwing the two poacher woman into the back of the Land Rover. Bob tells Helen to bring their rifle and he tells me to bring the poached deer. I do what I am told.

I can now see the poached deer clearly in the Land Rover's headlights. By, what a fine red deer stag he is too, he has twelve points on his antlers. This is what they call a 'royal stag'. I see a bullet hole at the back of the front leg, the stag has been shot through the heart. I see a slit in the base of the stag's throat. This is where the poachers have stuck a long-bladed knife in to bleed the stag. I see it has been 'GROLLOCKED', that's a slang word for taking out the guts, and this makes the carcass lighter to carry. So I now throw the poached royal red deer stag into the back of the Land Rover. Helen puts in the poachers' rifle and Big Jim's in there with the two poachers. I close the back door of the Land Rover and me and Helen go sit in the front, and off Bob drives.

We travel a fair distance along this narrow highland back road until we come to a lonely old cottage which is out in the wilds in the middle of nowhere. Out comes a chap from the cottage, 'Jock' they called him. It was Jock who informed Bob about these two poachers and Jock now telephones the police from his cottage.

I find out that Jock is also a shepherd for the Laird on his vast estate just like Helen is a shepherd for the Laird. This was the first meeting I ever had with Jock, I am told that the rabbits on Jock's part of the Laird's estate are in plague proportions, just like the rest of the Laird's vast estate. Bob tells me I can do the rabbit control for Jock also.

It appears to me that with all this rabbit controlling Bob is giving to me I will want a wagon to get all the rabbits home, leaving me thinking, with a lot of gratitude, I am a lot luckier at being caught poaching than these two women poachers Bob has just caught.

The police duly arrived at Jock's cottage and whisked away the two woman poachers to the local nick.

I remember that poaching incident happening as though it was only yesterday. The two women deer poachers were successfully convicted in court, their rifle was confiscated and they were heavily reprimanded. They also lost their tree-felling contract on the Laird's estate.

So now our successful poacher-catching evening is over, Big Jim heads on back home. Me, Bob and Helen head on back to Bob's cottage. As we travel along the narrow highland back road, I say to Bob his Land Rover is bashed about a bit by ramming the poachers' old van. Bob says, "It's the Laird's property is the Land Rover, he will get it repaired. I have orders from the Laird to ram the poachers' vehicles if necessary. The deer poachers must be caught at all costs."

We now arrive back at Bob's cottage, the Hunter's Lodge, and Bob tells me and Helen that our postponed rabbit lamping is now all on for this evening. I invite Helen to come for dinner this evening here at Bob's cottage. Bob looks at me and says, "Who's doing the cooking then?"

I look at Bob vacantly. I tell Helen to get here early and to bring her rifle with her all ready for the rabbit lamping and off she goes on her quad bike which takes her over the mountain tops and home.

Me and Bob now go off into his cottage and I look at the clock on the mantelpiece. It's 4 o'clock in the early hours of the morning and off to bed me and Bob do go.

I wasn't late out of bed the next morning. I look at the clock on the mantelpiece, 8 o'clock it says. And yet again Bob's beaten me up out of bed.

I go out into the courtyard to see if I can see him. I don't see him but I can hear him, he's playing holy hell at something. I peer over a wall and there he is, he's chasing a rat, he's trying to hit it with a big stick as the rat is fleeing trying to make its escape. Bob sees me watching and he says, "Can you catch these bloody rats with your ferrets?"

I tell Bob, "I don't have my ferrets with me."

I go across to Bob and he tells me the rats are eating all his pheasant feeder corn and the pigs' feeder meal. I weigh the situation up, now I can see how to catch some of these rats. I tell Bob I will try to snare some of these rats for him.

Bob says, "Good," and off he goes and leaves me to it.

All today I have nothing special to do, just killing time waiting anxiously for the rabbit lamping tonight. As I look around where these rats are, I see a large cluster of mushrooms out in the grass paddock. I think these will do for our dinner this evening when Helen comes for tea. The mushrooms are only small, they need my special treatment before I pick them.

I see some bullocks (BEEF CATTLE) grazing in the next field, so off I go over there. I want to gather together some old cow claps, that's the bullocks' shit which has dried out. They are as big as dinner plates these cow claps and stiff as a board on the outside, but underneath they are wet with cow shit.

I now go back to my large cluster of small mushrooms, I lay one cow clap over some of the mushrooms and do the same with the rest of my cow claps. The mushrooms now are set in perfect ideal conditions, the darkness and humidity will now encourage the mushrooms to grow at a fast rate, all within a few hours.

Now to snare some of these rats for Bob. Rats are usually quite simple to snare, and usually the snare holds them alive.

These rats of Bob's are living in a manure heap, it's nice and warm inside there. The manure heap is full of internal combustion caused by fermenting pig, horse and cow shit, but the manure heap is not on fire, just keeping everything like a large oven. It will be just like home sweet home for the rats inside there.

Bob keeps his pheasant and pig feed in a hut about fifty yards away from the manure heap and the rats are continually going backwards and forward from the manure heap to the hut. There are many rat runs all polished by many pounding feet, the runs are just like rat footpaths, which is just what they are.

I have some rabbit snares in my Land Rover all made by myself. I have some snares there made with only four strand wire, which are ideal for snaring rats.

I am now by the side of a rat run and I heel in the tether peg. The top of the peg must be level with the ground, otherwise the snared rat will chew through the tether peg. I now make a noose in the snare wire and nip it tight into the wooden tealer. I stick the tealer into the ground making sure the end of the tealer does not overlap the rat run. The snare is now stood over the run. I make the noose just big enough for the rat to get its head and front feet through. So now as the rat goes along its run the snare wire snags on his low-lying belly which tightens the noose around the rat's body, and the rat is well and truly caught.

I now carry on and set twenty snares altogether all along different rat runs, my snares are now all set and ready for the capture.

I want to catch these rats by late afternoon today if I can, which only gives me about seven hours to do the job. I am going out rabbit lamping tonight remember, so I have to have something to lure the rats out earlier than per usual.

Those two Tamworths that we slaughtered the day before, we put their guts in a bin. They will do nicely to lure out the rats early. So I go get the bin full of pigs' guts which are well away from these rats so they haven't had the chance to smell them.

I am now back at the rat runs with the bin full of smelly pigs' guts. The wind is blowing from the hut which holds the pheasant-cum-pig feed and blowing across to the manure heap. The wind's blowing just perfect. I empty the bin full of smelly pigs' guts at the side of the hut, the wind now is wafting the scent of the smelly pigs' guts across my snares and across the manure heap. That should tempt the rats out early.

I now leave everything quiet and head off back towards Bob's cottage. I see Bob in the courtyard, he wants to know if I will give him a hand to get some logs for the cottage fire. "Of course I will," I tell him, and off me and Bob go in his Land Rover.

We head on along a fir tree woodland side and we now have to walk and gather the logs as we go along. I see something odd, it's a branch stuck in the ground. That may not appear odd to the unlearned person but to me it tells tales.

As Bob is passing me by he picks up a log which is right by the side of this stick. Bob is oblivious of the stick which is positioned right alongside a main rabbit run. I tell Bob he has a poacher working around here.

Bob instantly acknowledges me, he says, "How do you know that then Doug?"

I don't tell Bob about the stick which he is oblivious of, not yet anyway. I say to Bob as I point, "Follow that rabbit run into the woodland and you will find a snare set." So off we both go into the woodland.

We go about ten paces and I see another stick stuck in the ground at the side of the same rabbit run. Bob is oblivious of this stick also. Bob bends low as he walks along the rabbit run scrutinizing as he goes, and there it is, a snare set over the rabbit run. Bob says, "But how did you know the snare was there in the first place?"

I now tell Bob. I point to the stick and I tell him that's a marker stick, it tells the poacher where his snares are set. Bob sees another stick further along the same rabbit run and there again is another set snare. We leave the snares untouched where they are.

We carry on further along the woodland and every good rabbit run we come across, sure enough we see more marker sticks alongside set snares. I point to one of them and sure enough we see more marker sticks alongside set snares. I point to one of the snares and I tell Bob, "That snare has just recently had a rabbit caught in it." I tell him, "Note how rough and ready the snare is set and note the bits of rabbit fur on the snare wire and on the tether twine. Also note the scuff marks on the run, that's where a rabbit has already been caught. The poacher hasn't had enough time to clean up his snares properly."

Bob looks captivated at what I am telling him, then we hear magpies squabbling in the woodland not far away. I am just about to tell Bob what the magpies are squabbling over, but Bob tells me first. "That's how I caught you rabbit poaching in the first place. It's where the poacher has paunched out his rabbits, that's what the magpies are squabbling over, and that was your telltale mark and how I captured you Doug."

We set off along the woodland side to investigate the squabbling magpies. As we go along the woodland side there are many rabbit runs leading from the woodland and leading way out into the grass meadow. Bob says, "Why didn't the poacher just set his snares here in the open grass meadows?"

I tell Bob, "The woodland conceals the snares away from your roving eyes."

Bob's now scratching his head at that reply.

We now arrive on the scene of the squabbling magpies, and off they fly cackling and squawking as they go. We peer into the undergrowth, and there they are, a pile of rabbit guts. The poachers had a good catch by the looks of it.

I pick up a paunch, I show Bob and tell him the rabbit was caught in a snare early last evening. Its stomach is empty, it never made it to the feeding grounds. I now pick up another paunch, its stomach is full. The rabbit has somehow managed to wangle its way around the set snares and get to the feeding ground, but this morning as it made its way back to its warren in the woodland its luck ran out. It got itself caught in a snare. I tell Bob to feel at the guts, they are still slightly warm. I tell Bob the poacher has just recently left the scene.

Bob looks at me and says, "You catch this poacher for me Doug."

So that's just what I did.

As I write this story it's the year 2008 but I can now look back through time. Remember all this happened in the 1970s.

I arrived at the scene of the poacher's snaring area early next morning. I went along the wood side and stopped just short of where I knew his first snare was set. I got myself hidden in the undergrowth and sat back and waited. The first light was just beginning to break through the overcast dark cloudy sky and I had a sneaky idea that the poacher would be an early bird just like myself.

As I sit there patiently waiting and watching every move with eagle eyes, I hear the blackbird cackling as they come out of their roosting trees. The blackies, as I call them, are always one of the first birds to rise in the morning. I hear distant jays calling deep in the fir tree plantation, I hear woodpigeon as they are flying from their overnight roost. I see carrion crows as they skim over the treetops above my head. Everything around me is by now coming to life. I hear the big fat pheasant calling as they are late from their roost.

When I am snare poaching rabbits, the first thing I do when I arrive on the poaching scene is to sit in the hedgerow and watch all the bird activity around me. They will tell me by their sign language if the keeper is around me, they don't know that I am hidden in the bushes.

By now dawn is well broken and I can now see out into the meadows. I see rabbits everywhere as they are feeding along the woodland edge. This massive estate of the Laird's is a rabbiter's paradise, everywhere I look it's rabbit galore. I notice a rabbit sit up high on its back legs, its got its ear pricked trying to locate a distant sound. I see it thumping the ground with its back legs, that's a sure sign there's danger approaching. I hear a jay screeching out in the tree plantation, woodpigeon come clattering through the fir trees. I look out on to the grass meadow, I see rabbits bolting for the safety of this woodland which I am by now squat low down in.

I oh so slowly lean out and look down the woodland side, a blacky comes tear-arsing down. It hasn't seen me as its looking behind itself and it nearly knocks my head off as it goes squawking and cackling past me. I see someone coming down the woodland side, he looks nervous and on edge as he comes towards me. He comes to his first marker stick which is stuck in the ground at the wood side, he stops and cagily looks around himself. He looks straight past me as I am hidden low in the undergrowth.

The poacher disappears into the woodland so I come out of my hiding and I oh so slowly move along the wood edge. I peer into the dimly lit woodland and I see the poacher. He has his back turned to me and he's squat down taking a rabbit out of a snare. I think to myself with a mischievous titter, I will have a bit of devilment with the poacher now.

I see some old mature Scots pine trees not far away from where the poacher is. Keeping myself at the back of the trees as I go so as not to let him see me, I carefully make my way through the woodland feeling my feet down on to the woodland floor making sure I don't make a sound or break any branches as I go. I get myself up the back of a big trunk of a Scots pine and I peep around the trunk. The poacher's only a few yards away from me, he hasn't a clue I am there. He's only a young fellow in his early teens by the looks of him.

As I peep with half an eyeball around the trunk I give out a long drawn out blood-curdling scream. I make this noise with my mouth and the poacher instantly turns around. I see him looking and scanning the woodland around where I am hidden. I am still peeping with just a quarter of an eyeball, I mustn't let him see me. I give out another wailing pathetic hare scream. The poacher raises himself into a stood-up crouch, he's pinpointed where the screaming is coming from, he's looking directly at the tree I am hidden behind. The poacher makes his move, he stealthily moves towards me.

He still hasn't seen me peeping with a quarter of an eyeball so I get myself completely out of sight behind the Scots pine trunk. I give out another long drawn out blood-curdling hare scream and then just lean casually with my back up against the trunk of the tree.

I hear him, he's just at the other side of my tree trunk. He's now brushing up the side of my tree trunk and as I look down I see the top of his head. I see him peer at my feet and he looks up and his eyes hit my eyes. He's a bumbling wreck, he's stuttering and stammering trying to get his words out. I tell him to calm down, I am not going to do him for poaching. But I do tell him the gamekeeper's on the warpath, and that he's gunning for him. I tell the lad to pick up all his snares and heed and be off. The lad couldn't be thankful enough for letting him go, he's wiping the tears from his eyes as he goes.

I think to myself, who am I to tell him what to do, I am only a glorified poacher myself.

I tell Bob later on that I came across the poacher and that he did a runner when he saw me, but I gave him a good chase for his misdeeds. I frightened the living daylights out of him and he will not be in a hurry to come back poaching on the Laird's estate.

Bob's now smiling with gratitude. I am now smiling because I let the poacher go free. The poacher will now be smiling that's he's got his freedom, so now we are all smiling.

Now back to my story. I was telling you readers earlier, me, Bob and Helen are going rabbit lamping tonight. It's still only early afternoon and Helen is coming for dinner later on. Remember me inviting her when Bob says, "Who's doing the cooking?" So now I have to prepare dinner and I now want them mushrooms I treated earlier. Remember when I covered them over with cow claps to force grow them?

When I reached the scene of where my mushrooms are, which is the same scene where I set my rat snares remember, I couldn't believe what I saw. I had a dozen rats in my snares. They were all alive with the snares around their bodies. I leave the rats where they are, I have a little trick up my sleeve for these rats later.

I have to prepare the dinner first so I go over to my mushrooms, I lift up a cow clap that's covering some of my mushrooms and what I see makes my eyes sparkle. The mushrooms have trebled in size so I gather them all up and off I go.

I now have no meat for the dinner so I call and look in Bob's game larder, there's plenty of meat in there. I grab a rabbit, a hare, a brace of grouse and a cock pheasant. There, that should be enough meat, and off I go into Bob's cottage.

I skin out all my carcasses, I cut all the meat into chunks and drop it all into a big tray. I then cover over all the meat with a thick onion gravy and pop some vegetables in to add a bit of taste.

I look around Bob's kitchen, and what do I see, there's half a dozen dumplings there that Bob had prepared earlier, so I pop them into the big tray too. I now pop the big tray into the oven at the side of the log-burning fire. There, that should be cooked by early evening, and to think Bob had thought I couldn't cook.

My ears prick up, I hear a motor bike pull up in the courtyard. I see it's Helen on her quad bike. She has her faithful bitch with her and her rifle strapped over her back. She's come all prepared for rabbit lamping tonight by the looks of her. I now see Bob pull up in the Land Rover, he has his small terrier with him, the one he goes foxing with. I go out to greet them in the courtyard and I say to Bob, "Have a peer over that wall there."

As I point with my finger, both Helen and Bob peer over the wall, and what Bob sees he's overjoyed at. "Look at those rats," he says, "all in snares. Let me go kill the buggers."

I tell Bob, "No. We will have a bit of fun with the dogs, they will kill the rats."

Helen, Bob and me are all for it, and off we go to meet the rats. Helen puts her dog onto a slipper lead. Bob gets a length of baling band, he throws half to me and I put my Pup on a on-the-spot-made slipper lead. Bob does the same with his foxing terrier. The dogs must be kept under control, once they see the snared rats they will be wanting to be at them.

We arrive on the scene, the rats see us and the dogs, the dogs see the rats, now it's pandemonium with barking, yapping, struggling dogs trying to slip their slipper leads. The rats are hissing and spitting back at the dogs as they fight to free themselves from the snares.

Bob and Helen take all three dogs about fifty yards out into the grass paddock and now the rats settle down a little.

What we are aiming to do is give the rats a fair distance to run to make their escape back into their rat warren in the manure heap. So I oh so carefully approach one of the caught-in-a-snare rats. They are big rats so I make sure I am on guard as I gingerly bend down and pull out the tether peg. I am now holding the struggling rat up off the ground as it dangles in the snare.

So far so good. I take the dangling rat over to Bob and Helen. I now have to release the rat from the snare which is around its body. This will then give the rat freedom to run fast as it makes its escape.

I have brought with me a stick which has a hook screwed in the end. I let the rat on to the ground and I put my booted foot gently on to the top of the rat. I don't want to injure the rat, I just want to hold it still. Now with my stick I push the hook under the snare wire, I quickly release my foot and lift the rat back up in the air. With the weight of the dangling rat pulling at the snare wire on the hook, the snare noose now opens up and releases the rat. The freed rat now hits the ground, it never even hesitates, it's off like a bat out of hell towards the manure heap.

The rat's now run a fair distance so Bob slips his snarling, growling, bloodthirsty terrier, and off it goes hell for leather after the fleeing rat. The rat doesn't make it to the manure heap. The terrier is now biting and chomping the rat in its mouth. I see Helen has a battle on in her hands herself, my Pup and her dog are pulling her arms out as they try to get among the action.

Bob puts his terrier back on the slipper lead and I go bring another snared rat. It's Helen's dog's turn now to catch a rat while Bob holds the other two dogs.

The released rat is now running, off it goes at helter-skelter pace. Helen is fumbling trying to release her dog, it's a modern technology slipper lead she has on her dog and it doesn't work. The rat's well on its way to freedom. I shout to Bob, "Slip the bloody dogs."

All three dogs are now mad crazy pulling and tugging and fighting their slipper leads. The dogs, they are off, all three of them together. One of the dogs grabs the fleeing rat and throws it up into the air, another dog catches the spinning bedraggled rat. It's squealing its head off but squeals no more.

I look for my Pup, where is she? She's over there is the damned dog, she's killing the rats in the snares. I race over to her, I grab her, she's killed four of the rats. I turn, I see the other two dogs, they have gone into a frenzy of bloodcurdling killing.

I now have gone into a frenzy of fear. In my carelessness I have ventured too close to a snared rat and the bloody thing has run up my trouser leg. I have my hands around my knee and the rat lays still just below my hands. I freeze motionless, I dare not move, I feel beads of sweat on my forehead. I just watch Helen and Bob chasing all three dogs about, they have gone into a frenzy killing. Now all the rats lay dead in their snares. Bob and Helen are puffed out with racing the dogs around, they are laughing and joking at the good entertainment they have just had.

They look across at me and I am not laughing, I have a stern solemn face on as I grip hold of my leg. I stand there in silence and speechless. They see the snare tether going up my trouser leg and Helen is now aghast with grief at what she sees. Bob says, "It's all right Doug, rats will not bite while ever they are left still and in the darkness."

I think to myself, it's not Bob who's got a rat up his trousers. Bob and Helen are now just stood there looking at me pondering the job. I can feel the warm body of the rat just under my knee. I can feel its claws sticking into my skin as it holds firmly onto me.

Bob says, "We will have to pull the rat out with the snare tether." I grimace at the thought. Bob says, "We want a straight pull so that the trousers do not obstruct the rat as it's being pulled."

So that's what they did, they got me laid on my back with my legs stretched out straight. I felt the snared rat move its position, I felt its claws digging even deeper into my skin.

All three dogs are now by my side, all three have got their noses stuck out sniffing, they can smell the rat up my trouser leg. They don't care about me, they are eagerly awaiting the kill.

Bob says, "Now when me and Helen pull, if the rat bites you it wont hurt much."

I grimace at the thought and give Helen and Bob a little forced smile. So Bob is now in position, he's going to pull me one way by my shoulders. And Helen is in position, she's going to pull the snare tether the other way at the same time with Bob. I see all three dogs are also in their position around me, they all have their tongues out panting. It looks to me as though they are laughing, they must think this is hilarious fun as they are waiting for the kill.

Now Bob says, "Are we ready, one, two, three, pull!" Bob gives me one almighty pull one way and I see him trip and fall over backwards. All at the same time Helen pulls hard at the snare tether. I feel the rat's claws scrawl and bite into my skin as it slides down my leg, then the rat leaps out of my trouser bottom. I see Helen's face, it's a picture of fear at what she sees. The rat's leaping straight for her and she trips in her anguish of fear and lands flat on her arse backwards. While the rat's still in midair leaping for Helen, all three dogs leap in together all at different angles. They all grab at the rat together, there's blood and snot and growling as they all laid in a heap on top of Helen.

Helen's by now all curled up in a ball with her hands over the back of her head. She can't see it's the dogs on top of her, she crying out, "Get this rat off me!"

I quickly get myself up from the ground and pull Helen away from the mad crazy, biting, growling dogs. I let Bob pick himself up from the ground, and that was the end of our rat catching expedition. Phew!

My leg was badly scrawled by the rat's claws, but nothing of importance, and off we all go back to Bob's cottage. As we walk in there is a strong aroma of cooking and Bob and Helen say, "What's for dinner then Doug?"

I get them seated at the table and out comes the dinner from the oven. They are now savouring the meat. Helen says, "Mine tastes like grouse."

I have a taste, mine tastes like pheasant. Anyway, whatever it tastes like we all got stuck in and had a good hearty meal.

After our dinner we had time to kill, it was still too early to go out rabbit lamping. So Bob pulls his armchair up in front of the log-burning fire and I pull up my armchair. There is no armchair for Helen so without asking she plonks herself on my knee.

Helen says to Bob, "I enjoy your poaching stories like the one you told me and Doug the other day. Tell us another poaching story Bob."

Bob says he gets quite a lot of poachers from the local village and that he is forever catching them. Bob smiles to himself and gives a little chortle. Then he goes on to tell me and Helen it's only fairly recently he had some poachers who were taking the odd pot-shot at game on the roadside. "I had seen them a time or two poaching, but every time I saw them I was always high up in the hilltops. I always had my stalker telescope with me and I could see very well what they were up to. There was always two of them working together from a small van.

"I had quite a few pheasants there on that long stretch of highland country back road. The pheasants would gather along the roadside picking up grit.

"These two poachers would come along the roadside picking off the pheasants with what looked like a small bullet rifle. The gun must have had a silencer fitted to it, I never ever heard a crack from their rifle. Then when they had shot a pheasant or two I would see the one in the passenger seat jump out of the van, make haste and run out into the rough grazing land quickly retrieving the pheasants. And he would be back in the van in double quick time and they would be off and out of sight before I had time to do anything about it."

Then Bob says, "So I decided to lay in ambush and catch them red-handed poaching."

Helen is clutching her arm around my neck, all in tension as she sits on my knee in front of the log-burning fire as Bob tells us his poaching story.

Bob carries on to say, "With there being two poachers I wanted to catch them both together, so I got Big Jim to assist me. I wanted to really throw the law book at these two poachers to show an example to other potential poachers who were also poaching the area. I wanted to catch these two poachers in possession of big game. The magistrates do not look lightly on big game poachers. So hopefully they would not look on these poachers lightly. That was my intentions anyway.

"The day arrived when me and Big Jim decided we would try to catch these two poachers. I calculated that they would be about today and they always poached this length of quiet country back road very early in the morning before anybody was around. It was only the estate workers who used this back road anyway. The road was out in the middle of nowhere in a sheltered glen surrounded by mountains.

"It was before daybreak when me and Big Jim set off. The day before we had had a bit of a shoot so I took some of this shot game with us. As me and Big Jim drove along this quiet country back road it was still dark. I pulled up and laid a couple of hares by the side of the road. The two poachers will now see these two hares and will hopefully pick them up. They will think they have been knocked down by passing vehicles. We drove along a bit further up the road and I dropped off three dead pheasant by the side of the road. A little further along the road I dropped off a couple of grouse and then four or five rabbits.

"Now for the big game to come into my reckoning. I had been out on the hills a couple of days before and found a dead stag. Why it had died I don't know, but he had a fine set of antlers on him. I took him purposely off the hill with the intentions to give him to the poachers. So again I pull up at the side of the road and drop off this dead stag. He looked just like a road casualty as he lay there by the side of the road.

"I purposely left the stag's guts in to make it look all realistic so that hopefully now the temptation will get the better of these two poachers. They will take all the trail of game I have left them along the road including the big stag. And by the time me and Big Jim catch them their little van will have plenty of game inside it, including the big game, the big stag.

"So now me and Big Jim get to the point in the narrow country back road where we intend, hopefully, to catch our poachers. We park our Land Rover up at the back of an old peat hag and it's now out of sight of the poachers' roving eyes.

"I have prepared myself for how I am going to catch these two poachers. I have brought with me a long wooden plank. About fifty yards away from the roadside runs a wide, fast-flowing stream. The poachers cannot see this stream from the roadside, it lays concealed below its banks. I lay this long wooden plank from bank to bank across the stream so the poachers can now cross over the wide, fast-flowing stream when they see the wooden plank.

"I have also brought with me three dead cock pheasants and I intend to lure the poachers into capture with these dead birds. I now cross over to the other side of the stream on the plank I have just laid across and I take these three dead cock pheasants with me. There's some willow trees growing by the side of the stream and I go over and break some long, slender branches from these willow. I now go to a point on the stream bank where the poachers can see this high part of the stream bank from the roadside. I get one of the dead pheasant and push a thin branch into the pheasant's mouth. I keep on pushing the branch and it goes right down its throat and long neck. I now push the other end of the willow branch into the ground. I now get another slender willow branch and push it well up the pheasant's backside and I push the other end of the branch into the ground. I now rearrange and adjust the pheasant until it looks all fit and well and just as though it's contentedly feeding. Then I do the same with the other two cock pheasants

"I have also brought with me three long lengths of fishing line. I tie a length of fishing line to each pheasant, run out the lengths of fishing line and throw them over to the other side of the stream. I now cross over the plank to the other side of the stream. I have also brought with me a long length of strong thin nylon rope. I tie it underneath one end of the wooden plank and run out the length of rope nestling it under the grass as I go.

"My poacher's trap is now all set and ready and it's by now just breaking daylight. It's now time for me and Big Jim to get laid squat and out of sight and wait for our poachers to hopefully arrive.

"Big Jim gets himself out of sight behind an old peat hag by the side of the narrow country back road. That's hopefully where the poachers will pull up in their small van. I have given Big Jim strict orders to lay still and not to make a move until he sees me jump out and grab my poacher.

"I now get myself laid squat out of sight at the back of the stream's bank and it's by now daylight.

"I am laid squat just a short distance away from the wooden plank and my three dead feeding cock pheasants. From where I am laid squat the pheasants look all realistic and just as though they are casually feeding.

"I now lay back and wait for our poachers to arrive. As I peer over the bank looking through the blades of grass, there's not a sign of Big Jim to be seen. I get myself to thinking, I hope Big Jim hasn't fallen asleep.

"I then look back down along the road. I have with me my deerstalking telescope, so I put my eyeball into the 'scope and scan the area. I see pheasants that have come to the roadside to feed on the grit. I see the big dead red deer stag, he's about a quarter of a mile down the road from where I lay squat. His antlers are so big they are holding his head up from the road surface. My attention is attracted by something further down the road way out in the distance. The early morning winter sunshine is sparkling on something in the distance. I carefully pull up my 'scope to my eye and I see a vehicle coming along the road. It's a small van, dark in colour just like the poachers' van. I see it pull up, I see someone jump out of the van, he's picking something up off the road. I zoom right in with my powerful stalking telescope, it's the poacher. He's picked up the two dead hares from the road and he's thrown them into the back of his van. I see the van set off along the road again.

"The poachers are doing exactly as I intended them to do. The more game they have with them when me and Big Jim catch them, the harder I can throw the law book at them.

"Thinking of Big Jim, I look across at the peat hag he is laying squat behind. There's not a sign of him to be seen at all. I look back along the road, the poacher's out of his van again, he's again picking something up off the road. He grabs one and then moves on and grabs another and then another. He's picking up the three dead pheasants I laid there on the roadside and he throws them into the back of van. I can now see there are two poachers and they drive on up the road again. They are forever getting closer and closer to where me and Big Jim are laid tight squat and there's still no sign of big Jim to be seen.

"I look back towards the poachers and they are now all but upon the pheasants I saw earlier which had come to feed on the grit by the roadside. I have my beady eye on them as I look through my 'scope and I see the poacher in the passenger seat of the van has got a gun and he's pointing it out of the window. I see a pheasant crumple as he takes a shot, it's flapping and fluttering about. The other pheasants are just stood there watching, they are dumb to the fact are pheasants. I never heard a bang from the poacher's gun so they must have a silencer fitted on it. I see the poacher taking aim again, I see another pheasant crumple to his shot, and still not a bang from their gun to be heard. In a matter of a few short seconds the poacher has four, five pheasant down. The other pheasants have finally come to their senses, they are up and off away from danger.

"I see the poacher jump out of the van and run out and pick up the shot pheasants. I look across at Big Jim's peat hag, there's still no sign of him to be seen. He's missing all the poaching action taking place here right in front of his very own nose. He must have fallen asleep the old devil.

"I look back along the road and see the poacher's back in the van with the pheasants. They set off along the road again, forever getting closer to where I lay tight squat and Big Jim is snoring his head off.

"I see the van stop yet again. The poacher's out of the van and he's gathering something up off the road again, it's the same two dead grouse I laid there. The poacher throws them into the van and they are off again. But they no sooner set off than the van pulls up again. The poacher's out picking up the dead rabbits I laid there. I think to myself with a smile on my face, go on, keep throwing all that game into your van, I will have you with or without Big Jim's help.

"I see the van move on again to where there's a slight bend in the narrow country back road. The dead red deer stag is laid just around the bend and I am eager to see their reactions when they see it.

"I glance across to where Big Jim is laid in hiding, he's not there, but then I see him. He's moved further up the peat hag, I can just make out the top of his deerstalker hat, and he's peering through the blades of grass as he's watching the poachers at work. I have my 'scope on him but I can barely make him out as he lays there, he's just like a sly old fox waiting to pounce on a rabbit. He's laid there waiting for the kill. I think to myself, good old Jim, I didn't think he would let me down.

"I look back at the poachers, they are coming around the bend in their small van. I hear their van screech to a halt, they have stopped in front of the dead red deer stag. Both poachers jump out of the van and they grab the deer from the roadside. They are struggling to carry him he's so large. They open the back doors of the van and in goes the red deer stag.

"There, I think, I now have them for poaching big game, just what the magistrates want to hear.

"The poachers' van moves off again and they are now nearly on top of us. They range up alongside of me as I lay squat low behind the stream's bank. Big Jim is at the other side of the poachers as he lays tight squat behind a peat hag. Their van pulls up, the poachers have seen the three pheasants which I have stuck up on the top of the stream's bank. They are about fifty yards away from me on the roadside. I see Big Jim at the far side of them, I can barely make him out as I peer through the grass blades as he is peering back through the grass blades.

"The two poachers haven't a clue what's laid in hiding for them. I hope Big Jim sticks to my orders, he mustn't pounce on the poachers until I pounce. I want to catch these poachers red-handed with the pheasants in their hands.

"I see the poacher wind down the passenger window of their van and I see him poke out the gun. It looks like a rifle from where I am laid in hiding.

"I gather together my three lengths of fishing line, one length in one hand, and two lengths in my other hand. I hear a dull thud as the gun is fired and I hear the bullet come whistling past me. I look at the three dummy pheasants and I see the bullet thump into the far pheasant. I pull one of the lengths of fishing line to tipple that pheasant. But I have pulled the wrong fishing line and the middle pheasant topples over the bank and out of sight of the poachers.

"I hear the poacher say to his mate, 'These sights are off on this rifle, I shot at the end pheasant and the middle one has fallen.'

"I sigh with relief, the poachers haven't tippled to what's going off. I see the poacher take aim again with his rifle. It's a .22 bullet rifle by the looks of it, and there must be a silencer on it, I hear no crack. The poacher shoots again, the bullet comes whistling past me again and I see it thump into another dummy pheasant. I pull another fishing line and this time I have got it right. The pheasant goes toppling over the bank and out of sight of the poacher. I see the poacher pull back the bolt on his rifle and slot another bullet into the chamber. He takes aim and fires and I see the bullet thump into the last remaining dummy pheasant. I pull my last remaining fishing line, the dummy pheasant topples over the bank and out of sight.

"I see the poacher quickly jump out of the passenger side of the van. He starts running over towards me, he's come right up to six feet away from where I am laid tight squat just over the stream's bank. As I am looking through the blades of grass at him, he hasn't seen me laid there. If he only knew, I am sure he would have a heart attack.

"The poacher sees the fast-flowing stream. He didn't know it was there, it was hidden out of sight from where he was shooting from by the roadside. I hear the poacher chuntering to himself. He's so close to me I could reach out and grab him. But I lay still, I want him to retrieve my pheasants. I see the poacher look up stream, he sees my long wooden plank I have laid there and he sets off towards it. He puts his foot on the plank to test its sturdiness but he doesn't see my thin nylon rope I have there nestled in the grass. The poacher goes over the plank and crosses the stream, he grabs the three cock pheasants which he thinks he has shot. He's in that much of a hurry he hasn't noticed the thin fine fishing line attached to the pheasants' legs.

"The poacher makes haste and races back to the wooden plank and I grab hold of my nylon rope. The poacher by now is halfway across the wooden plank. The fast-flowing water below him is fair swirling with all the flood water that has come of the surrounding mountains. The poacher is treading carefully as he crosses the plank, but not carefully enough. I give a good yank on my nylon rope, the plank topples, the poacher loses his balance and he topples over backwards and into the stream. The strong current of water is washing him down stream.

"I jump up and race out from my hiding place and I look across to the roadside. Big Jim has been watching my every move and I see him racing out from his hiding place and over to capture the poacher in the van.

"I race off down stream to capture my poacher. It looks as though he's drowning, he keeps disappearing under the fast swirling water then surfacing and gasping for air. I race past him down the stream bank and get to a point where I can reach out and grab him. I see him under the water as he is passing me by so I reach deep into the water and grab him as he surfaces. I have him by the scruff of his coat neck and he's gasping for breath. He's coughing and spluttering as if he's half dead. He's still clutching hold of the three pheasants as I pull him from the water and on to the bank, then I drag him over to their van on the roadside.

"I see Big Jim has dragged the other poacher out of the van and he's holding him in a bear hug from behind. He's a big strong man is Jim and he doesn't know his own strength. I see his poacher is red in the face and he cant' breath, Big Jim's holding him too hard. I tell him, 'Let him go, you're going to kill him.' Big Jim releases his bear hug of a grip and the poacher slumps to the road, he's spiflicated.

"My poacher's like a drowned rat. He's gasping for breath also as he falls by the side of his mate on the road, and they both lay there winded and in agony. They are both looking seriously injured and I say to Big Jim, 'Have we to call an ambulance to resuscitate them?' But after a short while both poachers recovered and they were both whisked off to the local nick."

Bob says, "A creature of habit gets caught, and these two poachers poached the Laird's estate once too often and got themselves caught.

"When these two poachers were summoned to court", Bob says, "I had to appear in court also to give my evidence against the two poachers."

Bob chortles to me and Helen as he his telling us his true-to-the-fact story as we sit in front of the log-burning fire in Bob's cottage. Helen readjusts her petite little bum as she's sat on my knee and we are now listening all intently to Bob's story. I hope you readers are enjoying this story as much as me and Helen are.

Bob says, "The two poachers stand in the dock in front of the judge who is browsing through the evidence against the poachers. He's tut, tut, tutting away to himself at all the misdeeds the poachers have been caught in the act of doing.

"The judge looks up at the poachers, looking over the top of his spectacles, and as he's looking he frowns upon the two poachers. He says, 'You were caught in the act of poaching and being in possession of two hares, eleven pheasants, two grouse, five rabbits...'

"One of the poachers raises his voice back to the judge saying, 'We did not poach them sir, we picked them all dead from off the roadside.' The judge retorts back saying, 'Silence in court.' Now the other poacher is shouting back at the judge, he's saying, 'I know my rights, it's legal to pick up dead game from the roadside. It's only illegal to pick them up if it's us that killed the game ourselves'. The judge says again, 'Silence in court.' By now the judge is going red in the face with fury, and he carries on to say, 'You were also caught in the act of poaching and being in possession of big game, a fine red deer stag you poached off the hill'.

"Now both poachers are objecting together as they stand in the dock. They shout to the judge saying, 'We did no such thing sir, we picked the dead deer up from the road'. Again the blood-red-faced judge says, 'Silence in court!'."

Bob says "Now the judge beckons me up to him and I show him a photograph I had taken of the poached red deer stag. I must admit to a bit of devilment myself, I had put a bullet hole through the stag's head and smeared hare's blood around the bullet hole to make it look all authentic and that.

"The red-faced judge looks at my photograph of the poached deer then he looks at the poachers in the dock. That judge absolutely threw the law book at them. The two poachers received the severest penalties the judge could give. The judge says to the escorting police officers of the two poachers, 'Take the buggers below and lock them up then throw away the key'."

Bob says, "That was two poachers well rid of from the Laird's estate and their punishment served as a warning to other potential poachers."

Bob's agitated, excited face now turns to a serious expression. Me and Helen gulp in anticipation of what Bob is going to tell us now. Bob went on to say, "There was a terrible incident happened on the Laird's estate not all that long ago. The Laird, who you know is my boss who owns the estate, went out one morning to do a spot of rabbit shooting. As the Laird was approaching a dry ditch, he sees a fleeting glimpse of a rabbit bolting across the top of the bank of the ditch. He picks up his twelve bore shotgun and lets fire. The Laird sees a glimpse of the rabbit fall over the bank and into the ditch. He goes over and sends in his retriever dog to bring the rabbit out of the ditch. The dog returns to him without the rabbit, it's whimpering and whining and would not go back into the ditch. So the Laird himself went into the ditch to retrieve the rabbit, and what the Laird saw was shock horror. He sees a young teenage lad lying there dead.

"The terrible incident was in due course all brought before the Magistrate's Court. It was found out the teenage lad was a local lad from the nearby village. He had been doing a spot of poaching, his purse nets and ferret were found on a small rabbit burrow in the dry ditch.

"Apparently what had happened was, when the teenage lad had seen the Laird coming he did a runner to make his escape. As the lad ran along the bottom of the ditch keeping himself low so as not to be seen, the lad had a funny shaped hat on his head. Unaware of the lad's presence, all the Laird sees is the top of his funny shaped hat as it goes along the top of the ditch. The Laird sees it as a fleeting bolting rabbit, and the consequences were fatal.

"The outcome of the verdict in the High Court was it was deemed as misadventure on the lad's behalf, and the Laird was exonerated of all blame."

So now as me, Bob and Helen sit in front of the log-burning fire in Bob's cottage, Bob looks at the clock on the mantelpiece and says, "Come on, it's time we were off lamping rabbits."

Me and Helen are all ready for the off. Bob goes to his gun lock-up cabinet and he pulls out his .22 rifle. He also pulls out a big, high-calibre rifle and says, "Where we are going there's liable to be a fox about."

So we are now all ready to finally go out lamping rabbits and I am eagerly looking forward to it. But as we make our way out of the cottage the telephone rings. I don't believe it, I hope that's not Jock again saying he's seen more poachers on the estate. Bob answers the phone and then says to me as he's handing me the phone, "Here, it's Lady Celia wanting you Doug."

Lady Celia is the Laird's wife. I answer the phone and she says, "Doug, I hear you are lamping rabbits tonight. Could you lamp the rabbits around the castle and the lawns?"

I tell her, "Yes, sure I will."

Lady Celia says, "I look forward to seeing you," and on that she puts the phone down.

I say to Bob, "I have never met lady Celia so how does she know me?"

Bob says, with a big smile on his face, "Watch her Doug, she is chasing you."

Helen grabs me by the arm and says, "Come on, let's go lamping bloody rabbits."

So off the three of us go out into the courtyard, we are going in the argocat and we all jump in. Bob is driving and I jump into the passenger seat. The argocat is open-topped with no canopy over and Helen jumps in the back and my Pup jumps in with her. We now set off for my long-awaited rabbit lamping.

Bob says, "We will lamp the castle grounds first."

We travel along a secluded old track that is only fit for the argocat by the looks of all the bumps and potholes in it. Bob ushers me by tapping me on the shoulder. The argocat shudders to a stop and there in the headlights I see three rabbits. I hear a thud and a rabbit drops dead. I quickly bring my rifle to my shoulder but before I even have time to shoot I hear thud, thud and the other two rabbits drop dead. It's Helen and Bob, they have beaten me to it.

I see my Pup race past my side, she's off to retrieve the rabbits and I struggle to get out of the argocat to give Pup a helping hand. I have one leg out when Pup arrives with a rabbit in her mouth. I stoop across awkwardly and take the rabbit from Pup and off Pup goes again. As she races away, I pass the rabbit to Helen in the back. I now have both my legs out of the argocat with my arse still on the passenger seat. I see Helen take another rabbit from Pup and I am now all about out of the argocat when I see Pup retrieve the third rabbit. Now Bob's setting off again while I am neither in nor out of the argocat.

These argocats are designed to float like a boat so there are no doors, so it's quite hard work climbing in and out. Bob drives on regardless of my dilemma.

As we travel along towards the Laird's castle there aren't many rabbits to be seen on this low-lying rough old track which runs along the foot of the glens. It's just about the only place on the estate which isn't infested with rabbits, by what I have seen anyway.

I think to myself as we travel along, this is the most perfect night for lamping rabbits. It's a pitch black night, you can't see a foot in front of your face and there's a stiff breeze picking up. That will take away the silence of the night. It's also starting to drizzle with rain, this will make the rabbits sit tight on the ground as they are feeding. All we want now is some rabbits to shoot.

We finally arrive at the castle gates. I look across at the castle and I see lights on in the upstairs rooms. Bob says, "The Laird's away grouse shooting on another estate."

This leaves me thinking, so it must just be Lady Celia at home.

Helen taps me on the shoulder. "There," she says.

We see a whole colony of rabbits feeding along the wood side. Bob manoeuvres the argocat down towards them and says, in a whisper, "We will lamp them outside of the castle grounds first."

Our rifles are now at the ready. The rabbits we have just seen should now be within range and Bob slowly turns the argocat's headlights across the pastureland. It picks up rabbits in the shade of the light. I no sooner see the rabbits when I hear a bullet go whizzing over my head. It's that bloody Helen at the back of me, she's too fast for me. I see a rabbit drop, I hear another thud and I see another rabbit fall. It's that bloody Bob, he's too fast for me too. And now all the rabbits we did see in the lights are now all laying dead.

Bob slowly moves the headlights around and I see a whole host of rabbits come into view. I hear bullets whizzing over my head and I hear the thud, thud, thud of Bob's rifle by the side of me. I look forward, I see one rabbit left standing so I quickly take aim and fire and the rabbit falls to my bullet. The rest of the rabbits now do a runner and disappear into the darkness of the night.

Pup runs out to retrieve the shot rabbits and Helen jumps out to give Pup a helping hand. Bob moves the argocat closer to the dead rabbits, it will save a lot of walking.

Between them Helen and Pup retrieve about a dozen rabbits. They are thrown into the back of the argocat and Bob drives on.

Helen is at the back of me and as she stands amongst the dead rabbits she has a good vantage point. She is looking down into the headlights and she can see what's coming before me and Bob can. She also has the advantage of resting her rifle on the argocat's roller bar which gives her steady aim. As Bob is driving along there's bullets whizzing over my head as I sit there in front. Helen's not missing a rabbit, she's a crack shot is Helen.

Bob pulls the argocat right alongside the rabbits she is shooting and I lean out and pick up the dead rabbits. Bob hardly has to stop before I have the rabbit and into the back of the argocat the rabbits do go. There are many rabbits around the surrounding pastures of the Laird's castle, I am sure the barrels of Bob's and Helen's rifles must be getting hot by all the shooting they are doing. I too am also adding to the bag with a bit of shooting myself and picking up the dead rabbits as Bob drives along.

Helen, I am sure, has done this before. When we first set off from Bob's cottage Helen insisted I sat in the front passenger seat. The little tinker, she knew I would have the job of picking up all the shot rabbits. I keep hearing her tittering at the back of me every time she shoots rabbits and I lean out awkwardly to pick them all up for her.

By now we have done the full surrounds of the Laird's castle and we arrive at the castle's main gates. We have many rabbits, the back of the argocat is full. As Bob stops the argocat, I hear a couple of quick firing bullets go whizzing over my head, I see two rabbits crumple. I hear thud, thud from my side. It's Bob firing and down go another two rabbits. I now have my scope on three rabbits sat together and I fire. I hear a thud, then I hear a bullet go whizzing over my head. I see one rabbit drop stone dead. Now Bob and Helen are claiming they shot the rabbit, but I know my bullet hit the rabbit also, so all three of us shot the rabbit together. That's bad discipline.

I tell Bob to turn off the headlights and I say to them, "We can't have this, all three of us shooting at the same rabbit. So what we will do is, when we get a lot of rabbits in front of us, I will shoot at the rabbits on the left, Bob will shoot at the rabbits on the right and Helen will shoot at the rabbits in the middle."

Now Bob is setting up a spotlight. It's positioned above us on the roller bar at the front of the argocat and it's plugged into a main power point on the dashboard. Bob turns it on, it's on a swivel, and the powerful spot beam instantly hits a rabbit bang in the eyes. I hear the click of Helen's safety catch being taken off her rifle. Then I hear the whiz of her bullet go flying over my head and the dazzled rabbit is no more.

I swivel the spotlight around a little and the light hits two more rabbits. It no sooner hits them when two bullets hit the rabbits and they both drop together. I swivel the light around a little further and it picks up another three rabbits. This time I am on the ball and I quickly aim and fire at the left-hand rabbit. I never hear Bob and Helen fire but all three rabbits drop together now we have our act together.

I turn the spot beam light the full circumference around the argocat and every rabbit that was sat there was eliminated. The rabbits do not know what's happening, there is no crack from the rifles to startle them, all our three rifles have silencers fitted on them.

Bob turns the argocat's headlights back on and we drive on further across the lawns. We are now upon the castle, all the lights are sill on upstairs and I see Lady Celia. Bob tells me everybody calls her 'CC' for short. CC looks very scantily dressed to me, she's wearing a sexy plunging neckline nightie and she's waving at us from the bedroom window.

Helen sounds disgruntled as she's telling Bob, "Drive on, we are rabbit shooting aren't we, not watching a striptease show."

Helen sounds bitchy to me. Bob does as he's told and we drive on. We pass on by the castle popping rabbits off as we go. There are many rabbits here on the lawns, it's a wonder there are any lawns left by the number of rabbits I see on them.

Earlier on as we were shooting the rabbits on the pastures that surrounded the outside of the castle grounds, all the rabbits we missed disappeared into the darkness of the night. They all ran through the belting of woodland that surrounds the castle and have now reappeared on the castle lawns. So it's rabbits adding to rabbits.

We are now driving around the back of the castle. The argocat's headlights shine way out across the lawns and what I see I don't believe. I see more than a hundred rabbits sat out feeding. Bob takes the light off them, manoeuvres the argocat around the feeding rabbits and heads towards the belting of woodland that runs along the edges of the lawns. This is the belting of woodland which I looked in when we came to the castle to meet the shooting men who were going grouse shooting that day not all that long since.

Do you readers remember, when I told you I saw all them large warrens inside the belting of woodland? The rabbits we see now feeding on the lawns have come out of these warrens.

Bob is driving the argocat slowly between the feeding rabbits and the safety of their warrens in the belting of woodland. He's cutting off their escape route.

We are by now just about within range of the feeding rabbits on the lawns and Bob turns the argocat in on to the lawns. The headlights light up the lawns and there they are, the rabbits are now all within range of our rifles. There must be more than forty rabbits sat there in front of us. I hear a bullet whiz over the top of my head, I see a rabbit drop dead in the centre of the bunch. That must be Helen keeping to our new found orders. I hear a thud from my right and I see another rabbit fall dead on the right-hand side of the bunch of rabbit. That must be Bob, he's keeping to our new found orders also. I pick my rifle up, I let fire, another rabbit falls on the left-hand side of the bunch of rabbits. I am keeping to the new found orders also and now none of us are shooting at the same rabbit.

Now there's bullets whizzing everywhere, now there's rabbits dropping dead everywhere. I see the other rabbits as they are looking around them. They hear no bangs to startle them, all they see is a dazzling light shining on them and their mates kicking and fighting about on the ground. They don't know there's danger around, not yet they don't anyway, they just sit there and look.

I have my scope on another rabbit and I see another rabbit sat directly at the back of the first one. I put the cross of the scope on the rabbit's head, the rabbit behind has got his head there also. I shoot and both rabbits drop dead, that's the power of these rifles. The bullet passes straight through the first rabbit and into the second rabbit.

As the bullets go whizzing and flying around there are now many dead rabbits laid around. The rest of the rabbits are now getting the idea all's not well around. They get the collywobbles and hop off across the lawns. I turn on the spotlight, I swivel it and shine it to one side of the argocat. The light picks up four rabbits, I hear a thud and a whiz and now there's only two rabbits standing. I keep the light on the remaining two, and a quick slot of another two bullets into their rifles and Bob and Helen have the other two rabbits down. I shine the swivelling spotlight all the way around the argocat and every rabbit the light picks up falls to a whizzing or thudding bullet.

We drive on in the argocat and manoeuvre around the lawns and every rabbit we see standing stands no more. The lawn's now empty of standing rabbits and we now have many, many rabbits laid dead on the lawns. I send Pup and Helen out to retrieve the dead rabbits. Helen is objecting but I tell her I am in charge of the swivelling spotlight. I will shine the light on the dead rabbits, it's her job now to pick them up. Helen is not amused but I have stopped her tittering behind my back.

There are many rabbits that have kicked and figged themselves to death and lay hidden in the shrubbery of Lady Celia's flower beds. I will find them in the morning in the daylight. Helen and Pup gather in many, many dead rabbits until the argocat is near on full to capacity. Helen and Pup now jump back into the back of the argocat. Helen is complaining yet again, now she's saying she's nowhere to put her feet. Me and Bob ignore Helen's moans. I look back behind me, I see my Pup, she's not moaning. She has a good vantage position, she is sat on top of all the dead rabbits.

Bob drives on towards the front of the castle. All these rabbits we are shooting, our aim is to put the bullet into the rabbit's head, that way the meat on the rabbit is not damaged. When I go homeward bound, which will be soon, I will be taking these rabbits with me. They will then go straight on to the meat market in my local town. So it's important that the rabbits are cleanly killed and as fresh as possible. The bullets we are using are called 'dumdum' bullets. They mushroom out on impact and the rabbit's skull shatters killing the rabbit instantly. But, boy, do they kick when the rabbit is hit in the head. The rabbit will jump two to three feet into the air, that's a sure sign of a headshot. The rabbit is dead but his nerves kick on and he will kick and fig maybe thirty yards away before he lays still well away from where I shot him. So they do sometimes take a bit of finding.

Me, Helen and Bob we are shooting the same make and type of

bullet. Doing it that way, if anyone of us runs out of bullets we can use the other's bullets. If we did use a different make or type of bullet in our rifles the performance of the rifle will alter and we would miss our target.

By now we are at the front of the castle again and we see more rabbits in front of us in the argocat's headlights. Bob drives closer into them and we can now see Lady Celia again up in the lit-up bedroom. She's waving frantically and she's half naked by the look of her. Bob is saying, "Is Lady CC trying to catch our attention, does she want something?"

Bob is that distracted looking at Lady CC he doesn't see the greenhouse and smashes clean into it. Bob quickly reverses back and we do a quick runner. We head across the lawns and the argocat is bumping and bouncing around. It's Bob, he's driving through the flowerbeds and he's breaking down the rose beds as we go. Lady CC has certainly made an impression on Bob! We carry on and finish back up at the main castle gates and Bob stops. Phew!

Now that we have finished lamping the rabbits on the castle grounds the night is still young so we are now going to lamp the main place where Bob says is absolutely overrun with rabbits. But first we need an empty argocat, so out come all the rabbits out of the argocat. It's near on full with rabbits so we take them and neatly lay them on the lawn by the side of the castle gates. The rabbits will cool off there in the cold chill of the night, and off we go and disappear into the darkness of the night.

We head on up the mountain side but where Bob is heading I don't know. Surely all the rabbits Bob speaks of will not be in the mountain tops, the altitude is too high for the rabbits to survive.

The drizzling rain is starting to come on heavy now and I have to protect my scope's lenses. If the rain fogs them up it will be impossible to carry on shooting rabbits. Bob and Helen do the same but they cover over their rifles with an old coat in the back of the argocat.

I have with me some tubes which I slot on to the ends of my rifle scope and these will keep the rain off the scope lenses. They are just simple tubes I made myself from a lightweight, stiff, waterproof canvas. I have stitched them into this tube shape which is a close fit when slotted on to the ends of my scope. At the far end of the scope the tube sticks out about three inches, that's ample to keep the rain off the lenses. At the near end of the scope the tube sticks out only one inch. This allows me to get my eye close into the scope, but still sticking out enough to keep the rain off the scope lens. The tubes are only a simple little thing but very effective.

By now we are at the top of the mountain and we can hardly see for thick overcast clouds that are swirling around us with the breeze that is blowing. Bob's now dropping down the other side of the mountain, and it's that steep and rugged where we go Helen and Pup are all but falling into the front of the argocat.

The ground now levels off and Bob's now going over what looks like a wooden walkway by what I can see in the argocat's headlights. It all looks precarious to me as I peer through the thick swirling low cloud. Now I feel the wooden walkway shaking, swaying and creaking as we go. We are now off the wooden walkway and on another mountain side by what I can see. Bob's now got the argocat facing upwards into the heavens and I see Helen holding on grimly as we go. She has hold of Pup so that she doesn't drop out.

The argocat bumps and bounces as it heads on upwards. We finally reach the top of where we have just come from, thank God, and now we are going down a mountain side. I see big white mountain hares in the argocat's headlights, and as we travel on down the mountain side I see dozens and dozens of mountain hares all in their white winter coats. Bob says, "We must not touch these hares."

As we reach the bottom of the mountain side the argocat's headlights are now shining across a large expanse of water. Bob says, "This is where the shooting men were stood when we were all out wildfowling that day not all that long since."

Do you readers remember? This is the loch where the shooting men were shooting the ducks and geese and then sending them over to us as we were shooting the ducks and geese on Bob's flight pond.

Bob's now heading out across the moorland. We come to a fence and then we get to a five-barred gate. The argocat's headlights are now shining into the grass pasture and Bob whispers, "This is it Doug, this is where all the rabbits are."

Helen goes and opens the five-barred gate and in we drive through the gateway, our rifles now at the ready. Bob drives on but we see no rabbits. There's a small hilly bank in front of us and as we climb the bank the argocat's headlights shine up into the heavens. Then as we drop over the bank the light picks up feeding rabbits. There's one that's not feeding for very long, a bullet goes whistling over my head and up in the air the rabbit goes. That's another rabbit down to Helen. Down goes another by its side, that's another rabbit down to Bob.

With us being on top of the grass bank, Bob says, "Watch this Doug."

I watch as Bob manoeuvres the headlights around the grass meadow, and what I see I don't believe. The grass meadow is vast and I must be able to see more than a thousand rabbits out there feeding as Bob flashes the headlights across them.

Bob drives down and amongst the rabbits and the bullets are at full blaze amongst the rabbits. I see rabbits dropping dead everywhere but the other rabbits are not running away, they are just sat there looking. I hear thump, thud, whizzing, whistling bullets, and I see rabbits kicking themselves to death everywhere. Bob had told me earlier these rabbits wouldn't be lamp shy, he told me they had never had a lamp across them before and boy is he right. The rabbits are just sitting there and letting us shoot them, they don't know what's happening. They will know less still when a bullet hits them in the head.

We leave the rabbits where they drop dead, we have to keep on shooting while the rabbits are dumb to the fact. I feel someone fumbling in my pocket. It's Helen, she's after more bullets. I have a big pouch full in there purposely for quick firing, it saves toilsome time having to take them out of the box one at a time.

Bob keeps on manoeuvring the argocat around the vast grass meadow and we keep on popping off the rabbits and leaving them where they drop. We range up alongside of a rabbit-proof wire netting fence line and we see twenty, thirty rabbits all together. They are all queuing up to go through a small hole in the wire mesh fence. I can see they are not all going to make it through the hole. There's rabbits dropping everywhere as the bullets go whizzing and flying at them.

Now the rabbits have all gone, all the alive ones anyway, I hear Bob chuntering away to himself. He says it's only recently he has had that fence line put in and look at it, the rabbits have already broken through it. He says, "If the rabbits can get the wire between their back teeth they have the power and will chew through the wire mesh."

Bob drives on disgruntled. We are now driving around the

grass meadow for a second time around and I don't believe it. The rabbits have come back out for us to have a second go at them.

We now have that many rabbits down laying dead on the ground from first time around, Bob is having to steer the argocat around them.

Now Bob is complaining yet again. He says he can't see through his rifle scope, it's all misted up. Helen's now complaining, she's also saying she can't see through her rifle scope either, they are fogged up also. It's all this drizzling rain that has caused it.

The scopes soon mist up in wet drizzly weather, but my scope is fine, I can see clearly through mine. My manmade tubes I have on each end of my scope have saved the day or is that night? I can continue on shooting, I now have all the rabbits to myself.

Helen is now the retriever with my dog Pup and they are now gathering up all the dead rabbits we shot earlier. The more rabbits Helen is picking up and throwing into the back of the argocat the more rabbits I am shooting and adding to her toilsome work. Now it's me tittering behind Helen's back.

The back of the argocat is now full to capacity, so what rabbits are left laying dead in the grass meadow I will pick up later when it breaks daylight. And there are many left laying dead I can tell you.

We set off now to leave this vast grass meadow, our lamping of these rabbits has now left its mark. Bob now drives on and just as we are leaving the meadow behind us Helen taps me on the shoulder and says in a whisper, "Look there."

As she point with her finger we see a pair of eyes shining in the argocat's headlights. Bob says in the lowest of whispers, "It's a bloody fox," and he tells Helen to pass him his high-calibre rifle. But by the time Bob has got his rifle up and ready the fox has gone.

Bob fumbles in his haste to turn on the spotlight and he shines it around frantically. There it is, it's heading across the grassland and it has a dead rabbit in its mouth. I hope that's not one of my rabbits it's got. The fox is way out in the distance about two hundred yards away but if the fox stops now Bob will have him. He's not too far away for the big rifle to pick him off. The fox has now jumped up on the top of a stone wall. It peers back at us with sparkling eyes and it still has the rabbit in its mouth.

Bob is fumbling and messing around. He's all fingers and thumbs, and by the time he does have the rifle up and ready to shoot, the fox has now disappeared over the other side of the stone wall.

Bob quickly gets out a small piece of polystyrene, he's now spitting on it, and he's now rubbing the polystyrene on the windscreen of the argocat. It's making a screeching sound just like screaming rabbit. Bob's now scanning the whole area around us with the spotlight. The fox is having none of that imitation rabbit screaming, the fox doesn't show himself.

I tell Bob in a low whisper, "Let me have a go." I tell Bob to turn of all the lights and we now sit all in the pitch black of the night. Now the argocat's engine is turned off, all we can now hear is the pitter-patter of the drizzling rain and the stiff breeze which is blowing off the moor. Then I give out a long drawn out bloodthirsty rabbit scream. I do this by drawing in air through a small hole in my bottom teeth, it's very effective I can tell you. You can chuck away all that polystyrene stuff, my screams are just like the true McCoy, I have had enough practice at it over the years.

For a good five minutes as we sit quiet in the darkness of the night I keep on sending out these bloodcurdling pathetic distressed rabbit screams. I now tell Bob to switch on the spotlight. Bob shines it around, and there it is, the fox has come back out from its hiding place. It's stood in a frozen position as the light glares on it and it's only a hundred yards away. As Bob fumbles with his big rifle, I say to him in a low whisper, "Come on you big silly pillock, hurry up. Have I to tell the fox to sit down for five minutes while you get your rifle ready?"

Bob now has the rifle on the fox and I now hear him chuntering away to himself under his breath. I say in the lowest of whispers, "Shoot man, shoot."

Bob replies in a whisper, "I can't, the scope lenses are all fogged up."

So now I have to take over with my .22 calibre rifle. I get the fox in my scope and I see him nice and clearly. My tubes on my scope have saved the day. But the fox is just a bit too far away for my rifle, it's only zeroed in at seventy yards.

I relax back and give out more bloodcurdling rabbit screams. The fox is not deterred by the spotlight shining on him and he moves in closer to the alluring screams. His eyes are shining and sparkling like green emeralds. As far as I know it's only human eyes that do not shine back in the dark when a light shines on them. It's to do with the retina at the back of the eye that reflects light back.

My long drawn out bloodthirsty rabbit screams have now lured in the fox to within seventy yards of us. I now have my scope on him and I have the cross on his chest. I want to shoot him in the heart but I can't, the dangling rabbit which he still has in his mouth is covering his chest up. The fox has his head lurched low, I give out another bloodthirsty scream and he's now coming in even closer. I keep the scope on him as I watch him. He raises his head, I gently pull the trigger. The fox shudders and slumps to the ground, and the fox is no more.

In my mind, a sad end to a magnificent animal. If the fox only knew not to take the gamekeeper's game birds or the farmer's chickens, just killing and eating vermin like rabbits and rats, I am sure most people would welcome the fox in the countryside.

Helen rushes out to pick up the dead fox. I take the rabbit from his mouth, I slit its lug with the knife and throw it into the back of the argocat with a whole pile of other rabbits. Now when I have time to sort out these rabbits, when I come to the rabbit with the slit lug I now know it may be chewed up by the fox, so I will skin it out to check it over.

Our mission now accomplished we drive on in the argocat. It's by now breaking daylight and we have been hard at it lamping rabbits all night long. We are now heading across the moorland towards Bob's duck flight pond. Bob wants all these rabbits' guts for ducks and geese to feed on.

As we travel along the moorland tops it's now turning out to be a lovely day. The drizzling rain has stopped and now the sun is coming up over the horizon. I see across the moor my old mates the blackcock, there must be about twenty of them out there on their lekking ground. I see they are sticking their chests out and throwing threats out to each other, as per usual. Bob says, "The Laird doesn't allow the blackcock to be shot. He is trying to preserve them so that they will breed on and spread further across the moorlands."

By now we are nearing Bob's flight pond. He's now crawling along with the argocat, he says he wants to see if there are any mink around. As we look over the bank of the flight pond we see many ducks and geese. They see us all at the same time and up they get from the water. The sky is now full of gaggling, honking, quacking ducks and geese.

Helen points and says, "Look there."

We see three great big rats, they are sat munching away on top of Bob's feeder bin. Helen says, "Let me shoot the big buggers."

I tell Helen, "Stop, you will only get one if you shoot. Let's all three of us shoot together." So that's just what we did.

Bob's and Helen's scopes on their rifles have now dried out and cleared now the drizzling rain has stopped. The three rats are about sixty yards away from us on the other bank of the pond. We are going to take good steady aim resting our rifles on the roller bars on the argocat. We are all going to shoot at different rats and all three of us now have our scopes on the rats as they are all sat together on top of the feeder bin. I put the cross of my scope on to the left-hand side rat, Bob does the same with the rat on the right, and Helen does the same with the rat in the middle. If only the rats knew what was happening, they would be off like bats out of hell.

We are now all ready for shooting and I say quietly, "On the count of three shoot. One, two, fire."

I only hear my rifle fire but all three rats topple over together. A bit of good shooting that, I thought, so off we go now to paunch the rabbits and throw the guts into the pond.

What a fine bag of rabbits we have in the back of the argocat, most of them head shots I might add. We have about a hundred and fifty rabbits here and there's as many again on the ground on the vast meadow we lamped through the night earlier. And not forgetting the near on argocat full we shot around the Laird's castle and left to cool off through the night on the lawn near the main castle gates. Together with a whole host of rabbits we did not pick up from the lawns. Wow, I reckon by the time I have finished picking up today I will have near on five hundred rabbits to take home with me in the morning.

Our rabbits now paunched and all the guts in the pond, the ducks and geese are going to have a birthday party when they see all this lot waiting for them. Bob's got his hand over the top of his eyes and he's looking at the willow trees I planted for him some time earlier. He says, "The willow trees are looking well Doug, they will help to draw in the ducks and geese and will give them shelter."

We now head on and back to Bob's cottage, the Hunter's Lodge, and this is where Bob and Helen leave me. Bob goes off into his cottage for a well-earned rest, and he takes with him his well-earned fox and drops it off outside of his cottage door.

I now have to say farewell to my beloved Helen, I am going home in the morning. Helen looks terribly bedraggled, her long blonde hair is all wet and tangled and her face is all smeared in rabbit's blood. After all, she should look like that, she has been out all night lamping rabbits in all that drizzling rain. But no matter what she looks like I think she's pretty anyway.

I give her a big hug and a big smacking kiss right on her lips and bid her farewell while next time I am up. That will not be long I am sure.

I now hang these rabbits in Bob's game larder, and with the argocat now empty of all its rabbits I now set off again to fill it back up again with rabbits.

Me and my Pup are now heading on back to the vast meadow we lamped through the night. I have to be early to gather all these rabbits up otherwise the marauding carrion crows will have them for their breakfast.

I go the same way Bob went and follow the argocat's track up the mountain side. Phew, what a climb it is too! I finally reach the top and I am certainly high up in the heavens up here. I follow the tracks Bob made across the mountain top until I reach the edge, this is the point where Bob went down. I look over the edge of the mountain side and I don't believe what I see. All that I see I have never seen before, remember I came over here in the darkness of the night. Down there in front of me is a great, deep bloody ravine.

I see gushing water cascading down the ravine, I see an old battered wooden bridge going over the ravine. This is what I thought was some kind of wooden walkway. I didn't know there was a deep bloody ravine down below us when we crossed it through the night.

I got the collywobbles from what I saw in front of me. But the thought of all my dead rabbits lying there in the vast meadow and the thought of all the marauding carrion crows eating them before I get there was enough to urge me on.

I had to cross the ravine, my rabbits are not far away at the other side. So I set off in the argocat with my Pup at my side. She is sat in the passenger seat and by the looks of her with not a care in the world. We have to drop down the mountain side a little to get to the bridge. It's sheer as we drop down and Pup has slid off the seat and on to the floor where the passengers put their feet.

The argocat bumps and bounces over the rugged mountain track until we reach the bottom. We are now at the start of the battered old wooden bridge.

Pup jumps back into her rightful place on the passenger seat and we are now just sat in the argocat standing still, contemplating the crossing ahead. Well I am anyway, Pup just looks nonchalant. The bridge is only about sixty yards long across the ravine so there will be nothing to it, it will be quite simple and I am now fully focused on my task ahead of me.

I set off across the bridge, it's only six inches wider than the argocat and there are no sides to the bridge, no handrails, no brushing boards to keep the tyres on the bridge. I carry on regardless, thinking, if Bob can cross it with just the headlights on then surely I can cross it easily in the daylight.

My eyes are now focused straight ahead keeping the argocat as straight as a die as we go. I can feel the bridge swaying with our weight, it's the bloody wind that's blowing that's pushing us over. I hear the bridge creaking and groaning and I am sure some of these wooden planks we are driving on are loose.

The fear of crossing this bridge has brought the sweat of fear on to my forehead. The sweat is now running into my eyes, I now can't see for sweat. I stop the argocat, I wipe the sweat from my eyes with my snotty, rabbit-blood-covered handkerchief. I open my eyes and I see we are only halfway across the bridge. I must admit to you readers now, I have a terrible fear of heights, what a time to admit it.

I peer over the side of the argocat and I freeze when I see what I see. It's a hundred foot drop down there into the ravine. I see waterfalls cascading over large massive rocks and boulders and I draw my eyes away from that view, oh so very slowly. As I am drawing my eyes away, oh so very slowly, I see the argocat's tyres, and what I see is shock horror. The tyres have half run off the bridge. I wince in fright and I pull my head back into the argocat and freeze motionless in fright.

There's sweat now pouring down my forehead, there's sweat dripping off my fingertips, my body, my clothes they are lathered in sweat. I am now sat there in a petrified position, I can't even move a muscle, I am doomed. I feel the old wooden bridge rocking and swaying, creaking and groaning. I see Pup out of the corner of my sweat-blurred eye, she is sat there like Lady Muck. She has her mouth wide open with her tongue hung out and it looks as though she's laughing at me. Then my ears cock up, I don't believe it, I can hear someone shouting. Saviour at last, I think. I look up with just my eyeballs, my head is petrified and frozen in one position, and what I see is my guardian angel. It's Helen shouting and waving to me from the far side of the ravine but I don't wave back. Helen keeps on waving, she's now coming across to me, she's now on the rickety old bridge, she's walking as though she's oh, so unconcerned.

She has half a dozen sheepdogs with her, there's tears of joy in my eyes now as well as sweat. Helen's now upon me, she has a great big smile on her face that must have stretched from ear to lug. She sees there is something wrong with me, I can't speak back to her, she sees I am petrified in the driver's seat. Helen can't get down the side of the argocat there isn't enough room so she just simply jumps on to the bonnet of the argocat using no hands.

She's now climbing over into the argocat and she says, with a smile on her face, "Move over ya silly bugger, let me take over."

But I can't move, I am petrified. Helen's now pulling and tugging at me, but my hands are stuck and welded to the steering wheel. Helen prises my hands from the steering wheel, she's now manhandling me and out of the driver's seat and I am now shaking and cowering in the passenger seat. Helen just simply jumps into the driver's seat and off she drives, her six dogs running and jumping as they are playing with each other. Running in front of us as we travel along the rickety old bridge. Helen is cosseting me with one hand while she steers the argocat with the other hand. Helen has no fears and sees no dangers and drives off the bridge as though there's nothing to it. All this simplicity from Helen brings me back to my senses. I feel better now we are off the bridge, but Helen doesn't stop she carries on in the argocat and starts climbing the sheer mountain side which takes us out of the ravine.

The argocat bumps and bounces its way up the rugged mountain track and Helen stops at the top. She leans over and puts her arm around me, and she's cuddling me that much I don't know whether she's mothering me or smothering me. I have now got over my terrifying ordeal and I tell Helen, "That bridge is dangerous, it's falling down."

Helen says, "It's a good strong bridge is that. It might just want a few nails knocking in it to hold it together, but that's all it wants."

So again Helen gives me a big smacking farewell kiss smack on my lips and again we depart. Helen jumps on her quad bike, she is off to tend to a flock of sheep over on that far lall hill. I look over to the lall hill where she's heading to, it's a bloody great mountain to me. And the deep, menacing ravine I have just crossed over, I suppose Helen will call that a lall gutter with a lall stream flowing through it.

So I now head off again to gather up all the rabbits we shot on the vast meadowland only last evening, following the tracks that Bob made with the argocat.

I begin dropping down the other side of the mountain and I see hares. There's hares everywhere I look and they are great big white mountain hares, they are in their full winter camouflage coats.

There are only three British creatures that turn white in the winter which acts as camouflage in the snow. One is these 'blue' mountain hares (they really are blue in the summer), the other two creatures being the ptarmigan, which are found up here in the Scottish Highlands, and the stoat which is called an 'ermine' when it's in its white winter coat.

I head on in the argocat further down the mountainside and I can now see the great loch in front of me. This is the first time I have seen this loch in the daylight and it's vast. I see many rafts of ducks and geese out there roosting in the middle of the water, and I see something else. I can't make out what it is so I pick up my rifle and look through the scope. It's a half-submerged boat in the shallows of the loch and I think, has it just sank, are there any people still on board? I scan the area with my scope, but I see no one. I will have to ask Bob about this shipwreck.

I now head on along the banks of the loch until I see the tyre tracks that Bob made with the argocat only last night. They lead out across the rough grassland and I follow the track which leads me to a five-barred gate. I recognize the gate, this is the one which Helen opened only last night, and I see the small grass bank in front of me, so I have now reached my destination.

This is the vast meadow where I have many, many rabbits lying dead from last night's shoot. I drive over the small grass bank and what I see I don't like. I see pesky marauding carrion crows, they are at my dead rabbits but they all scatter and depart when they see me. I now start picking up the rabbits and loading them into the back of the argocat.

There are many rabbits to pick up and I am in luck, the carrion crows have only been taking the eyes out of the rabbits. I pick and gather as I go along around the vast meadow with the argocat. Pup is working well, she is retrieving her share back to my hand.

It is a beautiful, glorious, sun-shining morning and I see rabbits sat out everywhere in the morning sunshine. I have my rifle in hand and I am picking off even more rabbits as I travel along. By the time I am three quarters way around the vast grass meadow the back of the argocat is full with rabbits. But still as I travel along I am picking off even more rabbits with the rifle.

I now have a big pile of rabbits with nowhere to put them. There is some baling band in the argocat so I get that and tie the rabbits into couples by their back legs. I now hang the rabbits up on the argocat's roller bars which go all the way around the top of the argocat. I keep on shooting even more rabbits and adding to the bag, and by the time I have finished hanging all the rabbits on the roller bars I can't see the argocat at all. It looks just like one big bundle of rabbit fur.

I force myself to put my rifle down otherwise I will have nowhere to put the rabbits. We are now travelling along towards a pine tree forestry plantation. I can't see where I am going, I have rabbits strewn all the way along the roller bar in front of me and I am holding the rabbits apart to see where I am going. I see dozens and dozens of rabbits in front of me, they are skedaddling to one side out of my way. Then they are stopping and looking back at me as though I am some sort of unheard of creature. Or do they recognize their mates as I pass them by in the argocat?

I am now at the forestry tree plantation side and I stop the argocat and have a breather. I don't believe what I see, there are hundreds and hundreds of rabbits sat along the woodland side, all out enjoying the morning sunshine. They are just sat looking at me, they have no fear of me. I peer inside of the forestry tree plantation and what I see I do not believe, there's rabbits, rabbits everywhere. There's even more rabbits inside there than there is on the meadow outside here.

The rabbits here are in plague proportions. I get myself to thinking, the Laird here on his vast estate has got one hell of a serious rabbit problem. So far, everywhere I have looked on this estate the rabbits are completely out of control. I could catch five hundred rabbits a day here on this estate and still not make an impression on the marauding rabbits. By the time the breeding season comes around the rabbits would breed on and be as bad as they ever were.

As you readers know by now, I am writing this story in the year 2008, and I can now look back through time gone by.

Mankind has tried hard to eliminate the ever-increasing marauding rabbits. Way back in time in the year 1953 mankind introduced a disease amongst the rabbits which was called 'myxomatosis'. This virus soon spread across England, Wales and Scotland, and in a matter of no time at all 99% of all rabbits throughout Britain were dead, all killed by the myxomatosis virus. As the years rolled on by, the 1% of the rabbits that remained built up a resistance to the myxomatosis virus and bred on. The rabbits went forth and multiplied, and now just look at them today.

Mankind's persecution of the rabbit kept on and in the year 1994 a new disease was spread amongst the British rabbits, it was called 'viral haemorrhagic disease', VHD for short. This disease spreads through the rabbit population when they are breeding, making the rabbits infertile. The outcome of the experiment amongst the British rabbits proved negative, they shrugged off the VHD just like a common cold.

So you readers now know just like I know that rabbits still flourish and breed on in the year 2008. Now back to my story.

I am on the vast grass meadow on the Laird's vast estate which is completely out of control with rabbits. I am fully loaded with rabbits on the argocat and I have difficulty finding the driver's seat with all the rabbits in and strewn all around the argocat. I have that many rabbits piled high on the passenger seat that my Pup is sat right on top. She has a good view up there as I look up at her because she's that high she can see over the top of the hanging rabbits which are hung on the argocat's roller bars. So off me and Pup go, we are now heading towards Bob's duck flight pond to paunch all these rabbits.

The argocat bumps and bounces across the rugged terrain of the upper moorland. Pup hangs on grimly as she bumps and bounces high up on top of the rabbits.

As we draw up alongside of the flight pond a whole host of geese and ducks fly up from where we threw the last lot of rabbits' guts in. I peer into the water and there's not a rabbit gut to be seen, the ducks and geese have scoffed the lot. These rabbits' guts are a real delicacy for the wildfowl, so I set to and give them another great pile of rabbits' guts to eat.

I am now all loaded up again with the rabbits all paunched out and on to Bob's cottage me and Pup do go. As we drive into the courtyard I see Bob through the rabbits which I am holding apart so that I can see. Bob looks startled at what he sees and he says, "Doug, Doug, are you there?" All Bob can see is a mountain of rabbits with Pup sat on the top.

"Here I am," I say, as I hold the rabbits further apart.

Bob says, "I thought for a minute that Pup was driving the argocat."

I now unload all the rabbits from the argocat and hang them up in the game larder with all the rabbits I hung in earlier. The game larder is getting really full by now, but there's more rabbits to come yet. I now have to go pick up all them rabbits we left on the lawn at the Laird's castle. This time I don't go in the argocat I go in my own Land Rover, it will be faster. So off to the castle me and Pup do head.

When I arrive at the castle gates I see all my rabbits still laid there on the lawn. I look at them, I think, I scratch my head and I look around. There looks to be a lot more rabbits than what we left there.

I load the rabbits up into the back of the Land Rover. There, that's another fine bag of rabbits, I think, and off I drive across the castle lawns. I pass on by the rose beds which Bob ploughed through with the argocat, but I see no rabbits lying dead on the lawns. There should be, we shot enough. I drive on further across the lawns, I pass on by the greenhouse which Bob smashed into with the argocat. What a mess it looks now the glass roof has caved in. I carry on across the lawns and turn around the back of the castle.

The lawns are big here and still I see no dead rabbits lying. There should be, me, Bob and Helen shot enough and just left them lying there on the lawns. There's something catching my eyes over in the shrubbery. I see a blonde head behind the bushes and I get out of my Land Rover and go across. I see a whole host of rabbits lying dead there on the lawn. I see a retriever dog, it has a rabbit in its mouth and it's taking it to the blonde head I see at the back of the bushes. I go take a look. It's Lady Celia I see, Bob has told me it's Lady CC for short.

Lady CC addresses me and calls me Doug. By, what a pretty lady CC is. She looks much younger than the Laird himself and she has long blonde hair just like my beloved Helen. Lady CC tells me she is gathering up all my rabbits for me and that she has added a lot to those rabbits at the main castle gates. Lady CC has a deep-plunging neckline on her tight-fitting blouse and my eyes nearly pop out when I see what I see. Her small, firm titties are nearly popping out as she bends down to take the rabbit from her retriever dog. I dash in and take the rabbit myself, I don't want Lady CC's titties dropping out, do I.

Lady CC has another retriever dog with her and it's coming out of the bushes with a rabbit in its mouth. Lady CC bends down with her back to me to take the rabbit from her retriever and my eyes nearly pop out when I see what I see. Lady CC has a pair of tight-fitting casual jeans on. By, what a figure she has, her pretty bum is all but bursting out of her tight-fitting jeans. I see a pair of sexy knicker tops showing above her low-fitting hipster jeans.

By, what I have seen is enough to make a dog sick. That is an old saying is that, "enough to make a dog sick", meaning how the opposite sex attracts the opposite sex, not only people but other animals too.

I remember once I went to my local pub for a pot or two of ale and I had my bitch with me. She was in season (ready for mating) and she laid at my feet as I sat in the pub. Who should walk in but my mate Ken and he had with him his lurcher dog. Ken got himself a pint pot of ale and came and sat down by my side. Now my bitch at my feet is getting giddy and she is pushing her arse over to Ken's lurcher dog, and all by natural instincts the lurcher responds. My bitch is teasing and tormenting him and she too is only being urged on by natural sexual instincts.

All this activity is going on underneath the table where me and Ken sit having a pot of ale. My bitch torments the lurcher dog so much, that when me and Ken see what is happening, Ken's lurcher dog is by now white foaming at the mouth. He's trying to be sick and now the Landlord is playing holy hell as Ken's dog is shitting all over the place.

That's now all taking place with me and Lady CC in the bushes in the castle ground. She's that pretty and sexually alluring it's enough to make a dog sick. But I have none of it and I tell Lady CC I have rabbits to gather in. As I am saying this Lady CC is looking me straight in the face. I have a small piece of chewing gum in my mouth and it jumps out of my mouth and gets stuck right between Lady CC's titties. Lady CC hasn't seen the chewing gum jump out of my mouth. I make a quick grab to get my chewing gum back and plunge my hand into her titties. Now Lady CC is aghast and blushing so I pull out the chewing gum and show her it. Now Lady CC is all frustrated, she was expecting the inevitable, but I now make my escape and I go gather the rabbits that Lady CC has gathered for me.

As I am loading them into the Land Rover Lady CC says that I smashed her greenhouse down last night with the argocat. I tell her, "It wasn't me driving, it was Bob. Him and Helen were so busy watching you up in the bedroom window. They thought you wanted something with all the waving you were doing. Bob was that distracted he smashed into the greenhouse."

Lady CC's now red-faced blushing again and she mutters, "I thought you were all alone."

And on that I jump into my Land Rover and make haste across the castle lawns. Phew! I look back and Lady CC's chasing after me across the lawns, and her titties are going to jump out, I am sure of it. In all my haste and hurriedness I am now ploughing through the rose beds but I keep on going and head on back to Bob's cottage. Phew!

I pull into Bob's courtyard and the first job I have to do is paunch all these rabbits I have in the Land Rover. I put all the guts into an old fertilizer bag. Bob can take them to the duck flight pond later. I now go to hang my rabbits into the game larder. I try to anyway, but there's that many rabbits in there now I have to squeeze them all up to get all the rabbits in. What a fine bag of rabbits they are too.

My mission is now accomplished. I have been hard at it lamping rabbits all night long. I have been non-stop hard at it gathering up all my rabbits until now. I look at my watch, it's two o'clock in the afternoon. I am knackered so I now go into Bob's cottage and lay up for the rest of the day.

It was early to bed that night and up early like a lark the following morning. I am homeward bound this morning, I have to get my rabbits home while they are still nice and fresh. They will be going straight on to the city's meat market as soon as I arrive home.

I now load up my rabbits on all my three decks in the Land Rover. I now have rabbits tied in couples, which I hang over the poles which are up in the Land Rover's roof. My Land Rover is now all about full.

Now for the first time I have to use my trailer so I couple it on to my Land Rover. In the trailer I have positioned some poles which go from side to side all along the full length of the trailer. The poles are positioned at the right height so that the rabbits hang freely. Again my rabbits are tied in couples by their back legs and I now hang my rabbits on the poles in the trailer. I easily get all my rabbits in. I now have a wooden lid which covers over the top of the trailer so if it rains now as I travel home my rabbits will be kept nice and dry.

So that's it, I am all ready and loaded for my homeward bound journey.

I must have more than five hundred rabbits loaded up there in the Land Rover and trailer together. I bid Bob farewell and say that I will not be long before I am back up again. Bob tips his hat to me and off I go.

I remember that morning very well. This was the most rabbits I had ever taken with me and I get halfway up the hill which climbs out of the glen and away from Bob's cottage and the Land Rover stops. I have that much weight on with rabbits the Land Rover can't pull it. But I know it has to so I slot my Land Rover into low gear box which automatically puts it into four-wheel drive. Then I slot it into the crawler gear, I give the engine a bit of juice and she starts creeping up the hill very slowly. She's doing a bit of coughing and spitting and I am sure my Land Rover is crying out, "I can't pull it, I can't pull it Doug," but I know she has to.

I hear moaning and groaning coming from the engine as my Land Rover crawled her way up that hill. And oh so slowly but oh so surely we reached to top of the hill. Phew, I thought for a moment then that Pup would have to get out and give us a pull. It's now plain sailing all the way home.

And that's what I remember of my first ever rabbit lamping I had on the Laird's vast rabbit-infested estate up in those Grampian Mountains in the Highlands of Scotland.

Do you readers think that my story is exciting? Remember all this happened in the decade of the 1970s. Read on, it gets even more exciting.

There was another time I remember I was up in them there hills on the Laird's vast estate and Bob was going to have a hare shoot high up on the hills on one of his grouse moors. The day before the hare shoot was going to take place, Bob was going to have a day of heather burning. There were many hares laid in this heather that Bob was going to burn and he wanted to get the hares out of this heather and push them across the moor and nearer to where the hare shoot was going to take place.

Bob asked me to help him with the heather burning. Bob does the heather burning all in a proper manner. He had informed the fire brigade when and where the heather burning was going to take place. Doing it that way, if the fire then gets out of control the fire brigade is prepared for any eventual emergency.

Bob had got a good team of men together to help him in the heather burning; he had got Big Jim, Jock and my beloved Helen. So this particular morning we all set off up on to the high grouse moor in the argocat.

Bob parked up the argocat well away from the burning area and out of danger. There was just a nice light breeze blowing across the moor, which is ideal for controlled heather burning. The heather that we were going to burn was tall and thickly growing and we got it blazing away in a nice controlled manner. We were doing what they call 'back burning', that meant the light breeze was blowing the flames away from the heather.

The heather was burning well but it was too slow for Bob's liking. He was wanting them hares up and running out of the heather double quick time and on towards the location for the next day's hare shoot. So Bob sent Helen way across the moorland to start her own fire. He also sent Big Jim and Jock way across the moorland in the opposite direction to start their own individual fires.

Bob now had a long stretch of the moorland on fire and in a controlled manner. We all had a long-poled 'fire shovel', a piece which controls the burning heather. The blue smoke was drifting across the moorland and smoking the hares out of the heather just as Bob had planned it. I could see many big white mountain hares running across the moorland. They stood out like sore thumbs in their white winter coats. The moorland is free of snow which does camouflage the hares in their white coats.

Mine and Bob's heather was burning nice and slowly in a sedate fashion. As we looked across the moorland we saw Helen laid down in the heather resting as her fire was steadily burning. We looked across at Big Jim and Jock, they were also resting up as their fires were burning well and under control.

Bob walked across the moor to have a rest up the side of the moorland wall and I went across to have a rest with him. As we stand there chatting away, I tell Bob that down in the South of England they call their heather burning 'swaling'. Bob nods in acknowledgement. We see a covey of ptarmigan in their white winter coats and I tell Bob that ptarmigan have a lot of feathers around their feet which act like snow shoes reducing 60% of their foot pressure. Bob nods in acknowledgement.

As we are stood there chatting away peering over the moorland stone wall, Bob points out a pair of golden eagles as they are sat

PTARMIGAN.

SUMMER COAT.

THE ONLY THREE BRITISH ANIMAL'S AND BIRD'S WHICH TURN WHITE IN THE WINTER ARE THE:- "BLUE MOUNTAIN HARE" "STOAT" AND "PTARMIGAN." ON THE SNOW CLAD MOUNTAIN TOP'S THESE BIRD'S TURN AS WHITE AS DRIVEN SNOW high up on the rocky crags. They are scanning the surrounding moorland looking for any potential prey. Golden eagles do sometimes work in pairs as they comb and search their territory and surprise-attack their prey. Bob points out a white mountain hare. As the hare was washing itself and having a good groom it was out of sight of the eagles' beady-eyed vision. The eagles took off into the air and started searching and combing the ground looking for a potential dinner.

The golden eagle has such good vision its eyes can spot the grouse blink as it lays tight squat in the heather from an amazing quarter of a mile away. That seems incredible to me. The Harris hawk can even go one better than that, it can see a rabbit twitch its ears at an incredible two miles away. There's no wonder there's that old saying 'eyes like a hawk'.

As I look back across at the golden eagles they are searching the ground and heading towards the hare which is sat out of sight over the hillside. If that mountain hare only knew what was approaching him. It is a big, strong, powerful bird is the golden eagle. It has the strength and power to fly along into the full force of a gale and not get blown back. The strength of the golden eagle's talons is phenomenal. Each toe has a pressure gripping power of 10,000 pounds per square inch. Compare that with the biting jaws of a fighting pit bull terrier which has a mere 5000 pounds per square inch.

The golden eagle will kill and carry away well grown red deer calves. They will kill and take the biting, snapping, wily old hill fox. Even the massive mad capper of a bird the capercaillie is not safe, not when the golden eagle is around.

As me and Bob are peering over the moor stone wall with only half an eyeball so as not to be seen, one of the golden eagles is by now nearly upon the unsuspecting mountain hare. The other golden eagle is combing and searching the hillside a little further away.

The first eagle was only about twenty feet from the ground as it soared over the hillside. It instantly saw the mountain hare and it plummeted down for the kill. But just as the eagle was going to strike the hare with its great big powerful talons, the mountain hare's all-round vision glimpsed the eagle coming. The eagle made its strike and in the flash of an eye the hare jumped to one side. The eagle careered past the hare and stumbled to the ground off balance. The white mountain hare raced off across the top of the

"GOLDEN EAGLES"
IN MID AIR COMBAT,
THEIR BEADY HOOKED BEAK
AND RAZOR "SHARP TALON'S ARE
CAPABLE AND WILL SNATCH AND KILL
WELL GROWN "RED DEER" CALVES
AND SNARLING BITING FOXES,
THEIR BEADY EAGLE EYE'S CAN' SPOT
A SQUAT "RED GROUSE" BLINK IT'S EYE'S
AT A QUARTER OF A MILE AWAY

"GOLDEN EAGLES" CATCHING THEIR DINNERS.

hillside and ran smack bang into the other golden eagle. That's just how the eagles like to hunt, surprise-attacking their prey.

The eagle instantly drops in for the kill, but the hare all at the same time leaps three feet into the air. Out of the heather leaps a white ermine stoat. The stoat misses the hare's throat by a fraction, the eagle's talons miss the hare's neck by a cat's knacker and the hare races on to take another breath of air. The predated animals around these parts have to have eyes up their arse or they are dead meat.

The mad, crazy, panic-stricken, white mountain hare raced across the mountain side as if there were no tomorrow. Me and Bob were gobsmacked as we watched on with half an eyeball as we peered over the moor stone wall.

I say to Bob, "Watch this." And as the white mountain hare races across the mountain side right in front of me and Bob, I give out a long drawn out bloodthirsty hare scream. For some reasons unknown to me, hares instantly respond to my screams and this hare does the same. It pricks its lugs on hearing my screams and it's now racing down the mountain side towards me and Bob.

By now both eagles are back up the arse of the hare. One eagle goes in for the strike but the hare turns instantly at an acute angle and the eagle again misses its strike. I give out another bloodthirsty hare scream and all at the same time the second eagle goes in for the kill. The hare turns sharpish and the eagle misses its strike. The hare's racing like a bat out of hell downhill towards us, acknowledging my screams, and it disappears out of sight into the long grass right in front of me and Bob.

As the golden eagles lost sight of the white mountain hare they soared and sped right overhead of me and Bob behind the moor stone wall. They careered vertically upwards into the sky and we got a perfect view of their mighty big hooked beaks. I can see their razor-sharp talons, I can see their golden nape feathers raised on their necks, and their mighty wings. That was one hell of a spectacle that me and Bob have just witnessed and all before our very own eyes. A sight once seen and never to be forgotten.

I remember an incident once happening with a hare. I was out training and teaching my young bitch, Nelly I called her. I like to teach my new bitches the tricks of the trade early doors.

As me and my bitch were walking over some rough grass, a three-quarter-grown leveret (young hare) jumped up. Nelly set off in hot pursuit after it. I was wanting to tease and urge Nelly on and teach her to catch the hare, so I started giving her bloodthirsty hare screams which I thought would urge her on and make her more keen on catching the hare. Nelly raced the young leveret here, there and everywhere, turning and twisting the hare as she coursed it.

I kept on giving her bloodthirsty hare screams, and each time I screamed the leveret appeared to turn towards me, but Nelly kept on turning it off course and away from me. Eventually, after a long hare course, the hare was becoming exhausted and Nelly was also tiring behind the young hare.

I kept on giving out these long drawn out hare screams. The leveret was acknowledging my screams and ran right up to me and got itself huddled up to my feet. This left me thinking, this hare has come to me for safety. Me thinking it was the hare screams that had drawn it in this situation touched me a little, so I picked up the leveret and held it high up to my chest so that Nelly couldn't grab it. The leveret huddled into my arms seeking protection. I let the leveret go when Nelly wasn't looking and off it went into freedom.

This hare here that I have just been screaming at with Bob, that also appeared to be wanting to run to us for protection. I will let you the reader decide for yourself what the screaming means to the hare.

Someone is tapping on my shoulder and I am aroused from my daydreaming. It's Bob, he's pointing frantically and I hear yelling coming from across the moor. I see big flames licking up from the heather, the wind has picked up and changed direction, the flames are now blowing fiercely across the heather. I see Helen, Big Jim and Jock, they are frantically waving their fire shovels, they are trying to put out the towering, licking flames.

The fire has got out of control. Me and Bob race across the moor and grab our fire shovels and we frantically try to dowse out the raging flames. The fire is raging across the heather with the wind blowing hard behind it.

I look across, I see Helen beating the flaming heather. She looks like a mad crazy woman as she is wielding her fire shovel.

I look across the other side of me to where Jock and Big Jim are but I can't see them, the thick blue smoke is shrouding the moor.

I see something running past me, it's a black rabbit. Oh no it's not, it's a white mountain hare covered in black soot.

I hear Bob yelling to me that the fire is heading towards some wooden butts he's just installed. He shouts, "Come on, hurry up, we have to save them butts!"

As me and Bob race along together with our long-handled fire shovels we pick up Helen on our way. All three of us now race across the moor towards this row of wooden butts.

These butts serve an important purpose on a grouse shooting day. If the wind is blowing in a certain direction the driven grouse tend to fly over these wooden butts instead of over the permanently built stone butts, so the shooting men stand in these wooden butts instead.

As all three of us are hastily making our way across the unburnt heather, I see the raging fire is upon the wooden butts. I look for Helen who is trailing behind me and Bob. She is only a small lass and she is having difficulty getting herself over the long heather and struggling to carry her long-handled fire shovel. I run back to help her. I grab her fire shovel with one hand and grab Helen's hand with the other to help her along.

I look at her and she looks at me. She looks a rare sight. Her long blonde hair is all in straggles and full of burnt black heather. Her face is all as black as the ace of spades and her big blue eyes stand out on her blackened face. She has a dead serious expression on her face and there's sweat running off her once lily-white cheeks. I pull Helen along and we head on after Bob.

When we reach the wooden butts they are ablaze. All the full row of what they call 'hurdles' are engulfed in the towering, licking flames. It is futile to even try to put out the raging flames.

Bob's now yelling again, he's frantically waving and pointing across the moor. I don't believe what I see, the fire is now raging across the moor and on towards the shooting box. This is the wooden hut where we all had our dinner that day when we were all grouse shooting. When I was ravenously hungry and I caused all that catastrophe with the waitress, remember?

Bob's now racing across the moor, he's yelling back at me and Helen, he shouts, "Come on, hurry up, we have to save that shooting box!"

Me and Helen race off after him. I can see Helen is exhausted, it would be quicker to give her a donkey ride on my back instead of pulling her along. As we are racing across the moor in a fashion, I see big parties of grouse striking up out of the burning heather. I can hear the grouse shouting out, "Go back, go back," as they head away to the safety on another part of the moor. I look further across and beyond the burning heather and I see white mountain hares everywhere as they stand out in their white winter coats. They are all heading in the direction of Bob's intention, on towards the valley where the hare shoot is to take place the next day.

We are by now all but upon the shooting box, the fire is raging across the moor and all but upon the wooden shooting box. I see Big Jim and Jock, they are wielding their fire shovels like mad crazy men. The heather there is tall, thick and bushy and the strong wind that is now blowing is fuelling the flames. The heat is so intense I see the tar on the brattice roof is melted and running. I see red hot sparks flying high up into the air from the roaring blazing flames. I see the shooting box roof ignite and the shooting box is now ablaze. There's nothing we can do but stand and watch.

I now hear Bob yet again yelling and frantically waving his arms. He's looking across the moor so I look across the moor, and what I see I don't believe. I see great towering, raging, licking flames around the argocat. Bob is yelling and shouting to us all, "Come on, hurry up, we have to save the argocat!"

So off we all go racing after Bob.

I will now hand this story over to the Laird. These are the exact words I recall the Laird saying as he told us his side of the story.

I knew Bob had a team of men burning heather up on the high grouse moor and I decided to take a steady walk up there to see how things were going on. As I am steadily walking up the long moor road, I see plumes of blue smoke on the moorland tops. Everything appeared fine and well but as I continued up the moor road I see the plumes of blue smoke getting thicker and thicker.

I now begin to grow a little concerned. I can see the wind beginning to whip up strongly and I see the thick smoke up on the high moor is getting thicker and thicker by the minute.

I begin to hurry along the moor road growing more and more concerned as I go. I now look up on the high moor and what I see I don't like. It's thick black smoke I see now which is filling the sky. I now begin racing up the moorland road and I now see big towering flames coming from where the shooting box is situated. As I reach the top of the high moor it's all dense with smoke. Then the wind whips up into strong gusts, it clears the smoke a little and I see men out across the moorland.

I race over to them, I see the argocat totally ablaze. I see my team of men frantically trying to put out the blazing argocat. I tell them all sternly to get away from the argocat, she's going to blow.

Everybody obeys my orders, all except Bob. I can see the dangers that he's in, so I go in and rugby tackle him and knock him clear away from the fireball of an argocat.

As we lay there strewn on the burnt, blackened ground we hear an almighty explosion. The fuel tank has blown on the argocat and now the argocat is one raging inferno of fire, but everyone is safe from injury. I tell Bob I am going to get out the fire brigade and off I race from the high moor. I head on down into the bottom of the glen to one of my cottages. I have a dairyman who lives there who milks two hundred cows for me, Buster they call him. I know he will be home, it's about midday, so he will be home for dinner. Without knocking I just rush straight into the cottage. I don't know who was the most surprised, Buster seeing me rush into the cottage or me seeing what I saw. Buster jumps up from the settee with no britches on, his wife Maria jumps up from the settee with no knickers on, and there's their old English sheepdog who jumps up with them.

I think to myself, there's no wonder Buster's always late back from dinner. I tell Buster the moors on fire and to get his britches on. I quickly telephone the fire brigade from Buster's telephone while Maria's hurriedly pulling up her knickers. The old English sheepdog looks all frustrated with himself, what he's been doing, I don't know.

The fire brigade arrived within minutes and off me and Buster go to meet them. There's only one fire engine arrives but it's well manned, I see six firemen inside the cab. There's no room inside there for me and Buster to get in, so Buster jumps on the footplate on the outside of the passenger side of the fire engine cab and I go and jump on the footplate on the driver's side of the cab, and off the fire engine races.

I guide the driver up along the moor road. The fire engine is bumping and bouncing as it goes along the moor road and the driver has his big emergency bell ringing as we go. Why he wants that ringing I don't know. There's no vehicles along the moor road to get out of the way of the fire engine. That's what the bell's for isn't it? The bell, it's a big brass shiny one, is ringing right in my ear hole and it's deafening me.

There's a fork coming up on the moor road and I tell the driver to take the left-hand turning. He can't hear me for some reason unknown to him. The driver's now wound down the window and is leaning out to me saying, "What you say?"

I tell him again to take the left-and fork. He's now leaning right out of the window and he says, loudly, "I can't hear you, shout up."

I tell him, "Turn the bloody bell off!"

Now the driver can hear me. The fire engine bumps and bounces as we go along the rough old rugged moor road. We see the moorland totally ablaze on the left-hand side of the moor road. The driver pulls up the fire engine well short of the blazing inferno and he says, "I will leave the fire engine here where it is safe. We have been trained in safety," he tells me.

I am now Doug who is taking over from the Laird's story.

Me, Helen, Bob, Big Jim and Jock are now sat on the side of the high moor watching what is going off below us. We see the fire engine arrive and Bob says, "That ringing fire bell certainly makes the hares run. I will use that bell in future when I have another hare shoot, it will save setting fire to the moor."

I must agree with Bob, the bell certainly makes the hares scarper, we must have seen hundreds of white mountain hares fleeing from the heather as the bell rang. Or were the hares running from the blazing heather?

The blazing-out-of-control heather is by now raging off the moor top and heading on downhill and on towards the firemen. The strong wind now blowing is fair lashing the licking flames down across the moor.

The firemen are using the moor road as a firebreak and we see them reeling out their long hosepipes. They are getting water from what they call a 'dew pond' from across the moor. Bob says the dew pond is always permanently full, it's fed by an underground spring. The firemen are bracing themselves to be prepared when the fast advancing wall of fire reaches the moor road.

I see the raging wall of fire disappear over a hill at the far side of the low moor and I think to myself, that's where the fire engine is. But I know they are trained firemen, they know what they are doing, they will have seen the wall of flame disappear over the hillside.

I look back at the firemen stood on the moor road, the Laird and Buster are assisting and helping them with their long hoses. The raging, roaring fire is now all but upon them and the firemen are dowsing water over the heather in front of them. There are firemen with their hoses on a long stretch of the moor road, these firemen know what they are doing. They have done it all before, you can see they are all well organized. Now when the roaring, raging wall of fire hits the now-dowsed-with-water heather the towering flames will just fizzle out, and then it will be all over.

The wind is by now blowing as strong as ever, it's blowing the flames way out across the heather in front as it advances. The heather is tall, thick and bushy just there where the firemen are. The roaring flames hit the tall heather right in front of the firemen and they are spraying the heather with water like mad crazy firemen.

The roaring, raging flames are now towering into the sky and I see big, red-hot sparks flying high into the air. These red hot sparks are landing at the other side of the moor road and igniting the other heather. The winds whipping it up into roaring raging flames, so now the firemen and the Laird and Buster have towering walls of flames at either side of them as they all stand on the moor road.

I see a fireman racing down the moor road and when I look to see where the fireman's racing to I don't believe what I see. The towering, raging flames have now raged up the hillside where I saw them disappear earlier and are now licking at the fire engine.

As the fireman races along the moor road to save his fire engine, he sees the rubber tyres are a ball of flames. The trained fireman sees his dilemma and he's now racing back up the moor road, the towering flames licking at him from either side as he goes. He's now rejoined the rest of his merry team of fire-fighters. They are now hurriedly discussing their next fire-fighting tactics.

It looks as though they have made their decision, they are doing a runner. With towering flames at either side of them they see a gutter leading away from the moor road. It's a bit of a firebreak and without even hesitating off they go and run up the gutter with the Laird and Buster following on behind. They race up the gutter and get in front of the raging, roaring wall of flames. Then they all now make a mad crazy dash across the moorland heading for the safety of the moorland ahead.

The roaring, raging fire is catching them up as they do their runner, and they are now racing like stags across the moor. The Laird can't keep with them, he's trailing behind and the raging, roaring flames are licking at his arse as he runs. We see the Laird running toward the dew pond and without any hesitation the Laird takes ones almighty leap and dive-bombs arse first into the dew pond. The raging inferno of towering flames race around the dew pond.

We are all full of anticipation as me, Helen, Bob, Big Jim and Jock watch on as we sit at the edge of the upper moorland. Where's the Laird? Is he dead, has he been burnt alive in the inferno of flames? We see the blue smoke clear around the dew pond and we all look on, optimistic and pessimistic, looking for the Laird. I see him, there he is, he's just got his head sticking out of the water. We cast our eyes further across the moor, all the firemen and Buster have reached the safety of the moor stone wall. We see all their faces peering over the wall as the raging, roaring wall of fire passes them on by. We hear an explosion, we look across at the fire engine, it's a massive ball of flames as the fuel tank blows up.

We look back across the moor and the raging, roaring, out-of-control wall of fire is no more. It came in like a roaring lion and has gone out like a lamb. What a fire we have just had, we all say as we sit on the moorland edge.

I turn and look at Helen, she looks at me. I say, "We have caused all this fuss."

Helen's face is as black as the ace of spades and her big blue eyes stand out where her lily-white face once was. Her green wellies are black and smouldering. I look at my boots, I have no laces in, they have been burnt out, my boots are smouldering just like Helen's wellies. The bottom of my britches are scorched. I look across at Bob and Jock they are as black as the ace of spades also.

I look at Big Jim. He had a big long bushy beard which stretched down to his chest but it's not there now, all I see now is burnt stubble on his chin. I think, where's Jim's beard gone? Then I look at our fire shovels and the big rubber flaps on them are smouldering with blue smoke.

I look at the surrounds of us, the moorland is just black and smouldering. I see the wooden butts where they stand no more; the shooting box at the back of us is now a pile of smoking rubble. I look across at where the argocat once stood in all its glory. It now stands a smouldering wreck. I look down off the moor and the once gleaming red fire engine now stands just a burnt-out chassis. We all gather ourselves together and that day we all had to walk off the moor and back into the glen bottom.

This was my first time I had been heather burning on the Laird's vast estate with Bob. Do you readers think we did a good job of heather burning that day? How does that old saying go, 'if a job's worth doing, it's worth doing properly'.

But there was one good thing that came out of that heather burning, Bob now had the hares in the location where he wanted them for the next day's shoot.

Me and Bob were up bright and early that morning and we got ourselves all prepared for the hare shoot that day. Bob had intended going up on to the high moor in the argocat, but not this time. The argocat was still up there all burnt out, so we set off in Bob's Land Rover.

We head on up to the Laird's castle, or what Bob calls the Boss's house, all the shooting men are meeting there. When we arrived the shooting men had not yet arrived. They were down at the Poacher's Arms having breakfast, that's the local pub in the village not far away.

While I was killing time waiting I see rabbits scurrying in and around the woodland that borders the castle grounds. I go across to take a closer look and I see rabbits scurrying across the large warrens everywhere I look. The amount of rabbits that we shot around here that night when we were lamping, it hadn't made much of an impression by the looks of all the rabbits that are still here.

I hear someone calling and I see it's my beloved Helen. She says, "Come on Doug, the shooting men are here." Helen has a flag in her hand and she says she is a flanker.

I see there is a good number of shooting men now gathering outside of the castle. This hare shooting day we are having is all well organized just like a grouse shooting day. Bob has nurtured and looked after these white mountain hares all purposely for this hare shooting day. This is all big business for the Laird, the shooting men have paid top money for this hare shooting day.

I see the shooting men having a quick toast of whisky before they leave for the hills. Lady CC is handing out the whisky to everyone, she is very smartly dressed in her family tradition Scots quilt skirt and jacket. Lady CC has now seen me, she hurries over and offers me a whisky from her tray. Helen comes over and stands between me and Lady CC. It appears to me Helen and Lady CC have a grudge against each other for some reason unknown to me.

As Lady CC is leaving our company she hasn't offered Helen a whisky, but Helen grabs one anyway. Everybody is now all ready, the shooting men hop into their four-wheel drive vehicles and Bob

WINTER COAT

SCOTTISH HIGHLAND'S BLUE MOUNTAIN HARES,

HYBRID BETWEEN MOUNTAIN HARE AND BROWN HARE,

SUMMER COAT

LOPPYLUGS THE LOWLAND BROWN HARE,

sends them off on their way.

The shooting men are going a different way to us, we are all loaded up into the beaters' trailer pulled by the tractor. There's about thirty of us all together and we are all crushed up as we all sit on the bales of straw inside the trailer. Now the snarling, growling retriever hunting dogs are thrown in with us and off we head into them there hills where the white mountain hares roam in out-of-control numbers.

We head on up the rough old mountain track bumping and bouncing as we go, dodging our fingers and arses as the biting, growling, snarling dogs squabble amongst each other.

By now we are in the high heavens of the mountain tops. We finally arrive at our destination and what I see is sheer beauty to my eyes. The scenery up here is out of this world. This is the place where the hare shoot is to take place. As I stand on the high tops of these hills, behind me is where we did the heather burning the day before. All the hares that were laid in that heather have now been driven to this location where I am now, in this vast area in front of me.

Bob had a canny little trick up his sleeve to keep the driven hares on course to here, he used what they call 'sewel lines'. These are simple, man-made lines made out of long lengths of baling band. Every six feet or so along the baling band is tied a strip of white polythene bag, the strips are about two inches broad and about two feet in length. The strip is threaded through the baling band and then a knot tied in it.

The day before the heather burning took place Bob had come up here into these hill tops and run out two great long lengths of sewel lines, each line must be about a mile long. One length of sewel line ran from where the heather burning ended right the way along to the front of me where I am standing now. The second sewel line Bob ran out is way out across country that far away I can't see it. That line also begins at the other side of the heather that we burnt. Both sewel lines are set in a funnel shape and they are very far apart where the heather burning took place. So now when the fleeing hare from the burning heather makes his escape, he's running in between the two funnel-shaped sewel lines.

These sewel lines are tied to the top of three foot high pegs allowing the strips of polythene to blow about in the wind. As the escaping, fleeing hare travels along he sees the sewel line. The polythene tassels are blowing and clattering together in the wind and the fleeing hare doesn't like what he sees and hears, it's all new to him. He's never seen that before so he gives the sewel line a wide berth, as he and his many mates travel along all in the direction Bob wants the hares to go. On the way all the hares now see and hear the other sewel line blowing in the wind. The hares don't like that either, it's all unusual to them on their territory. So the hares head away, and all the time they are heading on along between these two funnel-shaped sewel lines which eventually leads all the hares to this destination where I am now standing, just where Bob wants the hares to be.

The area between the two sewel lines is vast and there are still many, many white mountain hares within and between these two long lengths of sewel lines which have all been driven from the heather burning area of yesterday. So these hares have to be driven out. As we were coming up here this morning in the tractor-pulled beaters' trailer, where the heather burning had stopped and the sewel lines started Bob had dropped off a lot of beaters to drive down the vast area between the two long lengths of sewel lines.

As I stand there now on the side of the mountain range I see in the far distance the beaters are now approaching. I see their flags waving and I hear distant yelling of voices as they are driving the hares on. I see many, many white mountain hares below me as I watch. They are standing out like sore thumbs as they race along on the free-of-snow moorland. I see dozens and dozens of hares heading my way.

They are panicking to escape the beaters' yelling and shouting and waving flapping flags. They are trying to escape into the mountain tops to where it is safe but they now see the sewel lines flapping and clattering in the wind. They back off and head away. I see scores and scores of white mountain hares way over in the distance, they are doing the same as they approach the far sewel line. They are backing off and heading away, they are all heading the way of Bob's intentions.

These sewel lines are used by some pheasant gamekeepers throughout Great Britain. On a pheasant shooting day the gamekeeper will run out a sewel line through a woodland, it will run about twenty yards inside the woodland. When the pheasants are driven through the woodland and towards the waiting shooting men, pheasants are obstinate and often refuse to fly. But now when the pheasants come to the sewel line, they have never seen this before, it's all new to them. The polythene tassels on the sewel line are blowing and clattering about in the wind. This disturbs and upset the driven pheasants. They are frightened to pass underneath the sewel lines, and the beaters are urging the pheasants on from behind with their waving, flapping flags and their shouting and yelling. And here comes the beaters' hunting dogs. They are now upon the frightened, startled pheasants who have nowhere to go, only upwards.

They strike up into the air reluctantly which takes them over the top of the sewel line. The panic-stricken pheasants clatter through the treetops and high into the sky which takes them high over the waiting shooting men who are stood out on the meadow. And that's how the pheasant gamekeeper uses his sewel lines and here I am now watching all these white mountain hares being driven and guided between Bob's sewel lines.

Out in front of me where I stand, I see a vast flat-bottomed valley and all the hares that I see are now being driven by the beaters into that valley. I see the white mountain hares disperse way out in the distance across this valley and then they just disappear like white phantoms. They have got themselves laid tight squat in the heather and short, thick-growing moorland white grass.

I now see all the beaters loading themselves up into the back of the beaters' trailer, the tractor is taking them way out into the distance. I see a vast mountain range to where the beaters are heading, and I see flankers way out in the distance. They are spread out in a great long line across the mountain's foothills. I see flankers on my side of the mountain range. They are spread out in a great long line across the mountain's foothills, and I can now see the beaters way out in the distance. They are spread out in a great long line half way up the bloody mountain side. I see their flags waving and flapping as they descend off the mountain side. I see the smallest white dots you ever did see. They are darting about in front of the beaters.

I see flankers on either side of the mountain ranges, they are waving and flapping their flags at small white dots running past them. I see the beaters, they have now dropped off the mountain side and are now heading across the foothills. They are getting closer and closer to the vast flat-bottomed valley as they come. The small white dots that I see are getting bigger and bigger as they draw nearer and nearer.

I see waving, flapping flags everywhere I look. I hear yelling, shouting voices coming from the whole vast area in front of me where I stand.

I now see hundreds of white dots in front of the beaters. Wait a minute, I see a white dot coming towards me, it's getting bigger and bigger as it comes. I get myself squat low in the heather. The white dot is by now all but upon me and I spring up out of the heather. I don't know who was the most surprised, the white dot seeing me appear as if from nowhere or me seeing what the white dot was. It's a bloody great big white mountain hare. I surprise flag it and the hare doesn't know if it wants a piss, a shit or a haircut. It swivels around in its tracks and off it heads down into the vast valley in front of me.

I look up ahead of me and what I see it's hard for me to believe. I see hundreds of white mountain hares all racing about in front of the yelling, shouting, flag-waving beaters. I see all the hares head on down into the vast valley below them. They all disperse into the distance across the valley bottom and disappear just like white phantoms as they get themselves squat out of sight in the heather and moorland white grass.

As the beaters arrive back so does Bob and he comes over to me where I stand on the mountain side. I tell him what a lot of hares I have seen come off the drive him and the beaters have just driven, and how they have all scampered and disappeared getting themselves laid tight squat in the heather in the valley below.

Bob says, "Just where we want them." Bob's now pointing up the valley side and he says, "I want you, Doug, to go right up to the top of the valley head. You will see a line of stone shooting butts and I want you to stand high up on the hillside overlooking the end butt. You can flank there to stop any hares running out. When the hare drive is over I want you to gather in the shot dead hares. There will be plenty of helping hands there to help you. I have arranged for a gamedealer to be there and you can help him load the hares into his vehicle."

I nod to Bob and off I go. Bob shouts to me as I go, "Keep to the valley tops, we don't want the hares disturbing down in the valley."

As I head on the way Bob has just sent me, I look back and I see Bob and all the beaters loading themselves back up into the beaters' trailer. I carry on along the valley tops and I pass on by the flankers who are just stood there making themselves noticeable. They are there to stop any hares running out of the valley. The hares will be watching these flanker men with their beady eyes as they lay tight squat in the heather.

As I go along the valley tops I glance across at the beaters' tractor-drawn trailer. By now the beaters are back out of the trailer, I see them way out in the distance, they are just like small specks they are that far away. There's another great mountain out there and I see the beaters as they line across halfway up the mountain side. I see two great long lines of flankers well below and at either side of the beaters.

It looks to me as though Bob is having another hare drive on the other side of the valley. They are doing exactly the same as what they have just done on this side of the valley where I walk now.

I carry on along the valley tops and as I go I cast my eyes across the valley below me. It's vast, it must be well over a mile long, and it must be well over a mile wide. As you readers know now, there is bloody great mountains at either side of this valley. They are sheer beauty to my eyes. The foothills leading from the mountains run down to this valley top where I walk now and at the other side of the valley. The valley sides are sheer rock faces in most places.

The valley bottom is flat with short, thick-growing heather and short, thick-growing white moorland grass. I see there's not a single white mountain hare to be seen anywhere, but I know there's a whole multitude of hares laying tight squat in that vast valley bottom. I know that for a fact, I have seen them run in.

This vast valley as I look at it is sort of heart-shaped and where I am walking along to it tapers into like a bottleneck. This is where Bob has a long line of stone shooting butts. I arrive there now and I stand where Bob told me to stand, on the hillside well above the end stone butt. I get myself sat down in the heather and cast my eyes over the whole surrounding area.

I see the beaters. They have now dropped off the mountain side and are now driving down the foothills and on towards the vast valley in front of where I sit now. It's a hell of a long way across this valley to where the beaters are. Again I see whole multitudes of small white dots running here, there and everywhere in front of the mad, crazy, flag-waving beaters. I see a whole cluster of white dots, they are moving down across the foothills faster than the other white dots.

My eyes are distracted, I now see a large dark blob moving fast downhill from the beaters. Whatever can that large dark blob be, I think to myself. Now I see clusters of small dark dots moving fast down off the foothills.

My attention is now shattered by two bloody great big bangs from a twelve bore shotgun. I look down at the stone shooting butt below me and I see the shooting man, he has just shot two great white mountain hares running between the butts. Wait a minute, I recognise his face, it's the Laird himself shooting from the butt below me. I see the Laird's loader pass a second loaded gun to the Laird. Wait a minute, I know that loader's face, it's Lady CC, she's loading for the Laird.

I now look along the whole line of stone shooting butts. I see all the shooting men in them all have loader men with them. They must be expecting a lot of rapid shooting that's why they have loader men with them. I count the number of stone shooting butts I see. I count ten, all in a straight line which cover the full distance of the bottle neck of this vast valley. There's no escape for the hares, they have to run in between these stone shooting butts to escape this vast valley.

I note the stone shooting butts, they are further apart from each other than ordinary grouse shooting butts. The normal distance between each shooting butt is usually about forty yards, these shooting butts I look at here are about a hundred yards apart. They have been specially built for hare shooting, it gives the shooting men a more challenging long distance shot at the hares as they race between the butts.

I cast my eyes back over to the beaters and my ears prick up at the same time. I hear the familiar moorland sound of, "Go back, go back," and I see many coveys of red grouse winging there way down off the upper foothills away from the beaters. The red grouse are now settling into the short heather in the vast valley bottom. The cluster of small dark dots which I saw moving in front of the beaters was in fact these coveys of red grouse.

Wait a minute, what's that I see coming? It's a big covey of ptarmigan in their white winter feathers, they are winging their way down off the foothills away from the mad, crazy, flag-waving beaters. The ptarmigan glide themselves down and settle in the short heather in the vast valley bottom. The cluster of small white dots which I saw which were moving faster than the other white dots in front of the beaters were in fact this covey of white ptarmigan.

Wait a minute, what's that I see now? I see a big herd of red deer, they are racing themselves off the foothills away from the mad, crazy, flag-waving beaters. They are coming at breakneck pace down towards the vast valley below. They are now on top of the edge of the valley's sheer rock face and I see them stop and look down into the valley. They hesitate and then move on. I now see them all in single file move down the sheer rock face. They are going down a gulley which leads them into the vast valley bottom. This herd of red deer, they know where they are going. This is their domain, this is their territory. The big dark blob which I saw moving in front of the beaters was in fact this big herd of red deer.

What's that I see now? I don't believe what I see, I see great multitudes of white mountain hares running and racing around in front of the mad, crazy, flag-waving beaters. The hares are now upon the valley's sheer rock face side. They are milling around on the valley tops. Now I see the hares heading on down into the vast valley bottom. They are coming down the gullies in the sheer rock face. They are streaming down different gullies, it just looks like a stream of snow running down the gullies. The hares now in the valley bottom all disperse across the valley and just like white phantoms they disappear as they get squat low in the short heather and short moorland white grass.

The beaters' hare drive is now over, for now anyway. I now see the beaters heading across the far end of the vast valley. They are lining themselves out as they go, they look just like small dots in the far distance to me as I am watching from my good vantage point on the side of the hillside as I sit low in the heather. Wait a minute, what's that I see coming along the valley side? It's four great white mountain hares I see, they are making their way towards me as they come lolloping along the hillside. I get myself down low in the heather, I want to spring up and surprise them which will turn the hares and send them back into the valley.

Where I lay squat here on the hillside is only one of just a few places on the valley's side where they can escape. The land just runs down into the valley bottom with no obstacles like sheer rock faces. As I lay there peering through the heather the four hares are now all but upon me. I get myself all prepared to spring up out of the heather. I peer down at the Laird and Lady CC in the shooting butt below me. It's shock horror at what I see and my hair stands on end. The Laird has his gun pointing at the hares which are now right in front of me. Surely the Laird knows I am here laid squat in the heather.

I hear an almighty bang and I roll over and ball up on all fours. As I am hunched up with my hands at the back of my head for protection I hear another almighty bang. I lift my arm up and peer down at the Laird, I see Lady CC fumbling around trying to load the Laird's gun. As I am peering I see a hare right by my side, it's peering back at me as it goes by and I see it jump over the dead hare the Laird has just shot.

The hare that's just going by I see it crumple and drop quickly followed by a delayed almighty bang followed by another almighty bang. I hear pellets come pinging past me so I put up my flag and wave it from my crouched up position and I brace myself and sit up. The Laird sees me and he's now tipping his deerstalker hat to me as though there's nothing to fear.

I see four dead hares lying right against me, there's one so close I can reach out and touch it. Phew, that was too close for comfort.

Now recovered from my close encounter I see the beaters have set off to drive this vast valley bottom. I can barely make out the line of beaters they are so far way, but I can see their light-coloured flags waving and flapping around. I think to myself, this is going to be one hell of a massive hare drive is this.

I see white dots springing up out of the heather in front of the beaters as they advance across the vast flat-bottomed valley. I see the beaters' hunting dogs searching the heather as they go. These dogs that they are using will not pursue and chase the hares like most dogs naturally do, they are the sedate type of Labradors they are using. They will hunt out the hares and send them on their way and carry on hunting out more hares hidden in the heather.

I hear a lot of banging shooting guns coming from the shooting butts as early hares are racing through the butts. The hare drive has hardly begun yet and the banging guns have startled the herd of red deer, I see them come racing across the valley bottom. They are putting up hares galore out of the heather as they come.

I see the herd of red deer hurtling along at breakneck speed. They are strung out across the valley as they hit the shooting butts, there must be seventy, eighty, maybe ninety deer all racing and stampeding. I see multitudes of hares jumping up and racing and stampeding in front of the panic-stricken herd of deer. I see mad, crazy shooting going off as the hares race through the butts. And through the butts the deer do go, and off they disappear across the hillsides all unscathed by the shooting men.

But alas the racing hares do not follow, they have bitten the dust. The shooting men have obeyed Bob's orders, only to shoot hares. Just a minute, what's that I see coming now? It's a pack of red grouse I see, and as they come they are picking up more coveys of grouse out of the heather. Now I see one great big pack of red grouse, they are coming like high-powered bullets as they hit the butts. I hear them calling out, "Go back, go back" as they soar over the shooting butts. There's silent guns as the grouse pass over, the shooting men have obeyed Bob's orders yet again.

Just a minute, what's that I see trailing behind the red grouse? It looks like a flurry of snow to me. Oh no it's not, it's a covey of white ptarmigan. Off they go across the butts and way across to the mountain tops they do go, and not a shot fired thanks to Bob.

I look back across at the beaters, they are by now halfway through the hare drive. I see big mountain hares jumping up out of the heather everywhere. They are standing out like sore thumbs in their white winter coats. I see mad, crazy beaters waving and flapping their flags. I hear them shouting and yelling at the hares as they race hell for leather towards and through the shooting butts.

I hear bang, bang, banging of guns and I see hares biting the dust all the way along the line of stone shooting butts. I see the Laird in the nearest butt to me drop a hare then his old characteristic pause between shots and then bang, down goes another hare. The Laird will have to get used to holding the gun butt to his shoulder to claim a 'left and right' shot. I now see the Laird quickly passing his empty gun to Lady CC, she hasn't even got the other gun loaded yet. It's now loaded and the Laird grabs it from her. Lady CC is now looking at me up on the hillside. I point to my mouth, I am trying to tell Lady CC, in lip-reading fashion, to put the cartridges in her mouth to load the guns faster. I see Lady CC has got the message loud and clear. She's now got a great big smile on her face. She's kissing her hand and blowing me kisses. I think, the silly woman thinks I am blowing kisses to her.

I am distracted to what's going off out in the valley below me. The beaters have gone into a mad craze of flag waving. I look at what they are flagging and I see a fox, it's just jumped up out of the heather. It should have picked a better place to have a snooze. The fox is panicking, it doesn't know which way to make its escape, then it chooses to make its way toward me. I get myself crouched low in the heather, I see the fox coming across the valley bottom at helter-skelter speed. It's now coming up the hillside towards me. The breeze is blowing from me to him, he's only ten paces from me now, and he stops dead in his tracks. The fox hasn't seen me peering through the heather, but he senses danger, he's stood there staring into the heather where I lay. I see the fox twitch his nose, he doesn't like what he smells, he turns and off he goes back the way he came. He's a wily, crafty old hill fox is this.

The fox drops back off the hillside where I lay and he bumps straight into twenty, maybe thirty, great big white mountain hares. The fox stops dead in his tracks again. He's thinking, shall I catch my dinner now or try to save my life first? The fox is in a frenzy of fear. On one side of him he sees mad, crazy men waving flags, on the other side of him he sees trigger happy shooting men banging away with their guns. The fox looks back up the hillside to where I lay tight squat. The fox chooses to take me on and he makes a mad dash to freedom up the hillside. When he's halfway up he stops short of me and heads along the hillside passing below me and well above the Laird in his shooting butt. The fox knows he is well out of range of the Laird's gun, and off he disappears to freedom. He's a wise old hill fox is that one.

I look back at the beaters, the hare drive is now in full swing. I see hares, hares everywhere I look, great big white mountain hares. It looks to me as though we have just had a snow storm and the ground is covered in snow. The mad, crazy beater men have gone into a craze of flag waving, shouting and yelling. The hares are weaving and turning and racing headlong and full pace through the shooting butts.

I see shooting men bang, bang, banging away at the racing, fleeing hares and the hares are dropping like big-eared donkeys. I see loader men passing fully-loaded guns to the shooter men, I see the shooter men passing empty guns back to the loader men. And then I look at my poor little sweetheart of a woman Lady CC. She's trying her best to load the guns for the trigger happy husband of a Laird but the harder she tries the slower she goes. She's half watching what she's doing and half watching what I am doing. She's trying hard to blow another kiss but the Laird keeps on badgering and urging Lady CC on. He's playing hell with her, he's saying something like, "Will you pay attention dear, and load the bloody guns faster."

I hear a whistle blowing, I hear a hunter's horn blowing, it's signalling to the shooting men that the hare drive is now over. Phew, that was one hell of a hectic hare drive was that.

I see white dead mountain hares everywhere I look. I see dead hares strung out all the way along the front of the butts. I see dead hares in between the full line of butts, I see dead hares behind the full length of the butts. I see hares galore and they are all dead. But they are not exhaustible, they will breed on and go forth and multiply. There well may be more hares next year than there is this year, it's all good upkeep of the running and management of the Laird's vast estate. Everything must pay its way, it's a hard life in this world we live in.

I now see the shooting men come out of their butts, they are now gathering in the hares they have shot. As Bob told me earlier, there would be helping hands to help me gather in the hares all ready for the gamedealer to pick them up.

What's this I see coming across the moor? It's a large, covered-in box van. I get up from my good vantage position on the hillside and go down to check out the van. As I pass on by the Laird's shooting butt, there's the Laird and Lady CC gathering in their shot dead hares. I say to the Laird as I pass them by, "We will make a loader of Lady CC yet."

The Laird acknowledges with a tipple of his deerstalker hat.

The large, covered-in box van I saw coming is now reversing up to the shooting butts. I see writing on the side of the van, it says, in big fancy lettering, 'Gamedealer'. This is the man I am looking for. I introduce myself to the gamedealer and we start loading his large van with the shot dead hares. He wants the hares tied in couples by their back legs so that he can hang the hares on game rails inside his van.

I have many helpers of shooting men and loaders gathering in the hares from the surrounding butts. They leave them all in a great big pile at the back of the gamedealer's van. I tie the hares' legs together with baling band and keep on passing the hares to the gamedealer who is inside the back of the van.

The gamedealer says this is just how he wants the hares with their guts left in. I see the van is refrigerated and the gamedealer says when the hares get to their destination they will be deeply chilled and nice and fresh. I ask where the hares destination is. He tells me he is catching the late night ferry boat over to France and these hares will be on the French meat market by early next morning.

As I keep on handing in more and more hares to the gamedealer, he keeps on pushing the hares up tighter and tighter as he hangs them all on his game rails. He's having great difficulty getting all the hares in. Every time I pass a couple of hares to him he keeps on pressing a button. I ask him what the buttons for and he says it's a counter.

There, the gamedealer's refrigerated van is now fully loaded, it's fair busting at the seams with hung hares. The gamedealer looks at his counter and he says there's 561 hares. That's one hell of a lot of hares, I think, and off the gamedealer goes fully-laden with hares and all destined for the French meat market.

And that's what I remember about my first ever hare shoot I had for Bob on the Laird's vast estate up in them Grampian Mountains in the Highlands of Scotland.

Remember all this happened in the decade of the 1970s when I was in my prime of life in my twenties.

I remember another occasion I was up there on the Laird's vast estate, I had been rabbiting all day long and I then went into Bob's cottage to have a rest up. As I lay on the settee resting in front of the log-burning fire watching television, Bob asked me if I would give him a helping hand to cull out a red deer hind and its calf next morning. I jumped at the chance and agreed to help him. Bob says the hind has been injured and is in a very poor condition. He says the hind will not survive the cold winter and that the calf wouldn't make it either without its mother.

Me and Bob were up bright and early the next morning and Bob gave me the key to get a high-powered rifle out of the gun cabinet. When I looked, there were three high-powered rifles there. One was Bob's own personal rifle and Bob said the other two were spare rifles which were for the paying deerstalkers just in case their rifles got broken.

Bob's now telling me to go try out the rifle on the rifle range outside. So off I go outside into a paddock just beyond the courtyard. Bob wants to see if I can hit the bull's eye on the target, he says he doesn't want any deer wounding by bad shooting. Bob tells me the target is set at 200 yards that's the range the rifle is zeroed in at. I slot a big bullet into the chamber of the rifle, the bullets are much bigger than my .22 rifle bullets. The big telescopic scope on the rifle has a powerful magnification and it zoomed right into the target at 200 yards.

I got myself a good rest to take steady aim and put the cross of the scope bang in the centre of the bull's eye. Then I gently squeezed the trigger harder and harder so as not to snatch the rifle as I was firing. The high-powered rifle went off with such an ear-piercing crack it echoed all around the surrounding glens. The bullet had gone exactly where I had put the cross, bang in the centre of the bull's eye. Bob looked at the target and said, "That will do."

Bob tells me all the deerstalkers who come here shooting must test the accuracy of their rifles on this range before he allows them to go up into the hills stalking the deer.

Bob's now going into a grass paddock at the side of the rifle range and he's coming out with a couple of ponies. I say to Bob the crack of the rifle hasn't frightened the ponies. Bob says they are used to it and that the ponies are taken regularly up into the hills when they are deerstalking. He tells me the ponies carry the dead deer off the hills, it saves us a lot of heavy humping. Bob's now putting a harness on to the backs of the ponies, he says the special harness will hold the dead deer on the ponies' backs and will prevent the deer slipping off.

So we are now all ready for our deerstalking to take place and off we set up into them there hills. Each of us with a pony in hand and our high-powered rifles strapped over our shoulders. There is a good stiff breeze blowing which is ideal for deerstalking which will take away the silence and blow our human scent away from the deer.

We went a very long way along the mountain passes and down into glens which I had never seen before. My eyes were boggling at what I saw, every glen we passed through was absolutely overrun with marauding, out-of-control rabbits.

It appears to me everywhere I look on the Laird's vast estate it's just simply out of control with rabbits. And every time I see out-of-control, marauding rabbits Bob always says, "I want you to catch these rabbits Doug."

Bob's doing it now as we pass through these sheltered glens. He's saying in a whispered voice as we walk along, "I want you to catch these rabbits Doug."

It's one hell of a mammoth job Bob is giving me but I am not complaining. The more rabbits I have the merrier I will be I think.

As we climb up out of the mountain glens we approach the top of a high hillside and Bob ushers me to him in silence. He gives me his pony to hold and goes off in silence. He gets himself laid down and crawls and peers over the hillside. I see Bob take out his stalker's telescope and start scanning the glens below him. Bob appears to me to be keeping his telescope in one particular place

A FOURTEEN POINTER "WILSON STAG" LOOKS ON AS TWO RED DEER STAGS FIGHT IT OUT FOR THE HAREM OF HINDS

leaving me thinking, he must have spotted something.

Bob slithers himself back down the hillside and comes back to me silently. He whispers to me in the lowest of whispers, "There's a stag down there in the herd I want culling out." He says, "You will see two stags down there, there's one with part of his left antler broken, I want him culling out." Bob's now taking the ponies from me and he's whispering, "Go on, shoot it."

I couldn't believe it, Bob was giving me the task of shooting the red deer. I am not a bad stalker, I have done it many times, but only stalking rabbits until they are in the range of my gun.

Bob's now handing me a long-bladed, sticking knife, it's in a sheath threaded on a belt. I strap it around my waist and Bob whispers, "When you have shot the deer go straight to it and stick it and bleed it."

Bob's now ushering me off to go stalk and shoot the deer, so off I go with my high-powered rifle in hand leaving Bob stood there holding the two ponies. I get myself into a crawl just like Bob has just done and I peer over the hillside with just half an eyeball. I can see a good-sized herd of red deer, they are grazing in the bottom of a sheltered glen. They are about four hundred yards away which is far too far for accuracy. I need to take a closer look at the herd so I slowly pull my rifle up my side and oh so slowly point it over the top of the hillside. I look down at the herd through the high-powered scope on my high-powered rifle. I can pick out two red deer stags and I can see the stag with the broken antler. That's him I am after, the rest of the herd were all hinds (females).

The wind is hitting me smack bang in my face blowing my human scent away from the deer. I have to get myself in closer to the herd for a closer shot. I can see some hilly ridges further down along the glen side, that's where I want to be. I should be within range of the deer from there.

I very slowly slither my rifle back down and slither myself back down the hillside. I hand signal to Bob, who is still holding the ponies, I am going in for the kill. Bob acknowledges me back in silence, and off I go on my first ever deerstalk.

I feel like a poacher with permission to poach as I drop down the bank of the hillside. I make my way slowly along not daring to make a sound as I go. The wind is blowing perfectly across the glen hitting me in my left ear as I go. I reach the other side of the hillside all done in the silence of silence.

I now come to a narrow mountain stream and it's fair gushing down the hillside making a babbling sound as it flows along. I need to cross over the stream. I see rocks peeping up out of the rushing gushing water and I, oh so carefully and quietly, use the stones as stepping stones and reach the other side.

I now have to go up the hillside. I see loose stones as I go, one false footstep now and a stone will go rolling down the hillside and my cover will be blown. I have to go foot perfect as I go up the hillside. I am now safely at the top with not a sound made at all. I peer over the top of the hill with just half an eyeball and I see the herd below me. They are still grazing away, oh so unconcerned. If only they knew what was stalking them, they would be bats out of hell.

They are about 200 yards away from me now. This place where I am laid now will have to do to take my shot. I oh so slowly poke my rifle over the hill and look through my scope. I see my stag which I want, the one with the broken antler, but there's a hind stood right behind him. I have to wait and bide my time while the hind moves clear. If I shoot now, the bullet is so powerful it will go straight through the stag and maybe injure the hind.

As I lay there waiting, I have my rifle all in position and ready and I slowly slide the bolt back and cock the rifle. I look through my scope and I see the hind slowly moving away from my stag, but now my stag is in the wrong position. He's now got his arse facing me, and I don't want my bullet up there do I.

I patiently wait and bide my time, and I have my scope on him as I watch him. I see the second stag, he is the dominant stag of the hinds, and he starts roaring and blurting out at my stag. He wants him to move on and away from his hinds.

If my stag runs away now I will have blown my stalk so I quickly get the cross of my scope on my stag. I see the dominant stag racing over to my stag, he's gonna do a runner. My stag turns and as he turns I put the cross of my scope just at the back of his front leg. It's now or never. I gently but quickly squeeze the trigger and I hear one almighty crack from my rifle. It echoes all around the surrounding glens and all at the same time I see my stag crumple and drop dead in its tracks. And all at the same time I see the rest of the herd stampede away.

I have hit my stag straight through the heart, I can tell that because he dropped stone dead. He never even kicked his legs, which is a sure sign of a heart shot. I quickly go over to my stag, I

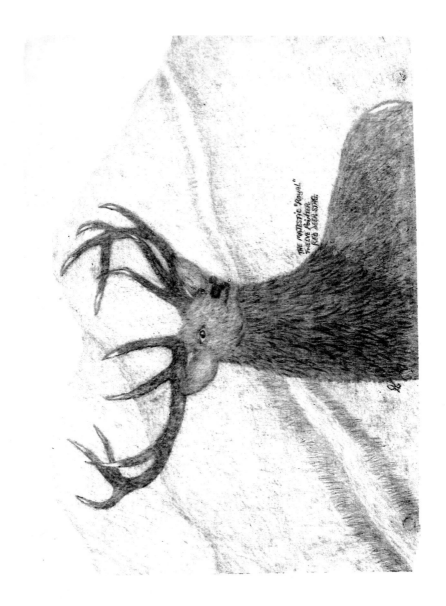

take out my sticking knife from its sheath and I stick the long blade into his throat at the bottom of his neck which is at the top of his chest. As I draw the knife out blood spurts and pumps out with it.

The end of an era for a majestic fine stag.

I now slit open his belly and grollock out the intestines making sure to leave the liver intact inside. As I look up I see Bob coming down the hillside with the two ponies in hand. Bob's now complimenting me on such a good stalk. He tells me that this stag had to be culled out of the herd because he kept fighting the dominant stag for the supremacy of the herd of hinds.

Bob's now pulling one of the ponies alongside the dead stag. He's now rubbing his hand into the pool of blood that's just come out of the stag and then rubbing his blood-covered hand on the pony's nose and up its nostrils. Bob says, "This reassures the pony, it lets him know what I am going to put on his back."

Bob gives the pony enough time to acknowledge the blood. We now pick up the heavy stag and manhandle it on to the back of the pony. Bob's now strapping the stag to the pony's harness. "There," says Bob, "the stag now can't slip off the pony's back," and on that off we set again.

We now resume our search for the poor hind and her calf. We search on and on along the foothills and the glens. We search here, there and everywhere looking for the hind and her calf.

Bob's now becoming frustrated with himself at not being able to find the hind and he says, "She's around here somewhere, I see her and her calf regularly. She will be in some secluded glen somewhere."

I say, "Maybe she's gone up into the tops of the mountains."

Bob says, "No, she'll not be up there, there are no midges around."

I say, "What's the midges got to do with it?"

Bob's reply was, "The reason red deer go high into the mountains is to get away from the marauding, blood-sucking midges. They descend on the herds of deer in their millions which is enough to send the herd crazy, which causes the herd to stampede into the mountain tops."

I say, "But won't the midges just follow the herd up there?"

Bob smiles and says, "No, the midges cannot fly in winds of more than 7mph, and more often than not it's always blowing hard up there."

I say to Bob, "It must get terribly cold up there in the mountain tops for the deer."

Bob replies by saying, "They are a hardy animal are the red deer. They have hollow strands of hair which keeps the deer insulated against extreme temperatures." Bob also adds, "Red deer will quite readily swim long distances across open waters to get from one island to another. The hollow strands of hair they have provide buoyancy and so prevent the deer from drowning in deep open waters."

And that's the end of a bit of history on red deer told by Bob as we search on and on looking for the elusive hind and her calf.

I look across the moorland and I see a large loch. Bob says, "That's the loch we were wildfowling on not so long ago."

Do you readers remember the duck shooting evening flight we had at Bob's flight pond when the shooting men stood on the loch and we were sending ducks and geese backwards and forwards to each other? Well this loch now that me and Bob look at is the loch where the shooting men stood. So I say to Bob, "So this must be the loch that we passed by in the argocat when we were out rabbit lamping that night."

Bob nods, leaving me thinking as I browse my eyes around the whole surrounding area, everything looks different in the daylight. As me and Bob walk along still on the lookout for the elusive hind and her calf we go along the side of a forestry fir tree plantation. I look up into the treetops and I see a massive great nest in the top of a large tall old pine tree. I point it out to Bob and he says, "It's an osprey's nest." He says, "The mating pair of ospreys haven't arrived yet, but they will be here for sure at the start of the breeding season." Bob continues on to say, "I have sat many an hour on yonder hillside overlooking the loch and watched the ospreys through my stalker's telescope.

"When the birds fist arrive, the first thing that they do is rebuild and strengthen their old nest and get it all prepared for their coming chicks. They come year after year to that same old nest. I have watched them bringing in big clumps of heather from the moor to line their nest with. I have watched them carrying great long branches holding them with their big powerful feet. There's some of them branches they try to carry they are so big they can hardly pick them up.

"I have watched them for many an hour as they are out on the loch fishing for their dinner. They have big, long, powerful wings," says Bob, "and at a distance they look all wings and no

OSPREY
A MASSIVE FIVE FOOT WINGSPAN,

body. He will patrol around the loch looking for fish just under the surface of the water. When he sees a fish you will see him start circling, he will pinpoint himself and lock on to the fish. You will see him hover briefly before he goes into his dive, his long powerful legs will be dangling below him. At the last moment before impact he will outstretch his big feet exposing his razor-sharp talons of claws, often submersing himself under water. The next second you will see him surfacing again, he will have a big fat fish clasped within his talons. Some of the fish they catch are good four-pounders, he will rise into the air with his prize clasped in his feet and give himself a good old shake to get rid of the water on his non-waterproof feathers."

As me and Bob stand there alongside of the fir tree plantation underneath the osprey's nest I see a large feather on the ground. I pick it up I say to Bob, "Is this an osprey's feather?"

Bob looks at it and says, "No, that's a golden eagle's tail feather."

This makes me smile with my thoughts. Now that Bob has told me his little story, I now want to tell him my little story, it's a story about eagles. I tell Bob about the North American Indians and about their feathered headdress they wear, and that they are made from eagle's feathers. Bob is all ears as he listens to me, so I carry on and tell him my story.

It's the Indian boy's job to go out and get the eagle's tail feathers for his father's headdress. The Indian boy will go out into the wilds of the mountains where the eagles roam and he will take with him a big, fat, dead turkey. He will make a small round hide from stones and on top of the hide he will place tree branches about three inches apart. On the top of these branches he will lay his big, fat, dead turkey. The Indian boy will now get himself hidden inside of his hide.

It's not very long before an eagle will come soaring overhead. The eagle sees the big, fat, dead turkey and soars in to have it for his dinner. The eagle lands on the wooden branches on top of the hide, and as the eagle stands there weighing up the turkey for his dinner, the Indian boy inside of the hide is watching the eagle up above him. When the eagle's not looking, the Indian boy will reach his hand through the branches and grab the eagle by its legs. He will pull the eagle's legs down through the wooden branches and hold him sprigged there.

The Indian boy now reaches through the branches with his

other hand and starts pulling out the eagle's tail fcathers. The eagle is squawking out and objecting but there's nothing it can do. The Indian boy will keep on pulling and tearing the feathers out of the eagle's arse until he's got the lot. The Indian boy now releases the eagle and off it flies with a bald, featherless arse. The eagles of North America have bright coloured tail feathers and off the Indian boy goes to give his father the feathers to make his headdress.

I look at Bob and he has a big broad smile on his face. I think Bob likes my little story of the Indian boy.

Bob says, "The eagles are all ragged-arsed but live to tell the tale." Bob's now reciting an old saying, "Kill not want not." Bob's now saying, "Come on, let's be off, we still have to search out the poor hind and her calf."

By now I am getting a little tired with all the walking we have done. We have been across and around a vast part of the Laird's estate, we have tramped up mountain sides and down mountain sides, in and out of glens. We have seen quite a few herds of deer but that elusive hind and her calf are nowhere to be spotted.

I notice the pony carrying the dead red deer stag is getting quite knackered also and I suggest to Bob we transfer the dead stag over on to the other pony's back. Bob acknowledges and we drop the stag off the pony and onto the ground. I now see Bob put his hand inside the slit where I had stuck the stag in the throat to bleed it. I see Bob's hand come out all covered in blood. Bob now goes to the other pony and smears the blood all around the pony's nose and nostrils. The pony hesitantly and warily smells the blood and it's now aware of the burden it's going to carry on its back. Bob now straps the stag on to the pony's back and says, "Come on, let's go have a sit down on that hillside over yonder."

As we sit and have our rest, it's a good view from up here which is overlooking the loch. I see a big building at the far side of the loch and Bob tells me it's a holiday hotel which is also on the Laird's vast estate. Bob's now telling me the hotel and the large loch is also owned by the Laird. This leaves me thinking, is there nothing around here that the Laird doesn't own?

As I sit there looking down on to the loch, I see that sunken boat again. All that is showing above the water is the cabin roof of the boat.

Do you readers remember me telling you about it, when I thought I will ask Bob about that boat? Well, this is a good time to ask Bob now. So I ask Bob and he chortles and gives a big smile. He says, "It carries a story with it does that sunken boat." So Bob tells me the story as we sit on the hillside overlooking the loch.

"Very early one morning not that very long ago, I was out in my courtyard back home when I heard the telephone ringing. It was the hotel manager from that hotel you see over the other side of the loch. He tell me there is someone out on the loch shooting deer from his boat." Bob points, "It was just below us here where the poacher was shooting the deer." Bob points again, "The hotel over yonder hires out boats to holidaymakers so that they can have a sail around this loch. The deer that graze here below us are so used to seeing holidaymakers in their boats they have become fairly tame. And this poacher was taking advantage of the tame deer, but this poacher was using his own boat."

Bob says, "On me hearing of these poaching activities going off by the hotel manager, I quickly ring Jock who lives in a croft just over the hills from the hotel. I informed Jock as to what was happening and arranged to meet up with him on the loch. I quickly grabbed my big rifle which I always carry just in case I come across a fox and I jumped into the Land Rover and raced across the hilltops to the loch here.

"As I looked over the hillside here at the back of us now, I saw the poacher out on the moor just down here below us now. The poacher had a red deer stag at his feet. I raced down this hillside where we are sat now, the poacher looked up and saw me racing towards him and he grabbed hold of the stag, threw it over his shoulders and made haste back to his boat. By the time I got to the water's edge, the poacher had by now gone out on to the loch. I shouted to him to heed and come back."

The poacher shouted back, "Like hell I am coming back."

"He starts revving the motor up on his boat and was about to set off back across the loch. The poacher hadn't heeded my warning to come back, so I picked up my rifle and put a bullet into his boat. I shot the bullet just under the surface of the water and water started gushing into his boat which quickly started listing and then sank. The boat rested on the bottom of the shallow loch just leaving the boat's cabin showing above the water.

"The poacher with his rifle slung over his shoulder scrambled on to the top of the boat's cabin," Bob says, "and as I am stood there on the bank of the loch, the poacher shouted, 'Help me, I can't swim'."

Bob carried on saying, "I didn't want to be had up for manslaughter so I went to his rescue. We have a boathouse further down the loch. The boats in there were used by us when we went wildfowling out on the loch. I started up the engine on one of the small motorboats and headed out to the poacher. On my way to him, I saw a red deer stag floating on the surface of the water. It was that poacher's stag he had just shot, it must have floated off the poacher's boat when it sank.

"I wanted this stag as evidence against the poacher, so I threw it into my boat. On my way to the poacher I saw a red deer hind also floating in the water, so I threw that in my boat also. The more dead deer I find the worse it will be for the poacher when I get him to court. I pulled my boat alongside the stranded, or is it marooned, poacher and I told him to jump into my boat. As the poacher is getting off his boat and on to my boat, he gives out such an almighty kick at me, knocking me reeling backwards. I tripped myself on the side of my boat and found myself under the water in the loch.

"By the time I had surfaced and gathered my senses, the poacher was sailing away in my boat. I clambered myself out of the water and up on to the cabin of the poacher's sunken boat, leaving me thinking, what a chump I was. Me and the poacher have now swapped places.

"As I look across the loch the poacher has disappeared out of sight in my boat as I lay there on top of the cabin of the sunken boat. I was soaked to the skin, frozen to death and shaking. I seemed to be there for ages when I heard the sound of an outboard motor engine approaching. When I looked I saw it was Jock who had come to my rescue. Jock started laughing his pants off as he saw me lying there marooned out on the loch.

"I jumped into Jock's boat which he had borrowed from the hotel and we headed across to the other side of the loch. We saw my boat floating empty out in the loch but the poacher was nowhere to be seen.

"I looked in my boat, the poacher had left my rifle in my boat but the two dead deer had gone. Jock's place was nearest to home, his croft was just over them lall hills, so I went with Jock to get myself dried out and warmed up at his place. As Jock drove along the main highland road, I saw a four-wheel drive vehicle approaching and it was towing an empty boat trailer.

"As it passes us going the other way, I look at the driver. It was him, it was the poacher, but it was no use me and Jock chasing after him. He was in a much faster vehicle and me and Jock were only in an old Land Rover. We quickly went to the hotel where I rang and informed the police. They picked up the poacher not long after and he had the two dead deer in the back of his vehicle. The poacher duly appeared in front of the beak, he was duly punished for his ill deeds and his rifle was confiscated.

"The poacher tried to summons me for damaging and sinking his boat, but the judge looked upon it in my favour," says Bob. "And the judge said I had put the bullet holes into the boat for identification purposes and I got away scot-free."

So now as me and Bob sit on the hillside overlooking the loch, I now know the history of that sunken boat.

Bob's now saying, "Come on, we have had our rest now," and off we go again looking in vain for this poor hind and her calf.

I ask Bob, "Why is the poor hind injured in the first place?"

Bob says, "The hind must have fallen over a rock face some time in the past and has injured herself so bad it's caused her to go to skin and bone. She won't make it through the cold bitter months on the mountain and the calf won't survive without its mother. So they both have to go."

After walking on for quite a while, Bob stops and ushers me to stay there and hold the two ponies. Bob's now going slowly and quietly to the mountain side where he gets himself sat down on his backside and rests his deerstalker scope on his knee. Bob's now scanning and surveying the hills below and he appears to concentrate on one place with his telescope. He ponders there a while and then comes back to me and says to me quietly, "There's a herd of red deer in the distance, there's a good chance that hind and calf will be among them. We will have to take a closer look."

So on we go getting closer to this herd of deer. We keep ourselves out of sight of the deer, keeping ourselves at the back of the hills. After circling a hell of a long way around the tops of the hills, keeping the wind blowing from the herd of deer and blowing to us, Bob stops and ushers me in silence to hold the ponies again. Bob slithers himself across to the edge of the mountain and pokes his scope over the top. He's now scanning the ground below him.

Bob's now coming back and he says to me in the lowest of whispers, "The hind and the calf are there with the herd. We want to be at the back of them hills," as he points with his finger.

We make our way around very slowly and quietly, we are now

on the mountain track, so as not to make a sound. We are now at the point where we want to be and Bob's now putting hobbles on to the two ponies. He puts the hobbles around each of the ponies front feet, around their ankles. The ponies now cannot wander away and they now start contentedly browsing on the heather. Bob's now beckoning me to load my rifle, Bob does the same and it's all done in the most silence of silence.

We are now both ready for the stalk and off we go together, we slither and slide ourselves along on our bellies to the top of a mound. We peer over the top with just half an eyeball, and there we see them. The herd is just below us contentedly browsing on the heather oblivious of our presence.

The wind is hitting us bang in the face, perfect. I now feel my heart pounding and the adrenaline now flowing through my body. The hind and her calf are feeding at the edge of the herd, they are at the side of the mountain track below us.

Bob's now putting his mouth right inside of my ear hole and his tongue is nearly licking my ear drum as he whispers, "You take the hind and I will take the calf. When I say 'now', shoot."

We both get our rifles in position. They are about a hundred and fifty yards down below us in the glen. They are both stood broadside on to us, perfect for two heart shots. Our rifles now on steady aim, I have the cross of my scope at the top and at the back of the front leg of the hind.

Bob says, "Now," and I pull the trigger

I hear one almighty crack which echoes all around the mountains and the herd of deer scatter and stampede away. The hind I shot at lays dead where she stood. I see the calf, it also lays dead where it stood. So Bob must have shot after all, but all I heard was one almighty crack. Bob goes down to stick and bleed the deer, I go get the ponies and join him down there.

As I meet up with Bob I see something coming along the mountain track and my two ponies start whinnying. I hear another horse whinnying back in the distance and I see a pony and trap coming along the mountain track. As it gets closer I see it's Lady CC and the Laird, they are out for a drive in their smart pony and trap. What a splendid sight they looked too as they pull up by our side. Lady CC looks a picture, she has one of the longest elegant dresses I ever did see, a shawl wrapped around her shoulders and with a pretty flowered scarf around her head.

The Laird looks equally as smart in his best tweed tartan plus

THE LAIRD AND LADY OF THE MANOR OUT FOR A MORNING DRIVE WITH THEIR SPLENDID APPALOOSA STALLION.

fours. He tipples his deerstalker hat to me and Bob and bids us both greetings. What a fine horse they have pulling their trap, it's a splendid Appaloosa stallion covered in black spots. By, what a fine set of English harness he has on him.

It's a magnificent two-wheeler trap he's pulling, all coach painted up in 'roses and stripes'. It looks fit for the king and queen to ride in.

As me and Bob stand there admiring what we look at, I say to Lady CC for a bit of a joke, "Can we get this dead red deer stag into your trap. We haven't enough room on the ponies' backs." Lady CC gives me a little ladylike titter and I say, "You can get its large antlers between your legs, I don't think you will get the horn."

Lady CC is taking me seriously. She's now standing up in the trap looking to see if she can get the stag in. As she turns and bends down her skirt gets caught on something and it pulls up high and reveals a grand pair of pink knickerbockers which stretch down to frills at her knees. By, what a sight for sore eyes as me and Bob looked on.

All at the same time, the Appaloosa stallion smells the blood from the stuck deer and it gets stricken with fear. It's now pauting the ground like a mad, raging bull; it's now blowing snot down its nostrils; it's now got itself bewitched; it's now rearing up in fear; it's now making a run for it. I see Lady CC fall backwards over her seat and she's now hanging on for dear life as her stallion stampedes away and off they go out of sight over the mountain tops.

Now that we are not distracted by Lady CC, me and Bob grollock out the deer, it will make them lighter to carry for the ponies. That job now done we head off back to Bob's cottage, the Hunter's Lodge.

Out in Bob's courtyard we hang the stag in the game larder, that's now waiting to be picked up by the gamedealer. The poor hind is skinned out, there's not much meat on her, but what there is Bob feeds to the dogs. What's that old saying, 'waste not, want not'.

Bob's now skinning out the calf, he's having this for his own table. Bob's now jointing up the carcass, he holds up a joint and says to me, "That's how venison should look when you are buying it from the butchers, well fleshed and a deep brownish red in colour." Bob's now telling me, "Venison, the meat of the deer,

RED DEER
STAG

FALLOW DEER
BUCK

ROE DEER
BUCK

MUNTJAC
DEER BUCK

originally meant any game animal killed for its meat, from the Latin *venatio*, to hunt. Venison is mentioned in the Bible, where it refers to a goat kid. The red deer is Britain's largest native land mammal, and lives for up to twenty-five years.

"A red deer hind (female) only comes into season five to six hours on one day in the whole of the year, so the stag has to have his balls about him and be on the alert." And on Bob continues, "There are five species of deer in Britain: red, roe, fallow, sika and muntjac. Depending on the species, the male deer is called a stag, hart, buck, or bull." And on and on Bob does say, "Fallow deer were first introduced by the Normans in the eleventh century for the nobility to hunt in their forests. This species is now the most widespread in the country." And Bob carries on saying, "The muntjac, introduced from China in the early twentieth century, is only eighteen inches high at the shoulder, or about the size of an Alsatian."

I can't stop Bob now he's got the chair and he says, "Every year there are approximately 1500 road accidents involving deer. Deer like to nibble on the bark of trees are such a problem in Poland that ICI sells a special 'tree paint' to help keep them away." Bob says, "Did you know Doug, that red deer kill the seabird called a shearwater to get calcium? The bird nests in burrows on inshore islands, visiting and courtship taking place at night to the accompaniment of unearthly screams and cackles. When the red deer move in, the screams and cackles may be a littler louder as the red deer take and kill them to get their calcium." Bob's now stopped talking.

Now I take the chair and that was a memorable day's stalking that I will never forget with Bob on the Laird's vast estate up in the Highlands of Scotland.

I must stop now, I have to tell you readers there's tears dripping from my cheeks and dropping on to the paper I write on. My faithful old rabbiting bitch, Pup, is dead. For the past few days now she has been poorly, and now as I write this story in May 2008, Pup has just crawled up to my feet and died. I am absolutely grief-stricken. It's a must now that I bury her safely underneath the back lawn of my home where she can now rest in peace with my other three old faithful rabbiting bitches that already lie there. That's Bess, Nelly and Sally. Pup who has just died, her name is Ella, she can now rest with them.

Here I am, I am back again. Pup's now gone to where the

rabbits roam free. "God Bless, Sweetheart."

The loose soil now on the lawn will wash away with the first rain and the loose grass sods I placed over her grave will soon knit together. You will then never even know there was a grave ever there at all. Pup will now drift further and further to the back of my mind and will be a distant memory, but will never be forgotten.

Now back to my story which all happened in the decade of the 1970s on the Laird's vast estate up in the Grampian Mountains in the Highlands of Scotland.

Bob Black or Black Bob who we all know as just Bob, he is forever telling me about the constant battle he has dealing with poachers up here.

I remember I was up there at one time or another, I was in Bob's courtyard when a chap calls. He introduces himself as James Macdonald and he tells me he has called in to see Bob Black. I tell James that Bob is not here, so me and James get chatting. James tells me he is surveying the estate for the Laird and that he manages the upkeep and running of the Laird's estate, checking and making sure there's a good healthy stock of deer and grouse on the moor, and also a good fish stock of salmon and trout in the river. This is all good management of the Laird's vast estate, which when this game is in the season of the year, is all big business for the Laird.

This reminds me of all the deer poaching that Bob gets and I say to James, "The gamekeeper has to be on his toes with all the poachers there are around these parts."

James tells me he was born and bred up here in these here hills and that when he was a lad there was nothing else to do up here but a bit of small time poaching. "But only taking game for our own pot," James says, with a little smile on his face. "Even nowadays I still come across the small time poachers up on the hills."

James is now going to tell us a true-to-the-fact story, and these are James's exact words I recall as he told his story.

"I remember I was on an estate one day, I was surveying it for the Laird just like I am surveying today for this Laird. I was up in the hills when low cloud rolled in and shrouded everything, you could say it was a Scotch mist. So I sat myself down for a rest and to wait while the mist cleared a little. After a while of sitting there the mist began to clear and I noticed someone sitting down further along the hill. As I looked at him and he looked and saw me he seemed to jump out of his skin. I went over to him and sat down by his side and he introduced himself as Hamish. He told me he was doing a spot of deer control for the Laird of the estate. Now I knew a poacher couldn't kid an old poacher like myself, but I went along with Hamish's story and said nothing.

"Hamish had three dead deer by his side. He had grollocked them, cut their legs off at the knees and cut off their heads, all to make them lighter in weight for easy carrying.

"Hamish had no rifle with him but again I asked no questions. I said to Hamish, 'I will give you a hand to carry the deer off the hill when the mist clears a little.'

"Hamish said, 'That's very good of you,' and he looked at me as though he thought he had kidded me on that he wasn't a poacher.

"I had seen some trenches cut out on the hillsides on this estate and when I was a lad," said James, "I myself would catch deer in these manmade trenches, tempting the deer into the trenches with a bit of bait. Once the deer is in the trench he can't get back out. I thought, this will be how Hamish has caught these three deer, but I ask Hamish no questions.

"I hinted to Hamish," said James, "that I like a bit of venison myself, thinking Hamish might give me a deer to keep my tongue silent. But Hamish offered nothing.

"As me and Hamish sat there on the hillside the mist began to clear," James said. "I saw someone fishing on the river below us and the fisherman was tucked under the river bank as he fished. It looks to me as though he is hiding as he fishes, I thought.

"I pointed out the fisherman to Hamish who quickly replied, 'Oh, that's only my brother Shamus is that'.

"At that moment Shamus hooked a big salmon and I said to Hamish, 'Is your brother Shamus controlling the salmon also?'

"Hamish nodded 'yes', with a sheepish-looking smile on his face. I hinted to Hamish that I liked salmon also, but yet again Hamish stayed silent. This left me thinking," says James, "how I could get a deer and a salmon for my dinner from these two obvious poachers.

"The mist had now cleared altogether so me and Hamish throw the deer over our shoulders and head off down the hill.

"Shamus was by now pulling in the big salmon he had caught. He looked up and saw me carrying a deer and appeared to go all in a panic. I said to Hamish, 'What's the matter with your Shamus, he looks a bit nervous to me?'

"Hamish says, 'He gets a bit uneasy with strangers'."

James says, "I see Shamus throw the big salmon on to the river bank and then he does a runner. There's a stone bridge that goes over the river nearby, it has a short bank that leads up to a quiet highland back road. Shamus sets off running up this short bank presumably to make his escape.

"As Shamus gets to the road, he goes all into a fluster and panics. There's a tractor coming along the road and Shamus dodges back and out of sight rather sharpishly. I said to Hamish, 'He sure is nervous is your Shamus. If I hadn't have known better, I would have said he was poaching,' and Hamish gave me a sheepish smile again.

"The tractor had now passed on by," James says. "Shamus looks back at me and sees me forever getting closer to him. He panics again and sets off running up the short bank again. As he reaches the road he throws his arms into the air all in a fluster, now there's a cop car coming along the road. Shamus panics so much he reels over backwards tripping himself as he went and finishes up splash bang on his back into the river.

"Hamish runs over and pulls him out saying to Shamus, 'It's all right, settle down, it's only James Macdonald who is giving me a hand to carry the deer off the hill'. Shamus had three big salmon caught on the river bank," James says, "and I hinted again, telling them both now, 'There's nothing I like better than a bit of venison and salmon'. Shamus is now silent as well as Hamish, there's no reply from either. They don't want to give me any of their poached game, I thought.

"They had their old van parked under a dry arch of the bridge, out of the way of the roving eye. They pulled it on to the quiet Highland back road and quickly threw the deer and salmon into the back.

"I thought, they are both in a hurry to leave without thanking me properly. I have to think of something and fast otherwise they are going to be off," James says. "I saw the cop car coming back along the Highland road and I seized my opportunity. I quickly open the back door of their van, I grab hold of one of the deer and hold it up high in open view to be seen.

"When Hamish and Shamus see what they see they panic and quickly jump out of their van. They snatch the deer from me and say, 'All right James, you can have a deer'.

"As they are secreting the deer back into their van, I quickly lean over them and grab a salmon and hold it high up into the air in open view to be seen. I see the cop car coming around the bend. Hamish and Shamus see the cop car coming around the bend, they also see their salmon exposed to be seen by the coppers. They say in a panic-stricken way, 'All right James, you can have a salmon also'. And they snatch the salmon from me and conceal it just in the nick of time before the cop car passes us by.

"The coppers acknowledge us as they pass, we acknowledge the coppers on their way, and the coppers are none the wiser as to what's just gone off. And off Hamish and Shamus go leaving me," says James, "with my hard-earned deer and salmon.

"Once a poacher always a poacher, choose which way it's got," says James Macdonald.

As James was telling me this story Bob had arrived and was listening to James tell his story. Bob now has a big smile on his face, he gives out a little chortle and says, "Poachers, poachers, we have poachers everywhere you look around these parts here. We get poachers who know they are poaching and we even get poachers who don't even know they are poaching."

Bob is now going to tell us another a true-to-the-fact story which happened up here on the Laird's vast estate. These are Bob's exact words I recall as he told his story.

Bob says, "I was up on the hilltops when I heard twelve bore shotguns being fired. I knew there should have been no shooting up on these hills that day so I went to investigate. I got myself to the top of a hillside and looked down below me, and what I saw I didn't believe. I saw a long line of men strung out across my best grouse moor. They all had a shotgun apiece in their hands and were shooting driven grouse as they walked them up in front of them.

"I raced over to them to stop them shooting and all the shooting men gathered around, they were all Chinese men. I asked them, 'What the hell do you think you are playing at? You can't shoot here'.

"They answered me back in some sort of Chinese tongue. They said, 'We out for a day's grouse shooting. We see it on television, "glorious twelfth" the start of the grouse shooting season, so we come to enjoy a grouse shooting here'." Bob said, "These Chinese men thought the television was telling them it's a free for all to go grouse shooting wherever they wanted to. So now you know," said Bob, "we even get poachers up here that don't even know they are poaching."

I remember yet another occasion I was up in them there hills on the Laird's vast estate in the Grampian Mountains in the Highlands of Scotland. Again I was in Bob's courtyard, which is at the side of Bob's quaintly-built stone cottage which is called the Hunter's Lodge, when who should walk in this time but the Laird himself. I told the Laird Bob's not at home but the Laird said, "It's not Bob I have come to see, it's you I want to see Doug." The Laird continued on to say could I catch some of the rabbits on the grounds that surround his home, him meaning his castle. The Laird said the marauding rabbits were making a terrible mess of his lawns and that they were making rabbit scats all over the place. Plus the rabbits are peeing everywhere making the lawns turn brown.

The Laird was saying, "The rabbits must be caught, they are creating a bad impression of the estate when the shooting men meet up there before a day's shooting."

I tell the Laird to leave it with me I will see what I can do.

The Laird has asked me at just the right time. I only arrived up at Bob's place the day before and I came up intending to do a lot of ferreting to the long nets. This is the game for excitement and getting big bags of rabbits, far more fun, far superior to ferreting to the purse nets. And I can assure you the ferrets absolutely love it too, working in a big team all together, all in one massive rabbit warren. The fesnyin of ferrets are in their element (that's what a group of ferrets is called, a 'fesnyin'). I have brought with me all my ferreting gear, and eight ferrets.

Helen is going to come with me for a day's ferreting. So I ring Helen and tell her about the Laird calling to see me and arranged to meet Helen up at the Laird's castle.

So off I go to get my eight ferrets I have brought with me for ferreting them rabbits out. I have them in a big caged hutch outside in Bob's courtyard. I put them all together into a big canvas shoulder bag with plenty of breather holes stitched in. The ferrets are content in there, I can hear them inside the bag, they are chattering and chanting to each other. They are excited, they know they are going rabbiting.

I meet Helen at the castle, she has come across the mountain tops on her quad bike to meet me here. Helen hops off her quad bike and hops into my Land Rover and off we head across the

Laird's fine big lawns and on towards the back of the Laird's castle. As we go we see many, many rabbits out feeding on the lawns. And as we travel along, the rabbits are bolting for the safety of their warrens in the belting of woodland that surrounds the Laird's castle and grounds.

Do you readers remember that night me, Helen and Bob went lamping in the argocat, when we lamped the Laird's castle grounds? All them rabbits we shot which was only twelve month ago, and now look at all the rabbits there is here again. They have all bred on and gone forth and multiplied.

I pull my Land Rover up by the side of the belting of woodland and into the woodland Helen, me and Pup do go. We see rabbits scampering everywhere, they are disappearing down into one big continuation of rabbit warrens, just where me and Helen want them.

This belting of woodland we now stand in is old mature pine trees and the ground is bare of cover, nothing will grow there. The pine trees must send out some kind of chemical from their roots, or maybe it's all the pine needles that fall from the trees which leave a thick coating of dead pine needles on the ground which smothers everything else out. Or is it the trees canopy that grows so thick it cuts out the daylight just like beech trees? Whichever or whatever it may be there is never much grows underneath these old pine forest woodlands.

All this bare ground makes easy work to run my long nets out and surround a big section of rabbit warren. I am using two one hundred yard nets so you can imagine how much ground I am covering. Me, Helen and Pup are now all ready. Out comes my big bag of ferrets. Helen takes four ferrets in hand and goes to the far side of the now netted warren. Helen is now doing the same as me, she's dropping a ferret of here and a ferret of there until she has dropped off all her four ferrets. All my four ferrets are now dropped off too.

We now stand back and look across the large netted warren and we see the ferrets smelling the ground around them and one by one they all disappear down into the holes and into the warren full of rabbits.

We now wait in silence for all hell to be let loose. I see a ferret emerge, it's running and chanting as it goes and its hair is stood up on its back as it smells the ground. It's been on to a rabbit and lost it. It now disappears down another hole. If I had have been ferreting to purse nets, I would have had to go over to where that ferret had just come out of and then straighten out and reset the purse net. That's the beauty about using long nets. There is no disturbance of me having to run over the rabbit warren which can make the rabbits obstinate in bolting.

I am distracted. I see a rabbit bolting out of a hole, but it no sooner appears than it disappears down another hole. It's no sooner disappeared when it comes flying back out of the hole, the rabbit has bumped into another ferret.

The rabbit is now terror-stricken as it bolts across the warren. The rabbit is not going to run down another hole, not to bump into another ferret and it's looking back as it goes to see where the ferret is. It hasn't seen the danger in front and now it's headlong and tangled in the long net.

It tries desperately to kick itself free, but alas Helen now has it in her clutches and the rabbit is no more. Helen's now taking the dead rabbit from the net and placing it safely at the other side of the net.

Its placed safely there so that a ferret cannot come up behind unseen and take the rabbit and drag it down another hole. It's so easily done, and when it is done, you have a lay up on your hands, and we don't want that do we. Helen has now straightened the net all ready for the next kill.

While Helen's back is turned I see four, five rabbits bolt from the warren, they all head Helen's way. Bump, one hits the net right by her side. The other rabbits are right up the arse of the first rabbit. Now Helen has four, five rabbits all jangling in the net together, all the rabbits now safely snottered. Helen now takes the dead rabbits from the net and places them safely at the other side. Helen now straightens the net out all ready for the next kill.

Now there's rumbling under my feet, it sounds like thunder that's coming to the surface. It's the ferrets chasing the rabbits about underground. Now I see rabbits bolting everywhere, they are heading for Helen again. My Pup is hot in pursuit and the rabbits are off as if there's no tomorrow. Bump, bang, thump as they all hit the net together, and a big crashing wallop follows. That's Pup who's hit the net with the rabbits. That will keep Helen busy for five minutes.

I now see rabbits bolting all over the warren, now the whole of hell has been let loose among the rabbits. I see a rabbit bolting out of a hole with the ferret up its arse. Down another hole the rabbit will go with the ferret following on after it. Now the same rabbit bolts out of yet another hole and it's brought out another eight or nine rabbits with it.

They are all panic-stricken with fear of the ferrets. There's rabbits like this all over the warren, they are darting here, there and everywhere as they make their escape away from the warren. But, alas, they make it no further than the long net that surrounds it. I see Helen at the far side of the warren, her net is full of bouncing, kicking, tangled rabbits. The woman's gone berserk, she's gone off her rocker, she's in a mad craze of killing rabbits. I see Pup, she's got herself tangled in the net again. She's laid all tangled up by the side of all the bouncing kicking rabbits. I hope Helen doesn't break Pup's neck by mistake.

I see ferrets out on top of the warren everywhere, they are racing here, there and everywhere as they are chanting around with their hair stood up high on their backs. The ferrets are all in a frenzy with each other, they are all enjoying the rabbit chase. I look at my side of the net, that surrounds the warren. It's full to the brim with bouncing, kicking, tangled-up rabbits. Now I am like Helen, I go into a mad craze of killing rabbits. A quick flick of the head backwards and the rabbit is dead. I carry on flicking and killing as I go, leaving the rabbits where I kill them.

I come to a great big ball of fur all tangled up in the net, it's seven or eight rabbits all balled up together. What a tangled-up mess they are in. I lift the net and give it a shake, it releases the rabbits a little and I can now put my hand in among them and break their necks.

There's one there, he's biting and snapping at me as I go in to break his neck. It's a big wily old buck and he's trying to bite my fingers is the old devil. I sneak my hand in at the back of his head, I grab him by the neck and shove his head back with my other hand and the wily old buck is no more.

I now look around me and the net shakes no more, the rabbits now lay dead in the nets. I look across at Helen, the mad crazy woman has now settled down. I see Pup, she's looking up at me as she lays tangled in the net by the side of a whole host of dead rabbits. Helen didn't break Pup's neck after all.

I see the ferrets now all on the surface of the warren. They have all worked well and I go to start picking them up. I count them as I pop them back into their big canvas shoulder bag. There's a lot more rabbits yet in this warren, we have bolted and caught the bulk of them but to send the ferrets in again will be risky. The rabbits down there in the warren may now be reluctant to bolt and the ferrets may kill in and lay up and we don't want that do we.

It's best not to be greedy, so I have now picked up my ferrets. I count seven ferrets, there should be eight, we have one missing and we have to find it. It's somewhere in this warren and I'll get Pup to help me, so I go and untangle her out of the net. Pup now goes searching around the warren, she has a good nose on her and she knows it's the ferret we are searching for. Pup puts her nose in this hole and that hole smelling and sniffing as she goes.

Before we started ferreting I had put locator collars on some of the ferrets. On the collar is a receiver and I have a handset in my hand which when turned on picks up signals from the receiver on the lost ferret's collar. I see Pup looking interested at a certain rabbit hole. Pup's looking at me and whining, she's trying to tell me something. I go over to her and turn on the handset, it starts clicking and bleeping, it's picking up the signal from the lost ferret's collar.

I criss-cross the handset around that area, the clicks and bleeps from my handset go louder and fainter as I move it about just on the surface of the warren. I go to the point where my handset was bleeping and clicking the loudest. I now have the exact point where the handset says the ferret should be.

The handset has a depth monitor on it, it says the ferret is two feet down. I now get my specially designed spade called a 'spit', it's only got a narrow blade which just digs out the essential soil. It's all easy digging in the soft soil of the warren and I am now nearly down to where the rabbits' tunnel should be. I now dig carefully, I don't want to cut the ferret in two with the spade do I.

The spade now drops through into the rabbit tunnel, and their she is, my bitch ferret is looking up at me all bleary eyed. 'Bitch' is slang for female, the proper name is 'Gill'. 'Dog' is the slang name for male, the proper name is 'Hob'.

So now I can see my bitch ferret in the bottom of the hole I have just dug and I reach down and lift her out. Her face is all covered in rabbit's blood. She's killed a rabbit down there, so I reach down and put my hand up inside the tunnel. I feel something warm and furry, I grab it and pull it out, it's a dead rabbit.

I get a stick and push it further up the rabbit tunnel where I have just taken the dead rabbit from and my stick touches something soft. I pull out the stick and have a look at the end. It's got all rabbit fur stuck on the end so I get my spade and dig a little further along the rabbits' tunnel. I can now see the arse end of a rabbit all balled-up and I reach down and grab it. I pull out a rabbit and it's still alive, well it was, I have killed it now.

I get my stick again and push it further up the rabbits' tunnel and again I feel something soft. It's too far up the tunnel for me to reach and grab it, so I dig in again with my spade and break into the tunnel further along, and their it is. I see another rabbit, I reach in and grab it, and this one is still alive also. I pass it to Helen who is watching on while I work, and as Helen grabs the rabbit with one hand she breaks its neck with her other hand.

That's three rabbits we have now dug out of this tunnel. I get my stick again and again I reach my stick up the tunnel and again my stick touches something soft. So off I go again breaking into the tunnel a little further along, and surprise, surprise it's another live rabbit. I do this on and on, working myself slowly but surely along the rabbits' tunnel. And by the time I have reached the end of the rabbits' tunnel we now have eleven rabbits.

What has happened is the ferrets have chased the rabbits around in the underground warren and the rabbits have kept on running down this tunnel which is a dead end tunnel. The rabbits now have nowhere to run to so they just ball-up, one at the back of the other until they are all in a long line in the tunnel. The ferret now comes along at the back of them and the ferret kills the last rabbit in the tunnel and holds all the rabbits in the tunnel.

And that's how ferreting to the long nets is done, far superior to ferreting to the purse nets.

Our eight ferrets are now safely found and put back in their carrying bag. Me and Helen now empty the nets of the dead rabbits, and what a fine bag we have too, I might add.

We now gather up the long nets and pop them back into their big sack, and that's it for this part of the warren. We now move on through the pine tree woodland and on to another section of the rabbit warren.

Me and Helen went on that morning and did a number of sections of the rabbit warrens and by the time we had finished we had a fine big bag of rabbits to show for our work. With several carries we get all our rabbits out of the pine tree woodland and laid out on the Laird's lawn. Then, for a bit of fun and for a bit of importance I empty the whole bag of eight ferrets out on to the now big pile of dead rabbits. The ferrets go marauding over the rabbits smelling at them and biting their heads and giving the rabbit's a good shake just to make sure they are dead. The ferrets will not damage the rabbits' flesh as they maraud over them, it's only the rabbits' heads they are biting.

This is all good for the ferrets, they know it's them who have caught all these rabbits. And for a bit of a complimentary bonus I take out a few hearts from the rabbits and smear the blood all over their little faces and now let them eat a few rabbits' hearts. They will not forget this day and will work as equally hard when they go rabbiting next time.

My faithful rabbiting bitch Pup is doing just the same as the ferrets, she too is smelling at all the rabbits and giving them the once over. She too gets the same treatment as the ferrets, I rub and smear the bloody hearts all over Pup's face and give her a few hearts to eat also.

I see Helen watching on and I have a handful of bloody hearts in my hands. Helen looks at me and she says, "Oh no, you're not doing that to me."

Incidentally my faithful rabbiting bitch I keep speaking of which I call Pup, it is not the same Pup which I told you readers about when my old Pup died. This is another Pup I speak of, I call all my bitches Pup.

Me and Helen now load up all our rabbits into my Land Rover. There's a good old fair bag of rabbits here and by the time they are all in they have filled up all three compartments of my Land Rover.

We now head off in the Land Rover and across the Laird's fine lawns we do go. We pass by a courtyard and I see fine horses with their heads over the stable doors. I see fine horse-drawn carriages everywhere, they are all gleaming and look in top notch condition to me. I see someone polishing them, it looks like a livery yard to me. Helen says, "They are all Lady CC's carriages, she likes to pick and choose which carriage she rides in."

We drive on by in my Land Rover. Now I see a large bird aviary and I see the Laird's inside with a big bird on his arm. I stop and me and Helen go over to him. The Laird tells me they are two Harris hawks which are well respected by people who fly birds of prey, they have the ability to catch large game such as pheasants on the wing. The Laird says he is just on the way out to give the Harris hawks a fly around.

The Laird invites me and Helen to join him and we head out

across the large castle lawns. The Laird is dressed very smartly in his plus four gentleman's suit. He has his deerstalker hat on and you can see your face in his polished shoes. The Laird has two Harris hawks, one on each arm, and has big thick leather gauntlets on his hands to stop the hawks' razor-sharp talons sticking into his wrists. I see the hawks have 'jesses' on their legs. The Harris hawks are big fine birds of prey, they look a picture to me.

We come to a wicket gate that leads out into a rough grass meadow. The Laird tells me and Helen both hawks are good at catching rabbits, but all the rabbits at this time of the day will be laid tight on their seats in the rough grass. I tell the Laird I will send Pup out to hunt in the grass to put up a rabbit for the hawks to catch. As Pup is hunting up and down in front of us the Harris hawks are watching every move Pup makes. Helen is gripping on to my arm in anticipation and excitement all rolled together.

I see Pup showing interest in and around some rough grass and I can tell by Pup's body language she is upon something. I tell the Laird in a low, quiet voice, "Watch out there's something going to get up."

I see Pup stop, she arches her back up, Pup sticks her nose into the air and scents the wind. Now I know Pup's ability to catch rabbits even before the rabbit has time to leave its seat. If Pup catches this rabbit she will spoil all chances of the hawks having a fly at the rabbits. So I quietly call her off and she slinks back to me. Pup must be wondering why I called her off the rabbit. I make Pup walk by my side, I go over to the clump of grass and I look back. Both hawks appear to be watching my every move. I see Helen, she looks as keen and interested as the hawks as she stands at the back of the Laird.

I give the Laird the nod to get ready and I go into the clump of grass and give it a kick. A rabbit instantly jumps up out of the grass and sets off like hell across the meadow. I look back at the Laird, I see both hawks flying over towards the fleeing rabbit, they are both coming like bullets as they whistle past me. I see one of the hawks dive straight down for the kill and it grabs the rabbit by the back of the neck with its pointed, razor-sharp talons. The rabbit kicks and fights but the hawk keeps its deadly grip on the rabbit all at the same time.

I see the other hawk swerve around with rapid wing beats and as I look across the meadow I see another fleeing rabbit. Pup is at the back of it, she must have put it up out of the grass. I see the

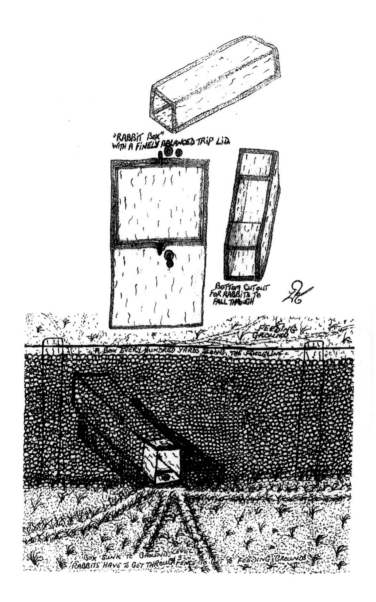

"RABBIT BOX"
WITH A FINELY BALANCED TRIP LID

BOTTOM CUT OUT
FOR RABBITS TO
FALL THROUGH

FEEDING
GROUND

A BOX EVERY HUNDRED YARDS ALONG THE HEDGELINE

BOX SUNK TO GROUND LEVEL
RABBITS HAVE TO GET THROUGH FENCE TO GET TO FEEDING GROUND

second hawk speeding towards the rabbit like a bullet cutting through the wind. I see the hawk whistle over the top of Pup's head and I see Pup's hair part as the hawk whizzes over her. I see the hawk stoop down at the fleeing rabbit and I see Pup. If the rabbit shits now Pup will get a mouthful. I see Pup grab at the rabbit, I see the hawk reach out with big-footed talons and both at the same time they grab the rabbit together. As the hawk's bodyweight impacts on the rabbit it knocks Pup skittling over. As she rolls with the rabbit still in her jaws, the rabbit rolls with her. The hawk is hanging on to the rabbit for dear life and the flapping, frustrated hawk rolls over with them.

I race over to them and there they are all tangled together. The hawk has the rabbit by the neck and Pup has the rabbit by its arse and neither will give up their catch. I go in to try to take the rabbit from the pair of them and now the hawk's striking at me with its great hooked beak. The hawk's now striking its hooked beak at Pup's eyes so I quickly roll over and cover Pup up. I see the Laird's now got himself here, and he's gone hysterical, he's shouting, "Get your dog off the rabbit!" But Pup's got a bloodthirsty grip on the now dead rabbit and it looks as though, because the hawk will not let go, Pup is not going to let go either.

The Laird comes up with a solution. He draws a knife from a sheath on his belt and stabs and slashes the dead rabbit into two halves. There that's two satisfied customers. Pup goes off with her half of the rabbit and the hawk goes up on to the Laird's arm with the other half of the rabbit.

I see the other hawk flying over to us, it still has its rabbit in its talons. It's coming in to land on the Laird's other arm and I see it's opened its empty foot with its large talons outstretched all ready to land. I see the Laird has still got his knife in that hand that the hawk's going to land on. The Laird hurriedly drops the knife and the hawk settles on his gloved hand safely, the Laird saying, "Phew!" in relief. "That was close," says the Laird.

The Laird is now going to tell us a true-to-the-fact story, and these are the actual words I recall as the Laird told me and Helen the story.

"One morning not all that long ago I was out flying one of my Harris hawks. My hawk had hunted well and had caught about six rabbits. As my hawk was hunting and searching around the surrounding area I decided I would paunch out the rabbits. I was opening up their bellies with a razor-sharp knife, when I looked up and I saw my hawk coming in to land on my arm.

"My hawk had caught me by surprise. I thrust out my arm for it to land on but my hawk landed on my hand. I still had my razor-sharp knife in that hand and before I even had time to realize it, my hawk clasped its big footed talons around my knife and gripped on tightly. My knife cut deep into a main artery in the hawk's foot and within less than a minute my hawk was dead. It had bled itself to death, a sad end," says the Laird.

Me, Helen and the Laird now head on back to the castle. The Laird puts his two Harris hawks back into their aviary, then says, "These Harris hawks have the finest eyesight. They can spot a squat rabbit twitch its ears at two miles away, absolutely incredible," says the Laird.

Me and Helen now head on over to my Land Rover which is parked nearby. The Laird follows us, he looks into my Land Rover and he sees all the rabbits that me and Helen have caught that morning from the warrens that surround the castle. The Laird says, "Have you caught all these rabbits here this morning?" The Laird carries on to say, "Bob tells me you are a good reliable rabbit catcher Doug."

I say, "Reliable maybe, but good I don't know."

The Laird gives out a gentleman's little chortle. The Laird's now looking at me with a serious look on his face and he says, "There's a post coming up for a full-time rabbit catcher for my estate." The Laird continues on with a serious tongue, "Doug, I am offering you that job now."

Helen's hung on to my arm and she's nudging me saying, "Go on Doug, go on, take the job, you can come and live with me."

The Laird interrupts Helen by saying, "I will supply a cottage for you to live in on the estate, it will be all free of charge with no rent to pay. I will give you your own Land Rover so that you can go around my estate doing your duties of rabbit catching. I will pay you a good yearly salary for doing your job and on top of all that every rabbit you catch will by yours which you can sell on and make yourself some extra money."

Now to me that was an offer of a lifetime, an offer that most rabbit catchers, like myself, wouldn't even think of refusing, but I did. I tell the Laird some serious facts about all the rabbits on his vast estate, telling the Laird the rabbits are in plague proportions and that they are totally out of control. The Laird nods in agreement with me. I tell the Laird about 'rabbit boxes' and the way rabbit boxes catch rabbits. The Laird is now all ears and listens to me intently. He appears impressed at what I tell him.

I ask the Laird if I can put some 'trial' rabbit boxes in on his estate and the Laird nods to me, agreeing with me wholeheartedly. The Laird then says, "You do as you wish Doug, and pass all the expenses on to me."

So on that me and the Laird shake hands and the business of me showing the Laird how to control rabbits on his vast estate was on.

As me and Helen are now leaving the Laird, Helen's playing hell with me for not taking the post as full-time rabbit catcher on the estate. But I didn't and that is my final word on this matter.

I must tell you readers, these rabbit boxes are the ultimate in rabbit catching. As you have already read in my story, since the year of about 1970 and onwards I have caught multi thousands of rabbits on the Laird's vast estate. It is now about the year of 1977 and the Laird has now allowed me to install a line of rabbit boxes for a trial. The multi thousands of rabbits I have already caught in the past six or seven years is a mere nothing to what I am about to catch from now on.

You the readers must now get yourselves all prepared to read the story of all lifetimes of stories in rabbit catching.

So now that me and the Laird have shook hands on our rabbit catching venture, I now have to get some rabbit boxes made. I go down into the local village where there's a small woodwork shop near on to the Poacher's Arms pub. I see the carpenter and tell him about the rabbit boxes that I want making. The carpenter's eyes nearly pop out when I tell him if these trial boxes are a success, which I know they will be, the Laird will want thousands of rabbit boxes making for the whole vast estate. I could see the pound signs rolling in the carpenter's eyes as he could see all the potential work I was offering him.

I tell the carpenter how the boxes should be made, giving him the specifications and the measurements the boxes want to be, and how the lids on the rabbit boxes must be on perfect balance.

I will tell you the readers how the rabbit boxes work a little later.

I specifically tell the carpenter not to put any creosote on the boxes once they are made as this will deter the rabbits from going anywhere near the boxes.

So the making of the rabbit boxes was all agreed and to start with the carpenter is going to make twenty trial rabbit boxes. Once these twenty boxes were in position and put into use, I could then convince the Laird how well the rabbit boxes catch rabbits.

I also wanted the carpenter to get me fence posts, rabbit netting wire mesh, staples and long lengths of bell wire. As I am bidding the carpenter good day, I tell him to send all the expenses to the Laird and he puts up his thumb in acknowledgement.

I remember this day very clearly in my mind. As I am leaving the carpenter's workshop there is the churchyard opposite. I see Helen coming out of the church, she is talking to the vicar. Helen has a pitchfork in her hand, this looked a bit devilish and fiendish to me, on Helen's behalf of course. Helen shouts me over and introduces me to the vicar. She tells the vicar that I am a rabbit catcher and the vicar replies by saying, "You want to catch these rabbits for me Doug, here in the churchyard? The rabbits are eating all the flowers which people put on the grave headstones."

And on that I set off to go the Poacher's Arms pub which is just across the road. The vicar went back inside the church and Helen jumped over the churchyard stone wall where she was tending some of her sheep that she had in the meadow there.

While I was having a drink of ale I got chatting to some people who were holidaying up here. They commented about all the rabbits they had seen running around in the countryside and they said they would have liked to have taken back with them some good eating rabbits for the table. I told them I had some rabbits hung in the game larder but they said they hadn't time to wait now, they were on their way home when they had finished their drinks.

I had a little think to myself, then I said to these people, "Just wait there, I will be back in two shakes of a lamb's tail." Then I went back and had a look over the churchyard stone wall.

By now there were quite a few rabbits out feeding. I had my .22 rifle with me, it was in my Land Rover parked nearby. I quickly got it and filled a magazine with bullets. I slotted a bullet into the chamber of the rifle and sneaked back up behind the churchyard stone wall. There was a stone water trough there which I rested my foot on and took steady aim by resting my rifle on the stone wall.

I put the telescope's cross on to the rabbit's brain and slowly pulled the trigger. A dull thud could be heard as the bullet hit its target and the rabbit jumped three feet into the air. That told me the bullet had hit where I aimed.

As the rabbit was now fighting and kicking itself to death the other rabbits sat up high on their back legs looking at their mate. Seconds later there was another two fighting and kicking themselves to death by the side of their once upon a time mate. I saw another two rabbits become aware of danger and make a run for it. When they reached the churchyard stone wall, they made a fatal mistake. Curiosity got the better of them and they stopped and looked back. A quick double shot and they were kicking themselves to death by the side of each other.

I looked across the churchyard and I saw Helen coming back over the churchyard stone wall. I shouted to her to pick up the dead rabbits and as she was gathering them, Helen signalled to me and pointed to the other side of the churchyard. I saw another rabbit so I picked my rifle up and aimed, but I didn't fire. The rabbit was laid low squat on the ground and it was looking straight across at me. If I put a bullet into its forehead the bullets are so powerful it would pass straight through the rabbit's head and through into its body which would damage the rabbit's flesh.

So I waited for it to move its position. Helen was looking across at me wondering why I didn't shoot. I gave out a low muffled rabbit scream with my mouth and the rabbit responded straightaway. It sat up on its back legs, I lined the cross up again and fired. The rabbit jumped three feet into the air, again the bullet had reached its intended mark.

Helen went over and picked up the rabbit and came on over to me. They were fine big healthy rabbits. Helen commented she had never heard a shot while she was tending her sheep in the meadow at the other side of the churchyard stone wall. That's how silent the silencer is on my rifle.

I quickly paunched the rabbits. I saw a freshly dug grave, so I threw the rabbits' guts into the grave and covered them over with a bit of loose soil. No sooner dead than buried, well, the guts anyway.

I remember, as I was climbing back over the churchyard stone wall, I saw something happen which really touched my heart strings.

I see Julie, she's a young pretty woman who lives in the village. Julie is blind and she has her guide dog with her who they call Lucky. Lucky, who has a harness on, is guiding Julie along the side of the churchyard stone wall. But what Julie doesn't know is that someone has left a barrow out on the pavement and a garden rake lays across the pavement just beyond the barrow and Julie is heading straight for them. Lucky is walking on the inside of Julie and I see Lucky bump into and nudge Julie's leg, Julie hesitates and stops for a second. There's a dog barking at Lucky at the other side of the road which Julie must think is what's distracting Lucky.

Julie carries on along the pavement bang on course to fall over the barrow. Lucky, the sensible dog, again bumps and nudges into Julie's leg. Julie again hesitates and does as Lucky bids her, she moves out across the pavement which takes Julie around the barrow. Julie's now trying to edge her way back to the churchyard stone wall but Lucky will not let her. She keeps on pushing and bumping Julie's leg for her to move over, and all at the same time the dog at the other side of the road is barking like hell at Lucky.

Lucky ignores the barking dog and continues on guiding Julie. Julie is now hesitating as to what to do. She carries on slowly but Lucky is still pushing Julie over. Julie obeys her dog and moves over. Now Lucky is pushing Julie off the pavement and on to the very quiet, traffic-free road.

Julie again hesitates but does as Lucky bids. Julie and Lucky walk safely around the garden rake which is lying right across the pavement. Now they are safely by the obstruction Lucky is now pulling Julie back up the side of the churchyard stone wall.

Wasn't that very intelligent of Lucky the guide dog? Watching that happen really touched my heart. Did my story on Julie and Lucky touch your heart readers? I am sure it did.

So now me and Helen head off to the Poacher's Arms pub with my quickly got rabbits. I peep my head around the pub door, I see the holidaymakers are still there, and I beckon them out of the pub. Their eyes nearly pop out when they see what I have got for them. They have a feel at the rabbits and they say they are still warm. They look down on the floor, blood is dripping from the rabbit's heads and on to the stone flags. I say, "They don't come any fresher than that."

They pay me and Helen some drinks over the bar, and off they go homeward bound and satisfied customers. Me and Helen are satisfied customers also. The vicar is also a satisfied customer, he now has no rabbits to eat the freshly laid flowers in his churchyard. So that now makes three satisfied customers altogether.

As me and Helen are quenching our thirst at the bar I think to myself my ale tastes a bit tarty, that means the beer tastes a bit sour. But I don't say anything, not yet anyway.

I look around the bar and I see a farmer and his wife sat in the corner, they are arguing and playing holy hell with each other. The farmer's wife looks dolled up looking as though she's been out on the town.

I see Old Squap who is a local who lives in the village. He's sat in another corner of the bar, so me and Helen go over to sit with him.

Old Squap has only got one eye, his other eye is a glass eye. As me and Helen sit down by his side Old Squap has his glass eye out cleaning it, which looked a bit gruesome to Helen, I could tell by the look on her face. I tell Squap about the rabbits I have just shot in the churchyard and that I threw the rabbits' guts into a freshly dug grave. Old Squap smiles to himself.

Old Squap is now pointing through the pub window. I look and I see a funeral cortege going by. Old Squap says, "That is old Jimmy going by in the coffin." But Old Squap is still smiling to himself and these are the exact words I recall Old Squap saying.

"Me and my neighbour who lives next door, we were both in this pub last night. We had both had a really big bellyfull of ale. I went home before my neighbour and took a short cut through the churchyard. It was that dark I could hardly see as I groped my way along and I tumbled and fell into a freshly dug grave. That's where they are putting old Jimmy now, on top of your rabbits' guts you have just put in.

"When I came to my senses from falling I see I am in old Jimmy's freshly dug grave. I jump and jump to try to get out but alas I couldn't. So I got myself huddled up into the corner at the bottom of the grave and went to sleep. Then all at once I am suddenly awakened. I open my bleary eyes and I see someone jumping up trying to get out of the grave. I see it's my drunken neighbour and as he is jumping and jumping trying his best to get out, I say, 'You will never get out.' This must have put the fear of God or the devil into my neighbour. In one almighty leap with the flames of the devil up his arse, he leapt out of the grave without even touching the sides." That tickled Old Squap did that as he told me and Helen as we sat in the pub.

I now get up and go to the bar to complain to the landlord about my tarty tasting beer. The farmer's wife is stood at the bar and she looks to me like a dressed up tart. Her tits are fair bursting out of her tight-fitting, low-plunging neckline of a blouse. As I am holding up my pint pot of ale telling the landlord about my beer, my eyes are transfixed on the farmer's wife's tits. I say, "That's tarty."

The farmer's wife says to me, "I hope you aren't talking about me. I will hit you over the head with my bloody handbag if you are." And off she goes and sits back down at the side of her farmer of a husband and off they go again arguing like cats and dogs with each other.

I intercept them and try to pacify them down a bit. I say to the farmer, "It's the livestock market day tomorrow, will you be taking in any livestock?"

The farmer says, "If our lass here had bigger tits I could take the cow in."

His wife screams back at him and says, "If you had a bigger cock we could get shut of the tractor driver."

Now there's all hell let loose between them and me and Helen slink off out of the pub and leave them to it. Outside the pub everything is all peaceful and quiet. The funeral of old Jimmy is now over and all the funeral mourners have gone.

As me and Helen are passing on by the churchyard we see the gravedigger by the side of old Jimmy's grave. He's chuntering away and playing hell with himself, and he's bent down wiping his boots. I ask him if everything is okay, and he says, "No, everything isn't okay. Old Jimmy's guts have all squelched out of his coffin and I have just put my feet all in them."

Me and Helen look at each other. The gravedigger has put his feet in our rabbits' guts but me and Helen say nothing and skedaddle out of the village.

My mission is now accomplished in them there hills on the Laird's vast estate. I have now arranged with the carpenter to make me twenty rabbit boxes for a trial experiment on the Laird's estate. All I can do now is go home and wait while the rabbit boxes are ready.

Its now early spring of about the year of 1977 and I don't have to wait very long at home before the carpenter contacts me and tells me my twenty rabbit boxes are ready. I am itching and eager to be off back up into them Grampian Mountains up in the Highlands of Scotland where the Laird's vast estate ranges.

I am taking back up with me my trailer. I know also that I am going to have a bit of devilment with moles on the Laird's fine lawns. So I put in my Land Rover some mole scissor traps and off me and Pup go heading for them there hills.

When me and Pup finally arrive up there, I see everything is all there prepared and waiting for me. The Laird has got me some local lads out of the village to help me install the rabbit boxes. My intentions are to install ten rabbit boxes around the outside perimeter of the Laird's castle grounds. These rabbits want cleaning up altogether, they are making a real nuisance of themselves. The Laird is pulling his hair out in frustration with all the damage the rabbits are causing.

I have chosen a special place for the other ten rabbit boxes to be installed. It's along the side of a large fir tree plantation. This woodland is just one big infestation of rabbits and there is just one big continuous rabbit warren that runs all the way along the inside of the woodland. A prime place to have a line of rabbit boxes.

There's a high deer fence on the edge of this fir tree plantation which stops the deer getting in and damaging the trees in the woodland. The rabbits are coming underneath this fence line, so me and the lads dig a six-inch deep trench along the bottom of the deer fence line. We then drop the bottom of the rabbit netting wire meshing into the trench and then back fill it with soil. We now lash and tie the rabbit netting to the deer fence line. Now the rabbits will not dig under the wire meshing.

On the inside of the fence line, inside of the woodland, we dig a hole big enough and deep enough to drop the rabbit box into. The top of the rabbit box is now at ground level and we now fill the sides in around the box with loose soil which nestles the box in position.

I purposely positioned the rabbit box on a main rabbit run which takes the rabbits out into the grass meadow which is the rabbits' feeding grounds. Now to assemble the lid on to the top of the box. This lid is finely balanced with a rod that goes along the dead centre of the lid. The rod sticks out a little at either end of the lid which then hangs in notches at the top of the box. The lid is now in perfect balance position. When one side of the lid is pressed down and then let go, the lid naturally comes back up level all because it's on perfect balance. That job's now done.

At the top of the box, on one half of the lid, lies a wooden tunnel. This is how the rabbit box now catches rabbits. The rabbit comes along its run and jumps into the wooden tunnel which will take it through on to its feeding grounds, or so the rabbit thinks. He puts all his weight on to his front feet on the balanced lid, the lid drops down, the rabbit drops with it and into the box below.

The finely balanced lid now naturally resets itself back into position all ready for the next rabbit into the wooden tunnel. And that's how rabbit boxes catch rabbits.

But firstly we have to complete our work, the wooden tunnel now needs attaching to the deer fence line. We cut a hole in the deer fence meshing and push the wooden tunnel through the hole which is a tight fit around the wooden tunnel. There, all completed. The rabbits can now pass through the wooden tunnel which takes them through the deer fence line and safely on to their feeding grounds. That is until I want them. Remember these finely balanced lids are locked off by me which allows the rabbits to pass through safely. When I do want the rabbits I just simply unlock the lids.

So that rabbit box is now in its final position and all finished with and you the readers now know how the rabbit boxes work.

Me and the lads now go on and put all ten rabbit boxes all the full length of the deer fence line. We install a rabbit box about every hundred yards or so and we now finish up with one great long line of rabbit boxes. Phew!

These rabbits here now will have to get used to their new found way of getting out on to their feeding grounds. They will hesitate and look at the wooden tunnel and back off but hunger will eventually give one rabbit the courage to go through the wooden tunnel. And after only a short while all the rest of the rabbits will follow on behind until it's their normal natural way of getting out on to their feeding grounds.

We have now finished here and it's now time to let these rabbits breed themselves out of control as per usual. I will be back for them come the month of September. Me and the lads now head away and on down to the Laird's castle.

We put in the other ten rabbit boxes all in the same manner but this time we have to put up a rabbit netting fence line which is put at the edge of the pine tree woodland. And when completed it stretches the full outside perimeter of the Laird's castle and the castle grounds.

We installed a rabbit box about every 150 yards and then the lads' work with me was completed. All twenty rabbit boxes are now installed and in position. The lads now want paying for their work and I tell them to see the Laird, he will pay all their expenses. The lads put up their thumbs to me and off they go heading for the castle.

All I have to do now to these rabbit boxes here at the castle is one final important job. That is to put a length of bell wire around the top of the fence posts which go around the entire perimeter of the castle grounds. This bell wire is stapled to the fence posts, about six inches from the top of the rabbit netting. Any would be rabbit that tries to jump over the top of the rabbit netting will then be knocked back by the bell wire.

Everything is made so that the rabbits have to travel over the top of the rabbit boxes to get to their feeding grounds. I can now put this bell wire up in my own time and leisure, I am in no hurry.

Now for me to have that bit of devilment with the Laird. He has no moles on his fine lawns, not yet anyway. So I go way out into the grass meadows to where I have seen a lot of freshly made molehills. I set half a dozen of the scissor traps I have especially brought up with me among and around these molehills. I must catch two or three moles here so that I can put my devilment into practice.

By the time I have set my six scissor traps it is by now coming into deep dusk of the evening. I go back to the Laird's castle, keeping myself under cover of the trees, to where all the rabbit warrens are. I have with me a sack which I will fill with good quality loose soil.

In the shadows of the darkness I sneak across the Laird's fine lawns which brings me to in front of the main entrance to the Laird's castle. I gingerly look around me, there is not a soul around to see me. So I get my sack and teem some of my soil on to the Laird's fine lawn. There, my pile of soil now looks just like a real molehill. I put small piles of soil here, there and everywhere around the Laird's fine lawn. Now my piles of soil look just like a whole host of real molehills.

I look around me, there's not a soul around to see what I have just done. My devilish mission now accomplished I sneak away and head off back to Bob's cottage.

The next morning I am busying myself in the courtyard outside Bob's cottage when Bob shouts across to me saying, "The Laird's on the telephone, he wants to speak to you Doug."

When I answer the phone, the Laird is rambling on about he has some moles on his best lawn and that they are right in front of his main entrance hall. The Laird rambles on that I must come straightaway and catch the little blighters. When I arrive at the castle I see the Laird marching up and down around some molehills on the lawns. He appears to be pulling his hair out with frustration, and says, "We have to get shut of them Doug, they will give a bad impression of the estate if my shooting guests see all these molehills." The Laird carries on saying, "I don't know where they have come from, they weren't here yesterday."

I tell the Laird not to worry, I will soon catch the pesky moles for him.

I got some more scissor traps from my Land Rover and set them around all the molehills which looked a real eyesore on the lawns. I think to myself, I have made a good impression on the Laird putting all these molehills here in the first place. And on that I went and started putting some of the bell wire on to the newly installed rabbit netting fence line. I'm not there long before Helen comes on the scene to give me a helping hand. We have to get this bell wire really taut from post to post and then staple it to hold it in position. Soon we need more bell wire so Helen goes off to get some.

As I am busying myself I hear a horse coming along the driveway, leaving me thinking, is that Lady CC on her sturdy steed? The clip-clopping of the horses hooves appeared to go on for some time. Then the serenity of the countryside where I was working ended abruptly.

All silence was broken and all hell was let loose. I heard a woman screaming her head off, leaving me thinking, there's a murder taking place here. I raced across through the woodland and out on to the castle lawns. I saw Lady CC, she was stood on the top of a picnic table screaming her head off. And who should be stood on the lawn puffing his chest out but my old mate that mad capper of a bird the capercaillie.

Lady CC was shouting, yelling and screaming, and she was waving and shooing at Capper. He was flying up in the air and flapping his wings at Lady CC up on the picnic table. Lady CC saw me and she yelled out to me, "Help me Doug, I am being attacked!"

I went to the fair maiden's rescue. I shooed my way through Capper's harem of hen capercaillie and I grabbed hold of Lady CC. I held her up high in my arms. And as I set off across the lawns towards the castle, the mad capper of a bird was flying up and pecking and fluttering his wings at Lady CC who was fair throttling me as she was clutching me tight around my neck.

Capper stands back on the lawn, he is now throwing threats

out at us. He gives out a loud 'pop' and a 'wheeze' followed by 'belching' and 'gurgling' noises. I could see Capper was in a terrible nasty mood.

I leave Capper stood there on the lawn with his harem of hens and make a hasty retreat across the lawns towards the safety of the castle. Lady CC is hanging on to me for dear life, and I am in so much of a hurry I trip myself on one of the mole traps I have set in the lawn. Me and Lady CC go hurtling forward, I lose my balance and we both end up in the flower beds.

As we are rolling about in and among the rose bushes, I look up and who should I see but my beloved Helen. And for the first time ever she wasn't giving me one of her big smiles like a breath of fresh spring mountain air. That mad capper of a bird has by now disappeared out of sight with all our evidence of why me and Lady CC were in the rose bushes together.

That appears to make Helen even more cattish towards Lady CC. There's no satisfying women, and I am not about to try to convince them.

I see Helen, her eyes are filled up with tears as she's walking away backwards. She trips herself on one of my mole traps set in the lawn, goes reeling and falling backwards and ends up herself in the rose bush flower beds.

I see Lady CC jump up with all thorns up her backside and she makes haste and runs off into the safety of her castle. I pull my beloved Helen up out of the rose bushes. She's all covered in red rose petals and she looks a real picture to me. I give her a peck on her rosy red cheek and off me and Helen go and disappear. As we go, Helen says she never saw the mole trap. I tell Helen about my mischievous ways of me putting the molehills on the Laird's lawn and she gives me a mischievous little giggle. She is all for it, saying it serves Lady CC right.

The mole traps I set the evening before aren't far away across the meadow so me and Helen have a walk across to see if the scissor traps have caught any moles. The first trap we come to the handles of the trap which show just above the ground are still closed up together. This tells me the trap hasn't gone off so we go to the next trap. We see the scissor trap handles are open, the trap has gone off. So I pull the trap out of the ground and there it is, a dead mole in the jaws of the trap.

I pop the dead mole into my pocket and we now go on and check the rest of my traps. We have another two dead moles in them and I pop them into my pocket. I now have three dead moles to do my bit of devilment ways with the Laird.

Me and Helen now set off back to the new rabbit netting fence line we have installed and begin putting on more bell wire. As we work, the serenity of the countryside is all quiet when out of the blue we hear shouting. "Yoo-hoo Doug, yoo-hoo."

It's Lady CC again, she has plucked up courage and braced herself, she isn't going to let Capper frighten her. This time she is prepared, she has an open umbrella in front of her and a bottle of wine on a tray in her other hand. Lady CC beckons me over to the picnic table, she hasn't seen Helen behind the bushes, but Helen follows on anyway.

At the picnic table Lady CC is filling up two glasses with wine when she sees Helen. I hear lady CC mutter to herself, "I thought she had gone home." Lady CC hands me a glass of wine and keeps the other glass for herself. We sit down to savour the wine but Helen isn't going to be put off. She plonks herself between me and Lady CC and starts swigging wine from the bottle. Their bitchy ways continue as I am trying to keep both women happy, both at the same time.

I see the Laird over by the main entrance to the castle, so all three of us take a stroll over the lawns to meet the Laird. I am now all prepared to put my devilment of ways into action. I now have three dead moles in my pocket and I am now about to convince the Laird he has a serious mole problem on his fine lawns.

I say to the Laird, "We will have a look at the traps set on the lawn to see if we have caught the moles." I wink my eye at Helen, Helen gives me a mischievous little smile back. I bend down to one of my traps and Helen moves in between me and the Laird and Lady CC to obscure their vision. I pull my trap out of the lawn and quickly put one of my dead moles into the jaws of the trap. I now turn and show the Laird and say, "Look, we have caught a mole."

The Laird gives a big smile that must have stretched from ear to lug, and I see Helen is about to burst out into hysterics with excitement. I give her a strong nudge and a serious look, and Helen settles back down.

The Laird by now has the dead mole in his hand and he says, "The mole has only pinprick eyes."

I tell the Laird, "The mole can only make out daylight from darkness, they have very poor eyesight. But what they lack in vision they make up for with a very powerful scenting nose."

As the Laird is busy looking at the dead mole, I bend to pick up another trap from out of the lawn. Lady CC is watching closely what I am doing. I give Helen the nod and she moves in and brushes Lady CC to one side to obscure her vision. I pull the trap out of the lawn and quickly take another dead mole from my pocket and put it into the jaws of the trap.

I now turn and show the Laird and say, "Look, we have caught another mole."

The Laird is over the moon with the success we are having, and I see Helen is getting herself excited again. As I pass over the dead mole to the Laird I give Helen a strong brush with my shoulder to silence her excitement. Helen calms herself down, and as the Laird takes the second mole from me he hands the first mole to Helen. Helen puts the dead mole into her pocket. As the Laird is now looking at the second mole we have just caught, he says, "Haven't the moles got a lovely furry coat on them."

I say, "The mole is called the little gentleman in his black velvet coat."

While the Laird is looking at the mole I bend down to pick up another trap out of the lawn. By now Lady CC falls over on to my back and she's groping my side with her hand. Her hand accidentally falls into my pocket and I see, shock horror, Lady CC has pulled out my third dead mole from my pocket. Lady CC shrieks out, "Look, a dead mole!"

I quickly grab it and as I stand up I make it appear that I have just taken it out of the trap. By now Lady CC is sprawled upon the lawn and she is laid there scratching her head. She is sure she has just taken that mole from my pocket, but she is too tickled and tipsy to realise what has just happened. She nearly gave my little game away, phew!

As the Laird takes hold of the last mole we have just caught, he hands the second mole to Helen who again puts it into her pocket. The Laird is now totally over the moon with all the success we have had catching the moles on his fine lawn. He hands the third dead mole to Helen who again puts it into her pocket. The Laird's now ushering me to one side. He's now pressing his cupped hand into my hand and highly praising and thanking me for the success I have just achieved in catching his moles for him.

As the Laird walks away I look to see what he has just given to me. It's a big roll of bank notes. Off the Laird goes with Lady CC back into his castle and off me and Helen go as two satisfied customers. We head on back towards the newly installed rabbit netting fence line and as we go I see Helen take the three dead moles from her pocket and throw them into the shrubbery of the woodland.

Me and Helen now start to put more bell wire on to the top of the fence line. I remember Helen went home early that day, which I thought nothing of and carried on working, and after a while I then myself packed in and went back to Bob's cottage.

The following morning I was in Bob's courtyard when Bob shouts across to me and says, "It's the Laird on the telephone and he wants to speak to you Doug."

So I go pick up the phone and the Laird's ranting and raving that he now has moles on his fine lawns at the back of his castle and that I must come straightaway to sort the little critters out.

When I arrive I see the Laird marching up and down around all the molehills that are upon the fine lawns at the back of the castle. The Laird is fair pulling his hair out in frustration. I see Helen stood there, she has a serious, innocent look on her face. The Laird looks at me, his face is a bloodshot red with blood pressure and he says, "Please, please Doug catch these bloody moles for me."

I think to myself, there is something suspicious going off here. I look at Helen and she has an expression on her face that is saying, "It's nothing to do with me."

I check these molehills out. I push my moleing bar into the lawn by the side of a molehill and my bar does not thump into the mole's run (a run is the mole's underground tunnel). I push my moleing bar into the lawn here, there and everywhere around these supposed molehills and there's not a run to be found. I know now there is some skulduggery going off around here. I know that someone has put these molehills here just like I did on the lawns at the front of the castle. But I say nothing to the Laird.

I set my mole scissor traps into the lawn around the molehills and tell the Laird, "I will catch the little critters for you," and off the Laird goes back into his castle.

Helen is now confessing to me that it is her who has put the molehills there. She put them there yesterday when she left me early to go home. I tell Helen she is a cheeky little monkey, upsetting the Laird like that.

We leave the traps set overnight and go back the following morning. The first job me and Helen have to do is go and retrieve them moles that Helen threw in the shrubbery in the woodland only the day before. We need these three dead moles to convince the Laird that we have caught the moles for him. We hunt and search in the shrubbery in the woodland but alas all we can find is one dead mole. The crows must have eaten the other two moles.

We see the Laird come out of his castle and go around to the molehills on his fine back lawns. This one dead mole that I now have in my pocket will have to do. Me and Helen go over to join the Laird at the back of his castle.

I bend down to pull a trap out of the lawn. The Laird is watching my every move from behind so I give Helen the nod. Helen moves in and stands between me and the Laird to obscure his view. I quickly take the dead mole from my pocket and put it into the jaws of the trap. Then I turn and say, "Look, we have caught a mole."

The Laird is overjoyed by our success. The Laird takes the mole from me and starts scrutinizing it. He says, "Doesn't the mole have big front feet."

I tell him, "The mole can have a territory as big as a football pitch. He will have tunnels all over that area so he has to have big shovels for feet to work the area the size of a football pitch."

The Laird appears intrigued at what I tell him. I can't get the dead mole back off the Laird, he's so intrigued at inspecting the mole. But I must have that mole so that I can put it back into another trap to convince the Laird we have caught his moles. It's the only mole we have so I have to have it back. Helen also knows this and she has her hand out hoping the Laird will give it to her so that she can pass it on to me. But no, the Laird keeps hold of the dead mole and says, "Lift some more traps Doug, see if you have caught any more moles."

I think to myself, how can I if you won't give me the bloody dead mole?

I stoop down to pull a trap out of the lawn and as the trap comes up I accidentally on purpose reckon to lose my balance. I go reeling forwards and give the Laird such a bump and accidentally on purpose knock his hand that is holding the dead mole. The mole goes falling to the ground, I fall on top of the mole and quickly put it into the jaws of the trap which I have just pulled out of the lawn.

I did all this out of the glimpse of the Laird's roving eyes and as I roll over on the lawn I have the trap in my hand above me and the Laird shrieks out, "Look you have another mole caught in that trap!"

Helen is gobsmacked with all that is happening in front of her very own eyes, and all so very quickly. And the Laird has taken it hook, line and sinker. Helen can't bear to let the Laird see her. She has her back turned to him, she is giggling and tittering trying her best not to laugh her knickers off. Her eyes are all welled up with laughter tears.

The Laird sees the funny side of it, or he thinks he does. "It was funny there," says the Laird, "how you fell."

So Helen's little bit of her devilment ways is now over and all accomplished. We have now caught all the moles for the Laird and he is now a very satisfied customer.

And that was one very memorable time I had with Helen catching the moles on his fine lawns that surround his castle. Moles that he didn't have in the first place.

I will now tell you readers about how these rabbits here at the castle grounds coped with the new rabbit fence line we have just installed.

With the Laird getting me the local lads from the village to help me erect and install the rabbit fence line, we put that fence line up in three days. How does that old saying go, 'many hands make light work'.

On the first evening of the fence line being erected, I packed in early from putting the bell wire on top of the fence line. I wanted to see how the rabbits reacted to their new found, rabbit-proof barrier of a fence line.

I got myself squat in the bushes and watched. After a while of it all being quiet I saw the rabbits starting to emerge from their massive warrens in the woodland. As you readers now know, the ground in this fir tree plantation is bare of undergrowth so I have a good view of all the rabbits in front of me.

The rabbits' first job when they emerge from their warrens is to sit at their hole end and have a good scrub up. They will have a good old scrat, a good old tongue licking coat wash and ear licking wash. As this is all going off the rabbits are vigilant of all that's going off around them, watching for any dangers that may be around them. As I lay squat in the bushes I watch all this take place. Now I see the rabbits make a move. They are getting on their runs that lead them from their massive warrens and take them through the woodland and out on to their feeding grounds, which is the large grass meadow on the outside of their woodland. But not this time.

My new rabbit fence line is stopping them. I see the rabbits are in a quandary as to what to make of this new found barrier and they won't go near the fence line. It's all new to them and they just sit and look and scent the wind for any danger that may be around. It's by now getting too dark in the evening for me to see, so off I go and leave the rabbits to their new found ways.

The following morning I am back to put more bell wire on to the top of the fence line. I purposely get there just as it's breaking daylight. I want to see if there are any rabbits running in off the grass meadows. If there are then they must have gone through the wooden tunnels which pass over the rabbit boxes and which will have taken them through the new fence line.

I walk along the wood side which is along the side of the new rabbit fence line. I go all the way around the full perimeter of the woodland which surrounds the Laird's castle. I see scores and scores of rabbits but they are all scampering around within the woodland. I never even see one rabbit on the grass meadows which surround, which is the rabbits' feeding ground.

Again that evening I purposely finish early putting the bell wire on top of the new fence line, which takes a bit of doing as I am going all the way around the full perimeter of the castle. And again I get myself squat in the bushes to watch the rabbits. Again I see the rabbits emerge out of their massive warrens, but this time it's a bit different to the previous evening when I watched them.

The rabbits emerge out of their warrens a little earlier and I don't see them have a wash and a scrub up like they normally do. I see them head on straightaway along their runs heading for their feeding grounds.

The rabbits by now are starving hungry, they haven't eaten for twenty-four hours. With the ground inside the woodland being bare of any food they cannot eat in there. They must get out on to their feeding grounds to eat.

I see the rabbits are bolder now, they are right up to the new rabbit netting fence line. I see them smelling and scenting at it. I see a rabbit, it's an old buck I see, I can tell that by his big round head, he's the dominant rabbit over all the rabbits here in this colony. I see him take one almighty jump to clear the new rabbit fence line.

He has his front paws on top of the rabbit wire netting, he pulls himself forwards and upwards but his nose hits the bell wire and alas knocks him back.

The old buck hits the deck and he's back where he started. I see him repeatedly try to jump the fence line but each time he jumps the bell wire knocks him back. There are many, many rabbits watching their bold leader try to jump the fence. But the bold leader of a buck cannot let his harem of does down, he has to get them out on to the feeding grounds.

I see the old buck go along the fence line smelling and sniffing as he goes. I see the old buck come to the wooden tunnel, he smells and sniffs at it. I see him look through the wooden tunnel, he can see daylight at the other side.

He can see his feeding grounds where him and his harem of does want to be. The bold old buck sits up high on his arse and weighs up the situation. His does are watching on. The bold leader of a buck, he's now got his head inside the wooden tunnel. His harem of does are watching and thinking, how bold their leader is. I see the buck take a hop and he disappears into the wooden tunnel.

I know the old buck is safe inside that wooden tunnel. The old buck will now be sat on the tippler lid, but I know the tippler lid isn't working, all because I have it locked off. I now see the old buck emerge out at the other side of the wooden tunnel. He's now on the grass meadow which is his feeding ground for him and his harem of does.

Through the now dim light of the evening it's getting too dark to see what's going off so I slowly move away from my hiding place in the bushes and leave the rabbits to their new found way.

I am back again the following morning and I intentionally arrive at daybreak. I want to see if there are any rabbits out feeding on the grass meadow. Again I walk down the woodland side which takes me alongside of the newly installed rabbit fence line. As I go around a bend of the woodland my eyes sparkle at what I see. I see eight, ten a dozen rabbits running off the grass meadow as they see me approaching. They are strung out across the meadow as they bolt for the safety of the woodland, and they are taking their old routine path across the meadow.

The rabbits have forgotten themselves as they make haste to reach safety. They now reach the new fence line which they had forgotten was there. I see them stop abruptly, have a little think and then they remember they have a secret wooden tunnel that takes them back through this new manmade barrier.

Off the rabbits head along the side of the new fence line to their secret wooden tunnel. They have to wait and join the queue while all the rabbits in front of them hop into their new found tunnel. And off they all go back into the woodland and to the safety of their massive warrens.

I continue on around the full perimeter of the newly installed rabbit fence line, which goes around the full perimeter of the Laird's castle grounds, and all the ten boxes we have installed on the fence line which all have a wooden tunnel over them. I see rabbits running in off the grass meadow and off they all go through their wooden tunnel into their own territorial part of the woodland and to their own private part of the massive warrens.

So now I know my rabbit boxes are a success, they are leading and guiding the rabbits to where I want them. It is by now the spring of the year and already I have seen young rabbits running around. They are born and bred here so these wooden tunnels they pass through to reach their feeding grounds is all a natural way of life to them. The young rabbits have known no different, they will now this coming summer grow up and breed on and go forth and multiply.

It's now time for me and Pup to go homeward bound and leave the rabbits to their new found ways. But me and Pup will be back at the end of summer when the rabbits will then be in their multitudes. We will be back come the month of September.

Now that I am at home I have to sit the long summer out and wait. I get myself reminiscing on the past experiences I have had with these so called rabbit boxes. They are used countrywide you know. Many keepers have them on their estates for controlling the rabbit populations. And also these rabbit boxes do tend to get poached from time to time.

I know of a gamekeeper from my neck of the woods, Mick they call the keeper. Mick has a long row of rabbit boxes along a wood side on his estate and there were many rabbits using his boxes. Mick had purposely left these rabbits alone, he was going to catch these rabbits at Christmas so that he would have a bit of extra pocket money. Mick would often pass by these rabbits in his Land Rover as he was going around the estate doing his chores. He would pass his eyes over the rabbits as he went by watching the rabbits getting fatter and fatter as they grazed in the grass meadow. Mick was rubbing his hands together at the thought of all the pocket money they were going to bring him in.

Early one morning as Mick was passing by his rabbit boxes he cast his eyes over the meadow where the rabbits should have been out feeding and there wasn't a rabbit to be seen anywhere. The alarm bells started ringing within Mick. He went over to his first rabbit box and his security lock on his rabbit box had been broken off. Mick, fearing the worst, went along all his rabbit boxes and they were all the same. All his security locks had been broken off and all Mick's rabbits had been taken. The poachers had dropped his boxes and taken his rabbits all in one night's work and all done in the silence of how the rabbit boxes work.

I don't wish any bad luck on Mick on how he had his rabbit boxes poached, but these rabbit boxes are such a temptation to poachers. They catch the rabbits so quickly and so easily and they take every rabbit that's there.

As you readers know I am a bit of a rabbit poaching lad myself and I remember very clearly around my neck of the woods where I live there is a big gamekeeper's estate there. They too have long rows of rabbit boxes installed all over the estate. I was on this estate early one morning and as I am walking along a woodland side I see many, many rabbits running in off the grass meadow. I look and I see all the rabbits are running over rabbit boxes.

Now how could I resist the temptation? These rabbit boxes were not locked off with security locks like Mick's were (I must tell you readers I am not a person who would break security locks off) so the devilment in me drove me on to poach these rabbits.

I went home early that morning but I was back early evening that same day, I needed a bit of daylight so that I could see to drop the boxes. I keep saying the word 'drop' the boxes, this is a slang word meaning activating the tippler lid so that it is set to catch rabbits. So I sneak along this woodland side dropping all the rabbit boxes as I go. I get a bit carried away with myself and by the time I have finished I have dropped twenty rabbit boxes.

It is by now coming into deep dusk of the evening. I stand at the wood edge thinking to myself, I have dropped too many boxes, I will have too many rabbits to carry when I empty them. But it's too late now, the boxes are dropped. By now I have been at the wood edge for quite a while pondering about the amount of rabbits I am going to catch.

It's by now the black of the night and as I stand there my ears prick up. I hear a faint thud and a faint clatter, that's a rabbit is that, dropping into the rabbit box which I am stood near on by. So the boxes are catching rabbits already. As I walk away to leave the rabbits to it, my ears prick up again. I hear a slight thud and a slight clatter, that's a second rabbit dropping into the rabbit box, and off I carry on and go home.

The time of year is deep winter time, the dark nights are long and drawn out so it gives me plenty of time to work under darkness. I while a few hours away at home giving the rabbit boxes plenty of time to do there work and then off I go again back to these rabbit boxes.

I have given myself plenty of time to work under the cover of darkness to empty all the twenty boxes, it will be three hours before it breaks daylight. I have driven my Land Rover purposely as near as I dare to these rabbit boxes just in case I have caught too many rabbits to carry. I hide my Land Rover under the trees and out of sight of any roving eye that may be around and I go to my first rabbit box. I hear a faint thumping coming from within the box as I climb over the rabbit netting fence and I slowly lift up the trip lid. I don't want any rabbits jumping out and escaping do I.

I peer through the dim gloom of the night, it's too dark inside the box to see anything. I put my hand inside and when my arm is only halfway down the box I touch something furry. I grab it, pull it out and hold it up in front of my eyes. It's a big fat rabbit I see. I quickly break its neck and throw it on to the grass meadow at the other side of the rabbit netting fence line.

Into the box I put my hand again and out comes another big fat rabbit. I put my hand in and out of the box and each time I dip my hand in I come out with a big fat rabbit. I am by now groping my hand deep within the box. I feel around the bottom and out comes my last rabbit and over the fence it goes with a broken neck to join the rest of the rabbits that have come out of the box.

I now have to fasten this box off just the same way as I found it. It had a big stone on the trip lid which stopped the finely balanced lid working. My work at this rabbit box is now over and there's now not a trace of me ever being here at all.

I climb back over the rabbit netting fence line and gather all my rabbits back together. I count fifteen, not a bad catch I do think. These rabbit boxes here are only small compared with most rabbit boxes I have seen. Usually the boxes are big enough to hold well over a hundred rabbits. These boxes here only hold about fifty rabbits when full.

I now leave these rabbits here to cool in the cold chill of the night, I will be back for them a little later. I carry on along the rabbit netting fence line emptying and fastening off the rabbit boxes as I go. I am getting six to fifteen rabbits out of each box and by the time I reach my last rabbit box, which is the twentieth rabbit box, I am running out of time. I look up into the sky, it's beginning to break daylight.

As I predicted, I have caught far too many rabbits to carry so off I race to get my Land Rover. I start her up not daring to put on the headlights for fear of being seen by any roving eyes that may be around. I back my Land Rover from out of the trees it's been hidden under and I can now see where I am driving. The sky is lighting up fast, I have to hurry. I travel along a hedge side which brings me to a gateway which leads me into the grass meadow to where my bag of rabbits are and I stop my Land Rover with the handbrake. If I put my foot on the foot brake pedal my red rear brake lights will come on and I don't want that do I. Everybody on the estate will see me then, that is if there is anyone around to see me.

I get out and close the gate behind me and I now drive on to my first lot of rabbits and pull up the Land Rover with the handbrake. I quickly pile the rabbits into the back of my Land Rover and off I do go on to my next pile of rabbits. And on and on I do go until I pile my last lot of rabbits into my Land Rover. The rabbits are by now piled sky high in the back of my Land Rover. I couldn't have got any more in if I had wanted to. Wow!

By now it's broken daylight and I am still on the estate. If I get caught now I will be hung, drawn and quartered. I race off out of the grass meadow which takes me through another gateway which leads me on to a private, dirt coach road which goes through a woodland. I now come to the dangerous bit. The coach road now passes on by the gamekeeper's cottage which is set back a little in the woodland. I head on with my fingers crossed for luck hoping and wishing the keeper isn't about as I pass on by his cottage.

As I pass I look into his yard. I don't see the keeper, thank my lucky stars, but I do see his dogs and they see me. They are now racing and barking behind my Land Rover so I put my foot down and get the hell away from there.

I am now passing on by a private hospital which borders on to the estate. I see nurses coming on to their early morning shift and the nurses see me. They see all the rabbits stacked high through the back windows of my Land Rover. The nurses are now putting up their hands to me in acknowledgement, they must think I am a bloody gamekeeper.

I head on and get the hell away from there and home I do go. When I get there, which is a village not far away, I look at my night's bag of rabbits. Phew, what a bag of rabbits they are too. I remember very clearly I counted 257 rabbits, not a bad night's work I do think. And where I took the rabbits from there's not a trace of me ever being there at all.

The gamekeeper will now go along his row of rabbit boxes and all he will see is there is no rabbits there at all. The gamekeeper should be more vigilant in looking after his game, not laid snoring and farting in bed.

Over the following two days I go out touting my rabbits everywhere. Nearly every household in my village has a couple of rabbits from me for their dinner, even the local pub puts them on the menu. I tout them around all the surrounding butchers' shops and they hang them on long game rails outside their shops. I tout my rabbits around all the local working men's clubs and pubs and by the time I have finished all my rabbits have gone.

I remember on the third day after catching this fine bag of rabbits I took a stroll through my village. Everyone I passed on by they were all talking about me and pointing their finger. I heard gossip, there was strong rumours going around my village about the Lord of the Manor on our local gamekeeper's estate, someone had poached all his rabbits. I passed the local village shop, there were two women stood there chinwagging and gossiping. They saw me passing them by, they were both pointing their fingers at me and saying, "That's him, it's Doug who has poached the Lord's rabbits."

I say in an innocent manner, "But it is not I."

One woman replies, "I have two of your rabbits in the oven now, roasting."

The other woman looks amazed, she says, "I have two of his rabbits in my oven too."

I say, "But, but…"

Both women now say together, "Never mind 'but, but', it is you Doug, you always have been a bugger for poaching rabbits."

I carry on passing the two gossiping women by and leave them to enjoy their poached rabbit stew dinners. I took heed from all the gossip I hear, I never went back on to that Lord of the Manor's estate for more than twelve months or more. I think, the keeper may be on the prowl. And then one early morning I decided to go back on to the estate, now that all the dust had settled.

I went back to that long row of twenty rabbit boxes and I looked and I saw rabbits, rabbits everywhere. They were all running from the grass meadow and passing through the wooden tunnels which took them over the rabbit boxes and into the safety of the woodland.

The rabbits have bred on since I was last here. I go over to have a look at the first rabbit box and I don't believe what I see. Someone has put a security lock on to stop the rabbit box working. I think, well what have they done that for then? I look at all the other rabbit boxes and they are all the same, they are all locked off with security locks.

Now as you readers know I will not break off locks, it is not my nature, but I do get a bit of devilment inside myself. I must have some of these rabbits I have just seen running in off the meadow. I have another trick up my sleeve and this is how I went about to poach some of these rabbits.

I set off from my home at midnight, I am all prepared and ready for the kill. I go on along by the private hospital and I see all is at peace as I peer across and see the lights dimly lit. I head on past the hospital which takes me through the main gates which is the entrance to the Lord of the Manor's estate.

I carry on up the dirt coach road which winds its way through the woodlands. I am now passing on by the gamekeeper's cottage which is set back in the woodlands a little. I peer through the darkness of the night and see the cottage all in darkness. Again the gamekeeper is laid snoring and farting in bed. When will he ever learn, he should be looking after his game. There could be poachers everywhere around this neck of the woodlands tonight.

I leave the gamekeeper to it and him peacefully tucked up in bed. I continue on up the coach road which brings me to the gate that leads into the grass meadow. This is where all the rabbits are, they will be feeding hard way out across the meadow, a long way from the rabbit boxes.

The wind is blowing hard across the meadow, blowing from the rabbits and on to me, and will now blow my human scent away from them. I head across to the first rabbit box, this time I am going to catch the rabbits in the wooden tunnels.

These wooden tunnels are about just short of three feet long and they are about five inches square, which is just about the right size for a rabbit to pass through them. I have brought with me twenty purse nets and I am going to use one purse net on each wooden tunnel, which is twenty wooden tunnels in all.

I open up one purse net and place it or set it over the end of the tunnel. This is all done on the grass meadow side of the tunnel. I now tie the anchor peg of the purse net to the rabbit netting fence line.

My intentions are to drive the rabbits from their feeding grounds which is out across the meadow. The rabbits will bolt to safety by them passing through the wooden tunnel which will take them through the rabbit netting fence line and on to the safety of their warrens in the woodland. But not this time. I have got the wooden tunnel covered by a purse net.

The fleeing, bolting rabbits will now race through the tunnel and the first rabbit in will hit the purse net. The rabbit will force itself through the tunnel but the purse net will clasp around the rabbit. I have made the length of the anchor line on the purse net just long enough so that it holds the netted rabbit at the far end of the tunnel. The netted rabbit now cannot move, it's stuck in the far end of the tunnel and the tunnel is now blocked off by the netted rabbit.

Its mate now comes racing along behind it and into the tunnel it goes, but it can't get through, its mate is blocking the tunnel. Now there's another rabbit bolting into the tunnel and it cannot get through either. Its mates in front are blocking the tunnel. The wooden tunnel is now full with all three rabbits.

They can hear a mad crazy man out on the grass meadow, that's me the rabbits hear. It feels dark and safe inside of the wooden tunnel where the rabbits lay, so they lay still and out of sight while the mad crazy man has gone.

So that's how I am going to catch some of these rabbits tonight. I now go along all the full row of rabbit boxes setting a purse net on the end of each wooden tunnel, which is twenty tunnels in all. It's all done in the silence and darkness of the windy night.

There, I am now ready for the kill. I have brought with me a long length of rope, it's the rope which I use when I am long-netting rabbits at night. I tie my rope to the rabbit netting fence line which is well to one side of the last rabbit box and off I go with my rope in hand. As I go I am dropping my rope off a few links at a time and I keep myself close up by the side of the hedgerow.

I now have my rope fully stretched out and stretching way back to the rabbit netting fence line. By now I am at the other side of the rabbits which were feeding hard on the grass meadow, but now the rabbits have picked up my human scent. Now the strong wind is blowing from behind me and straight across the rabbits and by now the rabbits are panic-stricken with fear. They set off hell for leather back across the meadow, they all want to be back into the safety of their warrens. But not this time, as you readers know.

I start whipping and lashing the rope across the meadow and then dragging the rope tight to the ground across the grass. There will be panic-stricken rabbits laid tight squat in the grass. One touch with my rope across its body and the rabbit will be up like a shot and bolting across the meadow and on to the safety of the warrens. But, alas, not tonight he won't. I whip and lash and drag my rope tight to the ground right across the meadow.

By now I have got myself back to the rabbit netting fence line. I pull and drag my rope until it's stretched tight up to the full row of rabbit boxes. All the rabbits make one final effort to escape from the mad crazy man out on their feeding grounds and into the wooden tunnels they do go. And off I go after them.

I come to my first wooden tunnel, I reach my hand in and, surprise, surprise, I pull out a big fat rabbit. I quickly break its neck and throw it on to the meadow. I now grope my hand back into the tunnel. This time I have to grope my hand further in and again, surprise, surprise, I pull out another big fat rabbit. I quickly break its neck and throw it with its mate on to the meadow. Again I grope my hand into the wooden tunnel. This time I have to grope my arm deep inside and, surprise, surprise, I touch another rabbit. I grab it and pull it out. The rabbit's all balled up in a purse net. Not for long it isn't. I quickly break its neck, take it out of the purse net and throw the rabbit to its dead mates out on the meadow.

This wooden tunnel is now empty of all its rabbits. I untie my purse net from the fence line and quickly put the net back into my pocket and off I race on to the next wooden tunnel.

I continue on and go along all the wooden tunnels taking and killing three rabbits from each tunnel. By now I am out of puff, I have raced about that much, and I stand and have a breather. I don't believe what I see, I look up into the sky and I see it's breaking daylight. Time does fly by when you're having fun. Off I race again, I have to get the hell off this estate before it breaks full daylight otherwise I am for the chop.

I now need something to carry my rabbits on, this time I haven't brought my Land Rover with me. I quickly jump over the rabbit netting fence line and into the woodland I do go. I see two long thin branches growing on a tree and I cut them off with my penknife at just the right length. Where I cut the branches from I smear the newly cut wood with loose soil from the woodland floor. I don't want to leave any tell-tale sign I have been around.

I now smooth off the small branches leaving me with two good straight poles and off back to my rabbits I do race. I now have to quickly leg my rabbits. I do this by making a slit at the back of the guider with my knife on the rabbit's back leg. I now push the other back leg through the slit and now the two back legs are locked together. I now slot the rabbit on to my pole.

I go along the rabbit netting fence line gathering my rabbits together as I go. I leg them and hang them and by the time I have finished I have two poles full of hung rabbits. Phew! I now have a sweat on with hurrying, but I can't stop for a breather yet. I am out on the open grass meadow, I am open to view and if there are any estate workers around I will be seen for sure.

I head on and reach the gate that takes me out of the grass meadow, there I can now have a breather. I am now in the cover of the woodland. As I wipe the sweat from my brow I cast my eyes over my rabbits, what a fine bag of rabbits they look too. I count them. I count twenty couples, ten couples on each pole, not a bad night's rabbiting I do think.

I now throw a pole of rabbits over each shoulder, get them all balanced up and off through the woodland I do go. I come to the dirt coach road which leads down through the woodland and past the gamekeeper's cottage. I hesitate and ponder. I think to myself, if that gamekeeper has now got himself up out of bed and he sees me walking past the front of his cottage with two poles full of his rabbits, he's not going to take very kindly to that is he?

So I head on a different way which takes me through the woodland and around the back of the gamekeeper's cottage. As I am passing by his cottage I see the gamekeeper in his backyard. I see he's doing something so I keep myself at the back of a tree and watch him. He's making rabbit snares. I have a good idea where he will be setting these snares. I will keep a close eye on him, I will have some of his snared rabbits.

I now head away feeling my feet down on to the woodland floor as I go so as not to break any hidden branches under my feet. One crack of a breaking branch now and the gamekeeper will have me for sure. I head on down through the woodland which brings me to the main entrance to the estate. I walked straight through these entrance gates at midnight last night, but not this time. It's now daylight, everyone could see me now, and I don't want that do I, not with all these rabbits on my shoulders. So I head on through the cover of the woodlands.

I am now passing on by the private hospital, the woodland I am in borders on to the large hospital lawns. I look across the lawn and see a woman over by the hospital buildings. She's seen me, she's watching me, she's now waving her hand and beckoning me over to her. She's dressed in some sort of uniform, she looks like a cook to me. I go over across the lawn towards her to see what she wants. She may be a fair maiden in distress.

She keeps on beckoning me to follow her and she beckons me on into the hospital building. It's the kitchen she has beckoned me into. She's now feeling at my rabbits on my poles and she's now telling me to lay a pole full of my rabbits on to the kitchen floor. She's now pressing her cupped hand into my hand, it's a handful of money she's giving me.

She says, "These will put some fat on to my patients' ribcages." She's now telling me to be on my way before the gamekeeper catches me. So I do as she bids and off home I go.

I hope you readers enjoyed my little stories on poaching the rabbit boxes. So now you readers know the capabilities and the workings of the rabbit boxes.

So by now I have been at home waiting while the long summer passed on by and it is by now the month of September and about the year of 1977.

I now have to go back up to the Laird's vast rabbit-infested estate in the Grampian Mountains up in the Highlands of Scotland. The twenty rabbit boxes which I installed on the Laird's estate way back in the spring of this year are now all ready for me to convince the Laird how well the rabbit box catches rabbits. Now let's get down to some serious business of rabbit catching.

It's midday when me and my rabbiting bitch Pup arrive up at the Laird's estate. I straightaway go on to drop my twenty rabbit boxes. I go first to my ten rabbit boxes that surround the full perimeter of the Laird's castle grounds. I leave Pup in the Land

Rover. I don't want the rabbits picking up her dog scent, it just may put the rabbits off of using their rabbit boxes tonight.

As I approach my first rabbit box, I am full of eagerness and optimism of what I may find. From now where I stand, which is in front of my rabbit box, I peer over the rabbit netting fence line which I installed in the spring of only this year. What I see in the fir tree woodland I do not believe. I see rabbits, rabbits everywhere I look on and around their massive warrens. They have bred completely out of control just as I expected.

As I peer on to the woodland floor what I see, I do not believe. I see well-used main rabbit runs leading from the massive warrens and all leading to this rabbit box where I stand. I look on the grass meadow where I stand and what I see I do not believe. I see well-used main rabbit runs leading from the wooden tunnel and leading way out across the grass meadow. By the looks of it, every rabbit in this vicinity is passing through the wooden tunnel, which passes through the new rabbit netting fence line, which passes over the rabbit box, which is sunk into the ground at ground level.

I get a serious look on my face. I know that just in this vicinity alone there are hundreds of rabbits here and I know this rabbit box where I stand will only hold one hundred rabbits when full. There's a sparkle comes into my eyes, leaving me thinking to myself, let me get at these rabbits! I bend down and drop the box, and as you readers know by now 'drop the box' means activating the finely balanced lid to catch rabbits. My rabbit box is now dropped and is now all ready for the onslaught of rabbits tonight.

As it gets late in the afternoon today, the rabbits will leave their massive warrens and head off down their runs heading for their feeding grounds which is the grass meadow. They will maybe stop in front of the wooden tunnel which they are all accustomed to by now.

They will have a good sit high on their arses having a good look to see if there is any danger out on the grass meadow. A rabbit will hop into the wooden tunnel and with its second hop its front feet land on the finely balanced trip lid. This time the trip lid is not fastened off, so with the weight of the rabbit the trip lid gives way and rabbit goes falling below. The trip lid will make a slight sound as it closes back into its normal natural position, all because it's all finely balanced.

The trip lid is now all ready and waiting for the next rabbit into the wooden tunnel. The rabbit that has just fallen into the box below makes a slight thud as it hits the bottom of the box. The other rabbits outside hear this slight thud and one will look down the wooden tunnel and think to himself, well where's my mate gone, he was in the wooden tunnel a second or two since. So the rabbit goes to investigate. All the rabbits outside hear another slight thud and now their mate has disappeared. As the afternoon goes on into the late evening the rabbits outside are getting thinner and thinner in multitudes until there are no rabbits left. They have all gone to join their mates inside the large rabbit box below.

So now that rabbit box is dropped and ready for the onslaught of rabbits this evening, I now move on and drop the rest of the rabbit boxes that surround the full perimeter of the Laird's castle grounds which is ten rabbit boxes in all. And every rabbit box I went to was just the same as the first rabbit box, the rabbits were in their multitudes. I now leave the vicinity of the Laird's castle grounds and head on to my other ten rabbit boxes which I installed on the deer fence line.

When I arrive there, I do not believe what I see. There's rabbits, rabbits, rabbits everywhere I look. These rabbits have bred themselves out of control, they are in plague proportions. They have certainly gone forth and multiplied since I was last here. And all these rabbits are all using the wooden tunnels which go through the deer netting fence line and over the rabbit boxes which are sunk to ground level.

I carry on and drop all ten rabbit boxes and leave the rabbits to it. I now head on and go back to Bob's cottage, the Hunter's Lodge. When I arrive there, I telephone the Laird on Bob's telephone. I tell the Laird that I have arrived back up on to his estate safely and that I have dropped all the rabbit boxes.

"What, all twenty of them?" says the Laird. He seems overjoyed at what I tell him and says he is looking forward to seeing how well the rabbit boxes catch rabbits. I arrange to meet the Laird up at his castle the following morning.

I remember that evening very clearly as I impatiently waited in Bob's cottage. I know, and you readers also know, but the Laird doesn't know how well the rabbit boxes catch rabbits. I could not sleep that night at Bob's cottage, I tossed and turned in bed thinking about all the rabbits that will now be dropping into my rabbit boxes.

Morning finally arrived. I am excited to be off and when I arrive at the castle the Laird is there all ready and waiting for me to arrive. I think the Laird is more excited than me and he straightaway jumps into my Land Rover.

I tell the Laird, "I think we may have caught too many rabbits for them all to go in my Land Rover. It's best if you take your smart four-wheel drive Range Rover also."

Off the Laird goes across his forecourt to get his vehicle and he looks full of spring and bounce as he goes. He looks as happy as a pup with two tails. The Laird now falls in behind me in his Range Rover and off we go.

As we go down the woodland side which takes us along the quite newly installed rabbit netting fence line, which is a rabbit proof barrier which surrounds the entire perimeter of the Laird's castle grounds, me and the Laird stop and park up our vehicles. We now set off on foot and as we go around a bend in the woodland and towards the first rabbit box, the Laird is aghast at what he sees. We see scores and scores of rabbits running in off the meadow. All the rabbits bolt and head for the wooden tunnel which leads them to the safety of their massive warrens inside the fir tree plantation.

I see the rabbits hesitate before entering the wooden tunnel and I know what they are hesitating for. I look at the Laird and he has a dismayed frown look on his face. He says, "The rabbit boxes do not work Doug, look at all the rabbits running over the rabbit boxes."

I say, "Don't you be too sure."

We are now stood in front of the rabbit box and I leave the Laird stood there on the meadow side of the fence line. I climb over the fence to get to the rabbit box which is sunk into ground level. I oh so carefully lift up the trip lid just enough for me to see into the box, and what I see is what I expected. The rabbit box is brimming full right to the top with rabbits. What has happened is that with the box being so full the rabbits have come right up to just underneath the trip lid. This has stopped the trip lid working and allowed the other rabbits to pass over safely.

I slip my hand into the box and pull out a rabbit, closing the lid behind me. I quickly break the rabbit's neck and throw it over the fence to the Laird. The Laird jumps back, aghast at seeing the rabbit, and says, "Oh, we have caught one rabbit then."

I oh so carefully lift up the trip lid again, I don't want the rabbits jumping out of the box and escaping, do I. I pull out another rabbit, break its neck and throw it to the Laird. Now the Laird has half a smile on his face. I keep pulling rabbits out of the box and breaking their necks and throwing them over the fence linc to the Laird. I see the Laird is keeping all the rabbits I throw neat and tidy in rows as I throw them.

I now see the Laird has a big smile on his face. As I am nearing the bottom of the box, I pull out a rabbit with its ears all chewed off. I know what has done that. I grope my hand around the bottom of the box, I touch something prickly, I grab its prickles with the tips of my thumb and fingers and pull out a hedgehog. Now that the new fence line is erected the wooden tunnel is now the main highway to get through the fence and there's many creatures now use this wooden tunnel besides rabbits. There's hedgehogs, stoats, weasels, even pheasants and they all fall into the box below when the trip lid is set to catch rabbits.

This rabbit box is now empty of all its rabbits and I now fasten the trip lid 'off' to stop it working. All the rabbits that have passed over the box through the night, will now be allowed to pass over the box again safely. That is until I come back again and drop the box to activate the trip lid. Eventually this rabbit box will catch every single rabbit in this vicinity.

I now climb back over the fence line to the Laird who is busying himself with all the rabbits on the grass meadow. He has them all neatly laid out in long rows and he says, "A 102 rabbits, phew!" Now the Laird has a smile so big on his face it must have stretched from ear to lug.

We leave the rabbits to cool off in the cold morning chill of September. There's an old saying used by rabbit catchers which goes, 'you only eat a rabbit when there is a R in the month'. September, October, November, December, January February, March and April all have an R in the month which are all non-breeding months of the rabbit. May, June, July and August are all the breeding months of the rabbit.

So me and the Laird now move on to the next rabbit box which is further along the woodland side. That rabbit box too was just as full as the first rabbit box. And on and on me and the Laird went emptying rabbit box after rabbit box until we empty and fasten off rabbit box number ten. All the rabbit boxes are now empty and all fastened off. I will be back at a later date to catch all these rabbits once and for all.

I now look at the Laird and he now has a great big smile on his face. I say to him, "That's a fine big bag of rabbits we have caught."

The Laird has been counting them as we have been catching

them. "1020 rabbits, phew!" says the Laird, as he wipes the sweat from his forehead with the sleeve of his fine tweed jacket.

Me and the Laird now leave all these rabbits here to cool off on the grass meadow and off we head to our other ten rabbit boxes on the deer netting fence line. As we head down the woodland and on towards the first rabbit box we see hoards of rabbits running in off the grass meadow. They are all queuing up to go through the wooden tunnel to reach their massive warrens inside the woodland. And again every rabbit box was full to the top with rabbits which stopped the tippler lids working. We empty the rabbit boxes of their rabbits and fasten off all the trip lids.

I have seen multitudes of rabbits here this morning all of which have escaped dropping into the rabbit boxes through the night. But I will be back at a later date to catch the rabbits altogether. I say to the Laird, "That's another fine big bag of rabbits we have caught."

The Laird has been counting them as we have been catching them. "1038 rabbits, phew!" says the Laird, as he again wipes the sweat from his forehead with the sleeve of his fine jacket. I now see the Laird doing calculations up in his head. "2058 rabbits we have caught altogether, phew!" says the Laird.

I now ask the Laird what he thinks about how well the rabbit boxes catch rabbits and these are the exact words I recall the Laird saying, "These rabbit boxes Doug, they catch the rabbits to the most upper part of excellence. I now want you to install rabbit boxes over the my entire estate. I want you, Doug, to rid my estate of all rabbits. I will get contractors in to install all the rabbit boxes and I will put you, Doug, solely in charge of the whole operation."

Those words I heard from the Laird were music to my ears. As you readers know by now, the Laird's vast estate is twenty miles wide and thirty miles long and all the low-lying glens throughout the whole of the estate are just one big mass of out-of-control, marauding rabbits. The Laird has given me one hell of a massive job, but that's just what I did.

Now back to these rabbits here that we have just caught in the twenty rabbit boxes, all 2058 of them. We leave these rabbits here to cool off on the grass meadow and me and the Laird now head on back down to the castle grounds. The Laird brings his smart Range Rover and we start loading up the rabbits. We throw rabbits after rabbits into his vehicle until the rabbits are piled nearly up to the roof.

The Laird says, "Stop, stop, the bloody front wheels are lifting up off the ground." He then says, "My motor can't carry any more."

I see his suspension springs are flattened out with the weight as the Laird heads off now with his load of rabbits. I tell the Laird to drop them off in Bob's courtyard against the game larder. I see the Laird's Range Rover's front wheels lifting and rising from the ground as he goes. I put a load of rabbits into my Land Rover and head the same way the Laird went.

When I arrive at Bob's courtyard, I see the Laird has gone but I do see Bob stood there scratching his head. He's looking at the great pile of rabbits the Laird's just dropped off. Now Bob sees my great pile of rabbits in my Land Rover and he says, "Don't be leaving all these rabbits here Doug. They want taking up to the duck flight pond and paunching the rabbits' guts to the ducks and geese."

I say to Bob, "I have a better idea, you paunch the rabbits and take the rabbits' guts up to duck flight pond later." I unload all my rabbits and throw them by the side of the Laird's pile of rabbits. As I leave to bring more rabbits in I see Bob still there scratching his head. Now Bob is looking at an even greater pile of rabbits.

It takes me many loads of rabbits to get them all from the grass meadows and back to Bob's courtyard and by the time I have gathered them all in they are piled high around Bob. I now give Bob a helping hand to paunch the rabbits. We throw the guts into fertilizer bags and by the time we have finished paunching we have many fertilizer bags full with rabbits' guts. We now gather up the rabbits and start hanging them in the game larder. We hang and hang until we can hang no more. The game larder is now bursting at the seams with hung rabbits but there's hundreds of rabbits still left on the courtyard floor. We have to leave the rabbits there. I lay them out nice and tidily, I will load them up in the morning into my Land Rover and trailer. I am homeward bound next morning.

Me and Bob have now finished paunching, gutting and hanging rabbits and we now go off into Bob's cottage. Bob's just about to use his telephone but I beat him to it. I now telephone the carpenter down in the local village and I tell him what the Laird has told me. The Laird wants thousands of rabbit boxes making and the carpenter is fair bubbling over the telephone. He tells me he will get in more carpenters to help him. I tell the carpenter to charge all the expenses to the Laird and that's that job done. The rabbit boxes for the Laird's entire estate are now being made.

I was off to bed early that evening at Bob's cottage and was up early the following morning. I am now homeward bound today and I get myself to thinking, I have too many rabbits to take home with me. So I decide to ask the gamedealer if he will take some of them. That's the gamedealer who takes Bob's game off the Laird's estate. I see Bob going to use his telephone but I am the nearest and I beat him to it. I ring and ask the gamedealer and he wants to know if they are fresh. "As fresh as the morning," I tell him. He now wants to know how they have been killed, he doesn't want shot up rabbits. I tell him, "They have all been killed with a broken neck." He now says he can't come and pick up just a few rabbits. I tell him there is about thirteen hundred rabbits. He's now coming straightaway to pick up the rabbits. And on that Bob takes the telephone from me and I now go out into the courtyard to load up my rabbits.

As you readers know I have all the rabbit carrying features in the back of my Land Rover and in my trailer. The three decks in the back of my Land Rover, I pile rabbits on them sky high. The poles in the roof in the back of my Land Rover, I hang rabbits after rabbits on these poles until there's no more room to hang anymore rabbits.

I now hitch my trailer on to the back of my Land Rover. As you readers know I have poles fitted in there also. I hang rabbits after rabbits on to these poles until there's no more room to hang any more rabbits.

I now look at the rabbits that are still left unloaded and I think to myself, the suspension springs on my Land Rover don't look too flat yet, maybe I can get just a few more rabbits in somewhere. I see Pup sat on the passenger seat at the front and I think, there's more room there. So I call Pup out of the Land Rover and start loading rabbits on to her seat. I also fill up the compartment where the passenger puts their feet. I now put Pup back in the Land Rover and up she jumps and sits on the top of the rabbits that are now upon her seat.

I now look at the rabbits that are still left unloaded. Surely, I think, I can get a few more rabbits in somewhere. I look at Pup sat on top of the rabbits and I see a gap between the top of Pup's head and the roof of the Land Rover. I can get more rabbits in there, so I call Pup back out of the Land Rover and pile more rabbits on top of where Pup was sat. I now put Pup back in the Land Rover and up she struggles on to the top of the rabbits that are upon her seat.

Pup's head is now touching the roof of the Land Rover.

My Land Rover is now full to the maximum and I see the trailer is bulging out with rabbits too. That's it, I am now fully loaded and not a spare space to put another rabbit.

I now see the gamedealer approaching with his wagon and I back him up to the rabbits that are still laying on the floor just outside the game larder. The gamedealer sees just a few rabbits laying there and is not happy at what he sees. He says, "I can't come up here just for a few rabbits like them."

I now open up the game larder door and what the gamedealer sees makes his eyes nearly pop out. Now the gamedealer's happy, he now has a smile on his face that stretches from ear to lug. I pass the rabbits to him as he hangs up the rabbits in a refrigerated wagon. Every time he hangs the rabbits he presses a button inside the wagon and he tells me it's a counter button which is tallying up the rabbits as he hangs them in the wagon.

The gamedealer now wants to know how I caught this big fine bag of rabbits and I tell him in rabbit boxes. He says, "What are they then?"

I now explain them to him and tell him we are installing the rabbit boxes over the whole of the Laird's estate. The gamedealer now appears impressed at what I tell him and he says, "You have a hell of a mammoth job clearing up all the rabbits that the Laird has on his vast estate."

I ask the gamedealer where he is taking these rabbits to and he says, "Glasgow meat market."

I ask him, "Will they fetch a fair price?"

The gamedealer says, "Wait and see, I will send you a cheque by post."

My rabbits are now all loaded up into the gamedealer's refrigerated wagon. He looks at the counter button he has been pressing and he says, "1308 rabbits." And on that the gamedealer closes up his wagon doors and off he goes.

I now see Bob looking into my Land Rover. He has a rare grin on his face and he says, "You will never make it home with all them rabbits on board Doug."

I now bid Bob farewell and tell him I will be straight back up to install all the new rabbit boxes once I have sold all these rabbits back home. And homeward bound me and Pup do go.

As you readers know by now, I have to climb the hill that leads from Bob's cottage which takes me out of the glen. I know the last time I climbed this hill I had just over 500 rabbits loaded in the Land Rover and trailer and my Land Rover only just made it up the hill. This time I have even more rabbits loaded in my Land Rover and trailer. What was the gamedealer's calculations? He's taken 1308 rabbits, I originally caught 2058 rabbits in the rabbit boxes, so that means I have 750 rabbits loaded into my Land Rover and trailer. "Wow! Phew!" I hear my Land Rover say.

I remember this day very clearly as though it only happened yesterday, but it was in the month of September of the year of about 1977.

I now head away from Bob's cottage. I look at Pup sat up on the top of the great pile of rabbits upon her passenger seat. Pup looks down at me. She doesn't look too happy to me. Pup likes to sit and look out of the window at rabbits in the fields as we are passing them by in the Land Rover.

I now have to get my Land Rover up that hill in front of me which takes me out of the glen. The track is flat for about three hundred yards before it comes to the hill. I decide to take a fast run up the flat track and hopefully my speed will get me up the hill. So here goes me and Pup at that hill. I rev my Land Rover engine to warm it up to the task ahead. I press the yellow button down in the cab which puts my Land Rover into four-wheel drive. It will give it more traction on the track. I put my Land Rover into second gear and off me and Pup go.

I put my foot down on the accelerator, I am now racing on at speed and I put my Land Rover into third gear. I am now racing even faster and my Land Rover is bouncing about as I hit potholes in the track. I look up at Pup and every time I hit a pothole Pup is bouncing and hitting her head on the roof of the Land Rover. I have to smile at her but I can see Pup doesn't think it's very funny.

My Land Rover now racing on at top speed in third gear and I now push her into fourth gear and press the accelerator flat to the board. My Land Rover is now racing on at top speed as we are now upon the hill.

Up the hill my Land Rover races. Oh no she doesn't, and I have to quickly drop her down into third gear and give her full throttle. She moans and groans and slows down rapidly. I quickly drop her down into second gear and give her full throttle again but she's getting slower and slower as she struggles up the hill. I quickly drop her into first gear and give her full throttle again, but alas she slows and slows until she grinds to a stop. Now me and

Pup are neither up the hill nor down the hill, we are stuck halfway in the middle of the bloody hill.

I look in my wing mirror and I see Bob coming up the hill in his Land Rover. He has a big smile on his face and he says, "I told you that you wouldn't get home with all them rabbits on board." Now Bob's hitching a tow rope between our two Land Rovers and he's going to tow me up the hill.

I now pull the red lever back in my cab, this now puts my Land Rover into low gearbox. I put my Land Rover into first gear, this is the low box crawler gear. Bob now starts pulling with his Land Rover and off we go moving up the hill oh so slowly. My Land Rover is coughing and spluttering and I see blue smoke coming out of the exhaust pipe. Bob keeps on pulling and I keep on driving my Land Rover hard and we eventually reach the top of the hill. I thank Bob for his kind gesture and again I bid Bob farewell, and off me and Pup head homeward bound.

Everything went champion after that. The main Highland roads were quite flat with no hills of significance to climb and then on to the motorway which is all flat.

The Land Rover's engine is purring along as me and Pup go along. I am sure I am leaving a groove in the road, I have been up and down it so many times. But then when we get about forty miles away from home the Land Rover starts struggling, and it starts slowing down. I look at the oil pressure gauge on the dashboard, that looks fine. Then to my shock horror, when I look at the water temperature gauge the needle is on red hot and by now the Land Rover engine is trying to cut out.

I quickly pull on to the motorway's hard shoulder and the engine stops on its own. I see a cloud of steam come from underneath the bonnet. I look under the front of the Land Rover and I see bubbling, red hot water running onto the road. I let the engine cool off for ten minutes and then take the radiator cap off. I see it's bone dry of water and I now have to get the breakdown service to assist me. I walk to the SOS box to telephone for help, the telephone doesn't work. It's the first time I have ever used an SOS telephone in my life, and it doesn't bloody work.

I have to find water for the radiator from somewhere. I manage to restart my Land Rover engine and I now go very slowly along the hard shoulder looking for water. I see the hard shoulder leaving the motorway at a main exit. The exit road runs up a hill to a roundabout and halfway up the hill my Land Rover can't pull all the weight with rabbits and cuts out again. I look across and down into a grass meadow and I see a pond, so off I go to get some water. I pour it into the radiator but the water spurts out of the bottom of the radiator as fast as I am pouring it in at the top. The radiator is bust.

With all these rabbits on board, I have to get help from somewhere, but I am out in the middle of nowhere. As I stand on this hill I can see a woodland down in the bottom of a valley and at the far side of the woodland I can see a farmyard. I have to go to that farmhouse and telephone for help. So off across the grass meadow as I drop down the valley heading towards the woodland below, I see someone crouched down in the meadow below me. This person has got his back to me and as I get closer and closer to him he hasn't seen me coming.

I see he is ferreting a small rabbit burrow. Now I know a poacher when I see one and I know he is poaching. This poacher who I am now upon turns around and sees me and he goes into a mad panic. His ferret has just shown out of a rabbit hole so he grabs it with one hand, grabs hold of four rabbits he has caught with the other hand and he sets off running down into the valley bottom toward the woodland. He is only a young lad in his teens, leaving me thinking, he needn't have run away from me, I wouldn't have shopped him.

The poaching lad made his escape along the woodland side and then disappeared. I carried on my way towards the farm which took me along this woodland side. As I was walking along the wood side I saw the poaching lad again, he was racing back towards me. He still had his ferret in one hand and the four rabbits in his other hand. When the poaching lad saw me again he panicked yet again and disappeared into the cover of the woodland. The poaching lad had no sooner disappeared when I saw another chap come racing down the side of the woodland. I was stood there out in the open watching all this take place.

The racing chap sees me and comes charging over. He has a gamekeeper's suit on and he says to me in a disgruntled voice, "There, I have caught you poaching my rabbits."

I am stood there gobsmacked and dumbstruck for words, but I do come out of my stupor of lost for words and tell the gamekeeper, "I have more rabbits than him."

He asks, "Where?"

I tell him, "In that broken down Land Rover over there."

Now the gamekeeper understands, so now I tell him what I am seeking and now he's directing me over to the farmyard. As I have got a distance from him I hear him shout to me, he says something like, "Watch out for the dog."

When I arrive at the farmyard I see the farmhouse, I head on over. It's very quiet here, there's not a soul to be seen. As I am opening the garden gate I hear a chain rattling behind me. I look around and I see, shock horror, a great big Alsatian dog springing a silent attack on me. As it leaps at me I leap to one side. It's a guard dog but it's now reached the end of its chain and it's now playing holy hell with me. It's barking and growling and spitting blood at me. It's gone off its rocker, it's gone barking mad. I see there's still nobody around so I decide to have a bit of devilment with the mad crazy dog.

I drop my britches down to my knees and turn around baring my arse to the dog. The mad crazy blood-curdling dog now goes to a whimper. Now it doesn't know what to do, it's never seen a bare arse before. I back myself into the dog and now it's doing a runner back towards its kennel. Now it's got itself all brave again and it's now racing back at me barking and growling. It would love to take a big chunk out of my arse, but it dare not. It's in such a dilemma as to what to do. It's causing such a commotion, barking, yapping, growling, baring its teeth, spitting blood at me when I hear a woman cry out. I look up and see a pretty young woman stood there. I see she is grief-stricken at what she sees. She comes racing over crying out, "Whatever are you doing to my dog?"

The mad, crazy Alsatian now wants cosseting by the pretty young woman, it's had such a terrifying ordeal with me. It's gone berserk in its head and it runs round and round the pretty young woman wrapping its chain around her legs. The whimpering dog now runs off into its kennel and the chain has pulled her short skirt while its neither on nor off.

As I stand there, my britches down to my ankles with my bare arse exposed and the pretty young woman showing plenty of knicker leg with hardly no skirt on at all, we hear a man's voice say, "Hi, hi what's going on here then?"

What could me and the pretty young woman say, we looked a real picture of guilt. I tell the man, "I am in a bit of a dilemma."

He says, "I can see that."

So as I am pulling up my britches and the pretty young woman runs off into the farmhouse pulling up her short skirt as she goes. I explain to the man, who I presume is the farmer, the predicament I am in. And to cut a long story short, I telephone the recovery breakdown service and off I do go out of the farmyard.

I head on back across the grass meadows the same way as I came. There's a thunderstorm brewed up and as I look up I see thick black rain clouds and the heavens open up bombarding me with hailstones that are hitting me like bullets. I race on and get back to my broken down Land Rover saturated. I now have to wait while the recovery truck arrives. I wait and wait, looking at my watch while I wait.

I look up at Pup who has by now made a nest in the top of the pile of rabbits and is now all curled up and looks all fed up with herself. She understands, she knows her Land Rover has broken down. The hailstones are pelting down hitting the Land Rover. Pup gives a big yawn and a bored whine. I look at my watch and me and Pup wait and wait until we are fed up of waiting. We have by now been waiting for more than an hour for the recovery truck to arrive.

I now see a truck coming up behind us as we are parked by the side of the road, the breakdown truck has finally arrived. The driver hangs his hook on to the front of my Land Rover and begins winching it up on to the back of the recovery truck. The winch struggles to pull my Land Rover and trailer and the driver says, "Is your Land Rover full of lead or something, it's taking some pulling."

The driver finally gets my Land Rover and trailer on to the back of his truck. Me and Pup now go sit in the truck cab by the side of the driver and off we go. The driver goes, or attempts to go, up the hill to a roundabout at the top. The truck struggles to climb the hill and the driver says, "Good God, my truck is struggling to pull your Land Rover."

I now tell him the Land Rover and the trailer are full of dead rabbits. The truck does just manage to get up the hill and around the roundabout we go which then leads us back on to the motorway.

As we travel along I get myself to thinking, when I get home the driver will just drop me off leaving me there with my broken down Land Rover, I will then have nothing to deliver my rabbits in. At this point I remember I did not dare to ask the driver to deliver them for me. At this point I remember the driver handed me over some paperwork and said, "It's just a simple form for you to fill in to say that I recovered you safely."

So as we travel along the motorway homeward bound I begin filling in this form. I come to a question which says, 'Our breakdown service guarantees we will recover you safely from the side of the road all within half an hour'. I point this out to the driver and I tell him he was more than an hour coming to my rescue. He says, "Put half an hour otherwise my contract I have with the company may be jeopardized."

I think to myself, I have got the driver beaten here. I tell him, "A favour for a favour."

He says, "What's that then?"

I say, "If I put down you recovered me all within half an hour, you return my favour by delivering my rabbits for me," and the driver agrees.

The place where I want my rabbits delivering is to a game shop owner called Steve. He has a game shop in the centre of a city near on to where I live. For a long time now I have regularly supplied him with forty or fifty rabbits and Steve is always saying he needs more rabbits to satisfy all his customers. Wait while Steve sees all this lot I've got for him, his eyes are going to pop out when he sees them.

Me, Pup and the driver are now in this city and I direct the driver around the city streets which leads us on to a busy street with one-way traffic. This is where Steve's game shop is. It's a main shopping street, always hustling and bustling with shoppers. The driver pulls up his recovery truck right in front of Steve's game shop.

I see Steve the game shop owner inside the shop. He's seen the recovery truck pull up and he's peering between the hares and pheasants which are hung in front of the large shop window. Steve comes out to investigate and sees me. I tell him I have some rabbits and now Steve looks happy. He says, "That's good, I have run out of rabbits."

I climb up on the back of the truck. Steve can see only the rabbits hung up on the rails in the back of my Land Rover, "By, they look a fine bag of rabbits," says Steve.

I unload all the rails that are holding these rabbits, all one hundred and fifty of them, and Steve now has them all laid tidily by the side of the pavement. Steve's now off inside the shop to get some money to pay me and I say, "Hang on a minute, I have more rabbits yet," and I now start unloading the rabbits from the three decks in the back of my Land Rover. By the time Steve has taken one deck he has rabbits laid and strewn all the way along the pavement. Now the shoppers who are passing on by are having difficulty passing by all the rabbits strewn on the pavement.

There's one old lady keeps on tugging at Steve's sleeve and asking him for a rabbit for her dinner. Steve keeps telling the old lady to wait a minute. There's Sue in the shop, it's Steve's wife, she keeps on shouting out, "More rabbits wanted in the shop." It's Steve's job to skin out the rabbits for their customers.

All at the same time, the recovery truck driver is pestering me to hurry up because he is going to get a parking ticket here.

I start unloading the middle deck in the back of my Land Rover. The row of rabbits on the pavement is getting longer and longer as I keep on passing Steve the rabbits. That deck of rabbits now unloaded, I now start unloading my bottom deck of rabbits. The recovery truck driver is now giving Steve a hand to unload the rabbits as I pass them to them. The driver is way up the street laying the rabbits in front of the shop next door and that shop owner is now playing hell with the driver for putting the rabbits there.

The dear old lady is still tugging at Steve's sleeve asking for a rabbit for her dinner. Steve is telling her, "Wait a minute love."

Sue keeps on shouting out from the shop, "More rabbits wanted for the shop."

My bottom deck of rabbits is now unloaded and Steve now has three hundred rabbits strewn and laid all the way along the pavement. Steve sees me closing the back door of my Land Rover and he sighs with relief, saying, "Thank God for that, all the rabbits are now unloaded."

I tell Steve to hang on a minute. I now go to my trailer and lift up the tarpaulin sheet that is covering my trailer full of rabbits. I now start handing Steve more rabbits and he is now handing the rabbits on to the recovery truck driver, who is now laying the rabbits in front of the other shop on the opposite side to Steve's shop. Now that shop owner has come out playing holy hell for laying all the rabbits in front of his shop.

By now it's getting really busy outside here on the pavement. The shoppers that are now passing by cannot get by for all Steve's rabbits strewn all along the pavement. There's cars behind the recovery truck that cannot get by and they are blowing their horns and playing holy hell. I keep on handing down more and more rabbits out of the trailer and Steve keeps on handing them on to the truck driver who is just laying the rabbits anywhere. I see rabbits strewn here, there and everywhere.

Now there's a copper come to the scene, he's now directing all the shopping people around the recovery truck. The driver keeps moaning on he is going to get a parking ticket, but I keep on unloading my rabbits from the trailer. The dear old lady keeps on asking Steve for her rabbit for her dinner. Sue keeps shouting out, "More rabbits needed for the shop."

Now to top all that, I see a traffic warden coming down the street. The recovery truck driver now panics, he's fearing getting a parking ticket and he makes a run for his cab. I keep on piling rabbits out of the trailer and just throwing them anywhere on the pavement. I hear the driver start up his recovery truck and I shout to him, "Wait a minute."

The driver's hung out of the cab window, he's revving his engine and I keep on throwing rabbits after rabbits on to the pavement. The traffic warden is now upon us, I grab my last two handfuls of rabbits out of my trailer and just throw them at Steve. As the truck driver races away I shout to Steve, "I will see you later," and as I look back the truck is racing away. All I see is pandemonium back there with seven hundred and fifty rabbits strewn everywhere in front of Steve's game shop. Phew, what a day.

So that was one memorable day I had delivering rabbits to Steve's game shop. I remember within a few days I got my Land Rover repaired and I went straight back up to the Laird's vast, rabbit-infested estate up in the Grampian Mountains in the Highlands of Scotland.

It is still the month of September in the year of about 1977 when I arrive back at Bob's cottage, the Hunter's Lodge. The Laird has arranged for a contractor to be there to meet me, and I have to show the contractor how and where to position the newly installed rabbit boxes. I take the contractor on down to the Laird's castle and I show him the rabbit boxes which I have recently installed. I tell him the rabbit-proof fence line must go along the edge of the woodland and around the full perimeter of the fir tree forestry plantation, and the wire mesh netting must be sunk in the ground about six inches at the bottom. This now acts as a rabbit-proof barrier.

I now tell the contractor how and where to position the rabbit boxes. The box wants sinking in to ground level and bedding in around the edges, and then the trip lid and the wooden tunnel can then be assembled on the top of the box. I tell him to position the rabbit box on a main rabbit run if possible and there wants to be a rabbit box about every hundred yards around the full perimeter of the forestry plantation. And I tell the contractor this must be done on every forestry plantation on the whole of the Laird's vast estate, which is twenty miles wide and thirty miles long.

The contractor says, "Phew!" I tell the contractor all this wants doing as soon as possible and again the contractor says, "Phew!"

The contractor now tells me, "It's a big job is this Doug, but I have plenty of men contracting for me, we will soon get the job done."

I now leave the contractor to get on with the work and I now go back to Bob's cottage. I have to contact the carpenter down in the local village. As I am going to the telephone Bob is too, but I beat him to it. I ask the carpenter how he is coming on with the rabbit boxes and he tells me he now has many carpenters in making rabbit boxes and that he has many, many rabbit boxes already made. I tell the carpenter about the contractors installing all the rabbit boxes and they will pick them up as fast as he can make them. The carpenter says, "Phew! It's a big job is this Doug. Phew!" the carpenter says again. I now leave everyone to their work.

Do you readers remember the words the Laird said to me not all that long ago? He said he wants me to eradicate all rabbits from his entire estate. I think to myself, miracles I can do straightaway, impossibles take a bit longer.

I know over time the rabbit boxes will eradicate all rabbits out of all the forestry plantations around the whole of the Laird's estate. But in between these forestry plantations, down in the bottoms of the glens, lay vast grass meadows which are the rabbits' feeding grounds. More importantly it's where the Laird's sheep and cattle graze. In these vast grass meadows are massive 'remote' rabbit warrens. There's some of these warrens which have more than a thousand holes to them.

Now I know I cannot catch these rabbits in the rabbit boxes but all these rabbits must be eradicated otherwise they will just breed on, go forth and multiply and then recolonize the whole of the Laird's vast estate. Here is how I went about eradicating these rabbits.

Do you readers remember Buster, he is the dairy cattle herdsman for the Laird? Where these dairy cows are milked twice a day in the milking parlour, this milking parlour has to be scrutinizing clean. All the milking cows will come into the parlour twice a day and each time they come in they will all have a shit. This cow shit is like a thick green soup and every day, twice a day, Buster and his merry men of helpers have to clean up the thick green soup of shit. They will take the shit and put it into a man-made reservoir called a 'cesspool', it's just like one big pond of thick green soup shit.

Now I want this shit to eradicate those rabbits in their remote rabbit warrens. Buster has got a big tanker which is mounted on wheels and is pulled by the farm tractor. Buster fills this tanker with the thick green soup of cattle shit, and off me and Buster go out on to the vast grass meadows and on to the first massive remote rabbit warren.

My first job is for me and Pup to dog the rabbits in that may be laying tight in the grass that surrounds the massive remote warren and then run the rope out to its full extent and start pulling the rope across the grass and around the surrounding area of the massive warren. Any would be rabbits now laying out in the grass will now get touched by the rope and up they will jump and race away and disappear down the warren, just where I want them.

Buster now backs the tanker up to the warren. The tanker has a thick pipe leading from it which is pushed down into the rabbit hole and the thick green soup of cattle shit is now pumped down the rabbit hole. On and on Buster goes filling every hole on the massive warren with thick green soup of cattle shit. Every single rabbit in that warren will now all be smothered to death, and that is the end of an era for them rabbits in that warren, totally eradicated.

Me and Buster carry on that day doing the same to each rabbit warren as we go. The cattle shit will eventually dry out and set like concrete and the warren will then grow over with grass. And in a matter of no time at all you will look and never even know there has ever been a rabbit warren there at all.

There's even more rabbits here on the grass meadows besides those rabbits in the massive warrens. These rabbits are holing up in the rocky crags and also cannot be caught in the rabbit boxes. But they are breeding stock and must be eradicated. I have to gas these rabbits using Bob's gas which he uses for pest controlling the estate with. It is a gas tablet which I am using and as the gas tablet comes out of a canister it is called 'aluminium phosphine' which sends off a harmless fume. But by God, the smell of them certainly gives you a thumping headache. I now drop the gas tablet into the rocks where the rabbits are. The humidity inside the rocks is damp and the gas tablet now activates from the dampness. Now the gas fumes are called 'aluminium phosphide', which is now a deadly gas.

The gas fumes which are heavier than air now sink deep below into the rocks where the rabbits lay. The gas fumes are so deadly one whiff of it from the rabbits and the rabbit breathes no more. I carry on dropping tablets in at all the entrance points in the rocks making sure I am downwind of all the gas fumes as I go. I don't want a whiff of the deadly gas do I.

That day I go on and gas more and more rocky crags but there are many, many more rocky crags like these on the Laird's vast estate. And many, many more massive warrens to be cow-shitted out on the Laird's vast estate. All these rabbits have to be eradicated.

You readers may be thinking, why bother to catch the rabbits in the rabbit boxes in the first place when I can just as easily cow-shit out all the rabbit warrens and gas the rabbits to eradicate them? The answer is simple. I think it is a sin and a shame just to kill rabbits and just throw them away or in this case leave them dead underground. On the other hand, the rabbit boxes catch the rabbits clean and fresh and, when there's an R in the month when the rabbits are caught, to be eaten. There's an old saying, 'kill not want not', and that is my way of thinking entirely.

So now while the contractors are busy installing the rabbit boxes all over the whole of the Laird's massive rabbit-infested estate, I also have another job to do. On the Laird's massive estate there is a long, outstretched hill which is roughly about 200 acres in size. This hill is situated right in the middle of a vast grass meadow and the number of rabbits I have seen running off this meadow is unbelievable. They are in plague proportions. They are now in their multitudes and magnitudes as I see them running to this hill which is just one complete rabbit warren under the cover of a pine tree forest plantation growing on the hill. To put the ordinary rabbit boxes here would be futile.

The standard size holding box would not be big enough to catch and hold these rabbits, so I am going to install rabbit pens to hold the rabbits instead of boxes. I get those lads again from the local village and they install a rabbit-proof wire netting fence line around the entire perimeter of this wooded hill.

I now go in and install the rabbit pens. I am going to make these pens large enough to hold five hundred rabbits. The wire meshing I am using is half inch holes which will keep out stoats and weasel which would kill and eat the rabbits. I also put a wire meshing top on to keep out the foxes and the marauding carrion crows. They too would kill and take the rabbits from the pen.

The trip lid which catches the rabbits is slightly different to the rabbit boxes. This trip lid is going to operate by weights and it is going to be hinged on to and underneath the wooden tunnel. So now that my pen is made I now slot the wooden tunnel through the holding pen and the rabbits can now come out and away from the wooded hill where their warrens are. They will hop into the wooden tunnel which will take them over the trip lid which I will have fastened off not to catch rabbits. And the rabbits will pass safely through the holding pen and out on to the grass meadow which is their feeding grounds.

Now when I want these rabbits I will simply unfasten the trip lid, which has an arm on it which I hang weights on. The rabbit now passes through the wooden tunnel, it hops on to the trip lid, the rabbit's weight is heavier than my balance weights, the trip lid drops and the rabbit drops with it. The rabbit is now safely held in the holding pen and the trip lid now resets itself by my balanced weights and it's now already for the next rabbit through the wooden tunnel. To you readers this may all sound a little complicated but it really is so simple.

I now head on and install a rabbit pen about every hundred yards until I have gone around the complete perimeter of this 200 acre wooded hill.

As time rolls on by, I keep on cow-shitting the remote rabbit warrens and I keep on gassing the remote rocky crags where the rabbits lay. And while all this goes on the contractors keep on installing more and more rabbit boxes on the Laird's vast rabbit-infested estate.

I remember when it got to Christmas time of the year of which is still 1977, or about that year anyway, I decide to get myself some Christmas rabbits to take home to make a bit of Christmas pocket money. I decide to drop them twenty rabbit boxes which we installed earlier. The ten which surround the Laird's castle grounds and the other ten rabbit boxes which go along that deer netting fence line. I know there is still many, many more rabbits to be had here and these rabbit have to be eradicated. All together I dropped all twenty rabbit boxes.

The following morning when I arrived back nearly all my boxes were three quarters full with rabbits. I emptied all the boxes and left them set for another night.

The following morning when I returned nearly all my boxes were now only a quarter full with rabbits. I again emptied my boxes and again I left them set for another night.

The following morning when I returned I now found only twos and threes of rabbits in my boxes. I again left the boxes dropped for another night.

The following morning I took the Laird himself this time, I wanted to convince him that the rabbit boxes do completely catch all the rabbits. That morning every rabbit box we came to was empty of rabbits and as we walked along all the rabbit boxes me and the Laird never saw a single rabbit. Now the Laird appeared pleased with himself and he said, "This is the first time in my entire life I have never seen a rabbit in these two vicinities."

I now tell the Laird that over the past few days I have had the boxes dropped and I have caught more than fifteen hundred rabbits. I was going to take them home for Christmas but my Land Rover and trailer cannot carry all this amount of rabbits.

The Laird gives me a big smile and he says, "Come with me," and off me and the Laird go to the castle grounds. The Laird goes over to some outbuilding, he's now opening up some big double doors and what I see is a bloody big army truck. The Laird says, "Use that to take home your rabbits."

Now the Laird is backing the truck out of the outbuilding and he's now showing me around it. He says, "It's all in good working order and fully tested for the road." He's now showing me in the back of the army truck, it's got all game rails fixed in there and the back of the truck is covered by a tarpaulin sheet. The Laird says, "We use this truck when we have a lot of beaters to take up on to the moor and when we have a lot of game to carry off the moor." The Laird now says, "It's yours Doug, this army truck will get your rabbits home."

And that's just what I did, I took the bloody great army truck and my fifteen hundred and some rabbits fitted into the back easily.

The winter of about 1977 passed on by and by the end of the summer of 1978 the contractors had completed their work. They now had thousands of rabbit boxes installed around all the vast fir tree forestry plantations over the whole of the Laird's vast rabbit-infested estate.

It's by now the month of September of the year of about 1978, there is an R in the month and now the rabbits are ready to be taken for the table.

And now, as I promised you readers earlier, get yourselves sat back comfortably. You are now going to read the story of all lifetimes of stories on big time rabbit catching.

I now go to a line of rabbit boxes which the contractors have installed. I purposely get there at daybreak, I want to see if the rabbits are using the boxes. When I arrive there I see hundreds upon hundreds of rabbits running in off the grass meadow. Now I see them all queuing up to get through the wooden tunnel, so now I know the rabbits are using the boxes. I also know that when I drop these boxes the underground box will fill up with rabbits and stop the tippler lid working.

I now have to do my calculations. I have calculated that my bloody great army truck will carry about 3000 rabbits. I know these boxes here are going to fill up with rabbits tonight, catching a hundred rabbits in each box. So I want thirty boxes dropping and that's just what I did.

I purposely arrive at daybreak the following morning, I want to see how many rabbits run in. I still see hundreds of rabbits running in off the meadow and I see them hesitate before going through the wooden tunnel. You readers now know why the rabbits are hesitating and, as I predicted, all my boxes were full to capacity which was stopping the trip lid working.

I now empty all thirty boxes and fasten off the trip lids. The rest of the rabbits that are still free will now pass through the wooden tunnels safely tonight.

I now paunch all my rabbits and hang them on the game rails inside my army truck. I reckon I have more than 3000 rabbits hung in there, but my army truck carries them well. And off me and Pup go with our fully-laden army truck full of rabbits and homeward bound we go.

I think my Pup likes this army truck. With the cab standing high Pup now sits on the passenger seat and she can now see over the hedgerows and see all the rabbits running around in the fields as we pass them by.

As the weeks now roll on by, I am now taking home two army truck loads of rabbits every week. That's more than 6000 rabbit's a week and I am flooding all the meat markets with my rabbits. The whole vast surrounding area of my home has many meat markets and gamedealer's shops.

I deliver rabbits to them so many times that now when they see my army truck coming down the road they all do a runner. They are sick to their teeth of seeing rabbits, rabbits, bloody rabbits. I do all the delivering of rabbits every week up to Christmas of the year of about 1978 and then I have a Christmas break.

On the second of January of about the year 1979 I return back up to the Laird's vast rabbit-infested estate. When I arrive at Bob's cottage, the Hunter's Lodge, the Laird is there to greet me. He's now telling me I have to catch more rabbits, he says, "The rabbits on my estate must be eradicated."

I now have to do some serious thinking. I have by now flooded all the meat markets with my rabbits back home. Now the Laird tells me I have to catch even more rabbits, but I have nowhere to take them. So what I did was I called in Bob's gamedealer. I tell the gamedealer the amount of rabbits I have been catching in the rabbit boxes and he appears amazed at what I tell him.

I tell the gamedealer the amount of rabbits that could be caught if wanted and the gamedealer is now raising his eyebrows at what I tell him. The gamedealer is now telling me his refrigerated game wagon will carry 5,000 rabbits. Now I am raising my eyebrows at what the gamedealer tells me. I now tell the gamedealer my army truck will carry 3,000 rabbits but I have nowhere to take them and that I have flooded all the meat markets back home. The gamedealer is now telling me to catch 8,000 rabbits, 5,000 for him and 3,000 for me. So that's just what I did.

Me and the gamedealer are now all loaded up with rabbits and the gamedealer is telling me he is taking his rabbits to the meat markets in Dublin and Belfast in Ireland. The gamedealer is now telling me to take my army truck load of rabbits down to the meat markets in Glasgow and Edinburgh. He tells me to tell the gamedealers down there that he has sent me, and on that we both go.

I arranged with the gamedealer to meet him back up here on the Laird's vast estate the following week. And when he arrives back I have another 8000 rabbits waiting for him. The meat markets where we delivered to the week before are now flooded out with rabbits.

Me and the gamedealer are now all loaded up with rabbits. The gamedealer's now telling me to follow him, he's now taking our 8000 rabbits to the meat markets at Liverpool, Birmingham and Manchester. We now flood them meat markets out with rabbits also.

Our next 8000 rabbits the following week we took to Nottingham, Bristol and London. Now them meat markets are flooded out with rabbits also. Every week me and the gamedealer flood 8000 rabbits into every corner of Britain and now the whole of Britain is flooded out with rabbits.

All this delivering of rabbits throughout Britain takes us through to the spring of the year of about 1979. Now the Laird is insisting we carry on catching rabbits through the summer months. Now you readers know that it is against my nature to kill rabbits just to throw them away, so I tell the Laird a firm, "No, it's a sin and a shame to kill rabbits for nothing."

The Laird now acknowledges my word as final, and all the rabbit catching stops for the summer.

I pass the summer on by at home and it's now September of the year of about 1979. Now there's an R in the month, now the rabbits are fit for the table. When I arrive back up at the Laird's vast rabbit-infested estate, I see the rabbits have bred out of control, they have gone forth and multiplied.

When I arrive at Bob's cottage, the Hunter's Lodge, and I pull into Bob's courtyard, I see the Laird there waiting to greet me. I also see Bob, Helen, Big Jim, Jock and Buster. The Laird is now telling me I have to catch even more rabbits than before. The Laird's now telling me the gamedealer now has **five** game wagons to take the rabbits away. I tell the Laird I cannot possibly catch enough rabbits to fill five gamedealer wagons.

Now the Laird's looking at Helen and he says to her, "I want you, Helen, to be in charge of all the rabbit boxes on your land. I want you to drop the amount of boxes Doug tells you to and I want you to empty the boxes of the rabbits the next morning. I want you to paunch all the rabbits and lay them tidily by the boxes all ready for the gamedealer to pick them up."

Helen says to the Laird, "But what about all my sheep?" the catching of rabbits is of the uppermost importance" says the Laird.

The Laird is now looking at Bob, Big Jim, Buster and Jock and is now telling them what he has just told Helen. Bob says, "But what about my gamekeeping and my deerstalking?"

The Laird tells everybody altogether, "The work you all do for me on my estate must cease. The uppermost of importance now is to catch rabbits, the rabbits on my estate must be eradicated."

I have to smile at Bob as I hear the Laird giving everybody their orders. Bob's bottom lip has dropped down. So I once was Bob's rabbit catcher, now Bob's my rabbit catcher.

Now the Laird's looking at me and is telling me, "Doug, I do not want you to catch rabbits. Your job now is to tell my work staff here how many rabbits you want them to catch to fill up the gamedealer's wagons."

So now the Laird has given us all our orders and I now go into Bob's cottage to use Bob's telephone to contact the gamedealer. He's now telling me he has got himself five new refrigerated game wagons and each wagon will carry 5,000 rabbits. The gamedealer now wants to know when I am going to fill his five wagons with rabbits.

I think to myself, that's 25,000 rabbits he's asking for, that's just like a sweet out of a bagful with all the rabbits there is on the Laird's vast estate. The rabbit boxes can catch them easily so I tell the gamedealer the rabbits will be caught and waiting for him to pick them up the following day.

I now get Bob, Helen, Jock, Big Jim and Buster to drop fifty rabbit boxes each on their land, which is really the Laird's land on his vast estate. And, sure enough, the next day everybody had 5,000 rabbits caught each. And each of these five game wagons went and picked up all 25,000 rabbits.

The gamedealer is now telling me he is catching the night ferry boat over to France. All his five game wagons are flooding the meat markets all over the entire of France. Unbelievable!

The following week I have another 25,000 rabbits waiting for him and the gamedealer is now telling me he is now flooding the meat markets in Belgium. The week after that he is now flooding the meat markets in Holland. And as the weeks rolled on by he flooded the meat markets right across Germany. And on and on the gamedealer went with his five game wagons and flooded all the meat markets across western Europe.

As the weeks rolled on by which rolled into months, I kept the Laird's merry team of men dropping rabbit boxes over the whole of the Laird's vast estate. And every week the five game wagons kept on coming and loading up with 25,000 rabbits each time they came.

Now the gamedealer is telling me he is flooding all the meat markets across the whole of Eastern Europe. All this carries on through the winter months and by the time we get to the spring of the year of about 1980 all the rabbits were 'gone'.

This is a sad day for the rabbits, now everywhere I look on the Laird's vast estate there's not a rabbit to be seen anywhere. I remember I was having a history lesson at school and teacher was telling us about Julius Caesar. His famous words were, "I came, I saw, I took." Julius Caesar must have been speaking of some far off land which he fought for and took. I remind myself of Julius Caesar, I 'came' here to poach the rabbits on the Laird's vast estate, I 'saw' all the rabbits and now I 'took' all the rabbits. So do you readers think I am a bit like Julius Caesar, 'I came, I saw, I took'?

I now have no reason to come back here on the Laird's vast estate, all the rabbits are now gone. But I will miss everybody I have met while I have been up here which was all in the 1970s. Such people as Bob, Big Jim, Jock, Buster, not forgetting Lady CC and the Laird. And then there's my beloved Helen. They will all be sadly missed.

I have to go now, there's a farmer contacted me in Australia he wants me to catch his rabbits for him. He tells me he has 'thirty-six million' rabbits on his farm.

I hope you readers have enjoyed my rabbit catching story which all happened on the Laird's vast estate up in the Grampian Mountains up in the Highlands of Scotland.

End.

Also available from the same author

THE LIFE AND TIMES OF A COUNTRY BOY

Available from all good book-selling websites and to order
through any reputable bookshop.
For the promptest response, order directly from the publisher:
www.upfrontbookshop.co.uk

Also available from the same author

THE LIFE AND TIMES OF A COUNTRY BOY

My own autobiography book, which was launched on the worldwide market in the year of 2006, tells of my love for the fields and countryside beginning when I was only a lad of seven years old, my devilment of doing a bit of worldly poaching, getting myself chased many many times by the gamekeepers for poaching their rabbits, continuing on into adult life for my passionate love affair with natures ways.

I tell of many characters I met along my way through life, spending many many years in the beautiful picturesque Yorkshire Dales. I tell of the true life story of a grouse moorland gamekeeper and his yearly cycle of the upkeep and shooting of his large grouse moor.

With me being a little green-fingered, I taught myself the unique art of growing wild moorland heather high up on the hilltops, cultivated heather grows in the same manner.
My big secret now exposed, the growing of heather will now be revolutionized to the world.

And then there's my love of horse dealing among the Romany gypsies, travelling the country to all the horse fairs together with my beloved Appleby Horse Fair up in Westmoreland.

Now, as I look back over those distant bygone years of yesteryear, I leave a long dusty road behind me as I put pen to paper and write of my bygone years.

A hardy 206 pages of action-packed true-to-the fact stories.
Happy reading!

Available from all good book-selling websites and to order through any reputable bookshop.
For the promptest response, order directly from the publisher:
www.upfrontbookshop.co.uk

Also available from the same author

MY OWN DOUBLE HEART
BYPASS OPERATION AUTOBIOGRAPHY

Also available from the same author

MY OWN DOUBLE HEART
BYPASS OPERATION AUTOBIOGRAPHY

Introduction

After my heart bypass operation, I continued on writing my other
three books. It was late 2006 when thoughts began drifting through
my mind about my operation. I had just recently had one memory
thought drifted onto another memory thought, and on and on my
memory thoughts went. I now scratch my head, I think to myself, I
have a good true to the fact story to write here and that's how this
story that you are about to read now was borne. Everything I have
written is purely from memory. I never wrote anything down at the
time of it all happening. I didn't know I was going to write a story
about it. I recalled all what the hospital staff had told me at the time of
it all happening; such people as the nurses, doctors, anaesthetist,
cardiologist, heart surgeon etc etc. I was always asking them questions
about what they were doing and why they were doing it, always
putting my nose in maybe when I should have kept my nose out, but
it all paid off in the end and now you can read my actual story of how
it all happened.
My natural way with people is always to bring out the best of humour
in them; all the hilarious activities I write of are all true. To the fact,
stories of what happened at the time, all purely brought on by me for
my devilment of bringing out the best of humour in people. I have
written my story in layman's terms, just like the patient sees it.
A very reassuring and knowledgeable story for future patients to read.